EMOTIONS IN HISTORY

General Editors

UTE FREVERT   THOMAS DIXON

Learning How to Feel

Children's Literature and Emotional Socialization, 1870–1970

UTE FREVERT, PASCAL EITLER,
STEPHANIE OLSEN, UFFA JENSEN,
MARGRIT PERNAU, DANIEL BRÜCKENHAUS,
MAGDALENA BELJAN, BENNO GAMMERL,
ANJA LAUKÖTTER, BETTINA HITZER,
JAN PLAMPER, JULIANE BRAUER, AND
JOACHIM C. HÄBERLEN

OXFORD
UNIVERSITY PRESS

OXFORD
UNIVERSITY PRESS

Great Clarendon Street, Oxford, OX2 6DP,
United Kingdom

Oxford University Press is a department of the University of Oxford.
It furthers the University's objective of excellence in research, scholarship,
and education by publishing worldwide. Oxford is a registered trade mark of
Oxford University Press in the UK and in certain other countries

First Edition published in 2014

Impression: 1

Published in the United States of America by Oxford University Press
198 Madison Avenue, New York, NY 10016, United States of America

British Library Cataloguing in Publication Data
Data available

Library of Congress Control Number: 2014934933

ISBN 978-0-19-968499-1

Printed and bound by
CPI Group (UK) Ltd, Croydon, CR0 4YY

Contents

List of Figures

Every effort has been made to trace copyright holders and to obtain their permission for the use of copyright material. The publisher apologizes for any errors or omissions in the above list and would be grateful if notified of any corrections that should be incorporated in future reprints or editions of this book.

List of Contributors

Magdalena Beljan is literary scholar and post-doctoral fellow at the Max Planck Institute for Human Development, Center for the History of Emotions, in Berlin. She works on her research project 'Ambivalent Emotions: Conflicts and Convergences in Dealing with Aids'. She is also co-editor of the online journal *Body Politics. Zeitschrift für Körpergeschichte*. In her dissertation she examined strategies of normalization and subjectivation of male homosexuality in the Federal Republic of Germany in the 1970s and 1980s. Her research interests are literary history from the perspective of media history, gender history, the history of the body in the nineteenth and twentieth centuries, and post-structuralist theories. Her publications include 'Unlust bei der Lust? Aids, HIV & Sexualität in der BRD', in P.-P. Bänziger, M. Beljan, F. X. Eder, and P. Eitler, eds., *Sexuelle Revolution? Zur Geschichte der Sexualität im deutschsprachigem Raum seit den 1960er Jahren* (2014); *Rosa Zeiten? Eine diskursanalytische Untersuchung zur Homosexualität in der BRD* (2014); 'Vorlesungen zur Psychiatrie/ Disziplinierung', in C. Kammler, R. Parr, and U. J. Schneider, eds., *Foucault-Handbuch* (2008).

Juliane Brauer is a researcher at the Max Planck Institute for Human Development, Center for the History of Emotions, in Berlin. She studied History and Musicology at Humboldt-Universität zu Berlin and University of Bielefeld. In 2007, she completed her Ph.D. in History at the Freie Universität Berlin on music in the concentration camp Sachsenhausen (*Musik im Konzentrationslager Sachsenhausen* (2009)). She is currently working on her habilitation project about Youth, Music, and the Cultivation of Feelings in a Divided Germany. In her main focus on music and emotions, her research interests include the history of children and youth, the history of education as well as the cultural and music history of the nineteenth and twentieth centuries. Her publications include: '"With Power and Aggression, and a Great Sadness": Emotional Clashes between Punk Culture and GDR Youth Policy in the 1980s', *Twentieth Century Communism* 4 (2012); 'Bilder, Gefühle, Erwartungen: Über die emotionale Dimension von Gedenkstätten und den Umgang von Jugendlichen mit dem Holocaust' (co-authored with Aleida Assmann), *Geschichte und Gesellschaft* 37 (2011).

Daniel Brückenhaus received his Ph.D. from Yale University in 2011. After a year as a post-doctoral fellow at the Max Planck Institute for Human Development, Center for the History of Emotions, in Berlin, he is now an assistant professor of Modern European History at Beloit College. Research interests include the history of the European colonial empires, the history of government surveillance, and the history of emotions. Daniel Brückenhaus has published articles on the history of trust, and on European memories. He is currently finishing a book manuscript on the transnational surveillance of anti-colonialists in early twentieth-century Western Europe, and he is working on a research project on the history of dignity, honour, and shame under colonialism.

Pascal Eitler received his D.Phil. in Modern History at the University of Bielefeld, and is currently working as a researcher at the Max Planck Institute for Human Development, Center for the History of Emotions, in Berlin on the emotionalization and politicization of human-animal relationships in the nineteenth and twentieth centuries. He is especially interested in the history of emotions from the perspective of the history of the body. His publications include 'The "Origin" of Feelings: Sensitive Humans, Sensitive Animals', in

Ute Frevert et al., *Emotional Lexicons: Continuity and Change in the Vocabulary of Feeling 1700–2000*, (2014); 'Tierliebe und Menschenführung: Eine genealogische Perspektive auf das 19. und 20. Jahrhundert', *Tierstudien* 2/3 (2013); '"Weil sie fühlen, was wir fühlen": Menschen, Tiere und die Genealogie der Emotionen im 19. Jahrhundert', *Historische Anthropologie* 19 (2011).

Ute Frevert is Director at the Max Planck Institute for Human Development and a Scientific Member of the Max Planck Society. From 2003 to 2007 she was professor of German history at Yale University and previously taught History at the Universities of Konstanz, Bielefeld, and the Freie Universität Berlin. Her research interests include the social and cultural history of the modern period, the history of emotions, gender history, and political history. Some of her best-known work has examined the history of women and gender relations in modern Germany, social and medical politics in the nineteenth century, and the impact of military conscription from 1814 to the present day. Ute Frevert is an honorary professor at the Freie Universität in Berlin and member of several scientific advisory boards. In 1998 she was awarded the prestigious Leibniz Prize.

Benno Gammerl is a historian and currently works on homosexuality and emotional life in rural West Germany between 1960 and 1990. In 2008 he completed his Ph.D. at the Freie Universität Berlin with a thesis on the legal and administrative handling of ethnic heterogeneity in the British and the Habsburg Empires around 1900. For the monograph based on this work Gammerl received the Wolfgang J. Mommsen Award in 2012. He has studied history, German literature, and economics in Freiburg, London, and Berlin. His fields of interest include oral history, comparative history, history of sexualities, citizenship, and nationality as well as post-colonial and queer theories. Among Gammerl's recent publications are 'Emotional Styles: Concepts and Challenges', *Rethinking History* 16/2 (2012), as well as 'Queer Romance: Romantische Liebe in den biographischen Erzählungen von westdeutschen Lesben und Schwulen', *L'Homme* 24/1 (2013).

Joachim C. Häberlen is assistant professor of modern continental European history at the University of Warwick. He received his Ph.D. from the University of Chicago in 2011. Before coming to Warwick, he was post-doctoral fellow at the Max Planck Institute for Human Development, Center for the History of Emotions, in Berlin. Among his publications are *Vertrauen und Politik im Alltag. Die Arbeiterbewegung in Leipzig und Lyon im Moment der Krise, 1929–1933/38* (2013); 'Contesting the Political: Conceptions of the Political in the Working-Class Movements of Leipzig and Lyon during the Interwar Period', *Contemporary European History* 22 (2013); 'Between Global Aspirations and Local Realities. The Global Dimensions of Interwar Communism', *Journal of Global History* 7 (2012). He is currently working on a project on radical leftist politics of emotions after 1968 in West Germany.

Bettina Hitzer is a historian and Minerva research group leader at the Max Planck Institute for Human Development, Center for the History of Emotions, in Berlin. Her research interests include the history of emotions, the history of medicine and science, the history of religion, and the history of migration in modern Europe. Currently, she is working on a book project which traces the emotional history of cancer in twentieth-century Germany. Her books include *Die Bielefelder Sozialgeschichte: Klassische Texte zu einem geschichtswissenschaftlichen Programm und seinen Kontroversen* (co-authored with Thomas Welskopp, 2010), *Zwischen Tanzboden und Bordell: Lebensbilder Berliner Prostituierter aus dem Jahr 1869* (co-authored with Michael Häusler, 2010); and *Im Netz der Liebe: Die protestantische Kirche und ihre Zuwanderer in der Metropole Berlin 1849–1914* (2006). She has published a special issue on *Feeling and Faith: Religious Emotions in German History* (co-edited with Pascal Eitler and Monique Scheer, *German History*/2014) as well as on *God in the City: Religious Topographies in the Age of Urbanization* (co-edited with Jochim Schlör, *Journal of Urban History*, 2011).

Uffa Jensen is a historian and works as a researcher at the Max Planck Institute for Human Development, Center for the History of Emotions, in Berlin. In 2003, he completed his Ph.D. in History at the Technical University of Berlin. Previously, he has taught at the University of Sussex and at the University of Göttingen. He has written on the history of German Jewry and anti-Semitism as well as on the history of psychoanalysis. His publications include: *Gebildete Doppelgänger: Bürgerliche Juden und Protestanten im 19. Jahrhundert* (2005); *Rationalisierungen des Gefühls: Zum Verhältnis von Wissenschaft und Emotionen 1880–1930* (ed. with Daniel Morat, 2008); 'Neuere Forschungen zur Geschichte der Psychoanalyse', *Archiv für Sozialgeschichte* 52 (2012), 765-800; *Das Selbst zwischen Anpassung und Befreiung: Psychowissen und Politik im 20. Jahrhundert* (ed. with Maik Tändler, 2012); 'The Lure of Authenticity: Emotions and Generations in the German Youth Movement of the Early 20th Century', in Hartmut Berghoff et al., eds., *History by Generations: Generational Dynamics in Modern History*, (2013).

Anja Laukötter is a researcher at the Max Planck Institute for Human Development, Center for the History of Emotions, in Berlin since 2010. After studying Modern History, Political Science, and Anthropology at the University of Cologne, Humboldt-Universität zu Berlin, and New University for Social Research, New York City she earned her Ph.D. with a study on the history of ethnological museums: *Von der 'Kultur' zur 'Rasse'— vom Objekt zum Körper? Völkerkundemuseen und ihre Wissenschaften zu Beginn des 20. Jahrhunderts* (2007). From 2006 until 2010 she was a researcher at the Institute for the History of Medicine in Berlin, working on projects on the history of human experiments and hygiene institutions during the National Socialism era. She is co-author of the book *Infektion und Institution: Zur Wissenschaftsgeschichte des Robert Koch-Instituts in der Zeit des Nationalsozialismus* (2009). Her current research concerns the transnational history of educational films, especially the link between emotions and knowledge. Her publications include: 'Wissen als Animation: Zur Transformation der Anschaulichkeit im Gesundheitsaufklärungsfilm', *Montage AV: Zeitschrift für Theorie und Geschichte audiovisueller Kommunikation* 22/2 (2013), 79–96, 'Moving Pictures and Medicine in the First Half of the 20th Century: Some Notes on International Historical Developments and the Potential of Medical Film Research' (together with Christian Bonah), *Gesnerus* 66/1 (2009), 121–45. Together with Margrit Pernau she is the editor of the internet portal on the history of emotions: http://www.history-of-emotions.mpg.de/en.

Stephanie Olsen is a research fellow at the Max Planck Institute for Human Development, Center for the History of Emotions, in Berlin. She is the author of *Juvenile Nation: Youth, Emotions and the Making of the Modern British Citizen* (2014) and has published a number of articles on the history of masculinity, childhood, education, and the emotions.

Margrit Pernau coordinates the India group at the Max Planck Institute for Human Development, Center for the History of Emotions, in Berlin. She teaches at the Freie Universität Berlin, where she also holds an extraordinary professorship. She was born in Madrid, went to school in Delhi and Paris, and studied History and Public Law at Saarbrücken and at the South Asia Institute in Heidelberg, where she finished her Ph.D. on Hyderabad under the last Nizam in 1991. In 1997 she moved back to Delhi with her family and spent the next six years tracing the history of nineteenth-century Delhi in the archives and in the lanes of the old city. The German version of her book has won the German Historians' Association prize for the best post-doctoral work in 2009 and the translation prize of Geisteswissenschaften International in 2010. Her other publications include *Family and Gender: Changing Values in Germany and India* (edited together with Imtiaz Ahmad and Helmut Reifeld, 2003); *The Delhi College: Traditional Elites, the Colonial State, and Education before 1857* (edited), (2006); and *Information and the Public Sphere: Persian Newsletters from Mughal Delhi* (edited together with Yunus Jaffery, 2009).

Jan Plamper is professor of History at Goldsmiths, University of London. After obtaining a B.A. from Brandeis University and a Ph.D. from the University of California, Berkeley, he taught at the University of Tübingen and from 2008 to 2012 was a Dilthey Fellow at the Max Planck Institute for Human Development, Center for the History of Emotions, in Berlin. He is the author of *Geschichte und Gefühl: Grundlagen der Emotionsgeschichte* [*History and Feeling: Foundations of the History of Emotions*] (2012; forthcoming in English from Oxford University Press); co-editor, with Benjamin Lazier, of *Fear: Across the Disciplines* (2012); and co-editor, with Marc Elie and Schamma Schahadat, of *Rossiiskaia imperiia chuvstv: Podkhody k kul'turnoi istorii emotsii* [In the Realm of Russian Feelings: Approaches to the Cultural History of Emotions] (2010). He has also recently authored *The Stalin Cult: A Study in the Alchemy of Power* (2012). His current research concerns the fear of Russian soldiers, especially during the First World War.

Prologue

This book is the product of the second collaborative research project conducted by the Center for the History of Emotions at Berlin's Max Planck Institute for Human Development. Having completed the emotional lexicons project (published by OUP in 2014), we became interested in the ways in which emotions are learnt, cultivated, and shaped in modern times. Two conferences on 'learning how to feel', in Berlin in 2010 and in Jerusalem in 2011, highlighted social institutions (from the family to the military) that had proven historically crucial for the emotional socialization of their members. It was Pascal Eitler's idea to use these broader insights and apply them to the study of a particular medium: children's books. All researchers were familiar with children's literature, either by remembering their own reading experiences or by reading, as young parents, aunts or uncles, to their children, nieces, or nephews. And everyone agreed that there was a wealth of emotional knowledge implicitly hidden or explicitly voiced in the stories of Robinson Crusoe, Pippi Longstocking, Slovenly Peter, and The Famous Five. But how could this emotional knowledge be retrieved? What kind of questions might be asked to understand what children learnt about emotions by reading books and engaging with their plots and main characters?

After collecting information on bestselling book lists in various countries, the group first agreed on a common corpus comprising about a hundred popular titles from around 1870 to 1970. On the basis of what all of us had read, we developed a framework of questions and identified epistemological problems that needed to be solved. We also decided on a set of major emotions that were for the most part continuously addressed in children's books, albeit with specific connotations and varying significance. These emotions were associated with the fictional characters, which allowed us to place them in specific time and place frameworks. Although focusing on one particular emotion at a time, we had to examine a wide range of complimentary and contradictory emotions concurrently. After all, in children's literature, as in real life, emotions usually occur in complex patterns. They are mixed rather than single, a notion which introduces a vast realm of historically specific research and discussion.

Research and debates spanned over two years. It took us numerous meetings, drafts, revisions, and re-readings to come up with what we present here. Such intensive collaborative work cannot be the product of conferences alone. It needs the constant presence and commitment of a group of researchers sharing basic interests and historiographic tools. And it needs the help of many others who order books, find out about translations and sales figures, check footnotes and references, and polish non-native English texts. A big thank you goes to (in alphabetical order): Christina Becher, Anja Berkes, Ilana Brown, Kate Davison, Karola Rockmann, Kerstin Singer, and all the student assistants past and present.

Introduction

Pascal Eitler, Stephanie Olsen, and Uffa Jensen

Bastian Balthazar Bux had always been a deeply anxious, unhappy, big little boy. After the death of his mother, he was practically left on his own, because his father was still mourning her death. This, however, was about to change, when one day—escaping from the usual bullying of his schoolmates—Bastian burst into a second-hand bookshop. Fascinated by a strange book, he stole it and began to read it in the deserted school attic. Living in his own dream world, Bastian had always been drawn to imaginative stories:

> Human passions have mysterious ways, in children as well as grown-ups. Those affected by them can't explain them, and those who haven't known them have no understanding of them at all. Some people risk their lives to conquer a mountain peak. No one, not even they themselves, can really explain why. Others ruin themselves trying to win the heart of a certain person who wants nothing to do with them. Still others are destroyed by their devotion to the pleasure of the table.... In short, there are as many different passions as there are people. Bastian Balthazar Bux's passion was books.[1]

As he is reading the book, the boy enters Fantastica, a world full of bizarre landscapes and odd creatures ruled by the Childlike Empress. She has fallen ill and her life—as well as the very existence of Fantastica—depends on a human child for help. Thus, the bookworm Bastian is literally drawn into the book: 'He, Bastian, was a character in the book which until now he had thought he was reading. And heaven only knew who else might be reading it at the exact same time, also supposing himself to be just a reader.'[2]

In Fantastica, Bastian Balthazar Bux is transformed into a handsome, resolute, and strong boy. After many adventures and challenges that make him almost completely forget who he really is, he finally returns to the human world as a better person, with a newly acquired skill: to love others as well as himself.

Michael Ende's *The Neverending Story* (1983; Ger. orig. *Die unendliche Geschichte*,1979) has been published in numerous editions and has sold more than ten million copies. The book has been translated into forty different languages, won numerous awards and inspired several movies. Its hero's journey develops into an *éducation sentimentale*—and, as such, it is concerned with many of the issues which *Learning How to Feel* addresses. *The Neverending Story* highlights some of the approaches necessary to understand the importance of passions or emotions in children's literature: the allure of strange and fascinating worlds that draw children to books, the knowledge children can gain through books about themselves and the world in which they live, as well as the emotional experiences learnt by reading about somebody else's pain and joy. In many ways, *Learning How to Feel* observes what children can feel through reading—much like we can observe Bastian Balthazar Bux reading the story of which he himself becomes a part.

Examining children and their feelings has a long history, starting before the end of the eighteenth century. Beginning slowly at first, the nineteenth and twentieth centuries witnessed the gradual emergence of an unprecedented level of activity in, and potential for, considering, understanding, and describing children's emotions, as well as shaping, regulating, coaching, or treating them with therapy. In diverse and changing ways, within the family or at school, in advice manuals, for both children and adults, and much later, under the influence of television or in self-help groups, children became objects of emotional training and optimization, and, at the same time, subjects of emotional self-development.

Against this background, it is possible to describe what has become a kind of naturalization of emotions: emotions are often regarded as something very basic, and essentially human. Children, it seems, quite simply just *have* emotions, not only from birth but—according to a popular assumption—even prenatally, within the uterus. Their emotional compass is said to react to the mother's stress and hormone levels during pregnancy. Furthermore, according to psychologists, the emotional experiences we have in our first years are crucial for our whole life balance and for our subsequent relationships.

The origins of this perspective can be traced back to the mid-nineteenth century, when children's emotions in particular became the topic of psychological, and later of neuro-psychological or bio-sociological research and discussion, and even of public debate.[3] Emotions became the purview of educational specialists, who advocated diverse methods of physical and socio-cultural emotional learning for the young. Immature or juvenile emotions were to be cultivated, nurtured, and optimized in various ways through a process of socialization or habitualization. Parents and society as a whole were, therefore, advised to tend very carefully to children who required particular professional help and educational advice.

Over the course of the nineteenth and twentieth centuries, children and their education became one of the central areas within which societies tried to understand and to shape their own emotional repertoires. During the 1960s and 1970s, professional, public, and political pressure on parents and adults grew significantly encouraging them to enable the emotional self-development of the children.[4]

This accompanied an historical concern among psychologists, educational specialists, and sociologists who devoted considerable attention to the study of children's emotions, an interest that lasts up to the present. As a result, one is tempted to draw the false conclusion that children's emotions have no history, when in fact they should be regarded as a welcome challenge for research into the past. It is to some degree surprising that, on the whole, children's emotions have not yet played a role in historical research.[5]

Within the fast-expanding field of the history of emotions, however, the topic is of utmost importance. Historians of emotions scrutinize the construction and societal framing of emotions, and the ways in which they are evoked.[6] They not only seek changes regarding the way in which the expression of feelings is ordered, but also question the traditional distinction between 'real' feelings that we cannot observe, and the 'mere' rules of display, or specific emotionology. They are concerned with the notion that emotions are 'natural'. This is not simply because their representation, perception, and taxonomy have been subject to variation over time. More importantly, emotions emerge as concrete effects of historical invention, as social products, and also—as it will be argued—as a question of practical knowledge.[7]

Against this background, the book tries to reconstruct what is assumed to be a critical element in the emotional socialization of children, focusing especially on the ways in which it changed between the mid-nineteenth century and the late twentieth century and extending beyond a traditional Western focus. We explore what kinds of emotions were offered to children through advice manuals and children's books, emphasizing the processes, specific discourses, and multiple practices involved in learning how to feel. How did young fictional protagonists learn and what kind of framework did children's books offer children as readers? What changes in that framework can be observed across space and time? Which particular emotions were learnt or at least taught as the most important for children and for which children? What role did age, gender, ethnic, and class background play? How can we understand the emotional repertoire offered to children by children's books and advice manuals within the context of large-scale societal developments in modern times, particularly between the 1870s and 1970s?

THE HISTORY OF CHILDHOOD AND CHILDREN'S EDUCATION

These questions are set within the framework of a much broader history of childhood and children, provoking some further, fundamental questions about age categories and how they impact emotional learning. The child is certainly not a fixed category and cannot be defined merely by biological or physical stages of the life-cycle.[8] Age categories can be better understood in terms of indices of cognitive or emotional development. But precisely who is marked out as a child, an adolescent, or an adult has enormous implications in terms of autonomy, selfhood, and power relations, as well as emotional development. Despite uncertain definitions, children, childhood, and youth are crucial categories of historical analysis. It is perhaps self-evident that concepts of childhood themselves exhibited significant geographical and temporal variation between the nineteenth and twentieth centuries. Large shifts have taken place in what it means to be a child, an adolescent, and a young adult. Changes have come about through government legislation, education, private initiatives, scientific expertise, and mass media, and have significantly affected the meaning of childhood at the level of society as a whole.

Historians have problematized the seemingly neat categories of the child and of childhood.[9] Youth, adolescence, and young adulthood are equally historically imprecise terms, and are often used interchangeably. Though the term 'adolescence' has had a much longer presence, its modern use—to categorize a liminal, problematic time between childhood and adulthood—did not emerge until the late nineteenth century and was effectively popularized by G. Stanley Hall's book, *Adolescence* (1904).[10] In legal terms, the end of adolescence is marked by the transition to adulthood, commonly pinpointed between the ages of eighteen and twenty-one, but in behavioural and emotional terms, the phase can be protracted. The period under consideration in Hall's *Adolescence*, for example, is between fourteen and twenty-four years of age.[11] Contemporary children are expected to be in school, obtaining literacy by the age of six. By sixteen, adolescence is in full swing, but legal adulthood starts two years or more later. This book is based on a childhood age range of six to sixteen to guide its investigation, and to define a starting point, but the authors have taken care to elaborate on the diverse and changing definitions of child and childhood, including those settings and periods lacking a concrete notion of the concept. In places and times in which such a concrete definition did exist, the book investigates whether children were construed as young adults or as innocent, idealized beings. Were they subjects who developed based on their own intellect or were they the objects of pedagogy, waiting to be transformed into adults?

In Western Europe and North America, narrowing definitions of childhood were commonly accompanied by increasing efforts to mould children in the 'correct' way. Children's socialization and enculturation, which had previously taken place primarily within familial and religious contexts, and, for lower-class children, also in the work environment, gradually became appropriated by educational authorities, and, conversely, by peer groups.[12] In the eighteenth century and in a large portion of the nineteenth century, education for children concerned mainly a male elite. The target of basic literacy for children, however, began to permeate class and gender boundaries, especially in predominantly evangelical regions as evangelism required its adherents to establish a personal relationship with God through the reading of religious tracts and the Bible. Gradually, literacy training became more systematic. In almost all the countries investigated here, there was a significant rise in literacy rates in the late nineteenth century. In India, literacy rates increased at a slower pace by comparison, with female literacy languishing even further behind. In Russia, literacy expanded significantly during the course of the nineteenth century, yet by the end of the century, the best estimates suggested that only 45 per cent of males could read, the most literate were between the ages of eleven and twenty. As in India, female literacy lagged behind. However, by around 1950 in Soviet Russia, 90 per cent of both men and women could read.[13]

The push for universal literacy in Western Europe and North America coincided with a substantial increase in mass education, often conducted first by religious or other non-governmental institutions. Eventually, education, mostly compulsory and free by the end of the nineteenth century, increasingly came under the purview of the state. In India, however, despite some attempts to establish compulsory primary education in some provinces, there was no system of universal education during the British Raj (1858–1947). In independent India, organized efforts were made to introduce free and compulsory universal education for all children up to fourteen years of age.[14] In Soviet Russia, education was not brought fully under state control until the 1930s and it was only in the late 1950s that the first eight years of schooling were made compulsory.[15]

These numerous efforts toward universal literacy and education produced a greatly expanded reading market, both male and female, and of all classes. The market was steadily supplied by a growing amount of reading material, including children's books and advice manuals. Children's books, in particular, proved to be an important genre in the process of constructing and producing emotions. Until at least the end of the twentieth century, children's books had a unique and, as this book suggests, significant function through which children were directly shaped. Today, other media are involved in the children's socialization process, introducing new techniques of learning how to feel. While cinema played a decisive role from the 1920s, for example, and comics from the 1940s, it was only from the 1970s and 1980s that other media began to have a wider social impact, especially television, audiobooks, and an ever-increasing plethora of computer games.

For the purposes of consistency throughout the entire period under consideration, the focus of this study is only on children's books and advice literature. The common work of the research group was based on a selection of approximately sixty very successful, widely recognized children's books, so-called classics of their time. Often transnational bestsellers, and many still in print today, they include *Slovenly Peter* (1850; Ger. orig. *Struwwelpeter*, 1845) and *The Jungle Book* (1894), *Peter and Wendy* (1911) and *Pippi Longstocking* (1945; Swe. orig. *Pippi Långstrump*, 1945), *The Famous Five* series (1942–62), and *The War of the Buttons* (1968; Fre. orig. *La guerre des boutons*, 1912), among others. One chapter focuses on various adaptations of *Peter Pan* across different genres in order to highlight the shifts in the concept of love and the changing emphasis on various kinds of relationships. Based on this selection, a detailed listing of which can be found in the reference section, each chapter considers a number of children's books and popular advice manuals, both those for children and for adults, pertinent to the particular emotion under examination in that chapter.

THE HISTORY OF READING AND READING WITH FEELING[16]

The focus of this volume is not so much on 'teaching by writing' as on 'learning by reading'. Instead of viewing the historical reader as a passive recipient of various forms of indoctrination, or at least socialization, we consider absorbed and enthusiastic reading as an active experience, through which readers can explore their imagination, participate in the production of the text's meaning, and exercise varying degrees of autonomy.[17] Historians of reading, including Robert Darnton, Jonathan Rose, and Martyn Lyons, have made great progress in reconstructing the history of readership, especially in Britain and France.[18] Crucially, the act of reading is now also acknowledged to engage and engender feelings; texts are not just interpreted, but also 'felt'.[19] As Rachel Ablow argues, 'in the mid- to late nineteenth century, reading was commonly regarded as at least as valuable as an affective experience as it was as a way to convey information or increase understanding'.[20] Rather than examining prescriptive norms, *Learning How to Feel* questions how writers and readers think about the experience of reading. Other scholars have looked beyond the meanings of texts to examine how readers respond to them. What makes one reader feel pity where another feels anger? The same text may move one reader to tears while another is unmoved. Susan Feagin explains affective responses to fictional literature in terms of appreciation, which she describes as the exercise of a set of abilities.[21] How do these emotional responses affect how we judge a particular text?

Describing when, how, and what children and adolescents read is a challenge. In the early nineteenth century, most children in Germany, France, and Britain learned to read with the help of simple primers and religious texts, usually the Bible and the catechism.[22] Only in middle-class families were more secular-oriented books available, first in the form of weekly magazines for children in the late eighteenth century, and later in the form of a specific literary genre for children. From the end of the nineteenth century, growing numbers of children from all classes—albeit to varying degrees in different countries—had easy access to children's literature.

At the same time, it is even more of a challenge for historians to portray the reading situations in which children read books. Undoubtedly, a broad variety of such settings existed, similar to the reading experiences of adults.[23] At times, children and adolescents read books on their own, once they were old enough, and had received the necessary education. In English and German nineteenth-century middle-class households, the children's room was only regarded as fully equipped once it contained at least one bookshelf that grew in parallel to its owner.[24] Books were sometimes read to children in groups, in public and in private. Bedtime stories, biblical or otherwise, became a custom in many families from the mid-nineteenth century. In other cases, children were asked by their teacher to read to their parents so that they could see the value of this newly acquired skill. In the instance of one middle-class family, the emotional (and almost sacred) significance of reading was quite evident, when the daughter was persuaded to listen to her father:

> When he reads something to you aloud, when he relates to you some of his achievements, when he radiates his warm feelings through song,—through prayer at the day's end—when his vocation enables him to read aloud to you from the Holy Scriptures or some other good book—; then let all that disturbs you fall from your hands, and be fully at one with your mind, spirit, feeling.[25]

The same book could be passed to multiple readers, making reading literature accessible and affordable to most children. This was not merely a middle-class practice. According to Robert Roberts' social-historical autobiography, for example, working-class youth frequently read school stories and those stories had a greater impact on them than anything else (including influential groups like the Boy Scouts). Boys internalized the public-school ethos better through these stories than by the teachings of their secular and religious leaders.[26] The same could be true, for example, of middle-class children reading about working-class characters, imagining themselves in various class- and race-specific settings depending on the inspiration they received from their reading matter.

PRACTICAL KNOWLEDGE AND MIMETIC LEARNING

But can the authors of this book really reconstruct and analyse learning processes by exploring children's books or advice manuals? Is it possible to get an insight into children's feelings, without exploring the concrete reception and different interpretations of these texts by their young readers? Can this book, in other words, describe more than mere teaching processes and a particular kind of emotionology of modern times?

Instead of emphasizing and overstating traditional distinctions between fictional and non-fictional literature, between scientific and so-called popular knowledge, or 'real' feelings and 'mere' feeling rules—binary distinctions that have been criticized for good reasons—this book underlines and focuses on the specificity of children and their emotional socialization. Children evidently learn in a more mimetic, imitative, and adaptive way than adults.[27] This applies to contemporary children, but it is our contention that similar processes were also at work in the nineteenth and twentieth centuries in Western Europe and North America, which, with some qualifications, were not wholly dissimilar to those at work in India or Russia.[28] It is assumed that within the period under investigation, children learnt emotions largely by trying to reproduce or echo the emotions they observed in others through bodily practices, mimicry, and gestures. They had to incorporate and— here we take up some fruitful ideas from Pierre Bourdieu—habitualize emotions in a concrete and situated sense, since these emotions were far from 'natural'.[29] As Christoph Wulf argues in this context, 'Mimetic learning...creates practical knowledge, which is what makes it constitutive of social...action.'[30]

From the authors' point of view, the important and productive question here is not so much *whether* children's books and advice manuals presented something other than a changing body of knowledge about children's emotions or learning processes, but what *kind* of knowledge they offered to children. In contrast to popular encyclopaedias or reference works, for example, children's books, in particular, did not deal with official or canonical knowledge, summarized into a more or less concise paragraph. Rather, they imparted and shared a situated and practical knowledge, telling children not necessarily *what* to feel but *how* this or that emotion occurs, what it looks like and the physical experience of it, in some level of detail.[31]

This practical knowledge was presented in varyingly complex conflicts, stories, and structures. From the middle of the nineteenth century onwards, more and more children's books began to deal not only with norms and their accompanying emotional or moral problems from the perspective of adults, but also set out to inform readers about serious clashes, changes, and long-term conflicts with or among children, who in turn emerge as the crucial actors in the stories. They offered solutions for these fights, originating first and foremost from the children themselves, rather than from the judging and correcting adults. Regardless whether children really had experienced these particular situations or not they could apply their own emotional knowledge to the stories and thereby expand upon this knowledge.

Drawing on the contributions of reception analysis, it cannot be assumed that children always learnt from children's literature or advice manuals precisely what authors or other adults wanted them to learn. In this sense, *Learning How to Feel* does not explore what children actually learnt from children's books or advice manuals in concrete—not only on the basis of the chosen sources, but with regard to children, particularly to small children, it would be very difficult to historically reconstruct the reception of the practical knowledge that was offered. Instead, this book advances the argument that children's books made available to their readers an extensive repertoire of experiences, expressions, and emotional practices that were learnt to a large degree mimetically in the absence of pre-determined outcomes. Mimetic learning was always subject to shifts and, to some degree, alternative interpretations.[32] The process of reproduction was also continually producing differences. Thus, the reading or listening situation is understood here more as one of *trying emotion* than coherent *doing emotion*.[33]

In the vein of Paul Ricoeur, René Girard, and the field of narratology more generally, the authors of this book assume that it was the manifold stories and their often complex narrative structures—stories that at certain historical points can also be found in advice manuals—that gave children the possibility and the time necessary to re-feel specific situations. By reading the stories told in these children's books or manuals in a mimetic, imitative way, from the bottom up, young readers were able to practice or develop an emotion accordingly, and to learn from their 'heroes' or their 'anti-heroes' how to feel.[34] As the characters in the stories developed, so did the reading or listening children. In this sense, the practical knowledge provided by children's books and many advice books could be adapted by children in a different way to what could be gleaned by adults, who, for example, read popular encyclopaedias. Children's books, in particular, did not only supply norms, but also offered detailed information about the feelings of their characters. It may be assumed that the reading or listening situation itself was, therefore, already generating experiences; it could initiate a concurrent learning process with sometimes strong effects on children and their bodies, from crying to laughing to trembling. The immense transformation within this genre during the nineteenth and twentieth centuries, especially in Western Europe and North America, into more and more polyvalent narratives, along with the growing market for children's books, created the space that enabled these experiences to occur. In this sense, the authors here regard the mimetic learning process not as a 'lower' or 'higher' stage of development within the history of emotions, but rather as a social opportunity to learn how to feel, to which different book genres and narrative structures in diverse periods and societies gave varying degrees of space. While this book focuses on reading situations within a more intimate context of children reading by themselves or in small groups of children and their carers, a mimetic learning process could also be initiated in much bigger, less intimate, group listening situations.

Children's literature in particular has been shown to assist children in coping with their own problems and dilemmas; psychological experiments seem to suggest this as well. Reading can increase children's emotional competence, raising their awareness of other people's emotional states.[35] This corresponds with earlier assertions of the (positive or negative) effects of reading on children and adolescents. Nineteenth-century advice literature regularly stressed the importance of books as powerful 'co-educators' and recommended those texts that made 'salutary impressions upon the heart'.[36] At the same time, authors incessantly warned of so-called bad and shameless reading that would allegedly spoil children's morality, 'pollute the mind'[37] and 'have an immoral effect on the heart'.[38] Such admonitions only attested, albeit in the negative, to the significant impact books were thought to have on children's emotional education.[39]

CHILDREN'S LITERATURE

While the beginnings of children's literature may be traced to the eighteenth century, the growing emphasis on childhood in the nineteenth century as a distinct, 'innocent' phase in the lifecycle, coupled with the mass expansion of child literacy, spurred a proliferation of literature specifically aimed at this distinct demographic. The period from the 1860s to the 1920s is often considered the 'golden age' of children's literature.[40] It also created a multiplicity of modes within that genre. Purely didactic and religious literature was supplemented and gradually replaced by stories that targeted the specific characteristics that children and adolescents were supposed to possess, informed by an ever larger quantity and variety of experts in the field.

Despite difficult categorizations, children's literature and its evolution provide a useful conduit for accessing changing expectations of youth over time and place. Children's literature does not exist in a 'vacuum', rather it is written and adapted for specific types of readers at specific periods in time, reflecting much wider societal concerns.[41] Children's literature is controlled by adults, no matter how subversive reading for youngsters may be.[42] Many of the books investigated here were deemed 'appropriate' by adult authority figures such as parents, teachers, reviewers, scholars, publishers, librarians, and various book-award committees. Some were written with a particular political, religious, or social audience in mind. Others were written to appeal to children's desire to be playful or to transgress. Many worked on multiple levels, rendering a straightforward analysis of their didactic purpose and intended effects or affects impossible. But how far can authors (and by extension, their intended readers) control how a text is read and understood? What literary devices did authors employ to get their emotional teachings across, and how did these affect readers' learning?

From its roots in eighteenth-century Britain and Germany, children's literature developed into a distinct genre by the mid-nineteenth century, with a vast commercial market not only in Britain and Germany, but also across the whole of Western Europe and North America.[43] From the beginning, many books of this genre were not intended exclusively for children, but were also meant to be read out loud among family members. Some books written for children were also popular among adults (the *Harry Potter* series being a recent example). Other books were originally written for adults, later to become children's classics in the nineteenth and twentieth centuries, such as *Robinson Crusoe* (1719) and *Gulliver's Travels* (1726), or much later, *Lord of the Flies* (1954), often in adapted or abridged versions for younger audiences. The sheer longevity of these classics along with their adaptability indicates their significance.

From the mid-nineteenth century onwards, children's books involved a greater number of complex and plural narratives, emotional and moral conflicts, and struggling heroes, and often in this context, learning processes and transitive feelings were expressed and reflected in great detail. In contrast to fairy tales or fables, which were traditionally characterized by a strong oral tradition, children's literature consisted predominantly of more prosaic, less symbolic narratives, presenting and discussing a concrete and practical kind of knowledge about feeling. It is worth noting in this context that children's books and advice manuals are indeed not the only possible sources for exploring the emotional socialization of children—one could also examine school books, religious sermons, educators' reports, or parents' diaries, for example. However, no other genre or medium offers such a rich insight into the learning processes and changing experiences with which members of this young audience could engage independently, at least when they were old enough to read for themselves, in their own time, in their own location, and under as little institutional pressure as possible.

Some of the simplest questions about this body of literature turned out to be the most difficult to answer.[44] While a rich research tradition on children's literature allowed the authors of *Learning How to Feel* to identify which works were significantly influential in various ways, in most cases information about sales volumes and other relevant data was scarce, at least until the latter part of the twentieth century. One of the few quantitative indicators came in the form of bestseller lists, yet such lists are often problematic and have their own complex history that needs to be taken into account.[45] Far from providing any insights into how bestselling books were actually received, at most they can only provide vague information regarding popularity. Harry Thurston Peck, the American editor of the journal *The Bookman*, invented the first bestseller list in 1895. He compiled monthly sales figures from various bookshops throughout the country and ranked the six most successful books. In other countries, the idea of judging literature by its commercial success elicited substantial opposition. In Germany, there were some short-lived attempts to establish bestseller lists in the 1920s, but they faced significant disapproval and were soon discontinued. A bestseller list appeared in the British publication *The Academy* between 1896 and 1899, but it disappeared, and similar lists did not re-emerge until the 1960s.

Even in the United States, specific bestseller lists for children's and juvenile literature only began to appear in the 1950s—with the exception of two short-lived attempts in *The Bookman* from 1909 to 1914 and *Publishers Weekly* from 1930 to 1932. The *New York Times* started to print lists of children's and juvenile bestsellers in 1952, at first once or twice a year. Data on bestsellers for other countries is even scarcer. Nevertheless, once underway, they left their mark. In her advice manual *Children are People* (1940), the American writer on etiquette, Emily Post, suggested to parents:

> When he is old enough to read to, don't let him miss the joy as well as the cultivating influence of *Alice in Wonderland*, the Just-So Stories, the books of A. A. Milne...Get a list of books proposed by the Child Study Association and select those which appeal to your children individually.[46]

Almost no effort was spared—and this is still the case—to find books deemed valuable and appropriate for children and young readers. In Germany, Britain, and the United States, a wide variety of recommendation lists were assembled to guide parents and educators in choosing the proper kind of literature. In some cases, (adult) readers were asked to name their favourite children's book and the resulting lists were published. Recommendation lists were also provided by experts. Moreover, every year new books for children received various prizes and awards as declarations of approval.

Literature for children and youth is a relatively transnational genre. In the *New York Times* bestseller lists for children and juvenile literature, the number of titles from outside the United States has increased over the years. In 1953, only one out of every sixteen books listed was by a non-American author. By 1973, however, eleven of the twenty books listed in two separate lists were non-American. Most of them came from the English-speaking world, with only few exceptions from France and Germany. The German *Libri-Index*, which registered the most popular books for the year 1971, contained twenty-nine books for children and adolescents among the overall top fifty books. Of those, fifteen were of foreign origin, though the overwhelming majority were written either by the Swedish author Astrid Lindgren or the English author Enid Blyton. One other indicator for the transnational dimension of the genre is that in the British *Time and Tide* recommendation list of 1938, the children's novel *Gay-Neck* (1927) by the Bengali author Dhan Gopal Mukerji appeared for the first time. The book had already received the American *John Newbery Medal* in 1928, with Mukerji becoming one of the first successful Indian writers in the United States. Several other authors received accolades for their work in more than one country.

Without a doubt, children's literature became an international success story. This was also true in other parts of the world, for example in Russia and in India, to which this book pays a special interest from a transnational or transcultural perspective. This transnational perspective is essential, as it focuses on unexpected translations and transgressions, global adaptations or regional modifications, and shifts within the socialization of children's emotions. Do particular children's books work better and more successfully in a transnational or transcultural context than others? Do some emotions play a different role in this context? Were there specific emotions that children could and should learn in Britain as much as in India, and in Russia as much as in Germany? Did this occur in the same way, and to the same degree, within the metropole as in the (former) colonies?

ADVICE MANUALS

In addition (and sometimes in contrast) to children's books, *Learning How to Feel* also investigates advice manuals on children's education and children's emotions. Advice manuals are significant sources for the normative and practical framing of childhood and, frequently, also of children's emotions. While it cannot be assumed that parents and other adults take advice on the education of their children at face value, the long-lasting popularity of the genre attests to its continued usefulness to readers.

The sources for this component of the study span a common corpus of approximately thirty of the most influential and most cited manuals, translations of which were also often published in numerous languages. These books were designed to guide or inform parents and teachers in particular, and in some cases they also directly addressed children or adolescents. As a genre, the range of advice manuals is nearly as diverse in content and form as children's literature, and includes manuals on sexuality, marriage, education, work, manners, and cooking.[47] The method of 'learning by reading', which was established by this genre from its emergence in the early modern period, profoundly transformed the processes of knowledge production, dissemination, and education.[48] It is not easy to identify the readership of this advice literature on childhood in any precise manner, although one of its main concerns has always been child-rearing.[49] Many books were clearly intended to be read by adults and above all by parents. This holds true for books about raising infants or young children (usually up to the age of three, in some cases up to age seven).[50] Other books, though, were intended to be read by young readers themselves, most frequently during their adolescence. Good examples of these are the books by the German physician and sexologist Max Hodann, and the American Lutheran minister and highly popular and prolific writer, Sylvanus Stall, both of whom published a series of advice manuals for older children.[51] In general, these texts almost always identified early childhood and adolescence as the most crucial periods of childhood, with less emphasis on the period of middle childhood (between five and twelve years of age).

As with children's literature, the nature of advice literature has been transformed greatly over time and in many ways. This is both a cause and an effect of the changing nature of childhood, as perceived by adults who educate, discuss, and provide advice concerning children. Rousseau's novel *Émile, ou de l'éducation* (1762), though inspired by other educational reformers including Locke, may be viewed as one of the first and most influential advice manuals for children, putting forward a specifically Romantic understanding of childhood. Rousseau is remarkable for his age-specific categorizations of emotional education and for his insistence on delaying the development of children as dictated by nature. Even reading, according to Rousseau, was damaging to the child and should not be introduced before the ages of twelve to fifteen.[52]

In the nineteenth and twentieth centuries, a number of developments resulted from the drive to professionalize the disciplines related to childhood and the forms of knowledge associated with them. The bodies of knowledge that informed the emotional enculturation of children also changed over the course of time. For a long period, one may observe a religious understanding of morality and education. From the late nineteenth century onwards, however, religion was gradually encroached upon by the sciences of the mind, and especially by psychology and pedagogy. A large part of advice literature for parents, as well as that for children and adolescents, was primarily focused on moral education yet presented its teachings in psychological terms. Conversely, psychologists of childhood and adolescence frequently relied on older understandings of childhood that had been informed by religion.

One of the most influential figures on the cusp of moral and scientific advice for children was G. Stanley Hall. His book *Adolescence* (1904) exemplifies the late nineteenth-century professionalization of the social sciences, of which Hall was a major propagator. With a theological background, Hall was a pioneer in scientific psychology and in issues relating to childhood and adolescence. He was also interested in pedagogy and in reforming children's education based on new theories in psychology.[53] In 1906, Hall published a shorter version of *Adolescence* entitled *Youth,* an advice manual for parents and educators on how to approach young people.[54] While striving to make his field scientific, he also popularized it among a wider audience of parents and young people. His books were widely sold in Europe, he had a large number of followers, and his views on the topic were quickly adopted by European social scientists. In many ways, however, Hall was not an innovator, but echoed older religious and moral ways of dealing with children and adolescents.

Over the course of the twentieth century, the academic professionalization of the social sciences, and of psychology and pedagogy in particular, altered the field of advice literature on childhood considerably. The influence of psychology was apparent in manuals on early childhood and infancy, not necessarily replacing religious or moral values, but often transforming them. The scientific orientation of knowledge about children's minds and their emotions also began to deeply affect the role of parents. In many ways, advice literature helped to create the problem it promised to alleviate. With traditional knowledge about childcare discredited, these books claimed that there was little to replace it with, unless parents began listening to the advice given to them by scholars and specialists. Such parental advice manuals and the advice genre in general worked by making the familiar unfamiliar. Toward the second half of the twentieth century, however, a critique of the scientific approach to childcare was strongly voiced within the genre of advice literature. Books like *Babies are Human Beings* (1938) by Charles Anderson Aldrich and Mary M. Aldrich encouraged parents once again to trust their own instincts.[55] Scientific knowledge could still be useful, the book suggested, but its task was first and foremost to educate parents about the naturalness of their role. However, if knowledge about child-rearing was instinctive, why was it necessary to read an advice manual? Advice literature failed to acknowledge that this approach would call into question the genre itself. Evidence also exists about how critically some parents approached and used this material. In the case of Benjamin Spock's famous *The Common Sense Book of Baby and Child Care* (1946), some mothers actually acted in accord with 'Spock's purported belief that they should rely on their own common sense in rearing their children' and stopped listening to his advice.[56]

A SUCCESS STORY? SIX MAJOR TRENDS IN MODERN TIMES

Over the next twelve chapters this book explores the changing emotional repertoire offered to children within these two heterogeneous genres, children's literature and advice manuals. Each chapter focuses on a single emotion, namely *anxiety, trust, piety, compassion, empathy, love, shame, pain, fear, bravery, homesickness,* and *boredom*, connecting it to other feelings and contextualizing it within broader historical shifts and changes from the mid-nineteenth century onwards.

The authors of *Learning How to Feel* have identified at least six major trends and significant topics within children's books and advice manuals: (1) the growing attention on and, as a result, the pluralization of emotions; (2) the changing role of morals, which, however, remained a constant feature in children's literature and advice manuals; (3) the struggle over more democratic relationships between adults and children and among children themselves; in this context (4) the influence of societal distinctions such as gender, race, class, or species and its changing role in teaching and learning how to feel; and (5) the growing importance of peer groups. Finally, while it might be tempting to interpret and portray these shifts and changes as a simple kind of success story, this book sheds light on (6) the growing responsibility of children for their own feelings and self-development over the past 150 years.

(1) The book does not assert that children's emotions as a topic was entirely absent from advice literature or children's books before the mid-nineteenth century, as several leading proponents of the eighteenth-century Enlightenment, including the German pedagogue, publisher, and bestselling children's author Joachim Heinrich Campe, observed. In recent times it has become accepted that children not only have emotions per se, but also experience and learn an ever wider variety of strong and serious feelings, as developed and almost as pronounced as in the case of adults.[57] Frequently, we can observe in both genres a remarkable extension, and

especially a pluralization, both of emotions and of ways to deal with them—that is, a changing and much more elaborate practical knowledge about learning how to feel. In Western Europe and North America above all, there has been a clear tendency to devote ever-increasing attention to children's emotions since the mid-nineteenth century. Some chapters reconstruct the growing interest in children's emotions, especially in the context of education and the family. It may be observed, for example, how certain feelings could bind children and adolescents to their families, while other feelings seem to detach them from their families. In this respect, advice manuals did not only inform parents about children's emotions, but also generated emotions—mainly anxiety and a feeling of responsibility—in parents.

(2) The increasing attention to children's emotions is very often marked by a simultaneous decrease in moralizing discourse within both genres. Indeed, there is a clear tendency during the period in question to deal with moral challenges in a different, often less strict way, highlighting not so much the problems and emotional or other competencies of adults, but those of children. Nonetheless this does not mean that children's books or advice manuals simply ignored moral or political topics. Children's education and entertainment in the late nineteenth and even until the end of the twentieth century operated at times in a considerably moralistic and didactic mode, with clear goals and strong rules of behaviour in public as well as private spaces, emphasizing in this context the distinctive, but changing, role of religion. Some chapters, for example, illuminate how children's books and advice manuals dealt with violence, suffering, and punishment, fields where moral judgements became evident. However, the way in which this happened was subject to change, allowing ever more space for the understanding of violence and suffering, not only of the victims but also of the perpetrators, even if the goal was almost always to reduce and control these woes.

(3) One of the most striking shifts in both genres at the end of the nineteenth century may be found in the trend toward less hierarchical, more democratic relationships and an associated emphasis on the empowerment of children, particularly in Western Europe and North America. Whereas it used to be the children who had to be taught how to feel by the adults, now the idea and sometimes even the imperative emerged, that adults should learn from children how to feel the 'right' way. In this way, both genres were deeply imbedded within some of the major societal tendencies of the late nineteenth and twentieth centuries, namely the increasing conflicts of social hierarchies, the emergence of emancipation movements, of democratic parties, and the advent of political participation in different fields—not only in the metropole, but to some degree also in the colonies. Such tendencies may be observed, for instance, through the transformation of the classical hero or heroine, whose fear becomes

increasingly legitimate. Some chapters highlight the changing role
of gender among children. However, the increasing equalization of
children—both in relation to adults and in relation to each other—was
contested. Due to the conflicting nature of these developments and
tendencies, it is not surprising to observe strong counter-tendencies for
less hierarchical relationships.

(4) As a rule, however, for the entire nineteenth century and a significant part
   of the twentieth century, the gender of children both as literary actors
   and as readers or objects of education played a crucial role in the ways in
   which they were intended to learn different kinds of emotions according
   to their traditional, supposedly appropriate, roles as the men and women
   of tomorrow. From the late nineteenth century onwards, as part of a
   much broader democratization process, gender distinctions slowly lost
   their overwhelming influence in children's books and advice manuals, at
   least in Western Europe and North America.[58] Other societal distinctions,
   normally strongly connected to gender distinctions, such as class, race,
   or species, often became less self-evident in this period. Sometimes
   these distinctions became much more a challenge for experimenting
   with unknown relationships than a platform for reproducing traditional
   binaries. Some chapters, for instance, demonstrate how learning how
   to feel with others, humans or animals, significantly gained historical
   importance in the metropole and the (former) colonies.

(5) Another very important and related shift in both genres is the growing
   importance of juvenile peer-group relationships. Within a broader shift
   towards the empowerment of children both as perpetrators and victims
   and against the background of a changing and expanding education
   system of kindergartens, schools, or boarding schools, other children,
   siblings, comrades, friends, or fighting groups took an increasingly
   central role in the emotional socialization of children in children's books
   and advice manuals. Even if the family, and especially parents, never
   lost their assumed key role in children's lives and education, there was
   a proliferation of stories and educational claims that offered alternative
   narratives about how children learn or should learn how to feel and to
   behave towards others. Some chapters in this book, for instance, reveal
   the role of boarding schools, especially in Britain, as a specific trope in
   children's literature from the mid-nineteenth century to the mid-twentieth
   century, with particular relevance for the peer-related emotional
   socialization of children. The degree to which this aspect of empowering
   children changed is demonstrated in the late twentieth century especially
   after 1968 with 'left-wing' children's literature. Here, the empowerment
   of children was a central goal; their feelings, wishes, and worries needed to
   be 'acted out' according to the individual needs of every single child in an
   'authentic' way.

(6) It could be argued that this 'authentic' way of feeling marks the outcome of processes that began in the mid-nineteenth century and should be interpreted as a kind of success story of empowerment and democratization, or liberation and participation. Although this book identifies some major trends and historical shifts, the authors of *Learning How to Feel* favour the argument that, first, these processes were neither linear nor homogeneous. They lacked a clear, historically determined goal and obvious counter-tendencies and conflicts may be found across the entire timeframe of investigation. Second, the authors wish to emphasize that these processes of empowerment and democratization should not be read exclusively as an unqualified success story. Becoming an emotional *subject*—and not so much an emotional *object*—with inherent rights and strengths meant that the children portrayed in children's books or advice manuals also had to become much more responsible for their own emotions and emotional well-being, and consequently their general behaviour and personal self-development. Against this background, our sources also allow us to analyse and to problematize what, in the spirit of Michel Foucault, one could call a therapeutization or flexibilization of children's emotions.[59] Some chapters therefore concentrate on the way emotions became more and more a pedagogical challenge and therapeutic mission. They came to be regarded mostly as an adjustment problem of the affected children and were thought to reveal something about their supposed psychological and emotional development.

Thus, the extension or pluralization of emotions evident in children's books and advice manuals from the mid-nineteenth century onwards was manifested not only as a chance for protagonists and readers alike, but these manifold opportunities and growing possibilities also became a new kind of duty. More democratic relationships between children and adults also confronted children with the demands of emotional or psychological self-development and of learning how to feel in an 'authentic' way. The growing number of possibilities to choose between different emotions in different situations and how to feel towards a variety of other actors opened the gates for a never-ending process of self-improvement and optimization. It demanded increasing flexibility in feelings. Far from trying to fix their emotions once and for all, both genres tried to make children adaptable to diverse challenges, always prepared for each new problem in their lives. Against this background, the authors of this book assume that both genres played an important, powerful and also intimate role in the emotional socialization of many children during the nineteenth and twentieth centuries. Learning how to feel—the 'right' way—in children's books and advice manuals, might have become less moralistic, hierarchical, or gendered, but evidently it also became much more contradictory and complex.

Whether these six major trends and significant topics discussed in the following twelve chapters continued to exist during the final decades of the twentieth century and well into the twenty-first century is a question for further investigation. However, children's books, as much as advice manuals, have certainly changed their societal function within the emotional socialization of children especially from the 1980s and 1990s onwards. Television and cinema, children's audio dramas, and computer games are not only continually gaining in importance from a quantitative perspective, the narratives about emotions or passions that these media try to unfold are becoming increasingly complex. Thus, computer games, too, nowadays the fastest growing global entertainment and education market for children and adolescents, are capable of initiating a mimetic learning process as much as children's books and advice manuals were and still are. The authors of this volume do not assume that children's and advice books have lost their impact on the lives of children in the present. Yet, any investigation into their role beyond the 'golden age' of children's literature would have to study them in relation to the multitude of media with which contemporary children learn how to feel.

NOTES

1. Ende, *Neverending Story*, 9–10.
2. Ende, 165.
3. On recent emotion research see, for example, Lewis, Haviland-Jones, and Barrett, *Handbook of Emotions*; Gross, *Handbook of Emotion Regulation*. See also chapter 1, 'Mrs Gaskell's Anxiety'.
4. This was particularly the case in the aftermath of '1968'. See, for example, Bookhagen et al., *Kommune 2*.
5. Of the few pioneers within this new academic field only one prominent historian, Peter Stearns, has paid serious attention to the emotional socialization of children. See especially Stearns and Haggerty, 'Role of Fear'; Stearns, 'Girls, Boys, and Emotions'.
6. Recent overviews in Frevert, *Emotions in History*; Frevert, *Geschichte der Gefühle*; Plamper, 'History of Emotions'; Plamper, *Geschichte und Gefühl*; Biess et al., 'History of Emotions'.
7. See, for example, Reddy, *Navigation of Feeling*; Frevert, *Emotions in History*. For more specific perspectives see, for example, Eitler and Scheer, 'Emotionengeschichte als Körpergeschichte'; Gammerl, 'Emotional Styles'; Scheer, 'Are Emotions a Kind of Practice'.
8. Davin, 'What Is a Child'.
9. Although his periodization of the 'discovery' of childhood is now viewed as problematic, Philippe Ariès' *L'Enfant et la vie familiale sous l'ancien régime* (1960; Eng. *Centuries of Childhood*, 1962) is often still acknowledged as the seminal text in this field. For persuasive reasons why historians should stop relying on Ariès, see Heywood, 'Centuries of Childhood'.
10. 'Adolescence'; Hall, *Adolescence*.
11. Hall, *Adolescence*, i, x.
12. See, for example, Gebhardt, *Angst vor dem kindlichen Tyrannen*.
13. Cipolla, *Literacy and Development in the West*, 72, 93.
14. Biswas and Agrawal, *Development of Education in India*, 835.
15. Anweiler and Meyer, *Sowjetische Bildungspolitik 1917–1960*, 44–51.
16. Feagin, *Reading with Feeling*.
17. Literary theorists like Wolfgang Iser, Stanley Fish, and Roland Barthes put forward theories related to reader-response criticism, whereby the focus is on the reader and on his or her response to the literary work, rather than on the content or the form of the

work itself. Thus, the meaning of a text is not in the text as such, rather in the reception of the reader or in the act of reading.

18. Darnton, 'First Steps Toward a History of Reading'; Lyons, *History of Reading and Writing*; Lyons, *Readers and Society in Nineteenth-Century France*; Rose, 'Arriving at a History of Reading'; Rose, *Intellectual Life of the British Working Classes*.

19. Ablow, *Feeling of Reading*, 4.

20. Ablow, 2.

21. Feagin, *Reading with Feeling*, 4.

22. Schenda, *Volk ohne Buch*, 73–85.

23. Schenda, 465–7.

24. Budde, *Auf dem Weg ins Bürgerleben*, 127–8.

25. Bahnmaier, 'Ein Wort für junge Töchter', 134 (all translations by the authors).

26. Roberts, *Classic Slum*, 160–2.

27. Different perspectives on this topic take up, for example, Saarni, *Children's Understanding of Emotion*; Suzuki and Wulf, *Mimesis, Poiesis, and Performativity in Education*; Nadel and Butterworth, *Imitation in Infancy*. For a good discussion of the concept of mimesis and mimetic learning see especially Gebauer and Wulf, *Mimesis*. A broad interdisciplinary overview offer Spariosu, *Mimesis in Contemporary Theory*; Garrels, *Mimesis and Science*. On the—modern, not the antique—'origins' of the concepts of mimesis and imitation within the literary and social sciences see the classics of Auerbach, *Mimesis;* Tarde, *Laws of Imitation*.

28. See the epilogue in this volume.

29. In fact, the concept of habitus has much in common with the concept of mimesis as Gebauer and Wulf, *Mimesis*, emphasize correctly. On the habitualization of emotions in the vein of Pierre Bourdieu, see, for example, Zembylas, 'Emotional Capital and Education'. See also, Scheer, 'Are Emotions a Kind of Practice'.

30. Wulf, 'Mimetic Learning', 56.

31. On the concept of practical knowledge and its links to the concept of mimesis, see, for example, Bourdieu, *Logic of Practice*.

32. See Wulf, 'Mimetic Learning'.

33. See Eitler and Scheer, 'Emotionengeschichte als Körpergeschichte'.

34. See especially Girard, *Deceit, Desire and the Novel*; Girard, *Mimesis and Theory*; Ricoeur, *Time and Narrative*, esp. vol. 1.

35. Trepanier and Romatowski, 'Classroom Use of Selected Children's Books'; Kumschick et al., 'Sheep with Boots'. As to the use of stories and plays to measure and increase moral emotions in pre-school children, see Malti and Buchmann, 'Entwicklung moralischer Emotionen bei Kindergartenkindern'.

36. Newcomb, *How to be a Lady*, chapter 16, quotation 158; Newcomb, *How to be a Man*, chapter 16; Blackwell, *Counsel to Parents*, 44–5; Anon., *Boys and Their Ways*, 199–233; Hughes, *Notes for Boys*, 121–30; Matthias, *Wie erziehen wir unsern Sohn Benjamin*, 168; Klencke, *Die Mutter als Erzieherin ihrer Töchter und Söhne*, 425–6.

37. Anon., 'Scene from Real Life', 82.

38. Klencke, *Die Mutter als Erzieherin ihrer Töchter und Söhne*, 572.

39. Vallone, *Disciplines of Virtue*, 4.

40. Green, 'Golden Age of Children's Books'; Carpenter, *Secret Gardens*.

41. Hunt, *Understanding Children's Literature*, 1–2.

42. See Rose, *Case of Peter Pan*, 2.

43. For a good overview, see, Grenby and Immel, *Cambridge Companion to Children's Literature*; Carpenter and Prichard, *Oxford Companion to Children's Literature*.

44. In this section, we are indebted to Karola Rockmann and Johanna Rocker for their valuable research assistance.
45. Eyre, *British Children's Books in the Twentieth Century;* Faulstich, *Bestandsaufnahme Bestseller-Forschung;* Vogt-Praclik, *Bestseller in der Weimarer Republik 1925–1930;* Egoff and Hagler, *Books That Shaped Our Minds;* Ferrall and Jackson, *Juvenile Literature and British Society;* Justice, *Bestseller Index.*
46. Post, *Children are People*, 182.
47. The available literature on the history of the twentieth century has primarily focused on sex advice: Bänziger et al., *Fragen Sie Dr. Sex;* Putz, *Verordnete Lust.* On the modern history of the effects of advice for the self: Maasen et al., *Das beratene Selbst.*
48. Messerli, 'Zur Geschichte der Medien des Rates'.
49. For a more general overview: Hardyment, *Dream Babies;* for the literature on the United States: Grant, *Raising Baby by the Book;* Hulbert, *Raising America;* on Germany: Fuchs, *Wie sollen wir unsere Kinder erziehen;* Gebhardt, *Angst vor dem kindlichen Tyrannen.*
50. For example, Isaacs, *Nursery Years.*
51. Hodann, *Woher die Kinder kommen;* Hodann, *Bub und Mädel;* Stall, *What a Young Boy Ought to Know.*
52. The one exception here is *Robinson Crusoe* (1719), which should guide the child's life in Rousseau's opinion. For an interesting discussion of the influence of Rousseau on nineteenth-century ideas on the child's mind, see Shuttleworth, *Mind of the Child*, 4–6.
53. Ross, 'Hall, Granville Stanley'.
54. Hall, *Youth.*
55. Aldrich and Aldrich, *Babies are Human Beings.*
56. Grant, *Raising Babies by the Book*, 225.
57. Compare, for example, Campe, *Robinson the Younger* (1781/2); Campe, *Ueber Empfindsamkeit und Empfindelei in pädagogischer Hinsicht* (1779).
58. See, for example, Clark, *Regendering the School Story;* Flanagan, *Into the Closet.*
59. See, for example, Martin, Gutman, and Hutton, *Technologies of the Self;* Rose, *Governing the Soul.*

1

Mrs Gaskell's Anxiety

Uffa Jensen

On the evening of 10 March 1835, the soon to be famous Victorian novelist Elizabeth Gaskell began to write a baby diary. She wanted to document the development of her first-born daughter Marianne and to keep a record of her educational influence on the child. She noted Marianne's mental and physical development meticulously. In terms of her personality, Marianne appeared to her 'remarkably good tempered; though at time she gives way to little bursts of passion'. Gaskell reflected upon any sign of her child's irritation. Marianne's crying always made her wonder about the causes and she expressed concern about her own response to her child's emotional outbursts. A few months later, she was still unsure about 'the best way of managing these sensibilities'. Very early on, Gaskell also noted how mutual their emotional dependence was: 'I had no idea the journal of my own disposition, & feelings was so intimately connected with that of my little baby'. She thus devoted much thought to the education of her child, as she wanted 'to act on principles now which can be carried on through the whole of her education'. Accordingly, she began to consult the latest advice literature on the subject, which included *L'Éducation progressive ou étude du cours de la vie* (vol. i, 1828; Eng. *Progressive Education, Commencing with the Infant,* 1835) by the Swiss educationalist Albertine Necker de Saussure, and *Principles of Physiology Applied to Health and Education* (1834) by the Scottish physician Andrew Combe. But the advice offered in these books frequently left her in despair. 'Books do so differ', she stated with irritation, as she tried to find some guidance on how to handle her child's emotional crises. Hence, another reason to keep the diary concerned Gaskell's own emotional management. She dedicated the diary—which she hoped her daughter would one day read herself, maybe as a mother—to her child, 'as a token of her mother's love, and extreme anxiety in the formation of her little daughter's character'.[1]

Gaskell was certainly an unusual mother for her time. Maids and servants helped her with the running of the household and with the care of her child. She was well versed in the latest scientific discussions, such as phrenology, which encouraged mothers to carefully observe their offspring for any physical irregularity that might indicate a mental aberration.[2] She was able to read Necker de

Saussure's advice book in French. This thorough study of the first three years of a child's life combined insights into the mechanism of children's development and the importance of parental authority with a general empathy towards children.[3] Such an empathetic parenthood seemed very much in tune with the Victorian family model of the emerging middle class. With the beginning of the Victorian age, it became fashionable to keep baby diaries at home.[4] Observational technique, diary-keeping, and advice books formed a fascinating alliance for a new form of childcare among middle-class Victorian parents. The coherent notion of this alliance was the idea of development: children's growth could be observed and documented and advice could be based on such observations, because the progress of development was based on certain mechanisms and principles. Gaskell's ambition to base her educational efforts 'on principles' reflected this fact.

The most pervasive emotions in Gaskell's diary were love and anxiety—and in many ways the two were intrinsically intertwined. On the one hand, '[t]he love which passeth every earthly love', as Gaskell herself described the emotion, fuelled the sustained resolution to observe and describe her child. Love was also meant to nurture the child's development. At this point, a new kind of regime—the regime of love, as it might be called—became evident. To support the child's growth with love and empathy meant to gain the child's compliance in the process of education. Loving attentiveness might be much more effective than violence in generating obedience. On the other hand, Gaskell's diary revealed a substantial amount of anxiety. In part, this resulted from the conflicting advice provided in the expert literature. Additionally, the new habit of closely observing children and their development created more occasions about which to be anxious. Nothing seemed trivial and everything seemed to bear consequences. Indeed, it was the very idea that a child's mental and physical capacities were in development and not predetermined that placed greater responsibility on the parents. Consequently, Gaskell was quite concerned when she addressed her thoughts to the future grown-up Marianne: 'And you too my dearest little girl, if when you read this, you trace back any evil, or unhappy feeling to my mismanagement in your childhood forgive me, love!'[5] It became a source of constant anxiety for Gaskell that she, with all her love for her child, might prompt the wrong kind of development.[6]

This anxiety-producing love was one aspect of the modern approach towards the development of children. A rather sustained criticism against such methods soon emerged. Excessive love was considered dangerous for children. In German advice manuals, this problem was called *Affenliebe* (literally: 'monkey love') or 'doting affection' and was closely related to the knowledge gained through zoology about apes.[7] Doting parents would always love their children more than they should. They would never be able to harden their children appropriately. From this perspective, it was deemed necessary to distrust the parents' (and especially the mothers') emotions and to undermine their educative authority. Modern childcare advice thus oscillated between these two models. Toward the middle of the nineteenth century, a hardening approach began to exist alongside an attitude that favoured affection and emotionality as the basis of the child-parent relationship.[8] Parents now had to ask themselves if their feelings represented what was good for their children—or if their feelings were, in fact, the real problem. Both models, however, relied on advice literature as the infallible authority that would not just provide parents with useful knowledge, but would also teach parents to either trust or distrust their inclinations and emotions. These distinct models manifested themselves in different advice on the various problems with which parents were confronted in raising their children: Should they inflict corporal punishment? Should they comfort their distressed child? Should mothers breastfeed their children under all circumstances? But it was not just the dependence on advice that the two models had in common. In their own way, both models actually produced anxiety. Did parents love their children enough or too much? Could they trust themselves or did they have to rely on others, because they were over-emotional as parents? The issue was not simply that the differences between advice manuals produced insecurities: such books also had to rely on the parents' need for advice in the first place.

KNOWLEDGE PRODUCTION ABOUT CHILDREN'S EMOTIONS

In many ways, Gaskell was writing her baby diary at the onset of a new knowledge culture about childrearing in the incipient Victorian age. Advice literature, on which this chapter focuses much more than the following ones, emerged as an ever-growing genre and book market.[9] In the early nineteenth century, middle-class readers primarily bought this advice literature, whereas in the late twentieth century its readership presumably expanded somewhat into the lower middle and, possibly even, into the lower classes. At least, this is what the growing sales figures for advice manuals suggest. The fact that Gaskell's observations frequently concentrated on Marianne's emotionality matches more general developments in the history of knowledge and science. By the mid-nineteenth century, the emotions of children had become a prominent topic in scholarly discussions, primarily in psychological, psychiatric, and pedagogical literature.[10] From this point onwards, various scientific disciplines, writers of fiction and advice literature, a fascinated public, and, especially parents formed a complex and interactive framework in which knowledge about children and their emotions was produced and circulated. Scientists such as Charles Darwin or William T. Preyer studied their own children and used their observations in scholarly treatises as well as in advice literature for parents. Like Gaskell, ordinary parents also collected observations about their children, frequently in diaries and questionnaires, a practice that was often encouraged by scholars such as G. Stanley Hall, who then collected the material creating more data on child development.[11] Writers of fiction, for instance Charles Dickens and Charlotte Brontë, not only benefited from this knowledge to write about children, but their stories also contributed further material to the discussions about child development. Ever since the German Enlightenment pedagogue Johann Heinrich Campe imbued Daniel Defoe's *Robinson Crusoe* (1719) with didactic significance in his own version, *Robinson der Jüngere* (1779/1780; Eng. *Robinson the Younger*, 1781/1782), writers of children's literature have frequently relied on pedagogical or psychological knowledge about childhood and childcare.[12] Journals, newspapers, novels, and advice literature increasingly came to inform the public about the latest studies and, in turn, also helped to set the agenda for subsequent enquiries into the minds of children.[13]

Advice literature played a pivotal role in this circulation of knowledge. In this genre, pedagogical and psychological knowledge increasingly merged. In fact, it is difficult to separate the two when it comes to childhood advice. A good example of the close intertwining of the two fields of knowledge was the intensive exchange between the movement for 'new education', or *Reformpädagogik*, and the psychological work of G. Stanley Hall, Susan Isaacs, and William Stern among others. Yet the two fields also differed somewhat in their interests. Whereas psychologists frequently concentrated on early childhood and infancy, as well as—to a somewhat lesser degree—adolescence and puberty, pedagogues were much more interested in middle childhood and the (early) school years. This is also reflected in the respective advice literature. Apart from scholars from the respective disciplines, who also published advice manuals with surprising frequency, many different professions were actually engaged in the production of this literature, in particular theologians, teachers, government officials, physicians, etc. While this chapter will primarily focus on the American, British, and German developments, it must be emphasized just how international the debates about childhood and childrearing were, at least from the late nineteenth century onwards.[14] American, German, French, British, and other authors collaborated with each other, cited each other's work and had their books translated into other languages. In some cases, knowledge reached even beyond the confines of the 'Western' world, as was the case with psychoanalysis, which became notably popular in South America, India, Japan, and Northern Africa.[15] Thus, knowledge about childhood and childcare was also adapted to these cultures.[16]

THE BEGINNING OF CHILD STUDIES IN THE NINETEENTH CENTURY

During the second half of the nineteenth century, child studies emerged as a scholarly field in countries such as Germany, France, Britain, and the United States. Growing scientific expertise in this area competed with older traditions of children's education and study in moral philosophy and religion. One of the first tasks was to collect data on the physical and mental development of children. The British-German physiologist William T. Preyer based his influential study *Die Seele des Kindes* (1882; Eng. *The Mind of the Child*, 1888/1889) on the detailed observations of his son's development until the age of three.[17] In the 1830s, long before Preyer, Charles Darwin had begun to keep meticulous diaries about his children, but he hesitated to use them for his studies on evolution, which he was formulating at the same time. It was not until 1877 that Darwin published his 'A Biographical Sketch of an Infant', which became the major incentive for the foundation of a veritable 'baby science' in the following decades.[18] Until the early decades of the twentieth century, the technique of keeping baby diaries for scientific analysis was widely utilized by psychologists. Such scientific diaries existed alongside educational and domestic practices of diary-based observations of children, which often continued for much longer into the twentieth century and are still in use today.[19]

As in the case of Elizabeth Gaskell, emotions played an important role in these baby diaries and, more generally, in the emerging concept of development, which had structured the discussions on the mind of the child since the mid-nineteenth century.[20] The work of the French psychologist Bernard Perez, for example, showed how different emotions, as well as emotionality in general, developed in a child. In his book on infants, he discussed the primary sentiments and the evolution of the affective sensibility in children, which included descriptions of fear, rage, envy, sympathy, and sexual and personal sentiment.[21] In an additional book on older children, Perez added a section on higher emotions in which he discussed aesthetic feelings and shame.[22] In such baby diaries, emotions were mainly an object of observation and came to be understood as specific elements at different stages within an overall developmental scheme. From an emotional base, the child was to mature toward cognitive capacities. Such views often reflected middle-class ideas about childhood—and, in particular, infancy—as the site of emotionality, and adulthood as the stage of rational self-control.[23]

Such notions of a developing emotionality—and the mind in general—were increasingly fused with an evolutionary perspective. Here again Darwin paved the way: 'May we not suspect that the vague but very real fears of children, which are quite independent of experience, are the inherited effects of real dangers and abject superstitions during ancient savage times?'[24] The American psychologist and most prominent protagonist of the American Child Study Movement, G. Stanley Hall, was a major advocate of such an evolutionary theory of recapitulation in child studies.[25] In his practical advice for childrearing, Hall exhibited a peculiar mixture of a Rousseauian tendency—the child needs to live through its 'savage' phase in a natural environment—and a belief in strict education with discipline, drill, and (corporal) punishment. It was only in adolescence that the savage child turned into a human being in the strictest sense—and, in 1906, Hall devoted an entire (advice) manual to the subject.[26] Like Hall, many authors compared the mind of a child to the mental structure of an animal, a primitive, an abnormal person, or to the mental state of the ancient past of humanity. In such notions of recapitulation, the development of an individual child (ontogeny) could always be correlated to, and ultimately, explained by the development of the species (phylogeny).[27] During the course of the nineteenth century and early twentieth century, this thinking linked the study of children to discussions about the impending degeneration of nations, civilizations and, eventually, humanity.[28] At the same time, the evolutionary perspective on child behaviour could also offer parents some comfort: seemingly incomprehensible actions of their children could now be 'explained' by an animal past. The general objective of children's education remained, however, unambiguous: to achieve the middle-class, western, civilized morality of a controlled, emotional, but not irrational, adult.

Toward the end of the nineteenth century, the interest in children's mental and emotional development grew further, while the field of scientific investigation became more complex. The hitherto prevailing qualitative studies of individual children were slowly replaced by increasingly large-scale surveys, for which statistical methods and testing were employed.[29] Additionally, infants and children became the object of experiments in professional laboratories, for example Francis Galton's *Anthropometric Laboratory* at the *International Health Exhibition*, which was opened in London in 1884. In general, these changes in the scientific organization of child studies reflected a move towards professionalization. This entailed a disregard for the involvement of parents in the process of gaining knowledge about children as well as an increasingly strict division of labour between researchers, parents, and practitioners.[30] For a subject so intrinsically intertwined with issues of domesticity and gender relations, professionalization also undermined the ability of mothers to observe their own offspring.

PEDAGOGICAL ADVICE LITERATURE AND THE EDUCATION OF CHILDREN

Children's emotions were long-established subjects in the discipline of pedagogy. Nevertheless, new ideas about the education of children began to circulate in the late nineteenth and early twentieth centuries in various European societies, in the United States and in many other parts of the globe. Terms like 'new education', *'éducation nouvelle'* or *'Reformpädagogik'* became a rallying call, prompting the emergence of a variety of movements for education reform.[31] The character of these attempts as a 'global education movement' needs to be noted, especially because they spanned not just the Western world, but reached well beyond.[32] For example, the concept of education employed by the Bengali poet and Nobel laureate Rabindranath Tagore for the founding of his university in Shantiniketan in 1918 was deeply influenced by ideas of the new education movement and by school reform projects.[33] From the very beginning, a broad array of influences from different cultures shaped the reformist agenda. The pedagogical work and school project begun by Leo Tolstoy at Yasnaya Polyana, his estate in the Russian countryside, in 1849 turned the Russian writer into one of best-known advocates for freedom in the education of children.[34] In 1900, the Swedish educator and socialist Ellen Key coined the central motto, the 'century of the child', for the ensuing debates: 'Adults will first come to an understanding of the child's character and then the simplicity of the child's character will be kept by adults.'[35] Understanding, kindness, and love were the emotional qualities with which parents were to approach the education of children.

In many societies, practical pedagogical experiments with 'youth republics' were promoted, in which young adults could establish autonomous structures (usually under the guidance of an adult): W. R. George's *Junior Republic* and Homer Lane's *Ford Republic* (later called *Boys Republic)* in the United States; Homer Lane's *Little*

Commonwealth and his follower A. S. Neill's *Summerhill School* in England as well
as Neill's German school experiment; Siegfried Bernfeld's *Baumgarten* home for
(Jewish) children in Germany; Anton S. Makarenko's *Gorky Colony* in early Soviet
Russia; and so on.[36] An emotionalized approach frequently accompanied these
projects, for example the 'loving attitude' towards children, propagated by Homer
Lane.[37] Such practical approaches directly informed much of the numerous new
advice manuals that focused on the idea of putting children at the centre of the
educational process. Lane's friend and disciple A. S. Neill utilized such concepts
in German and English reform schools, most famously at Summerhill, which he
founded in 1924.[38] Two years later, Neill published *The Problem Child* (1926), a
treatise for parents, which was printed in five editions over ten years and helped
attract more children to Summerhill. In his book, Neill argued that the problem
child is fundamentally unhappy.

> No happy man ever disturbed a meeting, or preached a war, or lynched a negro. No
> happy woman ever nagged her husband and children. No happy employer ever scared
> his employees. No happy man ever committed a murder or a theft. All crimes, all
> hatreds, all wars can be reduced to unhappiness. This book will be an attempt to show
> how unhappiness arises and how it ruins human lives.[39]

For Neill, only a 'philosophy of freedom' in education could produce happiness.
One German advice manual serves as an example of the same tendency: Heinrich
Lhotzky's *Die Seele Deines Kindes* (1908; Eng. *The Soul of Your Child*, 1924), which
was first published in 1908 and had sold at least 300,000 copies by 1938.[40] Here,
children were seen as equals to their parents, as friends.

Such examples of educational reform and emotional freedom show that a
reorientation of education was taking place at the turn of the twentieth century.
The intellectual dimension, while still important, lost its pre-eminence in
educational debates and the emotional as well as social learning of children gained
importance. However, this new focus on emotions in the 'new education' could
have adverse consequences. To trust a child to develop naturally could also produce
new insecurities, because it was difficult, if not impossible, for parents or teachers
to discern precisely what the nature of the child really was.

Educational debates around the turn of the twentieth century were not entirely
dominated by a reform-minded, child-centred approach. In Germany, Friedrich
Wilhelm Foerster—a Catholic professor of pedagogy combining the 'revolutionary and reactionary'[41]—was certainly the most prominent and widely read
author of educational literature. His advice manuals integrated a call for children's
self-government and self-control with a rigid moral philosophy that centred on
the teaching of a thorough suppression of emotions and desires. At the same time,
Foerster's work reflected the common plea to 'start from the child', which the
reform pedagogy of the time propagated so forcefully. The teacher of morality, in
Foerster's view, had to observe the child's character in order to identify the elements
that could be helpful for the development of self-control (*Selbstbeherrschung*).[42] For
Foerster, freedom of the child meant children finding their own way to rigidly
control their bodies, desires, and emotions, to choose their own tyranny. Arguably,

such appeals were far more widespread at the turn of the twentieth century than sometimes acknowledged in the literature on the reform agenda. In fact, the approach of hardening children in a hostile world was never absent from the pedagogical discussions.

CHILDREN AND THEIR EMOTIONS IN BEHAVIOURISM AND PSYCHOANALYSIS

The trend towards professionalization and empirical approaches peaked in the early twentieth century, particularly with the emergence of behaviourism. Its founder, John B. Watson, focused specifically on children's emotions. He criticized the older literature for studying infants exclusively from an armchair perspective and, thus, merely producing random observations outside of the scientific setting of professional laboratories. Instead, his approach entailed the extensive testing and detailed analysis of children's—mostly infants'—behaviour in a controlled laboratory atmosphere. He postulated that, 'An emotion is an hereditary pattern-reaction involving profound changes of the bodily mechanisms as a whole, but particularly of the visceral and glandular systems.'[43] This definition of emotion as a hereditary pattern—here, he only specifically referred to fear, rage, and love—did not rule out the idea that many aspects of emotions were learnt. Indeed, much of Watson's work with infants tried to prove that children and their emotions could be conditioned by training particular stimulus-response patterns. He attempted to prove this in his experiments with infants and children, which he planned and executed in part with a high degree of versatility and which involved considerable cruelty.[44] The most (in)famous case is certainly that of *Little Albert*: Watson and his assistant (and later wife) Rosalie Rayner conditioned the eight-month-old Albert B. to fear a white rat and, by association, furry objects.[45]

After his resignation from his post at Johns Hopkins University in late 1920, Watson went on to publish widely on child psychology, although he conducted no further experiments. His articles on childrearing were published in numerous popular magazine articles and were aimed at a wider public. His statements about the merits of scientific insights into the minds of children were sometimes quite radical. At one point, Watson provocatively announced that he could train any 'healthy infant, well-formed' into becoming any kind of professional—'doctor, lawyer, artist, merchant-chief' or 'even beggar-man and thief'.[46] In 1928, he and Rosalie published the advice book *Psychological Care of Infant and Child*, which sold some 100,000 copies in the first few years after its publication. Their intention was to 'help the serious mother to solve the problem of bringing up a happy child'. In their view, the 'modern mother' had only just begun to understand 'that the rearing of children is the most difficult of all professions'.[47] They insisted on the problematic effects of too much parental emotion:

> There is a sensible way of treating children. Treat them as though they were young adults.... Let your behavior always be objective and kindly firm. Never hug and kiss

them, never let them sit in your lap....Try it out. In a week's time you will find how easy it is to be perfectly objective with your child and at the same time kindly. You will be utterly ashamed of the mawkish, sentimental way you have been handling it.[48]

In such passages, Watson revealed the central mechanism of this advice manual for parents: to make parenthood seem unfamiliar, to instil insecurity and to promise improvement through advice. Overall, Watson's behaviourism certainly concentrated on the matter of children's emotions, turning them into a cornerstone of empirical investigation in a hitherto unprecedented fashion. The possible acquisition, strengthening, and diminishing of emotions in children through learning and conditioning opened up numerous perspectives for science-based childrearing practices. This approach opposed the 'naturalness' of the child-centred alternative in the tradition of Ellen Key, which denied the possibility of any true alteration of behavioural pattern and, indeed, of any learning in the fullest sense. In many ways, Watson subjected emotions to a programme of social engineering in order to achieve a mature and useful adult and citizen. For the ideal of a Fordist and Taylorist society, Watson's behaviourism and its child psychology could serve the goal of streamlining and rationalizing emotionality. In the first decades of the twentieth century, this view on children and their emotions was hegemonic in the United States, but also—albeit in a slightly different version, as will be discussed below—in Germany.

Psychoanalysis was another factor influencing child studies in the early twentieth century. Although psychological development during childhood and particularly infancy proved crucial for his theory, Sigmund Freud did not focus a great deal of attention directly on the study of children. Even the one major exception—his 'Analyse der Phobie eines 5jährigen Jungen' (1909; Eng. 'Analysis of a Phobia in a Five-Year-Old Boy', 1975), which became famous as the story of *Little Hans*—was not based on direct observation.[49] In the history of psychoanalysis, this case study has been perceived to confirm Freud's ideas of infantile sexuality, which he had first described in *Drei Abhandlungen zur Sexualtheorie* (1905; Eng. *Three Essays on the Theory of Sexuality*, 1949).[50] The Oedipus complex was of essential importance for classical Freudian theory at least: 'Hans really was a little Oedipus who wanted to have his father "out of the way," to get rid of him, so that he might be alone with his beautiful mother and sleep with her.'[51] From Freud's perspective the core of the development of—it must be stressed, *male*[52]—children, was marked by this Oedipal structure and thus, in fact, by an emotional story of love, envy, fear, and hatred. In this way, *Little Hans* stood at the onset of a psychoanalytical sub-field, the study of children's mental structure and specifically their emotions.[53] Some of Freud's female followers like Hermine Hug-Hellmuth, Anna Freud, and Melanie Klein developed the field further.

In many ways, child analysis served as a veritable alternative to the established practices of professional psychoanalysis. New psychoanalytical data could best be gained by observing children rather than engaging in therapeutic sessions with 'neurotic' adults. As such, child analysis also proved to be an appropriate starting point for lay female analysts who, in some cases, chose to analyse their own children.[54] In the late 1920s, Freud's daughter, Anna Freud, emerged as the new specialist in child analysis, quickly rivalled by Melanie Klein in Berlin and later in London.[55] In distinct ways, Anna Freud and Klein picked up the thread of the empirical tradition, through which the field of child studies had emerged in the late nineteenth century. Qualitative data collection through close observation gained prominence again through psychoanalysis, in contrast to the behaviourist tradition of testing and laboratory experimentations. Child psychoanalysts tried to create an atmosphere in their consulting rooms—with the help of, for example, toys or drawing utensils—that would encourage their child-subjects to play and, at the same time, would enable them to be observed.[56] While it is difficult to sum-marize how this varied and conflict-ridden research tradition discussed emotions, an important shift may be noted in the Kleinian tradition in particular, namely, the departure from the Freudian emphasis on drives, which in many ways prevented a conceptual appreciation of emotions.[57] This was slowly replaced by an emphasis on object relations, which brought the relationships of children—especially with their mothers—to the fore.[58]

Following the Second World War, with Europe in ruins and many, though not all, analysts having left the European continent, the post-war fate of psychoanaly-sis and its study of childhood was decided in the United States.[59] This change of scientific scenery transformed Freudian ideas in many complex ways.[60] Apart from a general medical reorientation of psychoanalytical theory and practice, the study of children was affected in particular by the more optimistic reading of these ideas. Freud's deep cultural pessimism about human nature never featured very promi-nently in the United States. Instead, a normalization of psychoanalysis took place in two important ways. In the post-war years, many of these ideas became part of the intellectual and even of the everyday mainstream. Additionally, it became much more accepted to study the psychological development of the 'normal' mind instead of sufferers of mental disorder. This resulted in a further boost in the popu-larity of the psychoanalytical study of children. On the one hand, the observation of children became an important instrument for the study of 'normal' behaviour—beyond the couch. On the other hand, psychoanalytical knowledge would now start to influence general childrearing practices.

THE NEW ROLE OF PARENTHOOD IN ADVICE LITERATURE

Toward the end of the nineteenth century and in the early twentieth century, much of the literature on childrearing was increasingly concerned with the psycho-logical well-being of children. The turn to scientific knowledge intensified, slowly replacing an older middle-class model of advice literature. Thus, in Germany for example, the bourgeois tradition of encouraging parents to emphasize the poten-tial self-formation and education of the child was succeeded by an increasing psy-chological expertocracy. The psychologist and educator Hildegard Hetzer, who had started her work with socially deprived children in the Viennese School of child psychology (together with the psychologists Karl and Charlotte Bühler), epitomized this trend with her various manuals, such as *Seelische Hygiene! Lebenstüchtige Kinder!* ('Mental hygiene! Children fit for life!', 1930).[61] However, this trend did not remain unchallenged. In 1934, Johanna Haarer published the first edition of her advice book *Die deutsche Mutter und ihr erstes Kind* ('The German mother and her first child'), which remained in print after 1945 (with the word '*deutsche*' removed from the title) until 1987 and sold a total of 1.2 million copies.[62] In the book, Haarer expresses her scepticism about the scientific and psychologizing trend, which prevents mothers from really educating their children. Here, the advice to restrain emotions is also very prominent: 'Beware of all too loud and intense a show of motherly feelings.' Parents should be wary of their child's emotions. They should fight against the child's natural desire for love and affection. Otherwise, they would create a 'domestic tyrant' (*Haustyrann*).[63] That such recommendations sound very similar to Watson's behaviourist advice to limit and control parental emotions should not be surprising. After all, Haarer, as well as Hetzer, stood in the same tradition of supporting the rationalization of childcare. What was specific about the German and the Nazi case was the ideological basis of such emotional control in the parent-child relationship.[64] Children were thought to be born into a hostile environment of social-Darwinian proportions. Therefore parents—and especially mothers—were to adhere to a rigid programme of toughening up their progenies. Excessive comfort, pampering, and emotions would ruin a child's ability to survive. This meant that parents—and, again, addressed primarily to mothers—had to learn to distrust themselves and their emotions.

A different approach emerged in the American advice literature of the 1930s, which eventually eclipsed these methods. During the 1920s, the psychologist Arnold Gesell had already begun to argue strongly against Watson's childrearing methods in favour of close child observation and individual development.[65] However, it was primarily Charles Anderson Aldrich and Mary M. Aldrich's advice book *Babies are Human Beings* (1938), which marked a clear departure from older concepts. Suddenly parents were encouraged to enjoy their child.[66] In Aldrich and Aldrich's view, the old style missed the obvious differences among children: 'If they were always entirely alike, ... [w]e might ... use the mass production methods of the chick industry and bring them up in huge infant incubators.' Parents should stop listening so much to advice literature and instead start responding to the natural development and other (emotional) needs of their child: 'To give a baby all the warmth, comfort, and cuddling that he seems to need; to meet his wishes in the matter of satisfying and appropriate food; to adjust our habit-training to his individual rhythm; and to see that he has an opportunity to exercise each new accomplishment as it emerges.'[67]

The Aldrich book served as an important inspiration for the most successful childrearing manual of all time: Benjamin Spock's *The Common Sense Book of Baby and Child Care* (1946), which has sold more than fifty million copies in over forty languages and is still in print today. Working as a paediatrician in New York in the 1930s, Spock had become increasingly sceptical about the behaviourist approach and began to develop an interest in Freudian ideas. Similar to Aldrich and Aldrich,

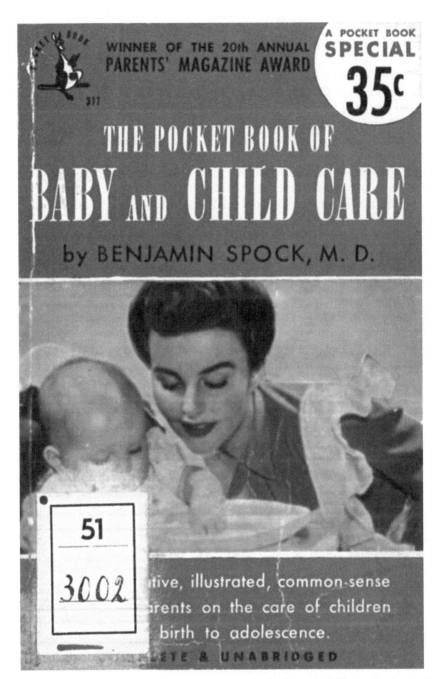

WINNER OF THE 20th ANNUAL PARENTS' MAGAZINE AWARD

A POCKET BOOK SPECIAL 35¢

THE POCKET BOOK OF

BABY AND CHILD CARE

by BENJAMIN SPOCK, M. D.

51

3002

...tive, illustrated, common-sense ...rents on the care of children ...birth to adolescence.

...LETE & UNABRIDGED

Fig. 1.1 Cover of Benjamin Spock, *The Pocket Book of Baby and Child Care*, Pocket Book 377 (New York: Pocket Books, 1946).

he wanted to encourage parents to trust their instincts in childrearing and to establish a trusting and loving bond with their child (Fig. 1.1).[68] However, his model was not a laissez-faire form of childcare. In many ways, his book was also concerned with the social engineering of 'useful, well-adjusted citizens'.[69] What was clearly different was the relationship between parents and children and the trust that parents should have in their own 'natural instincts'. Due to the emphasis on this natural dimension, the (biological) mother figured very prominently in this new tradition of advice literature. Because the child was in need of 'a steady, loving person', it seemed inevitable to Spock to claim that, 'in most cases, the mother is the best one to give him this feeling of "belonging," safely and surely'.[70] The role of the father was usually reduced to an auxiliary one and only later in the child's development was he seen as a crucial participant in childrearing, and even then mainly for the gender identity of a boy.

ATTACHMENT THEORY AND THE PRODUCTION OF KNOWLEDGE ABOUT CHILDREN

In scientific discussions, the alternative ways of raising children often developed in close relation with psychoanalytical knowledge, although not necessarily of a Freudian kind. The advances in psychoanalytical theory after Freud helped to open it up further to innovation in the study of children. One of the major theoretical departures in the post-war era came from the British psychoanalyst John Bowlby who was influential both in the United States and worldwide.[71] In his theory of attachment, emotions figured as the most important aspect in a child's development.[72] Bowlby was a trained psychoanalyst, psychologist, and psychiatrist who became the head of the children's department at the important *Tavistock Clinic* in London. In his early career during the 1940s, Bowlby was preoccupied with treating neurotic and deprived children. He tried to explain their neuroses by analysing their personal environments, in particular the bonds between mother and child. Even in 'normal' families where the mother-child relationship had not been severed by death, illness, or other traumatic events, children might display neurotic symptoms. Bowlby explained those as arising from a 'lack of the sympathy and understanding which the usual loving mother intuitively has'.[73] Instead, mothers might unconsciously feel hostility, resentment, guilt, jealousy, and even hatred toward their children, often originating in their own childhood experiences.

At the end of the Second World War, Bowlby was asked to conduct a study for the World Health Organization (WHO) on the needs of homeless children. His report *Maternal Care and Mental Health* was published in 1951 with a subsequent study *Child Care and the Growth of Love* published in 1953.[74] The later book was translated into fourteen languages and the English paperback edition sold 400,000 copies. From Bowlby's perspective, maternal love proved to be crucial for normal child development. While in some passages, he acknowledged that the biological mother could be replaced by a different mother figure, most of his formulations presumed that the biological mother would fulfil this function (Fig. 1.2). The

Attachment

John Bowlby

BASIC BOOKS, INC.
HARPER TORCHBOOKS TB 5035

Fig. 1.2 Cover of John Bowlby, *Attachment and Loss*, i: *Attachment* (New York: Basic Books, 1969).

father was reduced to a source of economic and emotional support for the mother, not the child. In addition to the presence of a mother, children needed a very specific kind of 'motherly love': an unconscious feeling which a mother 'intuitively' has for her child. If anything went wrong in the mother-child relationship, Bowlby would deduce that the mother lacked or had insufficient feeling:

> The provision of constant attention night and day, seven days a week and 365 days in the year, is possible only for a woman who derives profound satisfaction from seeing her child grow from babyhood, through the many phases of childhood, to become an independent man or woman, and knows that it is her care which has made this possible.[75]

The high demands which such theories placed on mothers and women in general have been subject to intense historical, scholarly, and political criticism, questioning the supposedly disastrous consequences of an absent mother.[76] Much of the later developments in attachment theory thus emphasized the broader social environment in which children grow up.[77] While the implications of a thoroughly gendered system of childrearing and its political significance for post-war notions of domesticity seem rather obvious, the emotional consequences of Bowlby's attachment theory are more dialectic: if motherly love is naturalized, it is no longer *love* in any meaningful sense of the word, but merely the mother's biological reaction.[78]

* * *

The study of child development from the middle of the nineteenth century frequently focused on emotions. Early scholarly attempts treated the emotions of children primarily as an object to be studied and examined with the help of various techniques, such as qualitative observation in baby diaries, experimental testing of children in artificial laboratory settings, or interaction with therapists in psychoanalytical sessions. While parents like Elizabeth Gaskell had been increasingly concerned with their children's emotions since the nineteenth century, in the twentieth century, the scholarly debate shifted progressively toward the emotional aspects of the child-parent relationship. Hence, with the advent of behaviourism, it seemed possible to advise parents on how to condition their children to have appropriate emotions. At the same time, psychoanalysis told parents how fragile and conflict-ridden their relationship to their offspring really was. Throughout this entire period, the production of scholarly knowledge was intertwined with popular and, often, ideological notions of childhood and childcare. In many ways, advice literature on childcare and development—either written by scholars themselves or influenced by their theories—served as a bridge between academia and the public. In some cases, however, it also generated knowledge on its own which then seemed to filter back into the scholarly discussions.

When Elizabeth Gaskell wrote her baby diary in 1835, she spoke much about her own emotional states of love and anxiety. Given the content of the advice literature which was available to her in the early nineteenth century, it already seemed difficult for parents to do the right thing. Nevertheless, throughout the nineteenth and twentieth centuries, the market for such books grew to unexpected dimensions, as an increasing number of parents assigned greater importance to this advice culture. But whatever this massive body of literature actually said about the importance of emotions in children and for children, the very nature of giving advice implied that those who received it were in need of it—and for this implication to work in practice, parents had to feel insecure and anxious. As a young girl, Gaskell had lost her own mother and her letters reveal the sense of loss she retained throughout her life.[79] Later, she had received some of her mother's letters which she cherished as a keepsake. Her private diary of the first days, weeks, and months after giving birth to her first child was supposed to be a similar keepsake, a token of her love, as she called it. And she wished that one day, when Marianne was a mother too, she would be able to cherish this gift and indeed be able to detect her own motherly love: 'I wish that (if ever she sees this) I could give her the slightest idea of the love and the hope that is bound up in *her*.'[80] Even so, the token had not just been one of love, but also of anxiety—an aspect of parental feeling, which Elizabeth Gaskell nevertheless seemed to try to hide from her child.

NOTES

1. Chapple and Wilson, *Private Voices*, 50, 56, 52, 50.
2. Wilson, 'Critical Introduction', 14.
3. Necker de Saussure, *Progressive Education*.
4. Wallace, Franklin, and Keegan, 'Observing Eye'.
5. Chapple and Wilson, *Private Voices*, 50.
6. For further scholarly work on fear in general, see, in particular, Bourke, *Fear*. From a different perspective, Peter Stearns has argued that parental anxiety emerged in the twentieth century in the United States because of the unclear social function of children, who—in contrast to earlier periods—no longer contributed to the family income; Stearns, *Anxious Parents*. For a detailed discussion of the role of fear in children's literature, see chapter 9, 'Jim Button's Fear'; chapter 10, 'Ivan's Bravery'.
7. For example, Matthias, *Wie erziehen wir unsern Sohn Benjamin*; Kay, 'How Should We Raise Our Son Benjamin'. For the most quoted zoological work see Brehm, *From North Pole to Equator*. For the role of animals in children's literature, see chapter 5, 'Doctor Dolittle's Empathy'.
8. For the alternatives of a 'Lockean nurture-is-what-counts school' of 'hard' advice and 'a gentler Rousseauian proponent of letting nature take its course in childhood', see Hulbert, *Raising America*, 9.
9. This chapter is primarily based on a selection of 42 advice books from the nineteenth and twentieth centuries. Most were published in the United States, Britain, or Germany, a few in France, and one in colonial India.
10. Scholarly work exploring the modern history of producing knowledge about childhood and about children's emotions in particular is sparse. See Herman, 'Psychologism and the Child'; Kössler, 'Ordnung der Gefühle'; Shuttleworth, *Mind of the Child*.
11. For a systematic discussion of the relationship between parents and psychologists, see Breeuwsma, 'Nephew of an Experimentalist'.
12. Defoe, *Robinson Crusoe*; Campe, *Robinson the Younger*. On Campe's advice literature, see Berg, 'Rat geben', 714–15. For a further discussion of Campe's *Robinson the Younger*, see chapter 4, 'Ralph's Compassion'.

13. On early advice literature in Germany, see Marré, *Bücher für Mütter als pädagogische Literaturgattung*; Fuchs, *Wie sollen wir unsere Kinder erziehen*; Höffer-Mehlmer, *Elternratgeber*. On advice literature in the United States, see Grant, *Raising Baby by the Book*; Hulbert, *Raising America*. On advice literature in Britain, see Urwin and Sharland, 'From Bodies to Minds in Childcare Literature'.

14. Brock, *Internationalizing the History of Psychology*. For the implications of this transnational dimension for the historical study of emotions in general, and of children's emotions in particular, see the epilogue in this volume.

15. Damousi and Plotkin, *The Transnational Unconscious*.

16. For example, in Calcutta one member of the local Bengali elite was very much interested in Freudian ideas and also in psychoanalytical understandings of childhood. In his popular introduction to this branch of analysis, Girindrasekhar Bose devoted an entire chapter to the psychoanalytical study of children; Bose, *Everyday Psychoanalysis*, 35–45. He also popularized these ideas in Bengali: Basu, 'Śiśur Man' ('The mind of a child', [1929]).

17. Preyer, *Mind of the Child*.

18. Darwin, 'Biographical Sketch of an Infant'.

19. Wallace, Franklin, and Keegan, 'Observing Eye'.

20. Kössler, 'Ordnung der Gefühle'.

21. Perez, *First Three Years of Childhood*.

22. Perez, *L'Enfant de trois a sept ans*.

23. Kössler, 'Ordnung der Gefühle'.

24. Darwin, 'Biographical Sketch of an Infant', 288.

25. For example, Hall, 'Study of Fears'.

26. Hall, *Youth*, which was based on Hall's major scholarly work, *Adolescence*.

27. Gould, *Ontogeny and Phylogeny*, esp. 135–47.

28. Olson, *Science and Scientism in Nineteenth-Century Europe*.

29. For example, Hall, *Contents of Children's Minds on Entering School*. Hall based this study on a survey of about 10,000 Berlin school children which had been published in the *Berlin Städtisches Jahrbuch* in 1870.

30. Breeuwsma, 'Nephew of an Experimentalist', 188–9; Wallace, Franklin, and Keegan, 'Observing Eye'.

31. On the history of 'new education' or '*Reformpädagogik*', see Röhrs and Lenhart, *Reformpädagogik auf den Kontinenten*; Brehony, 'New Education for a New Era'. For a critical assessment of the newness of 'new education', see Oelkers, 'Reformpädagogik vor der Reformpädagogik'.

32. Hermann Röhrs, *Die Reformpädagogik*, 98. On the impact of the German reform pedagogy in India, see chapter 3, 'Asghari's Piety'.

33. Kupfer, 'Rabindranath Tagore's Bildung zum Weltmenschen'.

34. Oelkers, 'Reformpädagogik vor der Reformpädagogik'.

35. Key, *Century of the Child*, 183.

36. Kamp, *Kinderrepubliken*.

37. Kamp, 119–22. See also Lane, *Talks to Parents and Teachers*.

38. Neill, *Summerhill*. For a discussion of Neill's concept of an education without fear, see chapter 9, 'Jim Button's Fear'.

39. Neill, *Problem Child*, 10–11.

40. Lhotzky, *Soul of Your Child*. See also Höffer-Mehlmer, *Elternratgeber*, 125–9.

41. Kamp, *Kinderrepubliken*, 88.

42. Foerster, *Jugendlehre*, esp. 15–23.

43. Watson, 'Schematic Outline of the Emotions', 165.
44. The proposed experiments to create fear in children were outlined in Watson, 'Experimental Studies on the Growth of the Emotions'.
45. The results were published in Watson and Rayner, 'Conditioned Emotional Reactions'. See also Watson, 'Experimental Studies on the Growth of the Emotions'. On the classic case of *Little Albert*, see Beck, Levinson, and Irons, 'Finding Little Albert'.
46. Watson, *Behaviorism*, 82.
47. Watson and Watson, *Psychological Care of the Infant and Child*, 14, 16. On the fundamental changes in motherhood, see Kay, 'How Should We Raise Our Son Benjamin?', 105–21.
48. Watson and Watson, 73–4.
49. Freud, 'Analysis of a Phobia in a Five-Year-Old Boy'.
50. Freud, *Three Essays on the Theory of Sexuality*.
51. Freud, 'Analysis of a Phobia in a Five-Year-Old Boy', 111.
52. Freud's position towards female sexuality (and, by implication, also the development of the female child) was certainly problematic. The male bias in Freud's concept of infant sexuality—i.e., his assumption of penis envy in girls—was criticized early on by female psychoanalysts such as Karen Horney; Horney, 'On the Genesis of the Castration Complex in Women'. This criticism has led to a fundamental feminist attack on (Freudian) psychoanalysis, which has steadily increased since the 1970s. See Appignanesi and Forrester, *Freud's Women*.
53. Wolman, *Handbook of Child Psychoanalysis*; Geissmann and Geissmann, *History of Child Psychoanalysis*.
54. On the history of female psychoanalysis, see Appignanesi and Forrester, *Freud's Women*.
55. Anna Freud's earliest work on the subject was published as *Introduction to the Technique of Child Analysis*. For Klein's approach, see Klein, *Psycho-Analysis of Children*.
56. Klein, 29.
57. Jensen, 'Freuds unheimliche Gefühle'.
58. Mitchell and Black, *Freud and Beyond*.
59. Kurzweil, *The Freudians*.
60. Hale, *Rise and Crisis of Psychoanalysis in the United States*.
61. Hetzer, *Seelische Hygiene*.
62. Haarer, *Deutsche Mutter und ihr erstes Kind*. For a scholarly discussion of the book, see also Benz, 'Brutstätten der Nation'; Gudrun Brockhaus, 'Lockung und Drohung'; Gebhardt, *Angst vor dem kindlichen Tyrannen*, esp. 85–99.
63. Haarer, *Deutsche Mutter und ihr erstes Kind*, 171, 176 (author's translation).
64. Gebhardt, *Angst vor dem kindlichen Tyrannen*, 99.
65. Gesell, *Mental Growth of the Pre-School Child*; Gesell, *Infancy and Human Growth*. For Gesell's major advice manual, see Gesell and Ilg, *Infant and Child in the Culture of Today*. For more on Gesell, see also Hulbert, *Raising America*, 154–87.
66. Hardyment, *Dream Babies*, 213–20.
67. Aldrich and Aldrich, *Babies are Human Beings*, 51, x–xi.
68. For the dimension of trust, see chapter 2, 'Dickon's Trust'.
69. Spock, *Common Sense Book of Baby and Child Care*, 484. See also Graebner, 'Unstable World of Benjamin Spock'. On Spock's approach towards corporal punishment and the effects of pain in children, see chapter 8, 'Lebrac's Pain'.
70. Spock, 484.

71. On the reception of Bowlby and attachment theory in the United States, see Grant, *Raising Baby by the Book*, 218; Hulbert, *Raising America*, 205. On the reception in Germany, see Gebhardt, *Angst vor dem kindlichen Tyrannen*, 166–73.

72. Vicedo, 'The Social Nature of the Mother's Tie'.

73. Bowlby, 'Influence of Early Environment', 164.

74. Bowlby, 'Maternal Care and Mental Health'; Bowlby, *Child Care and the Growth of Love*.

75. Bowlby, *Child Care and the Growth of Love*, 75–6.

76. Dally, *Inventing Motherhood*; Eyer, *Mother-Infant Bonding*; Vicedo, 'The Social Nature of the Mother's Tie'.

77. Bronfenbrenner, 'Ecological Systems Theory'.

78. Vicedo, 'The Social Nature of the Mother's Tie', 423.

79. Wilson, 'Critical Introduction'.

80. Chapple and Wilson, *Private Voices*, 50 (emphasis added).

2

Dickon's Trust

Stephanie Olsen

Dickon, the strong local boy who befriends and helps Mary and Colin in *The Secret Garden* (1911) is not only 'th' trustiest lad i' Yorkshire', which is already a strong claim, but the archetype of trust in children's novels. Those around him, young and old, rich or poor, define him by his trustworthiness, and several times in the novel he is described as 'such a trusty lad'.[1] His trustworthiness and the trust he engenders in others takes many forms. In the story, it is stressed that even though he is poor, he is of good character and good physique. He can be trusted to take care of feeble Colin's physical needs. More importantly, he can also be trusted with both Mary and Colin's emotional and spiritual needs, leading them by example to become better children and to develop their own personal character. Dickon is also the stalwart of true religion in the story. Through communion with the natural environment, Dickon leads at every spiritual and religious point in the plot, enabling the emotional growth of the two other children and the groundskeeper.

In children's literature and advice manuals, trust is described in various ways—as a belief, a hope, and a gift—but most importantly, as something to be learnt and felt. Trust is also relational. While one can trust in God, in country, in family, and in friends, trust is also built up in relation to others, including a personal connection to God. In order to learn how to trust, children needed to learn how to be trustworthy. Models of trust were frequently used to show children how to lead a moral life—to know right from wrong, good from bad emotions. In the texts, trust is also described using a variety of changing emotions: devotion, love, and confidence are repeatedly linked. Children could also learn about the dangers of distrust, misplaced trust, or untrustworthiness, to themselves and those around them. Often precisely through this tension within the plot around frustrations and problems caused by distrust or broken trust, children could learn how to trust and be trusted. Attempts to describe these emotions in various ways in order to intervene in children's emotional learning are tied in important ways to a changing understanding of these emotions themselves and their purposes in the education of children and youth.[2]

There is a growing body of work on trust in various disciplines, much of it showing that trust is not merely about rational choice and decision-making.[3] As the early sociologist Georg Simmel noted, there is another component required, 'a kind of faith'.[4] In trust there is a necessary interplay between knowledge and ignorance, because trust is unnecessary with full knowledge and impossible in complete ignorance.[5] Niklas Luhmann and others have pointed to the active choice of taking a risk inherent in trust.[6] This is compared to confidence, for which there is no alternative, and upon which individuals rely, consciously or unconsciously, in order to avoid disappointment. As we shall see, such a distinction is nuanced in the context of children's trust within literature and advice manuals, especially in their (changing) relationship to God. In both kinds of texts, trust in God, and devotion and love toward God, are always presented as an active choice, long before religious pluralism or atheism became real alternatives. In the earlier period, this was an active choice between morality and immorality, whereas in the later period, there was a greater variety of choices.

Historians are rather new to this topic, but have made an important intervention: trust is not a constant, rather it is a fluid concept that changes over time.[7] Much of the scholarly work on trust has focused on political or economic relationships in contemporary societies, or on the changes wrought by modernity. The conclusion is that in the nineteenth century, trust in God waned and was replaced by the trust essential for social relationships.[8] This scholarly rigour is helpful, but when looking at literary and advice sources for children and adolescents, it limits a full understanding of how trust was viewed by authors and narrators, what its educative function was, and how this changed over time. The focus here is on how trust was defined and how it was used as an educative tool to open up novel learning spaces for children and youth. Trust in childhood, though learnt through the texts as a means to developing the emotion as a mature adult, was in fact somewhat distinct from adult modes of trust. Children's perceived vulnerable stage in the lifecycle, combined with their perceived dependence on adults, made trust an essential emotion to cultivate. Although trust in God waned as a central theme over time, and a multiplicity of other relationships were presented, religious trust still provided practical learning models for children well into the twentieth century. Sources directed at children therefore provide a different kind of evidence for the history of trust.

The main focus of this chapter is on trust in a religious idiom, both in the affirmation and in the denial of organized religion or even of faith. It will trace how the models of trust, which prevailed from the beginning of the nineteenth century, were used to educate young people on how to cultivate character and self-governance and a belief in the authority of parents and educators. This later dissolved into mistrust and distrust as parental and familial trust and authority were put into question. In an increasingly post-colonial world, trust, which had become racialized and essentialized, also became more fragmented. Between two narrative bookends,[9] marked by *Tom Brown's School Days* (1857) and *Are You There God? It's Me, Margaret* (1970), this chapter demonstrates the changing emphasis in the desirable way that trust could be learnt during childhood, including some discussion of the context of Empire. The children's literature and advice manuals discussed here were chosen because, despite varied settings and periods, they all focus on one main character, his or her relationship to a group of peers, and to adults in authority, marked either by an adult's presence or absence. In this way each book represents a triangular relationship—the protagonist, the peers, and the family or authority figures—displaying hierarchical and horizontal relationships, but often in no clear-cut way. Children could learn from these relationship models or play out their own emotions in the context of their own relationships while reading. The books present the main agents of trust, whether authority figures or peers, and under what conditions children should place trust in them, or in themselves. Readers could also learn to distinguish trustworthy people from those who should not be trusted, in varied settings and periods.

TRUST IN A RELIGIOUS IDIOM

Although the same word is used, there is an implicit and sometimes explicit difference in children's sources between trust in an all-powerful God, trust in a fallible authority figure (with the possibility of fallibility increasingly acknowledged over time), or trust in a peer. Thomas Hughes's *Tom Brown's School Days* contains all three. It has become the exemplar of the English public school novel, promoting a version of boyhood character-building steeped in Christian morality. While the physical emphasis in muscular Christianity, a set of values through which boys were supposed to learn how to be both pious and manly, has been overstressed, the religious and intellectual components of character-building remain essential.[10] This view permeated British culture, and had a large impact on developing masculinity well beyond its original class confines. As Thomas Dixon argues, even after the Education Act of 1870 initiated the provision of mass education, prominent educational commentators like Alexander Bain and George J. Holyoake maintained that emotional education should not be part of the British school curriculum. For the masses, emotions should be taught in homes, churches, and society instead.[11] For elite boys, emotional education was provided in boarding school, but not necessarily in the classroom. Character development of this kind was only achieved by forming trust groups among peers.

Tom Brown and his best friend Harry 'Scud' East provide a good example of trust bonds among children themselves. They defend each other against school bullies, while encouraging each other to improve their characters and their abilities. However, in their case, as in many other children's stories of the mid-nineteenth century, this relationship was guided by authority figures: by their public school master, Arnold, and through their relationship with God. Tom and East did not arrive at this spiritual character development alone. They required the example of a new boy at school. Arthur, a frail and unpopular boy, trusted deeply in God. He had been spiritually guided by his father until the latter's death. As the narrator says, 'The spirit of his father was in him, and the Friend to whom his father had left him did not neglect the trust.' Entrusting his spirit and his character development to God through many tribulations, Arthur proved a positive example to the other boys in his friendship group, especially to Tom. In turn, Tom protected Arthur with complete devotion, turning this into an almost sacred trust: '[T]his trust which he had taken on him without thinking about it, head-over-heels in fact, was the centre and turning point of his school-life, that which was to make him or mar him; his appointed work and trial for the time being'. As the narrator explains, 'Tom was becoming a new boy', and although he frequently battled with himself he 'was daily growing in manfulness and thoughtfulness, as every high-couraged and well-principled boy must, when he finds himself for the first time consciously at grips with self and the devil'.[12] Courage, thoughtfulness, 'manfulness', and principles were the watchwords of Tom's character development, with trust (in peer groups, in authority figures, and in God) figuring prominently. A year later another public school book was published, Frederic Farrar's *Eric, or, Little by Little* (1858), clearly demonstrating the dangers of mistrust.[13] Like *Tom Brown's School Days*, this book is replete with various forms of trust, but unlike the positive example of good character provided by Arthur and Tom in *Tom Brown's School Days*, *Eric* provides an example for children to learn who not to be, and therefore to learn the virtues of being trustworthy. Eric is the son of British parents posted to India. As was common practice in the British Raj, the boy is sent to England to board at Roslyn School, where he is exposed to the best and the worst of boarding school education. Eric has an inherent moral goodness, but his decline really begins when he commits small moral wrongs causing authority figures at the school not to trust him. This loss of trust is the pivotal event that leads Eric down a path of destruction. Farrar makes no attempt to hide his stern moral and religious message: Eric's goodness is destroyed by the temptations of cheating, drinking, and popularity among peers. His eventual death is a warning to readers that they must learn to cultivate good character and religious piety, in order to engender the trust of others.

EXPORTING CHRISTIAN TRUST FROM THE METROPOLE

Uniting the learning of good character and the ability to trust in God was certainly not a novel concept in the Christian Socialism of Hughes, Charles Kingsley, and others.[14] In the early nineteenth century, Evangelicals produced many tracts and stories for children, tying individual heart-felt conversion (saving the child from hell-fire) to the learning of good conduct and morality for earthly life. Evangelicals quickly applied this rationale in their efforts to 'civilize' the racial Other. One popular example is *The History of Little Henry and His Bearer* (1814) by Mary Martha Sherwood, a children's book continuously in print for almost a hundred years and translated into many languages. Meant to inspire missionary action in children and adults, this story, like Sherwood's other popular tales, was a powerful blend of Christianity and the ideas of British pre-eminence, and consequently of Hindu and Indian inferiority. Sherwood's evangelical zeal throughout *Little Henry* insists on the importance of individual conversion and acceptance of God in the heart through an emotionally transformative experience. The story represents a sort of commonly produced obituary tract, which focused on the emotional conversion experience and subsequently—and inevitably—on Christian death.[15] This is evident both in the acceptance of Christianity of the little British orphan, Henry, who has no one to guide him in 'civilized' ways until he is introduced to a young English missionary lady, Mrs Baron, who acts as his surrogate mother, spiritual guide, and teacher in learning how to be 'civilized'. Little Henry, shortly before his death, then takes on the task of converting his native servant Boosy with missionary zeal. The narrator encourages young readers to be like Henry. Boosy finally admits that he is a Christian, teaching his grandson, whom he names Henry, about Christianity immediately before Boosy dies. Before this happens, however, the reader is told of trials and tribulations as he struggles with his feelings: he feels to his core that he must be Christian, but he is afraid of the ignorance of his native community, which is sure to ostracize him were they to know of his conversion. Most importantly, he strives to develop the trust required to believe that God would purify his heart as Henry had said. After Henry's death, Boosy seeks out Mrs Baron in vain. He wants to tell her of his trials and his persecutions by his own people because he had more 'confidence' in her than he had even had in his own mother and declares that 'I had this trust in her [Mrs Baron] because I believed her to be a Christian in heart, not in name only' and though he 'acknowledged the power of this religion', he could not yet state it publically.[16]

Boosy could trust true Christians like Henry and Mrs Baron, just as he could trust God. Entangling ideas of religious and racial inferiority and prejudice, Sherwood portrays Hindus as lying and cheating stock characters. Even Boosy's son is portrayed as mean and superstitious. Only through Christianity would Indians gain good character and civilization. Boosy's own prejudices and superstitions disappeared as the 'wall of separation between the white and black man was broken down' and he acknowledged that 'there is but one family of mankind, and one God and Father of all'.[17] Christianity was portrayed as a means to advancement, education, and socialization for Indians.

Similarly, native authors like Nazir Ahmad focused on the character development, prosperity, and good fortune that religious steadfastness would bring. In *The Bride's Mirror* (1903; Urd. orig. *Mirat ul Arus*, 1869), a popular Urdu and Muslim example of the value of trust and devotion to Allah, Ahmad's central concern was to correct the widespread gendered misconception of trust, saying, 'Men take it for granted that the female sex is not trustworthy.'[18] In various national and colonial contexts, trust as a wholesome social emotion and character trait was often gendered. Ahmad's main character, the young bride Asghari, is the most trustworthy character in the novel, in large part because of her religious piety. She proves her trustworthiness through her good household management, which is a manifestation of her good character. This form of female trustworthiness is repeated in numerous other stories from Europe and North America from the nineteenth century until around the mid-twentieth century.

The Bride's Mirror, though specific in its setting, could only have been written within the same context of British imperialism as *The Story of Little Henry and His Bearer Boosy* (1866). The worldly pay-offs of religious trust and devotion were just as desirable to a British audience as they were to an Urdu one: 'middle-class' domesticity and a colonial government job. British advice literature for Indian boys stressed similar goals. John Murdoch, a British missionary, spent much of his adult life in South Asia and produced many Christian advice manuals for Indian youth. His *Indian Student's Manual* (1875) includes many chapters that would have been familiar to British boys. There are prohibitions against smoking and drinking, for the good of the body and for force of character.[19] Though he peppered his text with Indian and Hindu examples, most of his advice could have been found in any British boy's manual: truthfulness (which he says is a particular challenge for Indians), integrity, frugality, purity (of thought, deed, and reading material), avoiding bad companions, temperance, industry, modesty and good manners, moral courage, and virtue were all stressed. Trust in God and the benefits of Christianity over other religions for the earthly future and for salvation are the central tenets of his advice manuals. Trust in individuals and in the self, he argues, is essential and is encouraged in Christianity while discouraged in Hinduism. In a chapter entitled 'Truthfulness', Murdoch declares that 'Confidence is the bond of society. Universal distrust would produce universal misery.' Trust, therefore, should be the end goal of moral and character development, for the individual as well as for society, and children should learn how to trust and be trustworthy, by word and by deed. Emphasizing that trust is not a stand-alone emotion, Murdoch cites Samuel Smiles to reinforce that it is one important component of 'good manners': 'Reverence... is alike indispensable to the happiness of individuals, of families, and of nations. Without it there can be no trust, no faith, no confidence, either in man or God—neither social peace nor social progress.' Social progress was tied to cultivation of the self and to learning through a process of character and emotional development (emotions like happiness, faith, and reverence predominated here).[20] Trusting in oneself, readers could learn, was an essential part of character development.

CHARACTER AND THE GENDERED NATURE OF TRUST

British and American advice manuals for youth promoted the same kind of learning. In the Victorian era, this was especially prominent among writers who promoted Christian Socialism, a brand of religious socialism based on the teachings of Jesus, whose proponents often supported muscular Christianity. Hughes's Christian Socialist counterpart, Charles Kingsley, promoted a similar regimen of learning and good character through trust in God.[21] He maintained that this would also manifest itself in social and familial relationships. Reverence, as with Murdoch, was brought about by trust, not by fear. This message is clear in the relationship between father and child, which was a proxy for the relationship between the individual and God. As Kingsley writes in *Health and Education* (1874), 'But which child reverences his father most? He who comes joyfully and trustfully to meet him, that he may learn his father's mind, and do his will: or he who at his father's coming runs away and hides, lest he should be beaten for he knows not what?'[22]

Predictably, advice for girls in this era was also centred on domesticity, often with a moralistic, gendered tone concerning typical female roles in the home and girls' future roles as wives and mothers. Girls could frequently read that in order to be trusted, they should work on being trustworthy, both in word and in action, and that this trustworthiness was a necessary trait for successful young women.[23] Like their male counterparts, girls were taught that they should rely on and trust in God to provide them with the strength they needed to grow into reliable, trust-worthy people.

Many advice writers of the period directed boys to learn how to emote and con-duct themselves in similar ways, masculinity being defined by moral strength and trustworthiness, not by physical prowess. Sylvanus Stall, a Lutheran minister and popular American writer of advice manuals, published a book for sixteen-year-olds, *What a Young Man Ought to Know* (1897), in which he maintained that youth needed to be trusted in order to succeed in life, and in order to be trusted they needed to be pure and temperate. Boys were also supposed to learn to respect girls and women and be chaste, because in order to trust their future wife, they should not be the 'criminal despoiler of [her] virtue' before marriage.[24]

Thomas Hughes himself wrote several advice manuals, the most pertinent being *Notes for Boys* (1885), which focused on the emotional and spiritual cultivation of manliness, leading to moral action. He repeated the Smilesian idea that 'Mutual trust is the very foundation of all human society.' It was therefore important to be trustworthy, and to be 'implicitly trusted' by conducting straightforward and truthful communication with others. It was also important to choose friends care-fully and establish solid bonds of trust. This trust involved mutual sympathy, interest in each other's joys, sorrows, and concerns.[25] Hughes had gone further in *True Manliness* (1880) stating that distrust is a form of cowardice. This is in direct contrast to the example of Christ: 'In Christ's life there is not the slight-est trace of such weakness or cowardice....And thus he stands, and will stand to the end of time, the true model of the courage and manliness of boyhood and youth and early manhood.'[26] Later, the father of child psychology, G. Stanley Hall, would disagree with Hughes that pious emotions were masculine. In *Youth* (1906) and other books, he cautioned boys to steer clear of such 'feminine emotions'. In *Adolescence* (1904), Hall named trust as one of the feminine emotions demanded by religion, perhaps lamentably defined as 'traits not involving ideals that most stir young men'.[27] He did, however, emphasize the importance of religious feeling, and pegged the liminal period of adolescence, between childhood and adulthood, as the crucial time when the emotions were most strongly felt, and character traits most strongly learnt.

Numerous texts from the nineteenth century to the mid-twentieth century provided children with a path to learning and development through trust and spiritual devotion. Johanna Spyri's children's books are thinly veiled lessons in the benefits of trusting in God, the transformative power of which would bring about good character along with civilized, middle-class and correct behaviour that was gender-specific. Her most popular novel, *Heidi* (1884/1885; Ger. orig. *Heidi's Lehr- und Wanderjahre*, 1880 and *Heidi kann brauchen, was es gelernt hat*, 1881), is no exception. Heidi is a little orphan girl who moves in with her gruff grandfather, whom she looks up to with 'trusting eyes', a model for children to learn to obey and trust their elders, but also to judge who to trust. For despite his crotchetiness, he shows her love and devotion for the first time through communion with nature. Heidi has to leave this idyll, however, in order for her education to progress. When she goes to Frankfurt to work as a companion for Clara, they develop a strong bond, and it is in Clara's home that Heidi learns how to read the Bible, to pray and, most importantly for her development, to trust in God. These skills have a transformative effect on Heidi's conduct and character, as well as on those around her. She brightens the life of her own grandfather and of her poor grandmotherly neighbour, who in turn reinforces her lessons on patience and trust in God, even in hard times, saying: 'I am sure He will help you in time, if you only trust in Him.'[28] In *Gritli's Children* (1887; Ger. orig. *Wo Gritlis Kinder hingekommen sind*, 1883 and *Gritlis Kinder kommen weiter*, 1884), Spyri again takes up the theme of trust in God, even when calamity and death are near. She teaches that 'only those can live happy and secure who have full trust in God, who holds all life in his hand, and who makes both joy and sorrow work together for good to those who love him'.[29] Children could learn through Heidi's example that they would be happy if they trusted in God, which in turn was tied to learning how to be trustworthy through good character.

Lucy Maud Montgomery's *Anne of Green Gables* (1908) is the bestselling Canadian story of another little orphan girl who desires love and acceptance in her new home and community. Like Heidi, her good character develops through accept-ance of gender norms, including emotional maturation, although Montgomery permits Anne a fairly large degree of independence and free-spiritedness within these confines. Her adoptive parents, siblings Matthew and Marilla Cuthbert, asked for a boy to help with their farm work, but received red-headed, imagina-tive Anne instead. Anne's journey from high-spirited girl to responsible and caring young woman is framed by the question of trust, especially as withheld or granted by Marilla. By the end of the novel, in response to judgmental Rachel Lynde's claim that 'There's a good deal of the child about her yet', Marilla, who in learning to trust and love Anne, softens from her former hard, Anglo-Canadian Protestant treatment of her charge, and is able to defend her: 'There's a good deal more of the woman about her.'[30] Anne's adolescence is thus played out on the road from Marilla's complete distrust to her absolute trust, even to the point where Marilla entrusts her own care (she is losing her sight), and the care of the Green Gables house to Anne. Though Anne is portrayed as good from the start, her character is only proven once she learns how to win Marilla's trust.

Early in the story, when Marilla loses her brooch, she falsely believes that Anne has taken it. Marilla declares to Matthew that 'It's a fearful responsibility to have a child in your house you can't trust. Slyness and untruthfulness—that's what she has displayed.' Matthew, Anne's constant champion, encourages his sister to trust her. But when Anne fails to be home and have supper ready for Marilla, she calls her untrustworthy again. This is a recurring theme throughout the novel and is only resolved when Marilla realizes Anne's true worth. As she says toward the end of the novel, 'she's real steady and reliable now...I wouldn't be afraid to trust her in anything'. As the narrator says, 'Marilla was not given to subjective analysis of her thoughts and feelings', but she is shown to be deeply religious and demonstrates her virtuousness by getting things around the house done properly. She expects the same demonstrations from Anne. Religious trust forms the background of this story, while the process of learning to trust among the main characters, and their shifting hierarchical relationships, are at the centre. Anne is not immediately trustworthy to Marilla because she does not have the outward signs of good character, as defined by early twentieth-century standards of girlhood and womanhood.[31]

This returns us to *The Secret Garden*. Colin does not seem as trustworthy as Dickon at first because he does not possess any of the outward signs of male trustworthiness, such as reliability or emotional control. Mary concludes, however, that since he wants a garden so badly, he can be trusted with it. Later in the novel she still asks him directly and solemnly whether she can trust him 'for sure', explaining that she had initially trusted Dickon because the birds trusted him. His answer came in almost whispered tones: 'Yes—yes!' Colin is then allowed into Mary and Dickon's circle of trust, and thus introduced to the secret garden.[32] Though in Burnett's own day *The Secret Garden* was not nearly as well known as her other classic, *Little Lord Fauntleroy* (1886), readers, especially girls and women, were ahead of critics in granting the book the status of a classic. In 1927, for example, it made the *Youth's Companion* list of favourites, and in 1960 it was voted one of the best books for children in the London *Sunday Times*.[33] In recent decades, the book has received more recognition from literary critics, and has been adapted for numerous film, television, and musical productions. It has thus proved more lasting than the sentimental portrayal of childhood in *Little Lord Fauntleroy*.

The Secret Garden is a good example of British imperial literature. Mary, deprived of 'civilization' in India, has become impetuous, imperious, and an angry loner. She diagnoses similar traits in Colin, who is repeatedly referred to as the 'Rajah', before his conversion to physical health and healthy emotions in the garden. This cure is achieved by the intervention of Mary, who has learnt to be 'civilized' first, and more crucially, through Dickon. Though he is working-class and ill-educated, he is the most trustworthy character, somehow in a state between civilization (in its effete, corrupting sense) and the state of nature (in its pure, curative sense). Dickon is trustworthy because he is in touch with his emotions and devoted to nature, to his friends, and to his family, not in a fawning, class-dictated way, but rather because of his good character, his care for humanity and nature. Colin is transformed, through his circle of trust with Dickon and Mary, into a boy who shows his neediness and insecurities, while at the same time becoming gradually stronger and more independent.

There are several obvious Christian and pagan religious allusions in the novel, especially related to Dickon's communion with nature and with birds and animals, in a circle under a tree, 'like sitting in a sort of temple'. His trustworthiness is clearly an outward sign of his trust in God and nature. Ben, the groundskeeper, affirms that the children's activities are of a religious nature as he thinks he has 'somehow been led into appearing at a prayer-meeting' and encourages Colin to exclaim his thankfulness at being well by singing the 'Doxology'. Indeed, Colin's healing through the garden takes on a religious quality of its own.[34]

In the 1920s, these earlier ideas of the connections between trust, character, gendered norms, and Christianity were afforded a prominence within the Scouting movement, which had become a huge international success among young people by this time. Known for its imperial and militaristic overtones, the Scouting movement also encouraged children and young adults to learn how to cultivate their minds and characters, according to the gendered, racial, and class-based expectations of the day. The founder, Robert Baden-Powell, himself a public school old boy, applied what he had learnt there and refined his own educational ideas in *Scouting for Boys* (1908) for a slightly more mature (in age) and more crucial readership: older boys and adolescents, who were seen, at least since G. Stanley Hall's work, to be in a precarious state, emotionally and otherwise. Baden-Powell's new book, *Rovering to Success* (1922), advised boys that what they needed most for their future lives as husbands, fathers, and citizens was an emotional maturation (characterized by restraint and 'appropriate' expression) which would build up their characters. Trust was essential here. Concerning work and advancement, for example, Baden-Powell advised that cultivating character, which he defined as 'absolute trustworthiness, tact, and energy' was more essential than even skill or training. He defined honour, so important within the military and the Scouting movement, in relation to trust: 'It means that I can be trusted to be truthful and honest in all that I say or do.' As with Kingsley and many other advice writers, he defined personal fulfilment and 'happiness' for men not in public terms, but rather within domestic life: '[T]here is intense happiness in the loving comradeship of a mate and the eager trusting companionship of your children'. The main image in *Rovering to Success* is that of a boy paddling his own canoe through the dangerous rocks of adolescent temptation. Baden-Powell advised that boys should not trust others to steer their canoes for them, but rather to 'go forward with good hope and trust in yourself'. Trust, in oneself and in God, was therefore a central component in cultivating happiness, which, according to Baden-Powell, should be the central goal in paddling the canoe to successful manhood. This happiness, however, is not an immediate gratification pursued through desire and temptation, but rather a future happiness centred on home life, satisfaction, and duty.[35]

Many children's books until the 1940s promoted gender norms and lessons influenced—whether explicitly or implicitly—by Christianity,[36] and by the 1950s these issues still dominated many texts, though their messages would become increasingly multivalent. This change reflected broader, gradual transformations in gender relations, religiosity, and a diminishing stress on hierarchy in social relationships. Veiled in the genre of fantasy, C. S. Lewis provides a conventional lesson in *The Lion, the Witch and the Wardrobe* (1950). Accused of writing a story that was too overtly Christian and moralistic, the book's initial reception by critics was lukewarm. It has nonetheless proven to be one of the most popular books of all time and has been translated into forty-seven languages. The story is set in 1940, where life is topsy-turvy and normalcy is overturned by the Blitz. Four siblings, Peter, Edmund, Lucy, and Susan, are evacuated from London to the countryside, where their adventure and their learning process begin. Trust in God becomes trust in Aslan, a lion and the true King of Narnia. In the end, in a scene reminiscent of Christ's crucifixion, Aslan sacrifices himself for Edmund, the boy who traitorously collaborated with the evil White Witch. The four siblings have a strong trust bond, which is interrupted by Edmund's treachery, until he learns to control his selfish emotions and feel for others. As the narrator says, for the first time he 'felt sorry for someone besides himself'. The other children are likewise exposed for the first time to a process of reconciliation after a significant breach in trust, negotiated through contrition, acceptance (handshakes), and the wisdom of a guiding influence (Aslan).[37] The narrative thus presents a model for the re-building of trust-based relations, even after acute betrayal.

In the second book in the series, *Prince Caspian: The Return to Narnia* (1951), Aslan returns, but is only visible at first to the youngest sibling Lucy, whose innocence allows her to trust him. Innocence, by this time firmly defining the ideal child, was shown to be an important characteristic in children's unconditional trust in God. Later stories, however, portray innocence as a source of potential danger, leading children astray through trusting too much, or through misplacing trust.

THE BREAKDOWN OF RELIGIOUS TRUST

Whistle Down the Wind, a popular novel from 1958 by Mary Hayley Bell, illustrates the questioning of traditional norms far more than the Narnia books. The story focuses on three young siblings living on an English farm who stumble upon a fugitive in their barn. Because of their trust in their religious teachings, they mistakenly believe that the man is Jesus. The man, who is wanted for murder, does nothing to correct them and an increasingly large group of children protects him, led by the eldest child, Swallow. A bond of trust is established among the children and with the man, in opposition to their distrust of all adults. They disregard warnings and lie to their father because of their complete trust in 'Jesus', fearing that adults would not understand and would crucify him a second time. The ten-year-old narrator, Brat, demonstrates throughout that children possess the common sense, devotion, and loyalty to be trusted, in contrast to adults. Brat declares that she thinks that grown-ups are 'mad' and that they 'kill [her]. They make so much out of nothing; and all that drink that turns them into idiots, laughing…about nothing at all'. Brat 'prefer[s] kids. They're more balanced; I mean, they really are. You see these grown-ups, heavy and downhearted about taxis and the state of the world'.[38]

The siblings decide that the only people they can safely trust with their secret about 'Jesus' are other children. Children from near and far, perhaps 'hundreds of them', having somehow heard the news, visit the barn and worship their 'Jesus'.[39] In the end the siblings learn to trust an adult, their father. They reveal their secret and he does not disappoint them. He becomes childlike and shares with them the experience of discovering a cross, left by their 'Jesus', on the wall of the empty burnt-down barn, which they interpret as the sign that he is free.

The book represents a complete breakdown of the model of religious trust shown in *Tom Brown's School Days*. Trust is misplaced and misguided, but remains a sign of children's true devotion and innocent purity. Through their adventures in misplaced trust, the child protagonists learn by themselves how to trust more effectively. Unlike the main authority figure in *Tom Brown's School Days*, Dr Arnold, who guides the boys steadfastly toward the discovery, seemingly by themselves, of true religion and who is implicitly trusted, the authority figures in *Whistle Down the Wind* preach both religious and secular trust, but they are not understood by the children, nor do they understand the children. The children are thus left to form bonds of trust with each other, and with their pseudo-Jesus. The only exception is at the end of the story: the children's father becomes an honorary child. This process of discovery—that they could indeed trust their father—unfolds in a revealing dialogue between Brat and her father toward the end of the book after the children had been successfully hiding the fugitive for a long time:

> 'Look here, you kids, can't you trust me?' he asked suddenly.
> 'We want to', I said miserably.
> 'Come on then. Tell your old Dad all about it. I won't eat you.'
> He smiled encouragingly.
> 'If we told you a secret would you swear to keep it?' I asked....
> 'Well then', I said, rather cheekily, I s'pose, 'we can't trust you, can we, since you asked?'...
> 'Is it about this man?' he asked.
> We didn't answer.
> 'Because maybe it's my business to tell someone else, and then where would I be if I'd sworn? Because if I promise a thing, I keep it. You know that.'
> We did.
> He looked at us hard for a long time.
> We looked stony.
> 'All right', he said suddenly, 'I promise'.[40]

At first the father presents himself as an adult, but by the end of the dialogue, he has entered their secret club, and can now be trusted as if he were a child. The children confirm that, despite everything that has just transpired, they still believed in their 'Jesus'. The father is moved by his children's religious fervour, and at the end of the novel, when asked if *he* had believed, he replies 'I believe that I did.'[41] Adults here are neither able to believe in children, nor even in God. It is children's imagination and trust in each other that allows them to believe in Jesus in an increasingly pluralistic age. In reading stories like this, children could safely explore and learn to develop feelings of trust, distrust, and belief in various contexts and in various hierarchical and peer relationships.

William Golding's *Lord of the Flies* (1954) provides a good example of a group of boys who operate without adult authority. The book's young, frightened characters temporarily form groups of trust, yet these groups become increasingly fractious and exclusionary. Belonging to the group eventually becomes a matter of life or death, as the boys slowly revert to a Hobbesian state of nature, or of savagery. Trust is consequently completely broken down, with only fear keeping the group together. Unlike *Whistle Down the Wind*, the boys cannot rely on the commonality of childhood experience in contradistinction to the adult world; childhood innocence has been destroyed, but has not been replaced by adult knowledge and cynicism.

For a time, Ralph, Simon, and Piggy form a bond of trust to protect themselves against the influence and violence of the other boys, led by Jack Merridew. The three boys long for a return to childhood innocence, where they can trust adults to make decisions for them. Their fantasy is of an ideal, adult world, where they can be protected and guided as dependent children:

> 'Grown-ups know things', said Piggy. 'They ain't afraid of the dark. They'd meet and have tea and discuss. Then things 'ud be all right—'
> 'They wouldn't set fire to the island. Or lose—'...
> The three boys stood in the darkness, striving unsuccessfully to convey the majesty of adult life....
> 'If only they could get a message to us', cried Ralph desperately. 'If only they could send us something grown-up...a sign or something'.[42]

In this story, not only is the religious model of trust broken down as in *Whistle Down the Wind*, but so is the entire structure of 'civilized' society, along with its emotional structures, its rules of conduct, and its age categories, all of which fall victim to a nuclear war. A breakdown in trust represents the breakdown of everything human, with the lack of civilization equating to animality.

While in time the hierarchical relationship to God, then parents and authority figures, becomes far less straightforward and unquestioned, power dynamics even among peers never disappear. Trust as a social emotion relies on the recognition of trustworthiness in others and in the self, and even in a relationship with God.

TRUST AND UNCERTAINTY

By 1970, much children's literature and advice had taken on the task of helping children and adolescents to adjust to a time of religious uncertainty and pluralism. Increasingly, personal trust in an all-powerful God was absent, or at least relegated to the background, and so were top-down interactions with authority figures.[43] The relationships that took their place were less hierarchical and more democratic; learning to trust and be trustworthy fed off these relationships. They demonstrated the possibility for children to learn how to make their own decisions about important matters, with less recourse to moral absolutes. Trust, therefore, underwent a similar transformation in this era, with the books themselves creating a trusting space to explore confusing emotions. In *Are You There God? It's Me, Margaret*, Judy Blume presents a main character who struggles with puberty and peer pressure, but also with a fractious religious heritage. As her Jewish and Christian grandparents struggle for influence, Margaret is left without organized religion. In a time of uncertainty in adolescence, Margaret yearns to get her period and be 'normal', but she also desperately wants to figure out whether she should decide to be Christian or Jewish. Interestingly, while she is going through these struggles, she prays to God every night and feels a presence when she is alone (and not when she is in church or synagogue). As with *Tom Brown's School Days*, Margaret quickly finds a group of friends in whom she can confide. Part of Margaret's journey toward adolescence from childhood, however, is to realize that she cannot completely trust her friends, especially her close friend, Nancy, who has lied about getting her period first:

> Are you there, God? It's me, Margaret. Nancy Wheeler is a big fake. She makes up stories! I'll never be able to trust her again. I will wait to find out from you if I am normal or not. If you would like to give me a sign, fine. If not, I'll try to be patient.... Thank you, God.[44]

Margaret trusts God, but she does not trust religious institutions, nor does she demonstrate complete trust in family and friends. Although she seems to have a functional relationship with her parents and occasionally confides in them, she goes through the emotional upheaval of puberty on her own, with her personal God.

This relational shift is made manifest in the advice manuals of the day. Catherine Storr, children's novelist and author of the handbook for parents and children, *Growing Up* (1975), explains that democracy has brought about greater equality, not just among various classes, but also among various age groups. 'Children don't feel themselves to owe immediate and unquestioning obedience to any authority', including parents, she writes, whereas parents 'no longer feel confident of their right to exert absolute authority over their children'.[45] Trust becomes the key in this sort of less hierarchical relationship between parents and children, especially at the stage of adolescence. As adolescents were granted more freedom, parents were advised to trust their children, in order for their children to trust them.[46] A decade later, another advice manual wrote to adolescents directly, as if in conversation, about the disappointment they might face when they realized that the trust they had placed in their parents' wisdom and knowledge might be misguided. Growing up, according to this view, was about learning to trust parents in a different way, more as equals than as superiors.[47] Here, learning to trust becomes about building social relationships, not about obeying authority or strictures. Later advice manuals put adolescents at the centre of their relationships with parents. In this teen-focused approach, it was easier for the young to feel like they were agents in their own relationships. Choosing someone they could trust for their first sexual experience, for example, was important.[48] Lengthy discussions of how teens wished their parents would trust them so that they could stay out later, or act according

to their own judgement (and not simply that of their parents) also figured prominently.[49] This kind of manual was often written with the goal of teaching teens
how to understand their parents and other adults, as well as their peers, and to
build relationships based on emotional understanding and empathy. This is in
sharp contrast to earlier advice manuals, which either instructed parents and other
authority figures how to comprehend the child/youth within a top-down understanding of the Other, or addressed youth themselves from a top-down, often
moralistic standpoint. This distinction shows a fundamental difference in how
authors and narrators viewed children and adolescents and consequently built up
trust within the books themselves. In the earlier part of the period under examination, an authoritative voice was meant to engender trust in the young reader
that the messages contained within were sound and to be followed. In the later
sources, trust was presented as a horizontal relational process: narrators, characters,
and young readers shared in the learning experience, building trust not by being
didactic, but by building up companionate relationships within the books themselves. This change in approach reflects larger patterns of changes in the concept
of the child and the adolescent, and changing educational norms. It also reflects a
changing understanding of the nature of trust itself, especially in the ways children
specifically should learn how to trust and develop trustworthiness.

* * *

Trust, devotion, and confidence cannot be isolated from the context in which they
are taught, narrated, and felt. In tracing the contours of the relationship between
morality, both in a religious and a secular context, along with trust and its varied
connected feelings, it emerges that the two concepts are embedded in children's
literature and advice manuals in an unstable way, changing in accordance with historical alterations in the status and meaning of the child and the family. If morality
is expressed through the emotions, both 'good' and 'bad', and if advice manuals
instructed children and their parents on how to feel in various situations in order
to judge what actions were moral, then an exploration of trust demonstrates how
morality and good character could be practically learnt by children, through often
unequal relationships with their peers, parents, and other adults. The outer manifestation of character was only part of the goal, explored alongside appeals to the
cultivation of children's inner selves.[50] Learning how to trust in God and in oneself,
as well as to be trustworthy and be trusting of others in an effective way, were all
components of a changing process in which children could develop the desired
characteristics for adulthood, the requirements of which were also historically contingent. *Tom Brown's School Days* still often resonates with the young, even in an
era long-since indisposed to elite schools, godliness, good learning,[51] and muscular
Christianity. Although changes in societal norms regarding gender, class, and age
have all had an impact on the meaning of trust, the model of trust shown by Dickon
in *The Secret Garden* has proven to be durable, despite its now largely outmoded religious and imperial underpinnings. Or perhaps, if not durable, Dickon's trust is flexible: the novel's unwaning popularity suggests the possibilities of new readings of
trust, and of learning how to trust and to be trustworthy, by an active readership.[52]

NOTES

1. Burnett, *Secret Garden*, 242, 141.
2. This chapter is based on more than a hundred works of children's and adolescent literature and advice manuals directed to youthful readers. The chosen works were published in Britain, with a focus on imperial literature and colonial India, North America, and, to a lesser extent, other European countries.
3. Misztal, *Trust in Modern Societies*; Fukuyama, *Trust*. Some scholars promote the view that trust actually increases as information flow improves, especially in urbanized economies; see Fisman and Khanna, 'Is Trust a Historical Residue'. Others note that trust can develop among strangers, but when people share a longer history, and possible emotional bonds, they no longer need to assess trust, but rather enact it in the habitual way, for example Sako, 'Does Trust Improve Business Performance?'.
4. Möllering, 'The Nature of Trust', 403; also useful for a discussion on how current trust research is moving away from a dichotomy between rational choice and more affective, moral bases for trust.
5. Simmel, 'Sociology of Secrecy', 450.
6. Luhmann, 'Familiarity, Confidence, Trust'.
7. Frevert, 'Trust as Work'; Brückenhaus 'Every stranger must be suspected'; Hosking, 'Trust and Distrust'; Shapin, *Social History of Truth*.
8. Frevert, *Does Trust Have a History*, 6; Seligman, *Problem of Trust*. For a discussion of how friendship and trust as moral ideals are defined by inversion in Western, urban societies, see Silver, 'Friendship and Trust as Moral Ideals'.
9. The argument here can be extended on both ends. *Tom Brown's School Days* represents the culmination of almost a century of ideas about emotions and character in children's literature. On the other end, *Lord of the Flies* (1954) and *Whistle Down the Wind* (1958) hint at processes of secularization and post-coloniality that became more pronounced later.
10. Boddice, 'In Loco Parentis'.
11. Dixon, 'Educating the Emotions from Gradgrind to Goleman'.
12. Hughes, *Tom Brown's School Days*, 267, 281.
13. Farrar, *Eric*.
14. For more on Hughes and Kingsley's works as the climax of literary treatment of muscular Christianity, begun in the previous century by Rousseau, Edgeworth, and Martineau, see Redmond, 'First Tom Brown's School Days', 8.
15. Cutt, *Mrs. Sherwood and her Books for Children*, 17–18.
16. Sherwood, *Story of Little Henry and His Bearer Boosy* [a combined and full version of *The History of Little Henry and his Bearer* (1814) and *The Last Days of Boosy, the Bearer of Little Henry* (1842)], 100–7, 80, 75, quotations 81.
17. Sherwood, 87, quotations 83.
18. Ahmad, *Bride's Mirror*, 14. See chapter 3, 'Asghari's Piety' for a more extensive discussion of this book and its context.
19. Murdoch, *Indian Student's Manual*, 107.
20. Murdoch, 121, 151.
21. See Newsome, *Godliness and Good Learning*.
22. Kingsley, *Health and Education*, 260.
23. Farningham, *Girlhood*, 121–6. Thanks to Kerstin Singer for finding this source.
24. Stall, *What a Young Man Ought to Know*, 47, 255, quotation 168.
25. Hughes, *Notes for Boys*, 13, 18, 98.

26. Hughes, *True Manliness*, 26.
27. Hall, *Youth*, 104; Hall, *Adolescence*, i, 225.
28. Spyri, *Heidi*, 78, 149. See chapter 11, 'Heidi's Homesickness' for a more detailed discussion.
29. Spyri, *Gritli's Children*, 196.
30. Montgomery, *Anne of Green Gables*, 426.
31. Montgomery, 136–7, 299, 347, 297.
32. Burnett, *Secret Garden*, 190, 237.
33. Bixler, *Secret Garden*, 10.
34. Burnett, *Secret Garden*, 303, 304, 342.
35. Baden-Powell, *Rovering to Success*, 126, 219, 18–19, 22, 111.
36. See, for example, Enid Blyton's description of gendered emotions in the trust bonds among the children in *Five on a Treasure Island*, 44, 40, 34, 48.
37. Lewis, *Lion, the Witch and the Wardrobe*, 109, 142–3.
38. Bell, *Whistle Down the Wind*, 4–5.
39. Bell, 136.
40. Bell, 131.
41. Bell, 151.
42. Golding, *Lord of the Flies*, 117. See chapter 7, 'Piggy's Shame' for more information on this book, its popularity, and its intended readership.
43. See chapter 12, 'Ingrid's Boredom'.
44. Blume, *Are You There God*, 111.
45. Storr, *Growing Up*, 13.
46. Storr, 118.
47. Powledge, *You'll Survive*, 72–3.
48. Farman, *Keep Out of the Reach of Parents*, 90.
49. Farman, 39.
50. See, for example, Jesse Prinz's theoretical pairing of 'virtuous character traits' and 'emotional dispositions'; Prinz, *Emotional Construction of Morals*, 15.
51. Newsome, *Godliness and Good Learning*.
52. For more on active readership, see Ablow, *Feeling of Reading*.

3

Asghari's Piety

Margrit Pernau

When Asghari enters the household of Maulawi Muhammad Fazl as a young bride in mid-nineteenth-century Delhi, she is almost overwhelmed by the difficulties facing her from all sides. Relatives scrutinize her every behaviour and even worse, a dishonest servant who has been with the family for many years and who now fears that Asghari's superior skills will uncover her frauds, works to sow discord between the young bride, her mother-in-law, and her husband.[1]

Asghari, however, overcomes all the difficulties, gets the servant dismissed, rescues the family from bankruptcy, and sets it on a path of affluence by cleverly and inconspicuously saving money. She convinces her husband to study hard and work his way up the British administrative ladder, establishes a school for the well-to-do girls of the neighbourhood, and finally succeeds in getting her sister-in-law married into one of the wealthiest families of Delhi.

Her father's education cultivated her natural disposition, enabling her to face all these challenges. This education stressed the importance of knowledge, which in turn developed her rationality and empowered her to establish firm control over her passions, while practical skills set her in a position to administer a large household in times of difficulties. Asghari's management of her emotions, her self-restraint, her modesty, her tact, her consideration for others, more than anything else, makes her successful in every situation.[2]

This novel by Nazir Ahmad (1831–1912) became an instant success. Originally written in Urdu for the education and edification of his own daughters, it won the prize of the government of the Northwest Provinces, became a standard textbook in girls' schools for many decades, sold more than 100,000 copies over twenty years, and was translated into a number of Indian languages.[3]

One might ask whether this book about a young bride can be classified as children's literature at all. The assumption behind the question, however, is that a clear demarcation exists between childhood and adulthood. This, in turn, finds its reflection in children's literature as a specific genre that should be modified for the nineteenth-century Indian context. Asghari is eight years old when she takes over the responsibility for her paternal household and she marries at the age of thirteen.[4] This was by no means an early marriage: the proposal to raise the age

of consent to twelve years of age in 1891 triggered storms of protest.[5] Instead of
entering into a debate about whether these are indicators of a missing childhood,
or if it might not rather be the case of a missing or delayed adulthood,[6] for our purpose it is enough to state that the three events traditionally taken as marking the
entry into adulthood—sexual maturity/marriage, the end of schooling, and financial independence[7]—did not come together in the Indian case, nor did they establish a firm boundary between stages in the lifecycle. As we have seen in the case of
Asghari, marriage took place at a very young age. While she had learnt everything
she needed before leaving her paternal house, her husband continues his schooling for quite some time after marriage.[8] Her sister, married to her brother-in-law,
had insisted on a separate house at an early stage, but this is one of the signs the
author uses to depict her lack of sense. Within a short time, her credulity makes
her an easy target for crooks, while her lack of housekeeping skills quickly leads
her into debt.[9] If the boundary between children and adults is not clearly demar-
cated, neither is the audience of the book. In his foreword, Nazir Ahmad depicts
his daughters reading it before they got married;[10] later in the book he reminds his
readers that it is suitable as a sermon for elders as well.[11]

    While we know that the book was read, and widely read, we know very little
about the reading practices of the time. These early novels were still situated at
the interstice between oral and print cultures. Even where the narrative structures
offer the possibility for mimetic reading—and *The Bride's Mirror* (1903; Urd. orig.
Mirat ul arus, 1869) certainly allowed its readers to try out how it felt to be Akbari
or Asghari—reading practices could either reinforce or hamper this process. Texts
like Asghari's story were rarely consumed privately, but read aloud collectively. We
know too little about the effect this has on the learning of emotions, but if the
argument of this book is that children's literature provided a space where emotions
could be tried without immediate consequences in the 'real' world, it seems at least
worth questioning how these processes play out differently according to the different practices of reading and listening.[12]

    The title of this chapter claims piety as the central category which holds the
narrative together—but is this a story about piety and even more importantly, is
piety an emotion at all? This chapter will investigate different emotions that can
come together under the label of the analytical category of piety, here referring
to a religiously motivated endeavour to lead a good life. Religion shall be taken
in a rather broad sense, including the right emotions towards one's fellow creatures and towards God. Contemporary readers would have recognized Asghari
as embodying the piety of the Muslim reformist project, though this does not
mean that they read the book only for pedagogical reasons and not also, or even
mainly, for the pleasure it provided.[13] Asghari's education is focused on the reading
of the Quran;[14] she prays regularly and keeps the religious fasts and festivals. She
acknowledges the omnipotence of God even though she relies not only on prayer,
but also on hard work to achieve her goals, and she finds consolation in Him when
two of her children die at an early age.[15] Still, her piety is less focused on a tran-
scendental relationship to God and more on her everyday comportment within
the extended family and the neighbourhood. While the nineteenth and twentieth

century European concepts of emotions increasingly distinguished emotions from virtue, this distinction was much less sharply drawn in the world in which Asghari lived. Virtue encompassed not only behaviour, but also the management of emotions that enabled a person to behave virtuously. Asghari's sister Akbari provides an example for what happens if virtuous emotion management fails, and a person is overwhelmed by her passions, by anger, by greed, by desires for food or costly clothes. She destroys the unity of the extended family, ruins her husband, and in the end only his nobility of heart keeps him from divorcing her.[16] Virtue thus bridges the distinction between interiority, which is the site of emotions, and behaviour, which is accessible to the external observer. Piety as an emotion-virtue encompasses both spheres and makes for their congruence.[17]

RELIGIOUS REFORM AND PIOUS ADVICE

Reform and education were the keywords of a public debate that had already started before the advent of the colonial power and gained momentum throughout the nineteenth century. Fictional literature and advice books come together under this goal. The genres, which seem so distinct at first glance, flow into each other upon further inspection. While Nazir Ahmad's *The Bride's Mirror* is usually acclaimed as the first novel written in Urdu, its very title links it to the mirror of princes literature, widely known in the Indo-Persian region since the Middle Ages.[18] As in those texts, we have seen how generous the author is in giving advice. On the other hand, hardly any advice book forgoes the possibility of enlivening the text with anecdotes and short (or not so short) stories.

The first group of texts we are going to consider can be linked to the Aligarh movement in its most encompassing sense. This movement aimed at catching up with modernization and progress through engagement with European culture and scientific knowledge.[19] Central to the movement was collaboration with colonial power. It found its focus in the efforts to establish the Muhammadan Anglo-Oriental College in Aligarh, but its aims were shared by people far beyond those directly involved with the College. Like Nazir Ahmad, who was Deputy Collector in the colonial administration, all of the authors of these texts held some position under the colonial power: Muhammad Mubarak Ullah was a clerk (*munsif*) in Badayun; Karim ud Din and Ayodhya Prasad worked for the education department of the Punjab and the North Western Provinces respectively; and Nur Ahmad Nur was a teacher at the Municipal Board School in Ambala. All of them benefited from the patronage of British officers and all of their writings were adopted as textbooks in government schools.[20]

Under these circumstances, it is hardly surprising that the books show the influence of Victorian values and feeling rules. What is more astonishing, however, is the extent to which this colonial influence is integrated into traditional Indo-Persian concepts of emotions and virtues. Mubarak Ullah, for instance, makes it clear that the aim of education and self-education should be the mastery of morality (*akhlaq*). *Akhlaq* consists of the beauty of the soul, of the cultivation of a way of being, which becomes an ingrained habit (*khalq*, sing. of *akhlaq*). These habits should at the very least encompass a knowledge of good and evil, the ability to restrain anger and desires within boundaries set by reason and justice. He further explains that justice is a balance that comprises everything, from the macrocosm to the fluids of the body, and not least the emotions of a person. These concepts hark back to Aristotelian philosophy that, through a long and complicated history of transmission and translation into Arabic and Persian, still formed the basis of morality teaching in nineteenth-century Indian madrasas. Mubarak Ullah's emphasis on knowledge as the basis of right feelings gives a central role to the correctly taught will. His insistence on the avoidance of both too little and too much of an emotion, and not on an absolute moral value of emotions, as well as his interpretation that emotions that matter are ingrained habits rather than short-lived surges, all sat at odds with contemporary Victorian ways of conceiving emotions.[21]

More easily agreed upon, in contrast, were the actual recommended emotions and virtues. The colonial officers in the education department would probably not have disagreed with a single one of the 150 admonitory sentences that Karim ud Din put together. Still, their selection once again shows a notably different way of approaching emotions. While Victorian emotion knowledge places feeling in the first instance in relation to the individual—even arguing that emotions are what constitute an individual, his most personal and private qualities[22]—for Karim ud Din, emotions and emotion management take their importance from their impact on social relations. Emotion management is never restricted to a person's own emotions: to avoid provoking anger is as essential as restraining one's own anger. Self-control of the eyes and tongue helps restrain one's own exasperation. The reason for this self-restraint is to avoid offending or shaming the interlocutor; and thus provoke him to uncontrolled passions. Greed and miserliness are not only bad in and of themselves, but are worse in their disruptive effects on the cohesion of a community. It is only at first sight that this emphasis on the social nature of emotions seems to contradict Mubarak Ullah's creation of the beautiful soul. The refining of the habits, the ultimate perfection of the soul, cannot be attained in isolation. Only through life in a community, through the shaping of emotions situated not primarily inside of individuals, but in the communicative space between them, can a person reach this ideal.

If the restraining of anger and greed and the cultivation of compassion and affection can qualify as piety, what about the most Victorian of virtues, economy and planned allocation of time (and money)? Nur Ahmad Nur devotes a long chapter to this topic, situated directly after the introductory praise of God and taking its tone from it.[23] It is the Almighty who gave man his span of time; it is man's responsibility not to waste it. Time is short and can never be brought back. A man who does not devote his youth to learning will be devoured by regret all of his life. Up to this point, the argument is traditional, and fleeting time evokes feelings of melancholy and nostalgic longing. The tone changes once the British enter the picture. Unlike the Indians, Nur Ahmad Nur tells his readers, the British make use of every moment of the day. They are always punctual, even decorating the walls of their houses with timetables.[24] This careful planning allows them to get much more work done—and if the Hindustani gentlemen would just look around, they would discover how much work there is to be done in their immediate neighbour-hood. Teaching, preaching, advising, and counselling those in need are clearly tasks marked out for pious men. Even more importantly, planning avoids confusion and imparts stability (*istiqlal*) to the temperament of a person.[25] As to how far planning and living according to rules take on not only an ascetic role helping to control the emotions, but create emotions of their own, would be worth exploring in greater detail than can be done here. Can we enlarge the history of emotions to encompass not only the study of anger and love, important though they are, but also the sigh of satisfaction at having organized the week's work and done one's duty?[26]

Piety, as a virtue or as an emotion, usually evokes a close link to a particular religion, and it is tempting to read the advice texts into the framework of Muslim reformism and even separatism. However, while references to God as the Creator and Lord of the Universe are abounding in all the texts, references to the Prophet Muhammad and quotations from the sacred scriptures of Islam are conspicuous by their absence. The piety they advocate travels easily across religious boundaries, be it as textbooks in government schools, or through translations into other Indian languages, which were even less exclusive to Muslims than Urdu. What comes more as a surprise (at least at this late stage), however, is the fairly substantial cor-pus of Urdu texts by Hindu authors, who use the Indo-Persianate reference frame of the *akhlaq* literature.[27]

The picture changes drastically once we leave the texts broadly linked to the Aligarh movement and consider those written by the Islamic reformist movement. Like the Aligarh movement's texts, they emphasize education, notably, but by no means exclusively, female education, which will enable women to avoid supersti-tion and excesses and lead a well-regulated life. However, here it is the Quran and the Traditions of the Prophet which have the sole moral authority. Piety means living and feeling according to those standards and is consequently accessible to Muslims only.

One of the most famous examples of this genre is a compendium written by Nawab Shah Jahan, the second of three female rulers of the princely state of Bhopal,[28] in which she aims at providing upper-class women with everything they need to know in order to lead a good and virtuous life from the cradle to the grave.[29] Similar to the *akhlaq* tradition, the *Tahzib un Niswan wa Tarbiyat ul Insan* ('The civilizing of women and the education of mankind', 1881) gives pride of place to knowledge. Religious knowledge paves the reader's way to eternal felic-ity and worldly knowledge—from how to avoid miscarriages and what to feed children, to which clothes to wear and how to sew and dye them, to the appropri-ate behaviour for every social occasion—and enables her to organize her house-hold successfully and uphold her family's respectability. Both religious and secular forms of knowledge come together in buttressing the social status of the family. Comportment inspired by religious precepts will also guarantee respectability.[30]

But besides these practical uses, the cultivation of knowledge, any knowledge, also strengthens reason and thus enables it to take control over desires and pas-sions. The emotional quality of the well-regulated life here gains a specific religious and emotional colouring, as it is closely linked to the example of the Prophet him-self: the lifestyle which at first glance seems almost devoid of feelings is at the same time one marked by an intimate community and communion with the Prophet.

Nawab Sultan Jahan followed her mother not only on the throne of Bhopal, but also in her educational endeavours, publishing her own book *Tarbiyat ul atfal* ('Training children') in 1914.[31] Without giving up on the project of Islamic piety, she distanced herself from its more rigorous expressions and drew closer to the Aligarh tradition which, in turn, had moved from its earlier, comparatively inclu-sive stance towards a more scripture-based piety.

Possibly under the influence of British ideas on education—Sultan Jahan men-tions an English book as her inspiration, but leaves us guessing as to what she might have read—this text shifts its emphasis from a general moral treatise, useful for all age-groups, to focused attention on children. Teaching children is still a parental duty, but as the title already indicates, the emphasis on imparting know-ledge (*talim*) is replaced by a more general education (*tarbiyat*). To be success-ful, the educator not only has to observe closely the natural temperament and inclinations of the child, but also be aware of the developmental stages of child-hood: approaches which work well for a five-year-old child can be quite inappro-priate for a toddler or a young person.[32] Virtues and emotions are initially learnt not through rules, but through experience. It is the parental duty to provide the child with the right kind of experience by surrounding it with virtuous people. By imitating and mimicking their behaviour, as well as by absorbing the atmosphere virtuous people generate, the child will learn to act and feel the right way. This process no longer accords a central role to the will: the classical sequence of 'to know—to will—to do/feel' is replaced by the new 'to do—to feel—to understand'.

Where verbal explanations and instructions are given, the parents should not rely on their implementation as a matter of course, but watch over the child and supervise his or her behaviour until the parents can be sure that a stable habit has developed. Exhortations and reprimands are necessary, but Sultan Jahan stresses that the child should never be shamed. Rather, admonishment should be given in private and in a way that does not damage the child's self-respect or self-confidence. Whenever possible, parents should resort to indirect forms of teaching, and to this end moral stories are unsurpassed. Therefore, the entire second part of the book is devoted to collections of anecdotes and short stories. Though they address the child directly, the narrative plots are underdeveloped and they read more like reminders of stories and experiences already known. The stories were possibly therefore not meant to be either studied silently or read out loud, but served as suggestions for tales to be developed orally. The field they cover is extensive and ranges from his-tory, both European and Indian, to the daily experience of children, and to narra-tives from the Quran and the Traditions of the Prophet. Lessons could be imparted to the children through a wide variety of situations and heroes: from a boy rid-ing a bicycle who can only direct his vehicle if he holds on to the handlebars; to Lycurgus and Cesar; the Prophet; Umar Faruq; the caliphs; and Captain Scott. By the beginning of the twentieth century, the colonial state and the spokespersons of the Muslim community agreed that childhood was the time for learning and that moral and virtuous emotions were the most important lessons imparted by the family, the school, and by children's literature.[33]

SUBVERSIVE LAUGHTER—THE TALES
OF AMIR HAMZA

If moral and instructive tales have a long tradition in the Indo-Persianate world, they were by no means the only, or possibly even the predominant, genre. Rather than teaching respect for hierarchies, as the *akhlaq* tradition did, popular stories make fun of figures of authority. They lampoon the religious scholar in the Mullah do Pyaza, and in the anecdotes circulating about the Mughal emperor Akbar (1542–1605), he is regularly outwitted by his minister Birbal.[34] Many of these stories have found their way into today's children's books, suitably sanitized. They were not, however, originally devised specifically for children, but rather transmitted orally in a wide variety of settings, ranging from the popular to the courtly.

The Amir Hamza is perhaps the best example of a story that is decidedly set in an Islamicate frame of reference, while just as decidedly marginalizing and even subverting pious feelings.[35] Amir Hamza is the son of the Prophet's uncle. Accompanied by his faithful companions Amar Ayyar and Muqbil Wafadar, his whole life is a series of adventures leading him not only through the Arabic and Persian world, but to India and China, and to the land of the fairies and jinns. While the three friends are Muslims and regularly ask their vanquished foes to convert to Islam, they do not feel too closely bound by the codes of Islamic (or any other) law and morality. The help they regularly receive from the netherworld does not come in the shape of God's miracles, but of magic.

This framework allowed storytellers to adapt their recitals to their audience.[36] The tales were performed in public places—in the nineteenth century, the steps of the Jama Masjid in Delhi were a regular meeting point for storytellers and their audiences—but also in private homes. Children listened to these performances, but before the second half of the twentieth century, there was no version of Amir Hamza written explicitly as literature for children.[37]

So how do these stories negotiate moral and pious emotions? The disregard for the social and gendered hierarchies that all the *akhlaq* texts and reformist narratives worked so hard to uphold is striking, as is the negation of the need to accord proper respect to authorities and avoid shaming anyone. By looking more closely at three stories, we shall point to different strategies of subversion inherent in the text, a subversion which may or may not contribute to the establishment of a different form of morality.

One day the emperor has a dream he cannot recall upon waking up. He summons his minister Alqash and all of his astrologers and threatens them with death if they cannot tell him the meaning of his forgotten dream. In his plight, Alqash remembers young Buzurjmehr, who has a miraculous ability to foresee the future. However, Alqash had killed Buzurjmehr's father, who had been his friend, out of greed—a fact that Buzurjmehr has found out without the minister's knowledge.

Summoned by the emperor, Buzurjmehr refuses to come unless Alqash is sent to his house, saddled as his mount, to ride to court. The children's version describes Alqash's shame and the jeering of the crowd in even more detail than the version for adults. Shaming, in this episode, works as retribution. Subversion exposes hidden sins and serves a higher morality. Revenge is induced by pious feelings, in this case love for the father and also the desire to re-establish justice. The story praises the young Buzurjmehr as 'pious and devout, of noble blood, courageous, and unrivaled...unsurpassed in wisdom and learning...upright, constant, and generous'.[38]

Subversion works differently in the second story. One day, the emperor goes hunting in the forest with his entourage and Dil Aram, one of his female companions. They meet a woodcutter who bears the same name as the emperor. Struck by the diversity of their fortunes, the emperor asks for an explanation. Buzurjmehr refers to the constellation of the planets at the moment of their respective births, but Dil Aram contradicts him and argues that the bad housekeeping of the woodcutter's wife is responsible for his plight. The emperor is incensed by the implication that in his life, too, the women of the palace might be the cause of his fortune and misfortune. He abandons Dil Aram in the forest, telling the woodcutter that he could have her. Living as the woodcutter's daughter for several years, Dil Aram advises him sagaciously and indeed, like Asghari in *The Bride's Mirror*, successfully improves his economic situation to the extent that his riches ultimately match those of the emperor.[39] The flouting of gender hierarchies and the shaming of the men involved in openly showing women's superior capability and influence (something that Asghari always avoided), might be read as a counter-narrative, a challenge to the dominant norms in the name of a different morality. The fact, however, that this story voices the concerns of the reformers, both their replacement of faith in astrology with the belief in the ethics of hard work and good planning, and their advocacy of the importance of women in the improvement of a family's status, makes it probable that it is an interpolation at the earliest from the second half of the nineteenth century. The story leaves open whose emotions the listeners would want to try out and at whom they would laugh.

The shaming stories most challenging to decipher are those woven around Amir Hamza's friend Amar Ayyar. He makes his entry as a baby by stealing a valuable diamond ring from Buzurjmehr, living up to the prediction that he will be 'unsurpassed in cunning, guile, and deceit...excessively greedy, most insidious, and a consummate perjurer. He will be cruel, tyrannical, and coldhearted, yet he shall prove a trustworthy friend and confidant to Hamza.'[40] In school, Amar not only refuses to learn anything and through his rambunctious behaviour keeps the other children from learning, but over and again shames his teacher by stealing food and attributing the theft to the teacher, thus disgracing him in front of the entire neighbourhood and reducing him to tears.[41] Amar does get punished, but in the end he comes out triumphantly laughing, and the readers laugh with him. The easiest interpretation would, of course, be to ascribe a cathartic function to these stories, allowing for an acting out of pent-up emotions, a sort of emotional refuge,[42] which releases the subversive energy while concurrently limiting it to specific times and places and thus as a part of a disciplining endeavour.[43] But reading it as a moral tale in disguise does not explain why the Amir Hamza cycle has evoked so much resistance, from Emperor Akbar's opponents to the protagonists of reformist piety and middle-class values. How then can we think about humour and subversion without immediately refolding them into the moral project as its opposite? How can we transcend the frame of modern middle class literature and bring back into view laughter for its own sake—and not just harmless laughter, but also laughter that shames and hurts without an ulterior moral agenda?[44] At the same time, Amar also shows how problematic an idealization of this subversion may become, as his laughter not only shames the teacher and mullah, but also transforms the rape of a girl child and her subsequent death into an occasion for laughter at the unbound virility of her rapist.[45]

SECULARIZING PIETY—THE PEDAGOGY OF THE JAMIA MILLIA ISLAMIA

The Aligarh movement, as we have seen above, set its hopes on collaboration with the colonial government in order to help the Muslim community reform and catch up on what they perceived as its educational deficit. While they initially shared these aims with other religious and social reformers, this common strategy gradually gave way to and was replaced by sharp distinctions and even antagonism, notably to the Indian National Congress. Things dramatically changed in the last phase of the First World War and immediately thereafter, when the Young Party from Aligarh joined the national movement under the leadership of Gandhi, and simultaneously took up the religious reform agenda of the *ulama*. The Jamia Millia Islamia in Delhi was the outcome of this movement, founded as a centre for the education of Muslims who would become both pious and ardent nationalists.[46] The 'new' piety was to be distinguished from a communal agenda and was no longer aimed at the well-being of the religious community. Instead, it was to focus on God and his commands, thus bringing people together in a common endeavour rather than dividing them. If secular is seen as the opposite of communal, as it is in much of the Indian discussion, it was indeed a form of 'secular piety' to which they aspired.

Zakir Husain, later president of the Indian Republic, was most influential in the development of the pedagogical ideas particular to Jamia. While studying in Berlin, Zakir Husain had come into contact with German reform pedagogy, notably the idea of a working school developed by Kerschensteiner.[47] As an international movement, reform pedagogy shared a number of core influences with the Indian national movement, particularly the ideas of Leo Tolstoy and of the Theosophists, but also a more general critique of Western civilization and modernization. If it did not have emotions in common, then it did at least share an emotional attunement or colouring, for instance, the place given to intuition and educating the heart, instead of rationality and the imparting of knowledge; a quest for salvation; the attempt to transcend the boundaries of the individual self; and to recover wholeness through fusion with, and even sacrifice for, a leader, a community, or the world.[48]

Jamia provided educational facilities from kindergarten to college. *Payam-e talim*, Jamia's children's magazine, was started in 1926. It contained poems, riddles and stories, but also articles on Indian and European history, on foreign countries and their people, on natural phenomena and on science, as well as suggestions for play and news from the readers' community. Compared to Jamia's innovative pedagogical concepts, the stories remained quite traditional in their message. Not unlike the moral exempla in the *akhlaq* literature, the stories are about virtuous heroes who come out victorious in the end and about the punishment met by those who lack the will or the self-discipline for these virtues. This can be shown through two exemplary stories. In the first, Khurshid Sultana tells the story of 'Nanha Tatu' ('Little Tatu', 1939), a little goat which lives just round the corner from six-year-old Jamil.[49] Seeing that the goat mother's chain is too short to allow her to protect her child, Jamil thinks it good fun to beat Tatu with his cap. However, the goat's owner sees what happens and when Jamil is gone, lengthens the chain. The next day, the mother goat beats up Jamil with her horns. The owner explains the risks of cruelty to the crying boy and teaches him how to befriend the animals. Avoiding cruelty is not enough; beyond this, children must also learn compassion.

In 'Tilismi Dawa' ('The magic medicine', 1939) a king's life can only by saved by water from a green pond guarded by dwarves. His three sons set out to search for it, but on their way, one after the other, they each refuse to help people and animals in distress—who, of course, turn out to be dwarves in disguise and who transform the offenders into stone. In the end it is the king's small and ugly daughter, humble and helpful, who returns not only with the water, but is also transformed into a beauty by the dwarves.[50] This story takes up the model of the fairy tale, situated outside of time and place. Its standard protagonists—the king, his family, his court and servants, the trader, the artisan, the old woman, the beggar—are not individual characters with individualized emotions. Their role is to transport the message and to render it self-evident by backing it up with their experience.

Compassion (*hamdardi*) with all suffering creatures, especially the lowly from whom no return can be expected, had become one of the central (if not *the* central) emotion-virtues of nationalist piety since the turn of the twentieth century. Compassion emotionally binds the community together without abolishing its internal hierarchies: the proper return for compassion is gratitude (unless, of course, the recipient is a dwarf in disguise who can bestow magical gifts).

Among the most poetic of the children's stories published in *Payam-e talim* are those written by Zakir Husain himself. 'Akhri Qadam' (c.1957; Eng. 'The Final Step', 2000),[51] too, starts out as a story on compassion. A noble man does not consider his wealth as his personal property, but as a gift God had bestowed on him as a trustee for the poor. He spends hardly anything on himself, but quietly gives to the needy, never bragging about his charitable gifts. This earns him the reputation of a miser and even the contempt of his friends. Though he feels hurt and his eyes fill with tears, he continues living in this humble way. His only consolation is his notebook, in which he keeps account of all his charitable expenses, hoping that his good character will be vindicated after his death. On his deathbed, however, he feels the shame of trying to shame the community, flings the book into the fire, and peacefully dies with a smile on his lips, just at the moment the muezzin proclaims Muhammad's Prophethood. Here, piety as an emotion-virtue has transcended the level of a possible division between feeling and doing, with both now leading the way to a transformation of a person's self. This self, in turn, is no longer limited by the boundaries of the individual, but merges in the community of believers, in the nation, and perhaps in the end, in God.

Abbu Khan ki bakri (1939; Eng. *The Bravest Goat in the World*, 2004)[52] is the story of an old man living high up in the Himalaya, with only his goats to keep him company. But like all mountain animals, the goats love their freedom more than anything. Neither the temptation of food nor the fear of the wolf could restrain them, and one after the other they run away and meet their death. Chandni is the most beloved of his goats and the old man is convinced that she, too, loves him. But she loves freedom more and one night she escapes. For a whole day Chandni roams the mountains, meeting other goats, intoxicated with her freedom. Nightfall brings the choice before Chandni: from one side she hears Abbu Khan calling her back to safety, from the other she sees the wolf's eyes glowing. She does not return to safety and stays, knowing that she cannot win against the wolf. But this is no longer important. 'Winning or losing is not in our control—that is in God's hands. What we can do is struggle.' And valiantly struggle she does, the whole night through, until the muezzin calls in the morning. The birds, who had watched the fight, all 'agreed that the wolf had won except one. A wise old bird, who knew that even though she had died, it was Chandni who had won in the end.'[53] Overcoming fear is all that mattered in the end—for Chandni, but also for the fighters in Gandhi's *satyagraha* campaigns, be they Hindu or Muslim. Piety is not mentioned in this story, with the exception of the reference to the muezzin's call. Nevertheless, in the context of the national movement it would have been read as a story deeply suffused with feelings of piety. This piety is not only present in the love of the homeland and of freedom, but perhaps even more in the sense of detachment from the fight's results.

The same message and the same emotions resound in a very different children's book which appeared roughly at the same time, Dhan Gopal Mukerji's *Gay-Neck* (1927).[54] Mukerji had migrated from Bengal to the United States as a young man. He wrote his stories for a specific section of the American public raised on the transcendentalism of Henry David Thoreau and Ralph Waldo Emerson (who were also important influences on Gandhi), spiritually close to theosophy and pedagogically to the reformist ideas of the *New Educational Fellowship*. The fact that *Gay-Neck*, read as a tale originating in oriental wisdom, won the prestigious *Newbery Medal* in 1928 shows how widely these entangled ideas had spread during the interwar years.

Gay-Neck tells the story of the friendship between a boy and a pigeon in the Himalaya; it is a story of a spiritual journey and of growing up. Gay-Neck is trained as a carrier pigeon and has to face the dangers of his calling, for example when he is attacked by hawks. Later he has to confront the horrors of the First World War in

the trenches, where his services are needed by the British Army. The central theme
of how to keep one's soul free from fear recurs throughout the book:

> [A]lmost all our troubles come from fear, worry and hate. If any man catches one of
> the three, the other two are added unto it. No beast of prey can kill his victim without
> frightening him first. In fact, no animal perishes until its destroyer strikes terror into
> its heart.[55]

This is not the fearlessness of soldiers, which enables them to continue the battle,
but a fearlessness which aims at overcoming violence, within the soul and outside of
it. More than controlling passions and bringing them into a state of balance, thus
bringing forth justice—the core of the *akhlaq* literature, as we have seen—what is
aimed at here is transformation, healing, and in the end, salvation. Fearlessness, and
the accompanying ability to act non-violently, is at the root of a spiritual life.

If the emotions these texts advocate are notably different from the pious feelings
favoured by the Muslim (or for that matter, the Hindu) reformers of the late nineteenth century, their quest for salvation, on the individual as well as on the social
level, is a re-interpretation of piety in the light of the cultural critique that marked
the interwar years. Most of the texts are too short to permit the kind of mimesis
the introduction of this book has laid out, drawing on Paul Ricoeur. Many, notably those stylistically drawing on a model of fairy tales, allow for learning through
identification with the hero or anti-hero. However, the lesson learnt will tend to
be cognitive as well as emotional: not a lengthy introduction into when emotions
arise and how they feel, instead happiness or grief as a result of right or wrong
behaviour, of acting with cruelty or compassion. The case is slightly different for
the stories from the core of the reform pedagogical project. Fearlessness is conveyed not so much through practical knowledge about the emotion, as through the
depiction of a dense emotional atmosphere which draws the reader into its spell.

CHILDREN'S BOOK TRUST AND PATRIOTIC PIETY

The transformation of childhood which had started at the beginning of the twentieth century gathered speed after 1947. This held true for the statistical indicators: the average age at marriage in India rose after independence, as did literacy
rates, both for girls and boys.[56] Childhood thus could not only be seen as clearly
distinguished from the responsibilities of married adulthood, but also from labour
(at least full-time labour). Instead, school came to be seen as the decisive and typical feature of childhood. Even if these experiences still did not reflect the day to
day reality of a substantial part of the population, notably in the rural areas, they
nevertheless developed a strong regulative impetus: this was the childhood that the
nation owed its children.[57] Against this backdrop, childhood began to be imagined
not only as a period of innocence and vulnerability, but also as a period of impres-
sionability.[58] It was the education of children which had to bear the brunt of building the nation and realizing the utopian visions of the Nehruvian era.

From the beginning, the new nation faced the challenge of poverty, internal disruptions, and conflicts, first between the religious communities, but eventually also between castes and language groups undermining the efforts of development. 'Emotional integration', a felicitous phrase created by Nehru, became the rallying cry:

> Let us, the citizens of the Republic of India, stand up straight, with straight backs and look up at the skies, keeping our feet firmly planted on the ground, and bring about this synthesis, this integration of the Indian people. Political integration has already taken place to some extent, but what I am after is something much deeper than that—an emotional integration of the Indian people so that we might be welded into one, and made into one strong national unit, maintaining at the same time all our wonderful diversity.[59]

The religious and emotional overtone of this message cannot be missed. As in religious reformism, every individual had to be transformed and work at his self-transformation. But where religious reformism had aimed at individual salvation—an individual salvation that was certainly only attainable in and through social relations—here the nation took over as the ultimate goal. It was for the nation's sake that every Indian was charged to transform not only his behaviour, but also his being and most importantly, his emotions. The nation took on an almost divine role as the ultimate goal of mystical experience.[60]

Therefore, to an even greater extent than during the colonial period, the state took over the responsibility of forming the character and the emotions of the next generation in order 'to produce good human beings' through schools and colleges, and also through children's films and children's books.[61] This was the background for the foundation of the Children's Book Trust, which owes its existence to the initiative of Shankar Pillai, a famous political cartoonist.[62] Already involved in a number of children's projects, Shankar was worried by what he perceived as the lack of good reading material for Indian children. Therefore, the aim of the Trust was not only to collect and publish books in English and in the different Indian languages, but also to generate the appropriate literature by motivating and training authors. The national agenda explains the exclusion of European and British books, which had come to dominate the market, from the category of 'appropriate'. Similarly, it is understandable that stories subverting the moral agenda of the state had to be either rejected or heavily sanitized. What is more difficult to explain is why prior development of children's literature in India, in English as well as in Indian languages, is silenced. This touches not only the projects around Jamia Millia described above (even if he did not read Urdu, Shankar must have been aware of its existence, as he belonged to the same circle of friends around Jawaharlal Nehru as Zakir Husain), but also the literature in Hindi, and with an even longer tradition, in Bengali, of which at least Rabindranath Tagore's contributions were available in English translation.

Instead, three-quarters of the books published in the initial phase of the Children's Book Trust were re-tellings of classical Sanskrit literature, the epic stories, and folk tales,[63] familiarizing children with what was defined as the nation's cultural heritage. A fascinating project of its own would be to follow up in detail how these stories were transformed by their transition from the oral to the written and their canonization into a national narrative. It seems at least possible that the eradication of regional variations and the homogenizing process that has been traced for the televised *Ramayana* in the 1980s[64] had its precedent not only in the comic books of the 1970s,[65] but publications of the Children's Book Trust in the 1950s.

What then were the emotion-values taught, and how were they related to the project of patriotic piety? Three examples, referring to three different genres, allow us to approach this question. Lord Krishna and Sudama had been friends in school. While one moves on to become a king, the other becomes a priest, too poor to feed his family, and too otherworldly to think of how to change this situation. After many years Sudama's wife, who was forced to take responsibility for the survival of the family, convinces Sudama to pay a visit to Krishna. In the joy of meeting his friend, and in listening to his tales, Sudama forgets to ask for his help. Krishna in turn never enquires about his friend's family. When Sudama finally returns home after many days, now worried about the fate of his wife and children, he finds them living in a palace, and provided with every luxury—Krishna had not waited for his friend to ask for help. This story can be read for its different emotions: the unquestioning love of the wife, Sudama's piety and detachment from worldly needs, the friendship between the two boys which survives a separation of many years, and Krishna's generosity that leads him to act without waiting to be asked.[66] At the same time, the patriotic piety which is to be taught through identification with the nation's heritage as well as to bring about emotional integration, remains coloured by specific religious traditions. *Krishna and Sudama* (1967) is simultaneously a religious tale embedded in *Vaishnava* Hinduism, and a story standing for the nation's cultural heritage. This nationalization takes place in the Children's Book Trust (and not only there) for selected elements of the Hindu and the Buddhist tradition, but rarely for others.

For younger children, correct behaviour and correct emotions are often taught through animal stories. *The Three Friends* (1969) extolls the virtues of unity. A rabbit, a mouse, and a squirrel live together in a forest. They love each other very much, are friends with all the other animals in the forest, and share housekeeping duties. As the rabbit is the eldest and biggest, the others recognize him as their leader. One day, a big black cat moves into the forest and threatens the small animals. Only by their quick wit and devotion to each other are they able to escape. When they have already decided to leave the forest, their friend the monkey succeeds in sending the cat down the river, tied to a plank of wood, by playing on the cat's greed and promising him a rich meal of fish further down the river.[67] Life holds deadly dangers, the children learn, but even the smallest and weakest members of the community need not be frightened, as love, solidarity, and innate intelligence will overcome every danger.

If one of the aims of the Children's Book Trust was to save Indian children from being overwhelmed by British books, notably of the Enid Blyton variety (without much success, if one looks at the distribution of books in any bookshop today and even in the Children's Book Trust's own library), this did not prevent the genre of the juvenile adventure novel to strike roots in India, albeit with some noticeable differences from the British adventure stories. Arup Kumar Datta's *The Kaziranga Trail* (1979), which in 1979 won the Shankar's Award, given by the Children's Book Trust to the best written work, narrates how three young boys follow the trail of poachers in Assam's Kaziranga wildlife sanctuary.[68] Like Blyton's Famous Five, they show courage and intelligence, and do not give up, even if adults initially do not take them seriously. Important though the children's contribution is, unlike the five friends they do not bring the mystery to its final conclusion on their own—in the penultimate phase the adults, the forest authorities, and the police take over to return the story to the proper social hierarchies.

But where has the patriotic piety—or for that matter, any form of piety—gone in this adventure narrative? While it still teaches some moral values, any reference to the nation or to religion is absent. In this, *The Kaziranga Trail* is only one example of a larger trend in post-Nehruvian India, at least as far as commercial and semi-commercial publications are concerned. The school textbooks seem to follow this trend only much later, if at all. Texts emphasizing religious and patriotic piety are certainly still written, but they are no longer mainstream. They neither become bestsellers, nor are awarded book prizes. If the story of Asghari, *The Bride's Mirror*, is still read by some, it no longer holds the power to shape a community's notions of piety and pious emotions.

NOTES

1. The research for this chapter would not have been possible without the generous help of many people. I thank C. M. Naim, M. U. Memon, Frances Pritchett, and Muhammad Khan Pasha for sharing their knowledge on children's literature and the Dastan tradition. Siddiq ur Rahman and Azra Kidwai, as always, have been the most generous of guides and friends. I thank Ghulam Hyder and Manorama Jafa for information on the Bacchon Ka Adabi Trust and the Children's Book Trust and sharing their books. The staff at the Zakir Husain Library, the library of the Jamia Hamdard, and the Children's Book Trust have been very helpful. Without the dedication of my research assistants Belal Asdaque and Dr Jalis Nasiri it would not have been possible to collect so much material in such a short time.
2. Ahmad, *Bride's Mirror*. See Lal, 'Recasting the Women's Question' with further reference to the corpus of studies on Nazir Ahmad.
3. Pritchett, 'Afterword'; Naim, 'Prize-Winning Adab'.
4. Ahmad, *Bride's Mirror*, 55.
5. Sarkar, 'Pre-History of Rights'; Nair, *Women and Law in Colonial India*.
6. Krishna Kumar, personal communication 1 March 2012.
7. Kohli, 'Institutionalisierung des Lebenslaufs', 7.
8. Ahmad, *Bride's Mirror*, 107.
9. Ahmad, 36–51.
10. Ahmad, 2.
11. Ahmad, 176.
12. For a glimpse of the way the text was not only still read, but also used in daily negotiations between girls and their parents in the 1950s, see Lal, *Coming of Age in Nineteenth-Century India*, 1–31, based on her interviews with Azra Kidwai.

13. Minault, *Secluded Scholars*.
14. Ahmad, *Bride's Mirror*, 20.
15. Ahmad, 86, 177–8.
16. Ahmad, 53.
17. This chapter is based on the reading of ninety-one children's books in Urdu and English, ten volumes of the journal *Payam-e talim* and forty-two advice books in Urdu and English.
18. Marlow, 'Advice and Advice Literature'; Hourani, *Reason and Tradition in Islamic Ethics*; Butterworth, 'Medieval Islamic Philosophy'.
19. Lelyveld, *Aligarh's First Generation*.
20. Information from title pages and prefaces of the books: Mubarak Ullah, *Tanbih at talibin;* Karim ud Din, *Pand-e sudmand*; Nur Ahmad Nur, *Anwar ul akhlaq*; Ayodhya Prasad, *Guldastah-e tahzib*.
21. Mubarak Ullah, *Tanbih at talibin*, 84–90.
22. Frevert et al., *Emotional Lexicons*.
23. Nur Ahmad Nur, *Anwar ul akhlaq*, 12–22.
24. Nur Ahmad Nur, 18.
25. Nur Ahmad Nur, 21.
26. For an exploration of the link between these middle-class values and the creation of a middle class in the second half of the nineteenth century, see Pernau, *Ashraf into Middle Classes*, esp. 241–69.
27. Besides Ayodhya Prasad, *Guldastah-e tahzib* see Munni Lal, *Shamin-e akhlaq*; Shankar Das, *Guldastah-e akhlaq*; Chaturbhuja Sahaya, *Maandan-e akhlaq*.
28. Preckel, *Islamische Bildungsnetzwerke und Gelehrtenkultur im Indien des 19. Jahrhunderts*; Lambert-Hurley, *Muslim Women, Reform and Princely Patronage*.
29. Shah Jahan, *Tahzib un Niswan wa Tarbiyat ul Insan*.
30. Shah Jahan, 146–7.
31. Sultan Jahan, *Tarbiyat ul atfal*.
32. Sultan Jahan, 49–62.
33. For a general introduction to Urdu children's literature, see Hanfi, 'Urdu'; Zaidi, *Urdu men bachon ka adab*.
34. Naim, 'Popular Jokes and Political History'; Oesterheld, 'Entertainment and Reform'.
35. Lakhnavi and Bilgrami, *Adventures of Amir Hamza*; Pritchett, *Marvelous Encounters*.
36. Khan, *Handbook for Storytellers*.
37. The first, as far as I could find out, is the edition in ten volumes in Urdu by Ferozons Publisher in Lahore, adapted for children from the fifth standard onward by Maqbul Jahangir (*Amir Hamza ke karnameh*).
38. Lakhnavi and Bilgrami, *Adventures of Amir Hamza*, 33.
39. Lakhnavi and Bilgrami, 34–45; Jahangir, *Amir Hamza ke karnameh*, i, 63–92.
40. Lakhnavi and Bilgrami, quotation 61; Jahangir, i, 123.
41. Lakhnavi and Bilgrami, 70–86; Jahangir, i, 134–69.
42. Reddy, *Navigation of Feeling*, 128–9.
43. Apte, *Humor and Laughter*, 220–31.
44. On the figure of the trickster, embodying chaos and freedom, as a necessary counter-balance to the king as the symbol for righteousness and *dharma*, see Siegel, *Laughing Matters*, 291–336. For a comparison to the European context, see Bakhtin, *Rabelais and His World*.
45. Lakhnavi and Bilgrami, *Adventures of Amir Hamza*, 358–60.
46. Hasan and Jalil, *Partners in Freedom*; Kumar, *Political Agenda of Education*.

47. Oesterheld, 'Zakir Husain'.
48. Brehony, 'New Education for a New Era'; Lawson, 'New Education Fellowship'.
49. Sultana, 'Nanha Tatu'.
50. Jalal ud Din, 'Tilismi Dawa, Part 1'; Jalal ud Din, 'Tilismi Dawa, Part 2'.
51. Husain, 'Akhri Qadam'; English translation: Husain, 'The Final Step'.
52. Husain, *Abbu Khan ki bakri*; English translation by Samina Mishra and Sanjay Muttoo as *Bravest Goat in the World*.
53. Husain, *Bravest Goat in the World*, 14, 16.
54. Mukerji, *Gay-Neck*.
55. Mukerji, 99.
56. See the introduction to this volume.
57. Nehru, 'Grow into the Heart of India', 12.
58. Bose, 'Sons of the Nation'.
59. Ministry of Education: Government of India, *Report of the Committee on Emotional Integration*, frontispiece.
60. Nehru, 'Making India Strong', 53.
61. Nehru, 'Unity and Harmony', quotation 277; Nehru, 'Meaning of Culture', 274.
62. Shankar, *Shankar*.
63. Berry, 'Value-Based Writing'.
64. Richman, *Many Ramayanas*.
65. McLain, *India's Immortal Comic Books*.
66. Shivkumar, *Krishna and Sudama*.
67. Ramakrishnan, *Three Friends*.
68. Datta, *Kaziranga Trail*.

4

Ralph's Compassion

Daniel Brückenhaus

In a vivid scene in his novel, *The Coral Island* (1857), Robert Michael Ballantyne depicts the emotional impact of the first encounter between European children and non-European 'natives'. Having grown up in Britain, fifteen-year-old Ralph Rover and two other boys are shipwrecked on a tropical island in the Pacific Ocean. With their previous, civilized education in Europe, the boys are described as resourceful enough to overcome even such an unexpected challenge; and their emotional maturity has allowed them to form a close bond. As Ralph states, in spite of their character differences, they have been 'tuned' to the 'key...of *love!*'[1] One day, however, the boys suddenly encounter wild non-Europeans. Canoes full of South Sea islanders appear at the coast. Hidden from sight, the British boys observe a bloody battle unfolding between two groups of natives. One party soon overpowers the other and takes prisoners. As the winners light a fire, Ralph—fearing that the victims will be burnt alive and eaten—is overcome by a 'dreadful feeling of horror', born out of compassion for the captives. As they are led to the fire pit, Ralph is almost overwhelmed by his emotions. He admits to being relieved when one of the prisoners is clubbed to death, because this at least prevents the victim from suffering a longer agony. When soon after, one of the 'savages' tears a child away from a female prisoner and tosses it into the sea, the mother's shriek of pain has a strong effect on the white boys. Suffering with her, Ralph's friend Jack emits a 'low groan'.[2]

Soon, the British boys are unable to simply watch; their compassion for the victims drives them to action. Utilizing their superior, 'civilized' sense of rational planning and coordination and the strong emotional bond between them, the white boys are able to overcome their enemies and to prevent further physical and emotional pain among the captured islanders.[3]

In condensed form this episode addresses two themes that form an important thread in European children's books from the late eighteenth century to the 1960s. First, during this period, many authors debated the role of feelings in imperial relationships. The central issue was whether Europeans should create an emotional connection with non-Europeans and, if so, what the effect would be on the power hierarchies between black and white people. Furthermore, Ballantyne addresses a second preoccupation of the time concerning the question of how to raise children. To what extent should parents insist on 'civilizing' their offspring from an early age? And what were the results if young people were allowed to live a carefree childhood, following their own emotional instincts?

Even though these two concerns might seem quite separate at first view, this chapter will show that they were in fact intricately connected to each other at the time. Novelists referred to the Empire in order to discuss how to educate children and they wrote about children in order to support their arguments about how to structure imperial relationships. Their books provided young readers with the opportunity for mimetic learning. Children could see non-Europeans through the eyes of the (mostly white) protagonists of the stories, and they could share the characters' emotional bond (or lack thereof) with non-white people.

It was above all by examining and debating 'compassion' that ideas about childhood education and imperial rule were brought together in this period. Compassion implied that someone felt sorry for another being. At the same time, this emotion did not necessarily depend on a thorough understanding of the other's emotional state. Moreover, compassion was often connected to condescension, as it was reserved for those who were thought to be unable to 'help themselves'. Meanwhile, the chapter also shows that in certain periods and among certain political groups, 'compassion' was rejected in favour of 'empathy' with 'natives'.[4] Compared to 'compassion', empathy could more easily be conceptualized in a non-hierarchical way and genuinely 'entering into another's soul' was more crucial to its definition. However, empathy could also be used in a strategic and manipulative manner; especially because, in contrast to compassion, empathy did not by definition require caring for the welfare of others.[5]

This chapter focuses on a sample of German and British children's books,[6] all of which were printed in considerable numbers during the period under consideration. Meanwhile, it is important to remember that access to these novels and their probable appeal to children of different social backgrounds, remained uneven. After all, especially before the twentieth century, not every family could afford to buy such literary works, and, in line with their 'imagined audience', only a minority of these texts was centered around poor or working-class protagonists.

The chapter shows that it is possible to distinguish several educational models based upon different assumptions about whether Europeans could and should feel compassion for non-Europeans. These systems of thought appeared at different points in time; however, newer models did not necessarily replace the older ones. Rather, they often overlapped, illustrating a process of pluralization of childhood emotions over the course of the nineteenth and twentieth centuries.

In the first such system, influential in both Germany and Britain between the late eighteenth century and the mid-nineteenth century, 'compassion' was central. White children were encouraged to feel sorry for 'unfortunate' non-Europeans. Such compassion was seen as a sign of civilizational development. Meanwhile, this model also implied a clear hierarchy in power and status: compassion was felt towards natives who were depicted as weaker and less mature emotionally than Europeans, at least until they had become fully 'civilized' and 'Christianized'.

Proponents of a second model, prominent among conservative British writers of the late nineteenth and early twentieth centuries, were more sceptical about the ideal of 'civilized-ness'. White children were now to be allowed to experience a free and 'wild' childhood. In the process, they were encouraged to adopt certain 'primitive' emotional characteristics of the 'natives', whom they encountered, for the most part, not in person, but solely through texts. As part of this argument, 'compassion' was now often rejected in favour of a special kind of 'empathy' structuring the relationship between Europeans and non-Europeans. However, this empathy was ultimately strategic, used precisely in order to protect imperial power hierarchies against challenges by the natives or by Britain's European rivals.

The third system of thought, introduced by progressive British writers of the late nineteenth and early twentieth centuries, used scenes of both compassion and empathy with (imagined) 'natives' in order to make a case for freedom in childhood development. Here, the message was not explicitly pro-imperialist; however, the ways in which imperial imagery was used in those books was still likely to confirm a view according to which imperial hierarchies were simply a 'given'.

Fourth, in late nineteenth- and early twentieth-century Germany, a controversy emerged concerning the value of compassion with 'natives', and its impact on 'character development'. Authors debated more actively, compared with the British novels of the period, about the value of Christian notions of 'brotherly compassion' with non-Europeans.

Finally, the chapter examines the impact of the Second World War and the decolonization period from the 1950s onwards on the portrayal of both compassion for, and empathy with, non-Europeans. As will be shown, these experiences led authors of children's fiction to question European notions of a built-in superiority over 'natives'. However, even in some of the anti-imperialist books of this era, the children's encounters with non-Europeans was incorporated into an inherently Western and/or Christian frame of reference.

COMPASSION AND THE CIVILIZING MISSION, 1770–1860

From the earliest modern children's literature in the late eighteenth century until the 1850s, depictions of European children's relationships with 'natives' were often employed to argue that compassion was a central tenet of 'evolved' behaviour. At the same time, however, the ability or inability to feel such compassion was also used in order to draw a stark distinction between those considered to be 'civilized', and those deemed 'uncivilized savages'. The boundary between Europeans and natives was defined in reference to two different kinds of emotional setups: while the 'civilized' Europeans were regarded as compassionate towards those around them, including non-Europeans, the 'uncivilized' natives were supposed to be devoid of any true feelings for others.

One example for this mind-set is presented by Johann Heinrich Campe's *Robinson the Younger* (1781/1782; Ger. orig. *Robinson der Jüngere*, 1779/1780). Based partly on Defoe's original *Robinson Crusoe* (1719), the book is often described as the first German novel written specifically for young readers and was still widely popular decades later.[7] One of the book's professed goals is to teach children and teenagers how to shape their emotions. Arguing against the 'fatal sentimental fever' of his age,[8] the author rejects certain un-civilized feelings as effeminate and weakening, such as overpowering, irrational fear. Meanwhile, there are certain 'enlightened' emotions that are portrayed as inherently positive, including 'compassion', which must be shown to every human being, independent of his or her background or race. One of the main themes of the novel is whether such compassion can and should be combined with colonial power hierarchies.

Like Ralph and his friends in *The Coral Island*, Campe's German Robinson also gets the chance to rescue a native; and, similarly to Ralph's case, it is compassion that drives him to do so. When Robinson observes some local 'savages' drag two native prisoners to a fire, Robinson's 'heart palpitate[s] with indignation and horror'.[9] At first, Robinson is paralysed by fear, but when one of the prisoners flees, Robinson suddenly develops unprecedented courage: 'Fire flashed from his eyes', and 'his heart urged him to assist the poor wretch'. He attacks and defeats the pursuers, and soon develops a close relationship with the native whom he has rescued and renamed 'Friday'.[10]

However, Robinson then quickly moves on to establish clear power hierarchies, conceptualized as a kind of enlightened absolutism. In spite of initial doubts, Robinson decides to accept Friday's act of symbolic submission, during which the islander places Robinson's foot on his neck. Resisting his impulse 'to overflow in caresses and tender embraces' towards Friday, Robinson decides to 'keep his...guest...for some time in the bounds of awe and subjection', and to 'play the king for some time'.[11]

For most of the novel, the relationship between Robinson and Friday remains contradictory. On the one hand, the author stresses the need for love and friendship in order to achieve happiness.[12] On those grounds, on many occasions throughout the novel, Robinson and Friday fling themselves into each other's arms and cry together, out of shared sorrow or joy.[13] On the other hand, during their stay on the island, the power hierarchy between them never breaks down. Robinson demands full obedience from Friday when it comes to decision-making; and while Friday is better informed about survival techniques,[14] Robinson is clearly superior in the 'higher' sphere of intellectual and spiritual matters. The fact that Robinson teaches Friday German, while never attempting to learn the native's language, is indicative of the higher value placed upon Western knowledge.

It is only at the very end of the novel, when Friday's civilizing process has been completed, and when the two characters have returned to Hamburg together, that Robinson can give up his position of authority. Showing that, for Campe, it is ultimately 'civilized-ness', rather than race that determines the Europeans' right to rule, from now on Robinson and Friday live and work together as master joiners being 'inseparable friends and assistants for life'.[15] Only now can paternalistic compassion be replaced by a mutual and equal friendship.

Upon closer examination, one may detect a similar argument underlying *The Coral Island*. As described above, Ballantyne does stress the compassion felt by the white boys for the pitiful non-Europeans. In an important twist, however, it soon becomes clear that it is precisely this willingness to feel for and with others that sets the civilized white boys apart from the 'savages'. Observing brutal scenes among the locals, including a native being eaten by sharks, or a drunken chief knocking out another native's eye, the narrator remarks that Europeans would be overcome with sorrow and anger when confronted with such misfortunes suffered by others. But on the natives' faces, Ralph cannot observe 'any other expression...than that of total indifference or contempt'.[16] The natives' habit of cutting off each other's limbs is symptomatic of their being cut off from each other emotionally. In *The Coral Island*, therefore, the white boys' ability to feel compassion, which might at first have been considered as undermining the colour gap, acquires the function of underscoring the distance and hierarchy between 'civilized' Europeans and 'heathen savages'.[17]

Again, however, the divide between Europeans and natives is not grounded primarily in their racial differences. To stress that fact, the author introduces a group of pirates who are described as 'white savages'.[18] Just like the 'natives', they lack the affective cohesion of the white boys.[19] The natives, in turn, though possessed of a 'natural depravity',[20] can overcome their negative character traits if put in the right educational context. Above all, it is the advent of Christianity on some islands that causes a kind of miraculous, instant transformation of the 'native character'.[21] Once Christianity has arrived, and once the natives have, in effect, become European in spirit, a bond of true, mutual understanding becomes possible; the natives then abandon their 'bloody ways' and are 'safe to be trusted' by white men.[22] Only at that point can real friendship blossom between black and white people.

The worldview proposed in *The Coral Island* may be viewed as typical of late eighteenth- and early nineteenth-century beliefs about colonialism and education. This period has been described as the British Empire's most 'liberal' and 'assimilationist'.[23] Proponents of the dominant British ideology saw little of inherent value in non-European traditions and cultural traits.[24] Non-Europeans, in their 'original' state, were not regarded as worthy 'partners in communication', nor could they teach much to Europeans. Instead, the goal was to help the 'natives' adopt as much European culture as possible (while excluding them from becoming part of civil society, as long as they had not gone through a sufficient 'civilizing process' yet).[25] European children should feel for those devoid of civilization, but under no circumstances should they be influenced by the emotional structure of the 'savages'.

REJECTING THE LIBERAL MODEL OF COMPASSION—CONSERVATIVE VOICES IN BRITAIN, 1860–1945

In the later years of the nineteenth century, a distinct feeling of crisis could be observed among many members of the British public. Suddenly, the old, straightforward belief in the assimilating powers of civilization that shaped novels such as *The Coral Island* was called into question. This change may be partly explained through the 'double shock' of the Indian uprising of 1857 and the Jamaican Morant Bay rebellion of 1865, which caused many British observers to feel betrayed by the colonized, who seemed to have rejected Britain's benevolent helping hand.[26] One might expect that the new, intensely racist views of the period would have led British observers to create an even greater emotional distance between themselves and those whom they saw as non-European 'primitives'. However, many conservatives now developed a new interest in building certain strategically conceived connections to colonized societies. Many writers claimed that one of the reasons for the uprisings in the mid-nineteenth century had been the insufficient attempts of the British to understand the 'native mind'.[27] British colonial ideology now progressed from the idea of assimilation to a new model, according to which British rule had to adapt to, and be integrated into, local cultural and political traditions to some extent.[28]

Moreover, in an era of growing imperial competition among European powers, fears about the weakening of the British nation through 'over-civilized-ness' were on the rise. On those grounds, conservative writers increasingly argued that one had to reintegrate a certain 'primitive' element into children's education and to allow children a free and 'wild' period in their youth to strengthen them against the dangers of decadence. This also implied a new emphasis on physical fitness. By the late 1820s, the American James Fenimore Cooper had combined a new model of muscular Christianity with stories of friendship between a white protagonist and Native Americans.[29] Books such as Thomas Hughes's *Tom Brown's School Days* (1857) introduced similar notions in a British setting.[30] While in adult literature, doubts and fears about Europeans 'going native' became increasingly influential from the late nineteenth century onwards, most famously expressed in Joseph Conrad's *Heart of Darkness* (1899), this does not seem to have been the case for children's books until after the Second World War. In many works of the late nineteenth century, the benevolent, yet condescending compassion for natives that characterized *Robinson the Younger* and *The Coral Island* was replaced by a call for a new form of 'empathy'. This empathy implied a greater respect for the strength of 'natives' in their 'original' state; yet it also abandoned the prospect of 'natives' ever becoming 'like Europeans' through the process of civilizing them.

The works of Rudyard Kipling, which became immensely popular in the decades preceding the First World War, may be considered typical of a new discourse in which a certain kind of 'primitiveness' was increasingly deemed positive for both a child's upbringing and for British performance in an imperial context. In *Kim* (1901), Kipling tells the story of a boy who lives 'between worlds', both culturally and emotionally. However, while the author's earlier *The Jungle Book* (1894) had focused on the inner turmoil and dividedness that stemmed from such a situation,[31] in *Kim*, this tension is resolved and 'made productive', allowing Kipling to write a more optimistic tale. Here it is precisely the white boy's emotional connection to non-European 'natives' that allows him to help maintain the rule of the British imperialists, to whom he belongs because of his race.

Throughout the book, Kim—born to white parents, but raised by an Indian woman—is described as a boy who has an unusual ability to form emotional connections to the different native groups around him. He is the 'Little Friend of All the World'.[32] As Kim becomes part of the Secret Service, he begins to make use of this skill for strategic purposes. The officials in the Service teach Kim that it is not hatred for, but a certain (instrumentalizing) empathy with, the 'natives' that leads to the white man's success and power.[33] Soon, Kim becomes a master at spying on the locals, based on his ability to 'enter another's soul'.[34] As Anne McClintock has argued, Kim thus performs a kind of 'anti-subversive mimicry'.[35]

In Kim's friendship with a Tibetan lama, Kipling's book also includes an example of a true and ultimately 'non-instrumentalizing' emotional connection with someone who is of a different race (even though, tellingly, this connection is reserved for a non-white person from a country that is not under imperial rule).

In Kipling's book *Stalky & Co.* (1899), however, only the strategic use of such emotional connections is portrayed. *Stalky & Co.* describes a school located in Britain, which is meant to be a training ground for future colonial officers.[36] While they are at school, the white students often seem more 'native' than 'British'. The boys are imbued with their own kind of 'native cunning', and 'with the stealth of Red Indians',[37] which allows them to carry out a hidden war against their teachers. Their 'savageness' is symbolized, at least in part, by the boys' style of emotional expression. In a way reminiscent of 'primitive' societies, they employ the 'simple...jests of the Stone Age';[38] and after successful pranks, they use a savage 'gloating ritual'.[39]

Once the boys have left the school, and, in most cases have entered the colonial service, it is, in fact, their past experience of 'being' and feeling 'native' that allows them to survive at the imperial frontier and 'beat the natives at their own game'. Stalky, the leader of the boys' group, continues to use the arsenal of tactics that he has developed and employed against the schoolmasters. He is able to sow mistrust between the natives of India, and he tricks them into attacking each other.[40] At the same time, Stalky also manipulates the natives in more subtle ways. He is able to 'play on' his soldiers and their feelings 'like a concertina'.[41] At times, 'Stalky *is* a Sikh'.[42] By gaining the natives' trust and devotion, Stalky is able to strengthen and extend British rule.[43]

Kipling's ideas about children adopting 'native' emotional characteristics resonated with numerous reformers of the period, who wished to counteract a perceived tendency toward 'over-civilization' and 'degeneracy' among the British population as a whole. To some, Kim's wild and carefree life seemed to provide a model for the 'right' kind of childhood, freed from overly restrictive rules. This fit well with the idea, supported by G. Stanley Hall and others, that, in order to develop a complete, civilized self, children first had to go through their own stage of 'savagery', 'recapitulating' earlier periods of mankind's racial development.[44]

The siblings Robert and Agnes Baden-Powell set themselves the goal of putting these ideas into practice.[45] Between 1907 and 1918, they founded the Boy Scouts and the Girl Guides, with separate sub-sections for various age groups. Justifying their plan, the Baden-Powells warned that Great Britain was facing grave dangers. According to Robert, modern life amenities tended to turn men into 'soft', 'feckless', and potentially degenerate beings.[46] Offering children the opportunity to live like 'wild natives' for a while could counteract such dangers. As part of this experience, Boy Scouts and Girl Guides were encouraged to 'fuse' their minds to some extent with those of the 'natives'. Among non-European emotional characteristics to be imitated, the Baden-Powells cite the honourableness and 'chivalrousness' characteristic of Japanese Samurai warriors, 'Red Indians', and Zulu warriors, traits which, in the authors' view, had faded in Britain.[47] British young people should strive for an active kind of happiness, which Robert saw realized more strongly than anywhere else among 'the Burmese'.[48] In this context, the Baden-Powells also brought forward an argument about gender norms. Agnes Baden-Powell specifically asks girls to adopt traits that in native societies were the reserve of *men*, integrating references to proud Indian soldiers and brave Japanese boys into the rituals of her group.[49] Given this attempt to draw from 'native cultures', it is not surprising that Kipling's Kim became the most important symbolic figure for both Boy Scout and Girl Guide groups.[50] The Guides' secret password was 'Dneir felt til'—'Little Friend' read backwards.[51]

However, according to the Baden-Powells, universal friendship was not a selfless goal. Just like Kim had built up emotional connections with the 'natives' in order to help the Secret Service keep them under control, one aim of the Scouts' and Guides' project of reintegrating 'native' character traits was to preserve British strength against the colonized.[52] The organization advocated that its members move to the colonies in later life,[53] and some of the Baden-Powells' stories were about Europeans whose ability to employ native skills and a native habitus helped them to prevail in colonial wars.

In order to understand the change in message of the 'new' children's literature of these years, as compared to the period of Campe and Ballantyne, it is helpful to examine how the Baden-Powells took up the work of Charles Dickens (who, incidentally, had been prominent in championing the cause of Governor Edward John Eyre, who had brutally suppressed the Morant Bay Rebellion of 1865).[54] On the one hand, Agnes Baden-Powell advocates for Girl Guides to do good deeds out of compassion for others; after all, she argues, no one is so badly off that there is not someone who is 'worse off still'. Agnes, however, specifies that such compassion should be reserved for white people in Britain only. As she tells her readers, she is not recommending that they become 'like Mrs Jellyby in Bleak House'.[55] In Dickens's novel *Bleak House* (1852–3), Mrs Jellyby's compassionate and maternal feelings for black people make her obsessed with charity work for Africa. Such engagement might have encountered the approval of writers such as Campe and Ballantyne. Dickens, however, describes Mrs Jellyby's stance as both dangerous and laughable, for her preoccupation with helping those in faraway lands leads her to neglect her duties as a wife and mother at home.[56] While the Baden-Powells were in favour of strategic empathy with natives, they joined Dickens in rejecting the concept of paternalistic compassion for non-Europeans.

In some ways, the system of thought outlined in the texts of Kipling and the Baden-Powells formed a curious mirror image of nineteenth-century Indian elite discourses. As Partha Chatterjee has argued in *The Nation and its Fragments* (1993), nineteenth-century Indian nationalists realized that, in order to compete with the West, they had to adapt to western-style 'civilization' in the 'outer' realm of technology and science. By contrast, these elites sought to preserve the core of their identity by protecting an 'inner' spiritual and cultural sphere from European intrusion.[57] For writers such as Kipling and the Baden-Powells, the opposite was required: in order to preserve the hegemony of western-style 'civilization', it was imperative to integrate some elements of 'non-developed-ness' into the minds of young Europeans.

COMPASSION AND EMPATHY IN BRITISH PROGRESSIVE NARRATIVES, 1890–1940

The writings of Kipling and the Baden-Powells were representative of a discourse that was prominent at the conservative end of the political spectrum. However, in the late nineteenth and early twentieth centuries, there were also a number of progressive British writers who published books in which imperial themes were combined with theories about emotional development in childhood. In contrast to the books by Kipling and the Baden-Powells, the Empire here appears in more abstract and symbolic ways. The stories are usually set in Britain rather than in the colonies. Moreover, while Kipling and the Baden-Powells stressed the value of a free and 'native' childhood for the preservation of the Empire, the reformist literature reverses this emphasis and focuses on using imperial images to argue the case for a freer childhood. A *strategic* use of empathy is not advocated here; and, in contrast to the Baden-Powells, charity and compassion with natives remains an inherently positive value. Nevertheless, on a more subtle level, those books still seem to have buttressed imperial ideologies.

The Story of the Treasure Seekers (1899) was written by Edith Nesbit, an author of reformist left-wing views and co-founder of the Fabian Society in Britain. Her book describes the adventures of six siblings who live with their father after the death of their mother. Although originally well-off, the family is now facing serious financial decline.[58] Throughout the book, the children appear as independent, funny, and strong characters. Out of compassion towards their sad father, they take the initiative to go treasure hunting to support their family.

Toward the end of the narrative, a selfless moment of compassion (seemingly) across the colour line rescues the family. The children get to know an 'Indian Uncle', an acquaintance of their father's. When their father invites the Uncle for dinner, the children assume that this must have occurred out of compassion for the visitor; after all, they have learnt from Alexander Pope's 1734 poem 'An Essay on Man' that Native Americans in general are impoverished and untutored. The children then approach the Uncle, tell him how sorry they are about his poverty, invite him to have a meal with them the following evening, and offer him the small amount of money they have saved.[59]

While the children initially insist on questioning the Indian Uncle about wigwams and beavers, they eventually realize that they have made a two-fold mistake: the visitor has actually never been to North America, but has lived in

India; moreover, he is a British white person who has profited from colonialism by becoming quite rich while abroad. The Indian Uncle, meanwhile, is so moved by the children's selfless (though condescending) gesture that he decides to invest in their father's struggling business. In the end, the roles are reversed: it is now the colonial superior who feels compassion towards the poor white children. The Empire appears in an inherently positive role. It becomes the source of rescue and delight, as the Uncle showers the children with presents from the Indian subcontinent.[60]

Writing in the inter-war period, Arthur Ransome also brought together ideas about 'free' childhood education and the Empire. As a writer for liberal publications such as the *Manchester Guardian*, and apparently sympathetic to the Russian Revolution of 1917, he wrote from a progressive and reformist perspective. His *Swallowdale* (1931) (part of the author's successful *Swallows and Amazons* series) shares a number of structural features with *The Story of the Treasure Seekers*. As in Nesbit's book, *Swallowdale* does not situate its protagonists in a 'real' colonial setting. Instead, the entire plot takes place during the children's summer holidays at a lake in northern England. In their games, the children impose an imaginary exotic geography upon the local landscape.

The novel is different from earlier ones by taking the terms 'natives' and 'Europeans' much less literally than before. In an ironic twist, grown-up people, with their different and 'strange' behaviour, are integrated into the children's imaginary reference system as 'natives', while the children appear as the superior colonizers. This indicates the extent to which the process of 'democratization' of the relationship between parents and children had developed at this point.

The children here use colonial metaphors to indicate their evaluation of different kinds of adults. The main characters feel a deep love for their mother who allows them to act out their own adventures without close supervision.[61] Accordingly, the mother is described at various points in the novel as 'the best of all natives'[62] and the 'most sensible native anyone ever knew'.[63]

At other times, in contrast, the relationship between 'colonizers' and 'colonized' is conceptualized in much less empathic terms and the stories reflect the antagonism and conflict between the two. This happens whenever the characters (and the author) wish to criticize a conservative approach to childhood education. Such a view is exemplified by the scary Great Aunt of the main characters' friends, who tries to force her nieces and nephews to be at home in time for all meals, thereby preventing them from going on their excursions. In the Great Aunt's presence, the children have to change from the rugged clothes of their wild adventures into formal attire, and they are forced to use excessively 'polite phrases'.[64] The children complain about being forced to 'go native';[65] and, they interpret the aunt's behaviour as 'native trouble'.[66]

In an interesting twist, associating the Great Aunt with violent natives in their most uncivilized state implies that the Great Aunt's behaviour is a thing of the past. The punctuality, politeness, and cleanliness that the aunt tries to enforce would in the mid-nineteenth century have been regarded as essential elements of white superiority, signalling the progress of Europeans towards a more developed future.

According to Ransome, however, these same norms of behaviour have now become outmoded. The main characters' mother, by contrast, is modern and happy that education is now based on forming empathetic bonds across generations, rather than on fear: 'how much better it was now that children could be the friends of their elders instead of their terrified subjects'.[67]

The novel makes a strong case for children's freedom. However, while imperial images have now become the medium for progressive educational messages, the colonial hierarchies underlying these images are never questioned. Children reading the novel might easily have learnt that, unlike the question regarding which educational models to employ, the distinction between colonizers and colonized was not up for debate.

CHRISTIAN COMPASSION AND BROTHERHOOD?—GERMANY, 1880–1918

As in Britain, German authors of children's books from the late nineteenth century to the early twentieth century continued to use imperial themes to write about 'correct' emotional childhood development. In Germany, like in Britain, writers also expressed concern about the dangers of over-civilizedness. The 'Life Reform Movement', for instance, began to stress the disadvantages of industrialization and urbanization, sometimes using language reminiscent of the Baden-Powells. Reformers recommended natural medicines and a simple, unpretentious style of dress. Concerning education, proponents of 'reform pedagogy' wrote in support of freer and more natural ways of raising children.[68]

While in British children's books Christian themes became less prominent from the second half of the nineteenth century onwards, in Germany, the notion of a specifically Christian compassion toward 'natives' remained central in shaping the terms of the debate. The question of whether or not such compassion should be taught to children led to a heated controversy, which drew heavily upon imperial themes. Two of the most successful children's books of the period that are situated at the opposite ends of this discussion may serve as examples.

In *Winnetou: Der Rote Gentleman* (3 vols 1893, Eng. *Winnetou I-III*, 2008–11),[69] Karl May describes how the German Old Shatterhand, who has recently arrived in America, symbolically comes of age in an imagined 'Wild West'. Even though May had not been to the United States at the time he wrote the story, his stereotypical and romanticized depictions of 'Indians' shaped the German popular image of North America. May's books became the most successful bestsellers in twentieth-century Germany.[70]

At first glance, *Winnetou* seems to open up the possibility for non-hierarchical and non-strategic empathetic relationships between Europeans and non-Europeans. The natives are described as possessing impressive, even superior emotional characteristics. These traits include great bravery in the face of pain and an inner balance that gives the eyes of the noble Apache Winnetou 'a tranquil, almost mild expression', indicative of 'a quiet, inner composure'.[71] Moreover, with Old Shatterhand's close friendship with Winnetou, May describes an adaptation to non-European cultures that goes considerably beyond anything described in earlier German novels, such as *Robinson the Younger*. Old Shatterhand enrols in Winnetou's 'Indian school', where he learns not only new warfare and hunting skills, but also Native American languages.[72] Eventually, Old Shatterhand does not only become an Apache chief but also Winnetou's blood brother[73] and this blood brotherhood symbolizes a deep emotional connection, going as far as to include romantic and erotic elements: 'We understood each other without having to verbally convey feelings, thoughts, and decisions to the other.'[74]

Nevertheless, the novel ultimately stops short of truly undermining the hierarchies between white and non-white people. In fact, one might argue that it indirectly reproduces older ideas about an 'assimilation' of natives to European culture. To be sure, the reader encounters a new, more 'muscular' form of Christianity here compared to *Robinson the Younger* and *The Coral Island*, reflecting the period's positive view of physical prowess and an untamed youth. Throughout the book, the main character forgives his enemies and refrains from killing them; but he does so only after defeating them in physical combat, proving his manly strength. Meanwhile, a strong belief in the transformative powers of civilization and Christianity still characterizes the book. As it soon becomes clear, when Old Shatterhand encounters the Apaches, they are actually no longer in their 'pure' primitive state, but already have been shaped by the influence of Klekih-petra, a German who went to live with them years before. At least some of the emotional restraint that the narrator admires in Winnetou stems from the influence of Christianity, as taught by the European visitor.[75]

As in *Robinson the Younger* and *The Coral Island*, a benevolent yet condescending compassion is central throughout the novel; and like in those early writings, this compassion ultimately does little or nothing to undermine colonial power. On the surface, *Winnetou I* goes quite far in its critical stance towards colonialist attitudes. Throughout the novel, the Native American Apaches are portrayed as being treated unfairly from a moral point of view, robbed of their land by white people. However, in the long run, Old Shatterhand's engagement with their culture turns into a more subtle kind of 'colonization of the mind'. Over the following volumes, Old Shatterhand's example gradually convinces Winnetou, the 'Red Gentleman', of the superiority of 'true' Christianity. And in more practical ways, too, Old Shatterhand's actions ultimately turn out to be in the interest of his white brothers. For instance, Old Shatterhand convinces Winnetou not to lead a violent uprising that would kill hundreds of thousands of white people. He thereby follows Christian norms of non-violence, yet also effectively protects further white expansion. In the end, the emotional connection that Old Shatterhand and Klekih-petra have formed with the Native Americans does not prevent them from seeing the inevitability of the disappearance of the natives. The mood of the novels is not one of rebellion, but of sadness; Klekih-petra's and the narrator's limited goal is to mourn the dying of the red race.[76] The narrator's compassion never goes as far as causing him to rebel actively against colonial expansion.

While the *Winnetou* novels do make an argument in favour of a Christian form of (limited) brotherly compassion, Gustav Frenssen's *Peter Moor's Journey to Southwest Africa* (1908; Ger. orig. *Peter Moors Fahrt nach Südwest*, 1906) provides an example of a second, quite different strain within German colonial youth literature.[77] Favouring a primitive 'struggle to the death' between white and black, the author explicitly rejects Christian values. Set in 1904, the book's German edition is dedicated to the German youth killed in the colony of South West Africa during the genocidal military campaign against the Herero people.[78] The protagonist, a military conscript in his late teens, volunteers to go to Africa to suppress the rebellion.

Parts of Frenssen's story may, in fact, be read as a recognition of the Africans' agency. In contrast to Peter's expectations, the Africans turn out to be formidable foes. They are equipped with modern weapons and able to kill many German soldiers. Moreover, in some passages, just like in *Winnetou*, the novel seems to accept the fact that from a *moral* standpoint, the Africans are in the right. One of the narrator's comrades likens the rebellion to the German wars of liberation: the Africans' rage is simply caused by the robbery of their land by strangers. Therefore they do not act any differently from the Germans resisting Napoleon in 1813; 'This is their struggle for independence.'[79]

However, such acknowledgments are not accompanied by any personal, empathetic connection between black and white characters, or by feelings of compassion. In fact, the protagonist repeatedly and successfully fights against his 'over-emotional' impulses that might diminish his skills as a tough fighter defending German imperial expansion.

When he meets Africans for the first time, Peter thinks 'that there could be at heart no possible understanding or relationship between' him and them.[80] However, especially in the second half of the novel, when the Germans regain the advantage and the war becomes increasingly genocidal, the narrator's emotional resolve is tested. Compassion toward Africans threatens to overwhelm him. Peter sees a large group of fugitive women and children and the fact that they are condemned to death sends 'cold shudders' down his back.[81] At another point, the narrator briefly picks up an abandoned two-year-old African child who has made a connection with him by establishing eye contact. However, the moment is cut short when the narrator decides to leave the child where he found it, stating, against all probability, 'I believe it had grown there in the bush without human help'.[82] A passage soon after implies that he has regained his own kind of 'hardness'. Passing by a dead African boy, the narrator and other Germans barely turn their horses to prevent treading on him. Peter comments that '[i]t is strange what a matter of indifference another man's life is to us when he belongs to another race.'[83]

In this framework, moral arguments become irrelevant. A German officer who has just shot an African prisoner acknowledges the immorality of his action according to Christian principles, but justifies it as a necessary part of a social Darwinist struggle of the races. For a long time yet, he argues, the Germans would need to be 'hard and kill' even against their moral principles and emotional impulses, while simultaneously striving toward 'high thoughts and noble deeds'. Then, at some point in the future, the Germans might be able to contribute to a broth-erly humanity.[84] This framework of interpretation, which transfers compassion to a utopian future, removes Peter's last doubts. The English translator tellingly omits the narrator's following statements: in the past, Peter Moor says, he had felt bad about 'the poor ill people' and 'all the dead'; but now he had achieved an 'understanding' of everything.[85] *Peter Moor's Journey to Southwest Africa* thereby becomes indicative of an especially brutal and 'exterminationist' form of racism. Here, unlike earlier children's novels, both compassion toward, and empathy with, natives are abandoned entirely. Instead, the *lack* of feelings for those different from oneself becomes a sign of 'tough' male maturity.

THE DISSOLUTION OF OLD CERTAINTIES—
BRITISH AND GERMAN COLONIAL CHILDREN'S
NOVELS AFTER 1945

In the second half of the twentieth century, the racist system of thought that was propagated by pro-colonialists such as Gustav Frenssen, and even more radi-cally by the Nazis, showed clear signs of dissolving. The decades after the Second World War saw the end of Britain's Empire as most colonies had gained their independence by 1970. At the same time, even more so than the experience of the First World War, the slaughter on the battlefields between 1939 and 1945, and especially the Holocaust, shattered traditional beliefs in Western cultural and/or racial superiority. As a further sign of the pluralization of views on childhood emotions, the reaction to this experience was not uniform. Two final novels—one from Britain and one from Germany—may shed light on the different potential responses to the new intellectual climate of the period. Both authors challenge old views of Europeans' innate superiority towards non-Europeans, yet one of them does so in an inherently pessimistic manner, while the other one is much more hopeful for the future.

While British novels from the inter-war period, such as Ransome's *Swallowdale*, had used imperial images to celebrate a 'free' and 'wild' childhood, William Golding's *Lord of the Flies* (1954) presents a dark vision of what will happen to children if they are left to their own devices.[86] The book tells the story of a group of British children who are stranded on a tropical island during a time of nuclear war and traces their intellectual and emotional descent into savagery. In the begin-ning, while the children are still under the influence of their earlier education and upbringing, they feel reluctant to hurt anyone, including animals. They are con-ditioned by the 'taboo[s]' of their 'old life', of 'civilization'.[87] Gradually, however, as the memories of their homes fade from their memories, it becomes increasingly difficult for them to resist their primitive impulses. For Golding these impulses constitute the children's 'true' selves that civilization had only painted over and fenced in temporarily. Increasingly, empathy and friendship among the children evaporate as they become overwhelmed by other emotions, such as aggressive anger and fear. More and more of them begin to revel in killing the local pigs, and over time, they are brutalized further, until they are ready to hurt and even kill their human opponents.

The book can be read as a dystopia directed against the idea—expressed both in *The Coral Island* and in *Swallowdale*—that children, if simply left alone, can maintain a community of mutual love and empathy, as long as they have previously been educated in a civilized, European environment. In fact, both works are cited in Golding's text to highlight this point. Early on in the tale, the children optimistically imagine that 'while we're waiting we can have a good time on this island', just like the children they've read about in *The Coral Island* and the *Swallows and Amazons* series.[88] In *The Coral Island*, the children's civilized 'Britishness' stood in clear contrast to the behaviour of the 'natives'. In *Lord of the Flies*, the children initially try to maintain a similar distinction: 'We've got to have rules and obey them. After all, we're not savages. We're English; and the English are best at everything.'[89] However, eventually, the white characters in Golding's account begin to act like the brutal 'savages' in *The Coral Island*.

When the surviving boys are rescued at the end of the novel, an officer first interprets the children's behaviour as 'fun and games', similar to the adventures in Ransome's books. Later, however, he realizes that the 'war' the children waged was very real.[90] The children's earlier intention to live in happy friendship like the protagonists of classic children's books has been overwhelmed by the 'darkness of man's heart'. 'Jolly good show', the officer remarks sarcastically, just 'like the Coral Island'.[91] Golding's account thereby rejects both the ideal of a free and unrestricted childhood and the (explicit or implicit) acceptance of imperial hierarchies that had characterized many earlier books.

Not all authors drew similarly pessimistic conclusions from the post-war decolonization era. Like *Lord of the Flies*, Michael Ende's two *Jim Button* novels (1960/1962) may also be read as indicative of an age in which old beliefs in Western superiority were crumbling.[92] Yet Ende tells a much more positive tale compared to Golding. While Golding argues that Europeans, too, are 'savages' at heart, Ende's novels convey the hope that it is possible for everyone to become enlightened enough to overcome racism and intolerance.

As has recently been shown, Ende's goal in writing these books was to attack the racism that had pervaded colonialism and the Nazi period.[93] More radically than any of the other writers discussed in this chapter, the *Jim Button* books propose that a non-hierarchical emotional bond with those different from oneself is an essential prerequisite for personal growth and maturation. This point is already clear through Ende's choice of his main protagonist. Unlike the books discussed thus far, the young hero is black. This creates an altogether new reading experience. In the earlier novels, white children had experienced potential compassion for, and empathy with, 'natives' through the eyes of other Europeans. *Jim Button* offers Western children a more far-reaching mimetic experience. Here, white readers can temporarily 'become' a black boy and see the world through his eyes.

Ende's *Jim Button and Luke the Engine Driver* is inspired by an episode in Charles Darwin's *The Voyage of the Beagle* (1838–9) in which Darwin describes how a South American native named Jemmy Button is first brought to England and then returned to his home country.[94] Like Jemmy, Ende's hero Jim is also of non-Western origin. He arrives in a postal package as an anonymous black baby delivered by accident to the tiny island of Morrowland. Similar to Darwin's companion, who is characterized by strong empathetic and compassionate feelings, Jim appears, throughout, as a character that can relate to, and build friendships with, those who are different from him. The central friendship of both novels involves him and Luke, the island's white train driver. Luke, with his face blackened because it is covered in soot due to his work, at first scares the child. However, as soon as Luke recognizes the boy as a person by greeting him with his new name, a direct emotional connection is built between them: 'And Jim laughed. From that day on they were friends.'[95] Together with Luke, Jim goes on many adventures, during which the boy learns enlightened moral norms. Ende here clearly subscribes to a democratization of intergenerational relationships. While Luke is older and wiser than Jim, their bond is consistently described as a non-hierarchical relationship of equals or near-equals, rather than as a father-son relationship.

Throughout the Jim Button novels, many more inter-racial friendships appear. Mrs Whatsay, the island's shopkeeper, quickly accepts Jim, and begins to love him as her adopted son. Jim, in turn, later falls in love with the Chinese princess Li Si. The theme of building friendships across seemingly unbridgeable barriers extends even beyond the boundaries of humanity. Luke feels so strongly for his train engine, Emma, that he and Jim follow her into exile; a half-dragon and a water creature overcome millennia of conflict and start working together. In this context, compassion towards those different from oneself plays a decisive role. For instance, Jim feels sorry for the lonely make-believe giant, of whom everyone else is afraid.[96] While some characters originally make fun of others because of their different outer appearance, such feelings are consistently portrayed as a sign of immaturity that needs to be overcome.

Ende's novels, therefore, may be considered a rejection of a Frenssen-style message of 'hardening' oneself against people of different backgrounds. This also becomes clear in the ways in which Jim and Luke treat their evil opponents. Both the pirates that form the 'Wild 13' and Mrs Soothsay, the dragon, are defeated and then pardoned out of compassion.

At the end of the story and as a final rejection of traditional age- and race-related hierarchies, the black boy Jim reaches the top of the social and political ladder. After the friends discover that he is the heir to the ancient kingdom of Jamballa/Jimballa, Jim begins a reign of universal tolerance. Children from all over the world arrive and form a multicultural society. Showing his willingness to incorporate foreign cultures, Jim and Li Si's palace on the island is in part a train station, in part a Chinese palace.

Yet the story's message is less straightforwardly anti-colonial than one might think at first glance. Not only does Ende repeatedly slip into racist stereotypes in his own writing, especially when it comes to his descriptions of China (which led his German publishers, in later editions, to change the country's name to the fictional 'Mandala'), Ende also clearly limits the 'strangeness' with which he confronts the reader.

First of all, it is made much easier for a German audience to empathize with the black protagonist by the fact that Jim arrives in Morrowland as a 'blank slate', and is then brought up in the inherently Western Morrowland culture. Moreover, Jim, whose combination of courage and mercy turn him into another example in the tradition of 'muscular Christianity', derives his own legitimacy as a ruler from Western Christian traditions. He has the right to reign because he is the descendant of the black king Caspar, who, according to the New Testament, had offered his allegiance to young Jesus. It might not be surprising, then, that at the end of the story, King Jim is taught and civilized by the most British character in the novels, Mister Sleeve, in a fashion similar to many formally independent colonial rulers who had their own Western 'advisors'. Therefore, while Ende's novel clearly rejects the pseudo-scientific racism of the nineteenth and early twentieth centuries, the book fails to truly question the superiority of Western cultural and religious traditions.

* * *

As the examples in this chapter show, imperial images were used effectively to make the case for a 'freer' childhood experience throughout the nineteenth and twentieth centuries. 'Colonial' novels provided children with 'wild' spaces in which they could imagine themselves as strong heroes outside the sphere of their parents' direct influence. Therefore, most 'imperial' children's books do indeed seem to have had a 'democratizing' effect on relationships between parents and children, as well as a 'liberating' influence on children's opportunities for emotional expression. This was the case even at times when a more top-down approach to education was still prevalent in children's books that were set in Europe.

By contrast, for most of the period under consideration, the effect of these narratives on European children's visions of non-Europeans was much more ambivalent. In the process of advocating a 'freer' childhood, many writers may well have strengthened the beliefs of European children in inherent power hierarchies between themselves and those of different skin colours. Only in the post-war era did most Western writers begin to question an explicit or implicit belief in their own superiority. Nevertheless, even authors such as Michael Ende, whose goal was to provide an anti-racist counter-narrative, found it difficult to escape their own rootedness in Western cultural traditions.

Even though several nineteenth-century writers, such as Kipling, continue to be popular among children today, contemporary authors of children's literature have largely abandoned imperialist visions of strategically employing emotional characteristics of the natives in order to reinforce Western world domination. Moreover, Frenssen-style polemics against any kind of emotional bond with non-Europeans have mostly become a thing of the past. Interestingly, however, the older model that was exemplified by *The Coral Island* episode at the beginning of this chapter may have proven to be more long-lived. Today, European children are no longer brought up to dream of imitating Ballantyne's Ralph in heroically rescuing powerless natives from being eaten. However, many present-day discourses about the so-called 'Third World' still bring forward a patronizing form of compassion for 'poor natives' who supposedly need to be rescued by more evolved Europeans. Rather than creating affective communities through an equal dialogue between people of different backgrounds, such arguments continue to use the language of emotions to create a false sense of Western superiority.

NOTES

1. Ballantyne, *Coral Island*, 118 (emphasis in original).
2. Ballantyne, 161–7, quotations 166, 167.
3. Ballantyne, 167–70.
4. Even though the word 'empathy' itself only appeared in English in the first years of the twentieth century, 'empathy' will be used in a broad sense here, encompassing earlier terms with equivalent meaning, such as 'sympathy'. See also chapter 5, 'Doctor Dolittle's Empathy'.
5. See Frevert, *Emotions in History: Lost and Found*, 177–8.
6. On the importance of the Empire in British children's books more generally, see Kutzer, *Empire's Children*, 10; Wallace, 'De-Scribing the Water-Babies', 176. See also MacKenzie, *Propaganda and Empire*, 198–226. On the prevalence of imperial themes in German children's books before, during, and after the period of German colonialism between 1884 and 1918, see Zantop, *Colonial Fantasies*; Friedrichsmeyer, Lennox, and Zantop, *Imperialist Imagination*.
7. Campe, *Robinson the Younger*; Zantop, *Colonial Fantasies*, 103.
8. Campe, i, vii–viii.
9. Campe, ii, 49.
10. Campe, ii, 51–2.
11. Campe, ii, 53, quotations 62.
12. Campe, ii, 93.
13. Campe, ii, 142, 247.
14. Campe, ii, 71, 94, 131.
15. Campe, ii, 263.
16. Ballantyne, *Coral Island*, 237, quotation 230.
17. Writers who belonged to European disadvantaged groups, including the eighteenth-century Jewish philosopher Moses Mendelssohn, had already alerted their compatriots to the hierarchical and potentially condescending quality of compassion; see Frevert, *Emotions in History: Lost and Found*, 183.
18. Ballantyne, 183.
19. Ballantyne, 189.
20. Ballantyne, 222.
21. Ballantyne, 201, 204.
22. Ballantyne, 209. For a more detailed discussion of trust as a religious idiom in British children's books of the period, see chapter 2, 'Dickon's Trust'.
23. See Metcalf, *Ideologies of the Raj*.
24. Macaulay, 'Indian Education', 722.
25. See Pernau, 'Civility and Barbarism'.
26. See Hall, *Civilising Subjects*.

27. See Bayly, *Empire and Information*. Bayly argues that the British loss of effective knowledge in the later colonial period derived, in part, from the colonizers' intensified racism, which led them to abandon earlier affective ties to Indian friends and partners who had provided them with useful information.

28. See Metcalf, *Imperial Vision*; Cohn, 'Representing Authority in Victorian India'.

29. See the books in James Fenimore Cooper's *Leatherstocking Tales*, published between 1823 and 1841.

30. See Hughes, *Tom Brown's School Days*.

31. Kipling, *Jungle Book*.

32. Kipling, *Kim*, 4.

33. Kipling, 188–9.

34. Kipling, 252.

35. McClintock, *Imperial Leather*, 69–71.

36. Kipling, *Stalky & Co.*, 210.

37. Kipling, 15.

38. Kipling, 87.

39. Kipling, 13–14.

40. Kipling, 20–1.

41. Kipling, 259.

42. Kipling, 252 (emphasis in original).

43. Kipling, 270–1.

44. See Hall, *Adolescence*.

45. On the influence of Hall's theories on Robert Baden-Powell, see Boone, *Youth of Darkest England*, 118.

46. Baden-Powell, *Rovering to Success*, 24.

47. Baden-Powell, *Handbook for Girl Guides*, 38, 351.

48. Baden-Powell, *Rovering to Success*, 10, 16–17.

49. Baden-Powell, *Handbook for Girl Guides*, 371. In this regard, Agnes's book was typical of print literature for girls of the period which showed an 'almost universal admiration for a promotion of active, physically strong girls'; see Smith, *Empire in Girls' Literature and Culture*, 12, 151–8.

50. Baden-Powell, *Handbook for Girl Guides*, 43.

51. Baden-Powell, 439.

52. As Elleke Boehmer has put it, 'Britain . . . [was], Dracula-like, to draw life force from subordinated cultures whose own vitality, arguably, . . . [had] been forcibly repressed'; Boehmer, 'Introduction', xxxvii.

53. Baden-Powell, *Handbook for Girl Guides*, 23.

54. Hall, 'Economy of Intellectual Prestige', 185.

55. Baden-Powell, *Handbook for Girl Guides*, 357.

56. Dickens, *Bleak House*, i, 47–64.

57. See Chatterjee, *Nation and its Fragments*.

58. Nesbit, *Story of the Treasure Seekers*.

59. Nesbit, 265–78.

60. Nesbit, 281–96.

61. Ransome, *Swallowdale*, 117, 208.

62. Ransome, 33, 39, 118, 132.

63. Ransome, 132.

64. Ransome, 222–3.

65. Ransome, 52.

66. Ransome, 27.
67. Ransome, 437.
68. See, for example, Skiera, *Reformpädagogik in Geschichte und Gegenwart.*
69. There are some translations of volume 1 and 2 but the first complete translation of all three volumes was published between 2008 and 2011 by Marlis Bugman.
70. Between 1892 and 1938, 7.5 million copies of May's collected works were published; Mosse, *Masses and Man*, 43.
71. May, *Winnetou I*, 59.
72. May, 231.
73. May, 222–3.
74. May, 223.
75. May, 67.
76. May, 1–4, 66–7.
77. Frenssen, *Peter Moor's Journey to Southwest Africa.*
78. Frenssen, *Peter Moors Fahrt nach Südwest*, 3.
79. Frenssen, *Peter Moor's Journey to Southwest Africa*, 77.
80. Frenssen, 34.
81. Frenssen, 159.
82. Frenssen, 193.
83. Frenssen, 228.
84. Frenssen, 234.
85. Frenssen, *Peter Moors Fahrt nach Südwest*, 101 [this paragraph is missing from the Ward translation].
86. See chapter 7, 'Piggy's Shame' for more background on this book and its author.
87. Golding, *Lord of the Flies*, 78.
88. Golding, 45.
89. Golding, 55.
90. Golding, 246.
91. Golding, 248.
92. Ende, *Jim Button and Luke the Engine Driver*; Ende, *Jim Knopf und die Wilde 13*. There is no English translation of the latter. See also chapter 9, 'Jim Button's Fear'.
93. See Voss, *Darwins Jim Knopf.*
94. See Darwin, *Voyage of the Beagle*, 222–54. Ende possibly first heard of Jemmy Button through Benjamín Subercaseaux's novel *Jemmy Button* (1954; Spa. orig. *Jemmy Button*, 1950).
95. Ende, *Jim Button and Luke the Engine Driver*, 11, quotation 15–16.
96. See chapter 9, 'Jim Button's Fear'.

5

Doctor Dolittle's Empathy

Pascal Eitler

Dolittle is a doctor, 'the best known doctor' of his town. The 'best people' come to him, and he and his sister Sarah, are thereby able to make a living. But Dolittle 'like[s] the animals better than the "best people" '. In his garden and in his house he keeps more and more 'pets', including fish and mice, rabbits and chickens, a lamb and a horse, a cow and its calf, a duck and a dog, a pig and a parrot, 'and many other animals'. As a result, he eventually loses all of his human patients, and with them his income. Facing their imminent financial disaster, his sister, who wants to cast the animals out of the garden and out of the house, decides to leave. Suddenly, Doctor Dolittle is alone with all his animals.[1]

At this point, his parrot Polynesia intervenes: 'Take care of animals instead...Be an animal-doctor', she suggests. With that Polynesia decides to induct the doctor into a much-treasured secret: 'Did you know that animals can talk?' she asks, and begins talking to him in this way for the first time in her life. Dolittle is surprised and fascinated to hear that every animal has its own language and that they can understand each other. But animals, so the parrot explains 'in a high voice, raising her eyebrows', 'don't always speak with their mouths.... They talk with their ears, with their feet, with their tails—with everything.' Dolittle is willing and curious to learn the various languages of different animals, beginning with the parrot, but he can only learn these languages and understand the animals—this is the central point—within a mimetic learning process of adapting and echoing their gestures and by mimicking their problems and emotions. The doctor thus has to both learn and possess empathy. As soon as the animals recognize that 'he could talk their language', more and more animal patients seek him out and find their way to him, where they tell him 'where the pain was and how they felt'.[2]

Dolittle therefore really does become an animal doctor, just as the parrot has suggested, and he cannot refuse the growing number of animal patients constantly crowding his garden and house, although he cannot afford the high expenses of the animals. In this regard, he also demonstrates empathy and compassion. And even when his financial situation changes dramatically and he becomes destitute, Dolittle is not troubled by being 'left all alone with his animal family'. More than ever before, he is very sure about his own feelings and those of the animals, and asks, 'What does money matter, so long as we are happy?'[3]

These opening paragraphs of Hugh Lofting's *The Story of Doctor Dolittle* (1920) provide a useful insight into the topic of this chapter: the meaning of empathy with animals within the process of children's emotional socialization, as it appears in children's literature and advice manuals from the mid-nineteenth century to the end of the twentieth century. The story highlights at least three things: first, it offers a stereotypical and consequential narrative that represents animals as *feeling animals*. This reflects an emotionalization of animals and, thus, a pluralization of emotions that was widespread mainly in Germany, Britain, and North America from as early as the end of the eighteenth century onwards.[4] Second, it shows or suggests how humans could and should approach these *feeling animals* as *feeling humans*, through empathy and compassion and therefore, in a manner typical for this period, emphasizes the function of language. The emotionalization of human-animal relationships encountered here most notably concerned the family and private sphere, but increasingly encompassed the fields of politics and morals, too.[5] Finally, the story claims a subtle, but strong, link between the emotions of the self and those of others—discovering one's own feelings not only through the feelings *of* others, but especially by feeling *with* others. Doctor Dolittle loses his sister, yet he is still 'happy' because he finds a new kind of family—his constantly growing 'animal family'.

This chapter aims to pursue the link between emotion in general, and empathy in particular, and to consider thereby the changing interplay between emotional practices and moral demands and the role of the family within this interplay.[6] If the emotional socialization of children is conducted through mimetic learning, then mimetic learning and feeling with others often go hand in hand. This was, at the beginning of the twentieth century, perhaps not so very different from the beginning of the twenty-first century. The process of learning how to feel with others is largely based on the construction of analogies and their narrative evidence.[7] Animals challenge this process because they seem to possess a higher degree of 'Otherness' compared to humans. Against this background, the process of learning how to feel *with* or *from* animals very often leads to a historically contingent anthropomorphization of animals.[8]

Although historical research and literary analysis may 'tend to ignore the animals therein',[9] animals are, in fact, not only omnipresent in Dolittle's garden or house, but may also be found nearly everywhere in children's literature not to mention in other genres and media,[10] especially from the mid-nineteenth century onwards in the countries investigated here.[11] If Lewis Carroll's *Alice's Adventures in Wonderland* (1865) may be described as a paradigmatic beginning of a new kind of children's literature in the 1860s and 1870s, which offered children the opportunity to interpret, experience, and construct an emotional situation or moral conflict in very different ways more than ever before, then it is no coincidence that Alice enters this wonderland by following an animal, a rabbit, deep down its rabbit hole. The period dubbed the 'golden age' of children's literature, spanning the last third of the nineteenth century and the first third of the twentieth century, signified a new opportunity and a great challenge for animals and human-animal relationships and their representation in children's literature, in two different aspects.[12]

First, it is striking that some of the most influential, most published, most popular, and most adapted children's or juvenile books of this period, which developed and established generation-bonding and genre-building narratives, dealt primarily with animals or human-animal relationships. This is seen not only in *The Story of Doctor Dolittle* (1920), but for example, also the earlier *Black Beauty* (1877), *The Jungle Book* (1894), *The Tale of Peter Rabbit* (1902), *The Call of the Wild* (1903), *The Wonderful Adventures of Nils* (1907; Swe. orig. *Nils Holgerssons underbara resa genom Sverige*, 1906/1907), *The Wind in the Willows* (1908), *The Adventures of Maya the Bee* (1922; Ger. orig. *Die Biene Maja und ihre Abenteuer*, 1912), and somewhat later *Winnie-the-Pooh* (1926). In fact, it was not only traditional fables and fairy tales, but also this new kind of children's literature that frequently contained so-called animal stories. It was only in the period under investigation here that animals often became the important protagonists of sometimes very complex narratives to a hitherto unprecedented degree.[13]

Second, even beyond these animal stories, from the mid-nineteenth century onwards, children were habitually surrounded and often directly accompanied by animals, in children's books and also, to some degree, in advice manuals. Animals gradually acquired the full meaning of the term 'companion animals' coined by Donna Haraway—veritable actors in a social world produced and reproduced not only by humans, but also by the animals themselves.[14]

Even though some children's books introduced 'negative' companion animals that had to be fought against, more frequently companion animals were portrayed in a 'positive' light, empowering children as literary actors with their friendship and camaraderie, wisdom or advice.[15] Sometimes these animals were heroic characters of almost unique courage and strength, such as the lion Aslan in *The Lion, the Witch and the Wardrobe* (1950).[16] But in most cases these animals were simply the children's so-called best friends, such as the bear Baloo in *The Jungle Book*, or the goose Martin in *The Wonderful Adventures of Nils*. Quite often these best friends took the form of horses, as in the book series *The Black Stallion* (1941 onwards) or *Fury* (1959 onwards), and dogs, most prominently in the book series *Lassie* (1940 onwards), which inspired the famous television series of the same title (1954 onwards).

While it might be expected that animals have a prominent role in certain books or book series, judging even by their titles or covers, this occasionally also holds true for children's books whose main focus is not to tell animal stories. This is the case for instance with Enid Blyton's *The Famous Five* (1942 onwards)—because without Timmy the dog, Julian, Dick, Anne, and George would only have been the famous four. In such long-lasting book series, animals accompany humans in emotional situations or moral conflicts almost throughout their entire childhood and adolescence. Perhaps an even better example in this context is Frances Hodgson Burnett's *Little Lord Fauntleroy* (1886). The little lord is almost always accompanied by a large dog named Dougal, and in relation to this animal he is introduced to his grandfather: 'There was a sudden glow of triumph and exultation in the fiery old Earl's heart as he saw what a strong, beautiful boy this grandson was, and how unhesitatingly he looked up as he stood with his hand on the big dog's neck. It pleased the grim old nobleman that the child should show no shyness or fear, either of the dog or of himself.'[17] Here the animal plays a significant role for the story as a whole, because it is the human-animal relationship between the child and the dog that shapes the relationship of the grandfather to his grandson from the very first moment.[18] Over the course of the story the little lord and the large dog very quickly become something like best friends, and at one point Fauntleroy explains the emotional meaning or function of his companion animal: 'Fauntleroy drew one hand from his pocket and laid it on the dog's head. "He's a very nice dog," he said. "He's my friend. He knows how I feel." '[19]

This relationship between young fictional heroes and their companion animals has become a classic topos in children's books, an emotional relationship between best friends, based on love or trust and a 'deep' and 'true' understanding between each other. The role of animals, nevertheless, varies from story to story, and also concerns the role of empathy or compassion for them. Animals are not always presented as children's best friends and the practical knowledge about different emotions and the different situations in which these emotions occur changed in this context in significant ways over time.

Human and animal characters acquired equal opportunities to occupy centre stage. Depending on particular narrative requirements, their feelings, desires or worries were portrayed either in more realistic or in more symbolic, figurative ways.[20] With this in mind, it is useful to distinguish, albeit provisionally, between four narrative patterns or interpretative frameworks, even if the borders between them are often blurred, and even if some stories use several of these patterns simultaneously.[21] The various ways of learning how to feel *from* or *with* animals are, as a rule, linked with different approaches in the representation of animals. Children's books and advice manuals differ markedly with respect to what they convey about which emotions, the empathy or the sympathy of their human protagonists, and the ways in which they display their emotions. They also differ as to how they connect emotional practices with moral demands, depending on which of the four interpretative frameworks they adopt (whether primarily or exclusively). Are animals, on the whole, portrayed more symbolically and is it therefore primarily a question of (1) their mere representative function as proxies for humans, or (2) also of the animals as animals and the emotional and moral framing of human-animal relationships? Alternatively, (3) should animals be portrayed more realistically, but not be the centre of attention? Or do more realistic narratives (4) concentrate in detail on animals as animals, but also as persons, in order to offer young readers a deep insight into the animals' supposed feelings, desires, and worries?

The question of how animals should be represented was thereby connected to an extensive debate about whether and how animals represented or expressed themselves. The great question was no longer 'Can they suffer?' but 'Can animals speak?'[22] Indeed, from the middle of the nineteenth century onwards, the notion that animals were equipped not only to experience sensations, but in certain cases also emotions, increasingly diminished as a serious point of contention.[23] But how could humans be really certain about whether animals could feel, and specifically what kind of emotions animals felt, if they could not speak about their emotions? Thus it is an important feature in children's literature, and especially in animal stories, that animals can speak—not only with each other, but very often also with humans, and primarily with children. In comparison, or in contrast, to Doctor Dolittle, children mostly do not have to *learn* how to do this, they simply *know* and make use of the different languages of different animals—as for instance in the cases of Mowgli in *The Jungle Book* or Nils in *The Wonderful Adventures of Nils*.[24]

The narratives in children's books constantly switch between a more realistic and a clearly figurative, more symbolic approach to the representation of animals and human-animal relationships and the forms and contexts in which animals speak are, thus, very diverse. The first two narrative patterns associated with more symbolic narratives are marked by the ability of animals to speak effortlessly and to conduct sophisticated conversations not only with humans, but also with other animals, even with multiple species. In contrast to what the parrot Polynesia explains to Doctor Dolittle, the animals within these kinds of animal stories speak primarily 'with their mouths'. Two ways of learning how to feel *from* or *with* animals emerge within the following more symbolic narratives.

'THE CHILD HAS AS FEW MORAL CONCEPTIONS AS . . .'—ANIMALS AS PROXIES

The first of these narrative patterns may be found in several famous animal stories as diverse as *The Jungle Book*, *The Wind in the Willows*, *Winnie-the-Pooh*, or *The Trip to Panama* (1978; Ger. orig. *Oh, wie schön ist Panama*, 1978). Here animals appear predominantly, or even exclusively, as proxies for humans.[25] This type of animal story opened up a potentially broad space for children to experience and experiment with diverse feelings—it set up something resembling a laboratory of emotions, for *doing*, and moreover for *trying*, all kinds of emotions.[26] This proxy pattern was based on a rather distinct anthropomorphization of animals, insofar as it barely focused on animals as animals, exhibiting many parallels to fairy tales or fables.[27] From the end of the nineteenth century, this interpretative framework was as widespread as it was successful, but reveals little about the practical knowledge of emotions and the specific contexts in which these emotions developed, as far as the meaning of animals and empathy or compassion for them is concerned.

These more symbolic narratives could initiate a mimetic learning process and evoke certain emotions or exposure to certain emotions insofar as children as readers could learn how to feel *from*, but not *with* animals by using commonly assumed analogies between animals and humans. Such stories emerged, therefore, through the ongoing emotionalization of animals, especially from the middle of the nineteenth century onwards.[28] The main point here is that these animal stories do not play an active role in the emotionalization of human-animal relationships, insofar as they do not directly impose any moral demands on human-animal relationships in contrast to the following three narrative patterns. In this framework animals only fulfilled a representative function as proxies for humans.

However, this first narrative pattern is not free of moral instructions to children, although it is much less explicit compared to many fairy tales and fables. These animal stories do not focus on traditional family structures, but on alternative family models, friendship, and camaraderie among peers. As a result, the feelings that animals or children have as literary actors in these stories are very multifaceted, as are those in which children as readers can imitate or recreate the feelings with which they need to come to terms—both their own and those of others. The various feelings and lifestyles embodied for example by Mole, Rat, and Toad in *The Wind in the Willows*, or Baloo and Bagheera in *The Jungle Book* complement rather than contradict each other. Thus, this kind of animal story allowed children as readers far more space for their own interpretations, combinations, and evaluations than fairy tales or fables generally did.

It is therefore no surprise that this way of representing animals and concerning family models within children's books only emerged in advice literature much later and to a limited extent because it tended to negate the moral instruction on traditional family structures with which the advice literature was often encoded, especially prior to the beginning of the twentieth century. One of the few early exceptions to this was Ellen Key, in what may now be regarded as her ground-breaking plea for *The Century of the Child* (1909; Swe. orig. *Barnets Århundrade*, 1900), when she claimed 'that the child in many cases has as few moral conceptions as the animal'.[29] To Key, this meant avoiding overburdening children, but it commonly meant to subdue children under rather strict moral expectations. Even throughout the eighteenth century, this kind of imagined resemblance between animals and children resulted from, and formed a part of, public discourse that shaped psychology and led to its great success in the nineteenth and twentieth centuries, and thereby also to the research on emotions. It is precisely during the 'golden age' of children's literature that we may observe an entangled evolution of child psychology and animal psychology on parallel paths, with effects to be traced not only in children's books, but also in advice manuals. In this spirit, in his very influential advice manual *Youth* (1906), G. Stanley Hall claimed: 'Psychology should be taught on the genetic basis of animals and children.'[30]

'BRINGING HAPPINESS TO THEIR FAMILIES'?—ANIMALS AS TEACHERS

Another way of representing not only animals, but also human-animal relationships, which had become widespread long before the middle of the nineteenth century, was more characteristic of the mass of childrearing advice literature in the period under investigation and could be observed beyond the writings of increasingly influential educational reformers or like-minded child psychologists from the beginning of the twentieth century onwards.[31] As a rule, children were constantly exposed to moral exigencies, albeit in increasingly subtle ways. Up to the middle of the twentieth century, it was often perfectly common in this genre to convey supposedly indisputable childrearing methods to parents, regularly promoting very hierarchical family structures. Serious meaning was often attributed to animals or rather human-animal relationships. Above all, living together with animals and especially with so-called pets, notably dogs, cats, horses, rabbits, sometimes birds, or even fish, was for example, supposed to establish a general feeling of responsibility in children—and until the beginning of the twentieth century it was very often within a religious framework.[32] It was in this sense, for instance, that in his widely circulated reflections on *What a Young Boy Ought to Know* (1897), Sylvanus Stall emphasized that '[w]hen we speak of animals, you will remember that man is an animal, although he is the highest in the scale of being, and God has placed him over all the other animals' because 'God has given him…a moral sense'.[33]

Within this second interpretative framework, it was not solely a question of the emotionalization of animals, but explicitly of the emotionalization of human-animal relationships. In this context, the coexistence of humans and animals became an important subject and increasingly acquired an intense moral currency. The preferred location of this coexistence between humans and animals was the family. Here, children—boys as much as girls—were supposed to learn how to feel not only *from*, but also *with*, animals. The focus of this increasingly discernible emotionalization and moralization of human-animal relationships did not apply to all kinds of emotions in general, but on empathy or sympathy for others in particular;[34] children were supposed to learn or deepen their understanding of the latter not least by way of their companion animals. An advice book for *Girls and their Ways* (1881), for example, explained that there would be 'no better test to apply to a young maiden than whether she loves God's visible creation. If she have [*sic*] no sympathy with it', the author admitted, 'I am always prepared for the revelation of some great mental or moral deficiency'.[35] Similarly, Adele Schreiber's *Das Buch vom Kinde* ('The book of the child', 1907) spoke of the 'love for even the most unremarkable living beings that we [the parents] strive to awaken in the child'.[36] In a similar vein and in relation to the concepts of empathy and, especially, philanthropy, the far less prominent author of the *Frauen-Bildungsbuch* ('Women's education book', 1921) identified the 'foundation stone for later active philanthropy', which was inspired 'when alongside corresponding instruction one charges the child [among other things] with the task of feeding starving birds'.[37]

Nevertheless, in childrearing advice literature, the coexistence with animals remained for the most part rather abstract until the mid-twentieth century. Indeed, animals as animals were an important element of this second interpretative framework, yet the central point here was not to provide a detailed description of the *animals* and their possibly very different feelings, but rather to convey empathy with them and a feeling of responsibility on the part of the *children*. In this sense, advice manuals represented animals and human-animal relationships through a more symbolic, rather than a realistic, approach. Furthermore, within the majority of the numerous advice books on keeping animals, and especially pets, published from the late nineteenth century onwards, children played only a minor role until well into the 1950s and 1960s. It was only in the second half of the twentieth century that cohabitation with animals began to be discussed in a wide variety of advice literature genres and in ever-increasing detail. Accordingly, *Der Kinder-Knigge* ('Children's code of conduct', 1938), for instance, urged young readers extensively to consider their responsibilities, because 'our animals at home want to be punctually and regularly taken care of. It is inconsolable to see little fish, living creatures, unable to express their agony through sound, eagerly gasping for air in a muddy and polluted fishbowl because their young owner has once again forgotten to maintain them.'[38]

With regard to learning the feelings of responsibility and empathy with others including animals, these pedagogical reflections and moral instructions were characteristic not only of a plethora of advice books, but also of numerous children's books between the last third of the nineteenth century and the first third of the twentieth century. Traditional family structures very often constituted the core of moral demands and a specific practical knowledge related to the emotional socialization of children. In one of the best-known animal stories of the twentieth century, *The Tale of Peter Rabbit* by Beatrix Potter, the mother of a young rabbit, Peter, explains that he 'may go into the fields or down the lane, but don't go into Mr McGregor's garden. Your Father had an accident there.' Eventually, Peter, very curious and 'very naughty, ran straight away to Mr McGregor's garden'. Mr McGregor nearly catches him in a wild chase through his garden: 'Peter gave himself up for lost, and cried big tears', but somehow he managed to flee back to his mother and their rabbit hole. 'He was so tired that he flopped down upon the nice soft sand on the floor of the rabbit-hole' and as a result of his insubordinate behaviour against his mother Peter became ill.[39] Felix Salten's story about the life of *Bambi* (1928; Ger. orig. *Bambi*, 1923)—famously adapted later as a film by Walt Disney[40]—promoted classic family hierarchies as well. Young Bambi has first to come to terms with the sudden, violent death of his own mother in order to then experience the support and recognition that he wished for from his father. Such clearly figurative narratives were compatible with much older narrative traditions such as earlier fairy tales or fables; the well-known *Fables of Aesop*, for example, were still very popular in Britain and elsewhere during the nineteenth and twentieth centuries.[41]

In a similar, but not identical, manner, Carlo Collodi's *The Story of a Puppet* (1892; Ita. orig. *La Avventure di Pinocchio*, 1883) and Selma Lagerlöf's *The Wonderful Adventures of Nils* focused on traditional family structures. Both stories begin with Pinocchio and Nils having damaged their families through their 'insubordinate behaviour' towards their parents. Interestingly, in both cases the adventures of these human protagonists begin with a reference to their violence against animals: Nils's against chickens, cows, and a cat, and Pinocchio's against a cricket—a wise cricket who will teach him 'that in this world, when it is possible, we should show courtesy to everybody'.[42] During his subsequent adventures—or rather odysseys—Nils yearns for nothing more than to become a son that his parents 'could long for'.[43] Nils, turned into a gnome, and Pinocchio, a boy made of wood, both experience a total, and above all emotional, conversion: during the course of the stories they finally become 'full' humans and 'good' children towards their parents. These changes are possible also because of the great help of their companion animals, a friendly goose in Nils's case, and a wise cricket in Pinocchio's case, both of whom act as a kind of 'transforming substance'.[44] Pinocchio's father Geppetto summarizes: '[W]hen boys who have behaved badly turn over a new leaf and become good, they have the power of bringing content [*sic*] and happiness to their families.'[45] Thus, within this second narrative pattern, animals appear at first as teachers of children, and, in the context of violence against animals, especially in the case of boys, restore them to their families and focus on traditional family values.[46]

Conversely, in the period spanning the last third of the nineteenth century and the first third of the twentieth century, one may observe a strong familialization of animals and human-animal relationships. Not only because of the emergence of pet ownership in a modern sense, but also because of the popular nature stories and animal encyclopaedias, such as Alfred Brehm's *Illustrirtes Thierleben*, which appeared in frequently revised and expanded editions between 1864 and 1893, and was later published in English as *Life of Animals*.[47] In this framework, too, it is possible to reconstruct and to problematize an ongoing anthropomorphization of animals.[48]

Thus, as much as animals might appear as more or less influential social actors in these stories, even within this second narrative pattern that might be referred to as the teacher pattern, the focus was never on animals. Children's books like *The Story of a Puppet* or *The Wonderful Adventures of Nils* were more about children as literary actors and also readers, about their 'insubordinate behaviour', their families, and finally—as the wise cricket puts it—the 'courtesy to everybody' which the human characters ultimately learn. Nevertheless, animals here represent something more than proxies for humans. This becomes especially clear by the fact that animals frequently become the victims of human violence—something that was generally absent in the first narrative pattern, but was quite common in the more realistic, third interpretative framework.

'IF YOU COULD ONLY TALK'—ANIMALS AS VICTIMS

The anthropomorphization of animals within more symbolic narratives in the interpretative framework of the proxy pattern tried to come to terms with very diverse forms of living together and thoroughly alternative family models. Within the teacher pattern, by contrast, the anthropomorphization of animals promoted primarily traditional family structures, and was supposed to teach children to learn from their parents, to be obedient, and to control their own feelings, worries, and wishes.

Nevertheless, the teacher pattern also allowed children to learn how to better understand their parents and their parents' feelings, as is evident in the cases of Pinocchio and Nils—but it was the more realistic narratives that enabled this as well. The story *Pucki und ihre Freunde* ('Pucki and her friends', 1936), for example, describes animals in a much less figurative way: the story deals with real animals from the human protagonist's everyday life as opposed to wise crickets. Nevertheless, this story, too, propagates a thoroughly traditional family arrangement, which generates a specific order of emotions constructed according to official gender models. At the end of the story, Pucki, a young girl, together with her father, watches a hedgehog, apparently female, rescuing its young from a burning heap of leaves and Pucki's father explains to her: 'It was about the life of her children. Every mother would sacrifice herself for that.' Pucki answers, deeply moved, 'She had so much motherly love that she would rather burn to death than live alone.' And she continues, 'I have known for a good while, what motherly love means, and today I have seen it again in this lovely little animal.' Emotionally distraught, she then goes looking for her mother, in order to affirm her own love, crying out of thankfulness. The story closes with one of the most central motifs of traditional family morals not only in the nineteenth, but also in the twentieth century: 'Since these events Pucki had grown somewhat quieter than before… Pucki had learned how well children are protected and sheltered, when motherly love is looking over them.'[49] Here it is, in fact, animals as animals that feature and significantly influence the progress of the story. Pucki learns how to feel from a real, or as such represented, hedgehog and in this case, too, through the production of analogies.

Within more realistic narratives, however, the children were not only supposed to learn how to feel *from*, but first and foremost *with*, animals. They addressed not only the family in general, but more so the children in their concrete relationships with their companion animals. This necessarily involved dealing with the propagated need for comprehensive empathy and active compassion for animals, and, more importantly, the role of animal welfare or animal protection in the emotional socialization of children. In contrast with the first and the second narrative patterns, this was a rather new development within children's books and advice manuals in Germany, Britain, and North America, especially from the mid-nineteenth century onwards, even though this emotionalization and moralization of human-animal relationships emerged gradually from the end of the eighteenth century.[50] Although more realistic narratives, too, tended to construct analogies between humans and animals, animals here appeared clearly as animals and not as proxies for humans. Unlike clearly figurative narratives, more realistic approaches pay much greater attention to the characteristics, skills, and circumstances of different animals as well as of different children. They portrayed children and their companion animals in their everyday life. At this point it would be useful to distinguish again two ways in which these more realistic narratives addressed the great question: can animals speak?

Within the third interpretative framework—which might be identified, for instance, in several popular books and book series such as Eric Knight's *Lassie*, Walter Farley's *The Black Stallion*, or Albert Miller's *Fury*[51]—the animals, mostly horses or dogs, can speak in the way that they normally use in order to communicate with each other. They bark and whinny, snarl and neigh, paw and scratch, lick and cuddle, run and duck. Exactly as the parrot Polynesia explains to Doctor

Dolittle, these animals speak 'with their ears, with their feet, with their tails—with everything'. Particularly children as literary actors seem to understand their animal best friends very well right from start. However, the animals in this narrative pattern do not engage in any complex conversations with the human protagonists or with each other. Thus, although some of these narratives do tell a kind of animal story, it is still the children rather than the animals that are central. Here, too, animals participate in the story only in relation to their young human counterparts. This third framework established a strong, but subtle, link between one's own emotions and the emotions of others. Children as literary actors could discover their own feelings by recognizing and identifying the supposed feelings *of* others but especially by feeling *with* others—and so could their child readers.

In this manner, children often have to speak up for animals, not only in the literal sense but also in a moral sense. It is, for example, little wonder that the human protagonist in *Fury*, a boy called Joey, meets his future animal best friend for the first time just as the horse, whose name is also the title of the story, is threatened by a rider. It is of even less wonder that over the course of the story, Joey saves Fury's life, who in a case of mistaken identity has been locked away and is due to be put down: 'As Joey looked out at the immobilized horse, his heart filled with pity for the innocent prisoner, who had been...unjustly condemned to death. Jim's heart-to-heart talk with Joey had not lessened the boy's despair', for the boy had not been able to convince Jim, his father, of the tragic identity mix-up. As Joey finally and secretly sets Fury free, he turns whisperingly to his animal best friend: 'If you could only talk...then they'd have to believe me.'[52]

Although philosophical and pedagogical reflection on animals, cruelty to animals, and animal welfare or animal protection has a longer tradition, extending as far back as the end of the eighteenth century, especially in Britain,[53] it is only from the mid-nineteenth century onwards that we begin to find children's books regularly dealing with animals as victims of human violence, for instance in popular stories such as Wilhelm Busch's *Max und Moritz* (1865; Eng. *Max and Maurice*, 1897) or Heinrich Hoffmann's *Struwwelpeter* (1844; Eng. *Slovenly Peter*, 1891).[54] Reworked and published in over a hundred editions by 1876, and translated into English by, among others, Mark Twain in 1891 as *Slovenly Peter*, the story addresses not only questions of personal grooming and hygiene or eating etiquette, but also the theme of cruelty to animals such as in 'The Story of Ugly Frederick', for instance, (see Fig. 5.1):

> O waly me! O waly me!
> Just such a boy I ne'er did see.
> He caught the flies, poor helpless things,
> Made hoppers of them, minus wings.
> He killed the birds, where'er he could,
> And catless made the neighborhood'.[55]

Through stories such as 'The Story of Ugly Frederick' the process of emotionalizing human-animal relationships in the second half of the nineteenth century enjoyed an unprecedented popularity. The trend of what might be described as

Die Geschichte vom bösen Friederich

Der FRIEDERICH, der Friederich.
Das war ein arger Wüterich!
Er fing die Fliegen in dem Haus
Und riß ihnen die Flügel aus.
Er schlug die Stühl' und Vögel tot,
Die Katzen litten große Not.
Und höre nur, wie bös er war:
Er peitschte seine Gretchen gar!

Fig. 5.1 'Die Geschichte vom bösen Friederich' ('The Story of Ugly Frederick') in Heinrich Hoffmann, *Der Struwwelpeter oder Lustige Geschichten und drollige Bilder* (100th edn, Frankfurt am Main: Literarische Anstalt, 1876), [7] not paginated.

a victim pattern turned animal-human relationships into a pedagogical and also political issue, promoting not only empathy in general, but also active compassion for animals in particular, propagating the abolition of cruelty to animals.

Thekla von Gumpert's book series *Die Herzblättchen* (1855–7), widely read especially in Germany, highlights the link between this victim pattern and a religious framework until the early twentieth century. In the very first volume, with the subheading *Erzählungen aus dem Familienleben und der Natur für kleine Kinder* ('Stories from family life and nature for small children'), the Ten Commandments are flanked as a matter of course in the instructions of a father to his children: 'You should be diligent', 'You should be polite', and last, but not least, 'You should not be cruel to animals'.[56] But while the protection of animals here as in *Slovenly Peter*,

Max and Maurice, or Johanna Spyri's *Heidi* (1915; Ger. orig. *Heidi's Lehr- und Wanderjahre*, 1880 and *Heidi kann brauchen, was es gelernt hat*, 1881) remains at a private level, in Elpis Melena's *Gemma* (1877), for example, which was well known within the animal protection movement, or in Karin Michaelis's internationally successful book series *Bibi* (1929–39), the protection of animals reaches a political level, too. Controlling and criticizing the animal transports and the cruelty to animals perpetrated by drifters at the harbour, the human heroine of the story, a girl named Bibi, explains to her father, 'if they are not decent to the poor little calves, I am going to write to the King and put in a picture of the way they do to their tails. That is cruelty to animals.'[57]

Thus, from the mid-nineteenth century onwards this emotionalizing process and pedagogical approach to human-animal relationships could also shape and emphasize a politicization of these relationships that was entirely absent in the proxy and the teacher pattern. Although the teacher and the victim pattern may appear similar, such a nexus of emotional practices and moral demands, which was directly connected to significant changes in the political sphere, was only possible within more realistic approaches. From this period, more than a few children's books in detail, or in passing, deal very directly with the animal protection movement that slowly emerged in Britain during the 1820s, in Germany during the 1840s, and in North America during the 1860s.[58] Emphasizing the 'compassion of children'[59]—as in Anton Kienast's *Gespräche über Thiere* ('Conversations about animals', 1855), which was hardly known even by contemporaries—might focus on a single animal protection organization such as the *Münchener Verein gegen Thierquälerei* ('Munich Association Against Animal Cruelty'), or on the great number of so-called *Bands of Mercy*. Marshall Saunders thoroughly reported on these *Bands of Mercy* in his internationally successful bestseller *Beautiful Joe* (1893), and G. Stanley Hall informed his readers a short time later in his advice book on *Youth* (1906) that there were approximately 35,000 in North America.[60] In fact, the movements for the protection of children and of animals very often went hand in hand.[61]

This third way of learning how to feel in this case not so much *from*, but more *with*, animals was equally popular in children's books and advice literature. As early as the end of the eighteenth century, under the rubric of religious derivation and encoded in his treatise *Practical Philosophy of Life* (1794; Ger. orig. *Über den Umgang mit Menschen*, 1788), Adolph Knigge warned 'that no living being has a right to *sport wantonly* with the life of a fellow-creature, inspired with breath by the Eternal Source of Goodness', and 'that an animal is possessed of as acute feelings of pain as man, and perhaps is even affected more sensibly by tortures than ourselves...How desirable is it that man should universally be sensible of all this, and open his callous heart to the heavenly sentiments of mercy and pity towards every creature.'[62] Countless etiquette and childrearing advice manuals championed his rebuke.

The point for these childrearing advice manuals, especially between the mid-nineteenth century and the early twentieth century, was not only the allegedly positive consequences of empathy for others in general, but also the apparently negative effects and moral dangers of cruelty to animals—in the first place for the cruel children themselves, but subsequently also for the families of these children, and finally, purportedly, for society as a whole. They were deeply embedded in public discourse on the early recognition of 'born criminals' and thus part of bio-political efforts at societal hierarchization.[63] It was in this spirit that in her repeatedly republished *Das Buch der Mütter* ('The mothers' book', 1867), Marie Susanne Kübler demanded that children should not only learn 'to be mindful and to love' animals as 'creatures of God', but also to 'feel sorry for' them, and in this context she feared that 'callousness towards animals can easily lead to callousness towards fellow humans'—to 'inner barbarism'.[64] According to Liane Becker in her also repeatedly republished *Die Erziehungskunst der Mutter* ('The art of a mother's education', 1908), this 'inner barbarism' would supposedly find its obviously necessary expression at some point 'in brutality against the weak and defenceless'—a child, who 'deliberately hurt animals' must therefore be 'strictly punished'.[65] Under no circumstances should one 'tolerate, that a child... even become at all guilty of cruelty to animals. The whole essence of the child requires diligent monitoring.'[66]

Between the end of the eighteenth century and the middle of the nineteenth century, mainly in Britain and Germany, and a little bit later in the United States, a specialized book market developed for animal protection advice manuals and pamphlets that were predominantly devoted to allegedly observed cruelties by children to animals and their supposed moral and political dangers, often in connection with the animal protection movement.[67] One entry on the concept of animal protection in a German encyclopaedia of 1886 reads like a commentary on this development: 'The education and upbringing of humans should be regarded as the most effective means for the prevention of cruelty to animals.'[68] And yet as much as cruelty to animals had to be abolished and animals within this more realistic approach of representing animals and human-animal relationships became something very different from proxies for humans or teachers of children, childrearing advice manuals and pamphlets on animal protection had little to say about the possibly very different emotions of animals—their primary concern was still the 'raising of the human'.

'MY HEART WAS NEARLY BROKEN'—ANIMALS AS PERSONS

Only within the fourth narrative pattern did some children's books or juvenile literature try to offer a detailed insight into the assumed manifold emotions of animals as animals and not as proxies for humans. This person pattern, as it might be called, may be found in popular animal stories such as Anna Sewell's *Black Beauty* (1877), Marshall Saunders *Beautiful Joe* (1893), Mark Twain's *A Dog's Tale* (1904), Jack London's *The Call of the Wild* (1903) and *White Fang* (1906), or Eleanor Atkinson's *Greyfriars Bobby* (1912), as well as some less popular animal stories such as Dhan Gopal Mukerji's *Gay-Neck* (1927). Only within the more realistic or even naturalistic narratives presented within this interpretative framework do animals occupy centre stage in every aspect of these stories. Some of these stories are told by an omniscient—neither human nor animal—narrator, while in other books it is the animals themselves who tell their own stories. Within these animal stories, presented as realistically as possible, the animal speaks directly to its human readers, as a person or as the author. Only in the second instance do they address members of their own species and seldom members of other species, but they never talk directly to children or other humans as literary actors.

In precisely this sense, *Black Beauty*'s subheading is *The Autobiography of a Horse*. This book was not the first, but probably the most inspiring, of these animal autobiographies and, thus, an animal story in the full sense of the term. Such animal autobiographies, which were not invented, but were established, in the 'golden age' of children's literature,[69] offered complex stories, in which the meaning of animals and empathy or compassion for them changed significantly. Autobiographical narratives enabled a mimetic learning process for their young readers to a degree previously unknown. In these autobiographies, the animals introduce themselves to the young readers as if they were persons telling the story of their own lives, for instance, the dog in *Beautiful Joe*: 'My name is Beautiful Joe, and I am a brown dog of medium size.'[70] Declaring how inspiring *Black Beauty* had been to him, he carries on:

> I am an old dog now, and am writing, or rather getting a friend to write, the story of my life. I have seen my mistress laughing and crying over a little book that she says is a story of a horse's life, and sometimes she puts the book down close to my nose to let me see the pictures.[71]

Yet, Joe's 'own story' does not begin with his mistress Laura, but rather with his very first master, a man named Jenkins. It is a story of pure cruelty to animals—of violence and death, grief and hatred:

> One rainy day, when we [he and his siblings] were eight weeks old, Jenkins...came into the stable and looked at us....Mother watched him anxiously, and fearing some danger to her puppies, ran and jumped in the middle of us, and looked pleadingly up at him....He took one pup after another, and right there, before my poor distracted mother, put an end to their lives. Some of them he seized by the legs and knocked against the stalls, till their brains were dashed out, others he killed with a fork. It was very terrible....I was the only one left.[72]

His mother, pale as death from mourning, also dies some weeks later.

> As I sat by her, feeling lonely and miserable, Jenkins came into the stable. I could not bear to look at him. He had killed my mother....She would never again look kindly at me, or curl up to me at night to keep me warm. Oh, how I hated her murderer!...My heart was nearly broken, and I could stand no more. I flew at him and gave him a savage bite on the ankle....He seized me by the back of the neck and carried me out to the yard where a log lay on the ground....He laid my head on the log and pressed one hand on my struggling body....There was a quick, dreadful pain, and he had cut off my ear, close to my head, so close that he cut off some of the skin beyond it.[73] (See Fig. 5.2.)

Fig. 5.2 Dust jacket of Marshall Saunders, *Beautiful Joe* (New York: Grosset & Dunlap, [c.1920]).

Never before had such detailed and brutal descriptions of cruelty to animals been written in such internationally successful children's books or juvenile litera-ture as in these much discussed animal autobiographies, which spanned especially the last third of the nineteenth century and first third of the twentieth century. And never before, on the basis of these descriptions, had such stories tried to make it easier to develop and deepen empathy and compassion for an animal as a person and the feelings it was supposed to have. To some degree, similar to anti-slavery narratives, these animal autobiographies tried to inflict 'emotional wounds' within their young readers.[74] As the pigeon Gay-Neck in *Gay-Neck* (1927) explains, all that young readers need in order to enter a mimetic learning process here is 'the grammar of fancy and the dictionary of imagination'.[75]

Thus, the mimetic learning process that these animal autobiographies tried to instigate was aimed not so much at the link between emotion and empathy in general, but much more at the link between empathy and compassion for animals in particular. Animal autobiographies such as *Black Beauty* or *Beautiful Joe* not only describe cruelty to animals, but also try to mobilize sentiment against it. It is therefore no surprise that a young man, who hears Joe barking and howling, storms into the yard and liberates the dog from the clutches of its cruel master. During the course of the story his new mistress joins an animal protection society—the local *Band of Mercy*.[76] The story offers not only practical knowledge on how to *feel*, but also on how to *deal* with these feelings. Thus, the emotionalization of animals within this person pattern might also lead to a very concrete politicization of human-animal relationships.

While this fourth interpretative framework had already broken fresh ground in the children's literature of the 1870s, it was not until much later that it reached the field of advice manuals, in some cases as early as the 1920s, but generally not until the 1960s or 1970s. Consequently, this development is reflected not so much in advice manuals about children, but rather in advice manuals about animals—mainly about pets. Yet, in parallel with children's psychology and advice manuals for raising children, an increasing emphasis on, and permanent extension of, the so-called 'emotional life' of animals may be observed in the field of animal psychology and advice manuals for raising animals.[77] It is precisely in this sense, for example, that in his reflections on the psychology of pets, *Zur Psychologie unserer Haustiere* ('On the psychology of our pets', 1939), Bastian Schmid emphasized that the issue had been plainly 'underestimated', especially on the premise that the emotional life of animals is solely based upon the existence of pleasant and unpleasant sensations. 'In reality', he claimed, animals experience 'joy and sorrow, envy based on food, things and gender, affection and aversion, fear and anxiety, attachment and loneliness'.[78] In his *Seelenleben unserer Haustiere* ('Emotional life of our pets', 1922), Theodor Zell, one of the most important protagonists in this development, expressed his amusement about the fact 'that now the age of the child has dawned'—an obvious reference to the title of Ellen Key's ground-breaking book, *The Century of the Child*—adding that 'those who know animals must laugh about it, for in the allegedly backward animal world the age of the child has existed since the year dot'.[79]

* * *

From the 1960s onwards and in the vein of this person pattern, a growing market for advice manuals concerning the understanding of 'neurotic' dogs or the care for 'depressive' cats may be observed.[80] Regarding this ongoing therapeutization of certain animals, namely pets, and their supposed emotions, it might also be appropriate to speak solely of an anthropomorphization of animals; this, however, would in principle disclaim the possibility for empathy, at least empathy with animals. To do this would mean to distinguish a priori between humans and animals, and to be unable to view and to problematize this distinction and its consequences as historically contingent and socially contested.[81] The person pattern is not only based on an anthropomorphization of animals, but could also lead to the collapse of a seemingly impregnable border between humans on the one hand, and animals—all animals—on the other. The fact that the 'Otherness' of animals challenges the question of empathy to a very high degree does not imply that empathizing with animals is necessarily impossible. From a historical perspective it is at least remarkable how far some children's books and advice manuals went in their attempt to understand the feelings of animals, to 'really' feel with 'real' animals. *The Story of Doctor Dolittle* thus faces the possible criticism of anthropomorphization, in that it introduces the character of a translator: the parrot Polynesia. For Doctor Dolittle, the acts of understanding the feelings *of* others and of feeling *with* others—in this case with animals—go hand in hand: empathy is always an act of translation and imitation, of carry-over; it is at least partly the result of a mimetic learning process.[82] And perhaps in modern times, not only children, or humans in general, but also certain animals, especially pets, have to learn how to feel and how to display their feelings in a manner that humans can understand and respect in a social world produced and reproduced not only by humans, but by these animals, too.

However, the evolution of 'new kinds of reading' that guided people to 'new experiences', a topic that was recently investigated in relation to the historical invention of human rights, may also be applied in this context to the diversely described, and repeatedly enforced, empathy with animals and the recent history of public discourse about animal rights. Whether empathy was based only on an anthropomorphization of animals or not, this empathy was an 'imagined empathy'.[83] This chapter therefore considers the emotions of empathy or compassion, too, as the focus of historical analysis, instead of attributing them to a biological, evolutionary endowment on the part of humans and a few other assorted animals.[84] Not only the fact that in the context of numerous children's books and advice manuals between the mid-nineteenth century and mid-twentieth century, the promotion and learning of empathy and compassion for animals went constitutively hand in hand with strictly hierarchical family structures demonstrates clearly the validity of reconstructing, differentiating, and problematizing the emergence and transmission of these emotions within a specific historical context.

NOTES

1. Lofting, *Story of Doctor Dolittle*, 5, 4, 2.
2. Lofting, 9, 11, 15.
3. Lofting, 17, 22–4, quotations 23, 24.
4. For an overview, see, for example, Bourke, *What it Means to be Human*; Buchner, *Kultur mit Tieren*; Eitler, 'The "Origin" of Emotions'.
5. See Ritvo, *Animal Estate*; Perkins, *Romanticism and Animal Rights*; Boddice, *History of Attitudes and Behaviours Towards Animals*; Kean, *Animal Rights*. Against this background we have to critically reflect the tendency toward racism within *The Story of Doctor Dolittle*.

6. See also, chapter 4, 'Ralph's Compassion'. The following analysis is based on the review of some seventy children's books and around forty advice manuals in German or English. For their help and critical advice, I thank Kate Davison, Michaela Keim, Karola Rockmann, Monja Schottstädt, and Jakob Schottstädt, to whom I dedicate this analysis.
7. See especially Breithaupt, *Kulturen der Empathie*. For an overview, see, for example, Coplan and Goldie, *Empathy*.
8. See, for example, Rothfels, *Representing Animals*; Daston and Mitman, *Thinking with Animals*.
9. Borkfelt, 'Colonial Animals and Literary Analysis', 557.
10. See, for example, McHugh, *Animal Stories*; Burt, *Animals in Film*.
11. See, for example, Mangum, 'Narrative Dominion'; Brown, *Homeless Dogs and Melancholy Apes*; Rudd, 'Animal and Object Stories'; Borgards, 'Tiere in der Literatur'.
12. See especially Cosslett, *Talking Animals in British Children's Fiction*. See also Römhild, *Belly'chen ist Trumpf*.
13. See also Grieser, *Im Tiergarten der Weltliteratur*.
14. See especially Haraway, *When Species Meet*.
15. With a focus on dogs, see, for example, Superle, 'Animal Heroes and Transforming Substance'; Oswald, 'Heroes and Victims'; Mangum, 'Dog Years, Human Fears'.
16. See also chapter 9, 'Jim Button's Fear'.
17. Burnett, *Little Lord Fauntleroy*, 71.
18. Burnett, 71–5.
19. Burnett, 84.
20. For similar differentiation, see, for example, Borgards, 'Tiere in der Literatur'; Superle, 'Animal Heroes and Transforming Substance'. On this whole issue, see Cosslett, *Talking Animals in British Children's Fiction*.
21. A very difficult case is, for example, Adams, *Watership Down*.
22. Bourke, *What It Means to be Human*, 19–63. For an overview, see, for example, DeMello, *Speaking for Animals*; Wild, *Tierphilosophie zur Einführung*. On Jeremy Bentham and his great question 'Can they suffer?', see especially Boddice, *History of Attitudes and Behaviours toward Animals*, 121–54.
23. See, for example, Eitler, 'The "Origin" of Emotions'.
24. See, especially Cosslett, *Talking Animals in British Children's Fiction*.
25. While in *The Jungle Book*, for example, it was a colonial context, in *The Trip to Panama* it was the so-called 'alternative milieu' against which background we have to historically reconstruct these stories.
26. See the introduction to this volume.
27. See also Baker, *Picturing the Beast*, 120–86.
28. For an overview, see Cosslett, *Talking Animals in British Children's Fiction*; Kete, *Beast in the Boudoir*; Bourke, *What it Means to be Human*; Eitler, 'Weil sie fühlen'.
29. Key, *Century of the Child*, 138.
30. Hall, *Youth*, 318. See also chapter 1, 'Mrs Gaskell's Anxiety'. See, for example, Perty, *Ueber das Seelenleben der Thiere*.
31. See also chapter 3, 'Asghari's Piety'.
32. See, for example, Eitler, 'Weil sie fühlen'.
33. Stall, *What a Young Boy Ought to Know*, 75–6, 78.
34. The terms 'empathy' and 'sympathy' or 'compassion' and 'pity' were often used synonymously throughout the period under investigation.
35. *Girls and their Ways*, 276.
36. Schreiber, 'Die soziale Erziehung des Kindes', 226 (all translations by the author).

37. Kutsche, König, and Urbanek, *Frauen-Bildungsbuch*, 220.
38. Tesarek and Börner, *Der Kinder-Knigge*, 25.
39. Potter, *Tale of Peter Rabbit*, not paginated.
40. See, for example, Whitley, *Idea of Nature in the Disney Animation*.
41. Budde, *Auf dem Weg ins Bürgerleben*, 129.
42. Collodi, *Story of a Puppet*, 224.
43. Lagerlöf, *Wonderful Adventures of Nils*, 367. See also chapter 11, 'Heidi's Homesickness'.
44. Superle, 'Animal Heroes and Transforming Substance', 174.
45. Collodi, *Story of a Puppet*, 232.
46. Here, in the context of violence, we can clearly observe a gender bias concerning the topic of this chapter.
47. See especially Brehm, *Illustrirtes Thierleben*; Brehm, *Brehm's Life of Animals*.
48. See, for example, Baker, *Picturing the Beast*.
49. Trott, *Pucki und ihre Freunde*, 139–41. See also chapter 6, 'Wendy's Love'.
50. See especially Kean, *Animal Rights*; Roscher, *Königreich für Tiere*; Zerbel, *Tierschutz im Kaiserreich*.
51. While these book series were transnationally successful, others were only nationally successful—for example, Tina Casparis's *Bille und Zottel* (1976–2003).
52. Miller, *Fury*, 104–5.
53. See, for example, Boddice, *History of Attitudes and Behaviours Towards Animals*; Perkins, *Romanticism and Animal Rights*.
54. For an overview, see Eitler, 'Weil sie fühlen'.
55. Hoffmann, *Slovenly Peter*, not paginated. See also chapter 8, 'Lebrac's Pain'.
56. Gumpert, *Die Herzblättchen*, i, 79.
57. Michaelis, *Bibi*, 241–2. This book series was published between 1929 and 1938 originally in Denmark, with several of the series' books later translated in German and English.
58. See, for example, Roscher, *Königreich für Tiere*; Pearson, *Rights of the Defenseless*.
59. Kienast, *Gespräche über Thiere*, 3–6. See also Oppel, *Thiergeschichten*; Knauth, *Lose Blätter und Blüten*.
60. Hall, *Youth*, 232.
61. See especially Pearson, *Rights of the Defenseless*. See also Flegel, *Conceptualizing Cruelty to Children*.
62. Knigge, *Practical Philosophy of Life*, 332. See also Trimmer, *Fabulous Histories*.
63. See also Eitler, 'The "Origin" of Emotions'.
64. Kübler, *Das Buch der Mütter*, 423.
65. Becker, *Die Erziehungskunst der Mutter*, 80.
66. Klein, *Wie soll ich mich benehmen*, 41–2.
67. The animal welfare movement sought out direct contact with children, for instance, in the form of child-oriented calendars and short stories.
68. 'Tierschutz', 693.
69. See also *Biography of a Spaniel*; Hoffmann, *Life and Opinions of the Tomcat Murr*.
70. Saunders, *Beautiful Joe*, 13.
71. Saunders, 14.
72. Saunders, 22–3.
73. Saunders, 23–4.
74. Noble, *Masochistic Pleasures of Sentimental Literature*, 126. However, concerning animals I find that children's literature is not about masochistic pleasures in these emotional wounds.

75. Mukerji, *Gay-Neck*, 55. See also chapter 3, 'Asghari's Piety'.
76. Saunders, *Beautiful Joe*, 166–74.
77. See, for example, Grier, 'Childhood Socialization and Companion Animals'; Kete, 'Verniedlichte Natur'. See also Levinson, *Pet-Oriented Child Psychotherapy.*
78. Schmid, *Zur Psychologie unserer Haustiere*, 19.
79. Zell, *Seelenleben unserer Haustiere*, 123–4.
80. See, for example, Baker, *How to Live with a Neurotic Dog.*
81. See especially the fruitful discussion in Daston and Mitman, *Thinking with Animals.*
82. See also the epilogue in this volume.
83. Hunt, *Inventing Human Rights*, 32–4. See also Breithaupt, *Kulturen der Empathie.*
84. See, for example, Waal, *Age of Empathy.* See also Shapiro, 'Understanding Dogs'.

6

Wendy's Love

Magdalena Beljan and Benno Gammerl

Mr Darling loves Mrs Darling, who loves Wendy, who loves Peter, who does not really love anyone: not Tiger Lily, not Tinker Bell, not the Lost Boys, not even his forgotten or non-existent mother. And, most certainly, the eternal boy, who is 'gay and innocent and heartless', does not love his opponent Captain Hook.[1] These connecting and disconnecting chains of affection that run through the stories about Peter Pan create many different constellations, within which various forms of love are expressed and experienced through diverse words and gestures. 'Peter', Wendy asks while she is busily mothering the Lost Boys in Neverland 'what are your exact feelings to me?'[2] Peter, whose role within the family game they play in their home under the ground oscillates between that of a son and that of a husband and father,[3] replies cautiously, 'Those of a devoted son.' This answer upsets Wendy. 'You are so queer', Peter tells her.[4] He fails to understand what Wendy wants to be to him if not his mother. As Wendy, claiming the status of a 'lady', refuses to explain to Peter what the problem is, he decides to ask his friend Tinker Bell. This flamboyant and jealous fairy unfortunately happens to be yet another female seeking his love. Hence, her reaction to Peter's question whether she wanted to be his mother does not come as a surprise to readers who have already gained some experience in matters of love: ' "You silly ass!" cried Tinker Bell in a passion.... "I almost agree with her," Wendy snapped.'[5] Peter's ignorance obviously frustrated various creatures that approached him with different kinds of love on their minds: there was motherly care, friendship, jealousy, and bridal affection, not to mention seductive and fatal love[6] or the one kiss on the lips of Wendy's mother which was not for her husband, but reserved for Peter. Thus, it is quite a difficult task—for the eternal boy, as well as for the audience—to find out whom they should love, how, and how much.

FROM TUT-TUT TO TÊTE-À-TÊTE OR LEARNING HOW TO LOVE

These explorations into the intricate stories of Peter Pan indicate some of the issues around which the chapter analyses how children were taught and learnt to love from the late nineteenth century onwards. Love demarcates quite a wide area, especially with regard to works of fiction and advice literature for children and adolescents.[7] This chapter does not focus on romantic or any other limited notion of interpersonal love, employing instead a comprehensive perception that ranges from affection between parents and children stretching to fondness within couples, and further to friendship among peers. Which patterns and practices of love did children and youth of different generations mimetically learn from the books they read? The somewhat distorted family game that Peter, Wendy, and the Lost Boys play in their home beneath the ground aptly demonstrates the potential of such learning processes. By mimicking adult behaviour within their joyful role play, the young protagonists offer readers, listeners, and viewers opportunities to re-enact the emotional interactions between family members on multiple levels and to distance themselves from, or identify with, certain positions in these relational networks. Thus, it is worth asking, what verbal formulas or physical gestures were offered by different books and were thereby either propagated or discouraged in matters of love. Which situations accompanied, environed, and shaped moments of affection and how did differences in age, gender, and sexuality influence these constellations?[8]

The first section follows the shift in emphasis from affectionate relationships between children and adults to those among peers.[9] The age difference between lovers is crucial for determining which emotional bonds they can legitimately establish. While the caring father and the friendly teacher display appropriate forms of attachment, the paedophile sports coach violates fundamental rules when expressing her or his feelings. Whether certain intimate practices are considered acceptable among peers also depends on whether they are pre-school children or teenagers. This shows how decisive the absence of erotic or romantic love is for contemporary perceptions of childhood.[10] Learning to love in a specific way is thus itself crucial for growing up and is intimately intertwined with notions of puberty and adolescence.

The second section scrutinizes the growing relevance of communication and negotiation within the family as well as between friends and partners. After the mid-twentieth century, the democratic ideal of equality demanded accepting and respecting the personality and the needs of the beloved Other. Therapeutic culture was instrumental in promoting these practices. Thereby, the 'psycho-boom' of the 1970s turned not only sexuality, but also self-awareness, emotions, and partnerships into issues that needed to be explored and continuously tended.[11]

The third section addresses the growing flexibility and diversity of love models, which complicated the successful navigation of affectionate landscapes. Especially in the last third of the twentieth century, the range of possible family constellations widened and hitherto clear distinctions between feminine and masculine emotional styles became obscure. Simultaneously, the evaluation of homo- and heterosexual constellations shifted significantly. Is it appropriate to interpret the therapeutic turn and these pluralizing tendencies as liberating individuals from moral constraints? Or should one rather speak of normalization processes that not only granted additional room to manoeuvre, but also produced specific sub-jectivities by exposing them to various demands and by stimulating continuous self-advancement?[12]

This chapter will address these issues by analysing stories about Peter Pan as well as works of fiction and advice manuals for children and youth. From the late nine-teenth century, both genres underwent significant changes that influenced how the young learnt to love. First, the narrative voices within children's books tended to discard their omniscient and heterodiegetic, somewhat distanced style, allowing readers to explore the interior ambiguities of individual characters in more detail. In a similar vein, advice manuals moved from didactic—a 1914 manual contained the handwritten inscription 'For your consideration!'—to rather companionable and conversational styles.[13] These trends increased the opportunities for mimetic learning as they offered a widening and ever more easily accessible array of situa-tions that readers could re-enact. These invitations for testing different roles were furthermore accompanied by a shift from warnings against imprudent love affairs to an emphasis on the rewarding aspects of affectionate relationships.[14] Second, a largely transnational style of writing and advising emerged in the second half of the twentieth century that levelled earlier differences between English- and German-language models of affection.[15] In terms of the questions discussed here, West and East German advice books also largely concurred.

Third, the relevance of class distinctions diminished. The Darling family clearly follows—albeit with ironic undertones—a middle-class ideal and, in the early dec-ades of the period under consideration, numerous manuals similarly presumed a middle-class background where children should train their affective abilities, for example by treating domestic staff with fairness. Other books explicitly addressed working-class readers, by, for instance, criticizing bourgeois moral standards as a means of oppression.[16] From the 1960s, such clear references to class became even rarer. Especially in the case of teenage love, social positions seemed to be increas-ingly irrelevant, at least for the authors of advice books. Whether the readership continued to be mainly middle-class is, of course, a different question.

Fourth, boundaries for the genders were also reconfigured. It is striking that the gendered specificity of advice was increasingly challenged by unisex manuals from the mid-twentieth century. Although separate chapters on female or male issues persisted, these could now be inconspicuously examined by all readers. Works of fiction addressing single-sex audiences also became rarer. This holds true for boys' boarding school novels that highlighted friendship and camaraderie, as well as for the German *Backfischliteratur* (teenage girl literature), and the English tomboy genre that informed their female readers about motherly care and romantic senti-ments.[17] This diminishing gender specificity of books contributed to a gradual reshaping of gender relations that unsettled the clear-cut distinction between the passive role of the female and the active role of the male in amorous encounters.

The stories about Peter Pan also demonstrate that learning about love has changed considerably since the late nineteenth century. Peter acquired his iconic status via a twisted path across diverse formats and media. His tale was written, rewritten, adapted, and modified by numerous authors.[18] Present-day versions of Peter's and Wendy's characters combine J. M. Barrie's texts, various stage performances, the Walt Disney film, and other adaptations of the story. Thus, Peter's very first appearances in *The Little White Bird* (1902) and the 1924 silent film have been largely forgotten.[19] Whereas his fame in the English-speaking world was primarily based on the theatre play, he was next to unknown in Germany before Disney brought an animated Peter to the screen in 1953.[20] This was just the first apex within a number of Hollywood films about the eternal boy.[21] Thus, the global popularization of the story corresponded with its Americanization. These translations and transformations also influenced the ways in which love was dealt with and displayed. Early versions emphasized Peter's longing for motherly love as embodied by Wendy Darling. The Disney film, though, gave greater prominence to Peter's jealous fairy Tinker Bell by portraying her as a blonde, scantily dressed little vamp instead of representing her as a glimmering light as she had been in past manifestations. This shift turned her into one of the most iconic characters—besides Peter (and Hook)—and boosted the presence of romantic and erotic love within the story.[22]

'MY HEART BELONGS TO DADDY'—FROM INTERGENERATIONAL LOVE TO LOVE AMONG PEERS

A shift in emphasis from intergenerational affections to romantic relationships among peers may be traced in various adaptations of Peter Pan throughout the twentieth century. Within this process, physical gestures of intimacy also gained a new and specific relevance. Early versions highlighted motherly care and were reluctant to display physical intimacy. Nobody was allowed to touch Peter and he refused Wendy even a hug.[23] When she still offered him a kiss, Peter did not know what kisses were.[24] This ignorance stemmed from the absence of his mother.[25] Motherly care was generally a prominent theme in the early versions where Wendy embodied not only Peter's wife, but also replaced his and the other boys' absent mothers, by virtue of her being a 'motherly person'.[26] The 1953 Disney version of the story continued to highlight motherly love: Wendy explained to the boys what a mother was, the pirate Smee longed for his mother, and Mrs Darling cared deeply for her children. Simultaneously, the movie emphasized patterns of romantic and erotic love focusing on Tinker Bell's jealousy, the mermaids' seductiveness, Tiger Lily's affection, and Wendy's adoration. These features should add a taste of 'adult romance' to the story, as grown-up test viewers had suggested during the production process.[27] The romanticizing of Wendy's relationship with Peter reached its climax in P. J. Hogan's 2003 film, in which Wendy's kiss on Peter's lips (Fig. 6.1) enabled him to defeat Hook. This kiss no longer signifies motherly

Fig. 6.1 Shy—Daring—Passionate: The Transformation of Peter Pan and of Kisses.[28]

love,[29] but a romantic bond, which empowers Peter to perform deeds that normal boys could not accomplish.

This significant reinterpretation of love was accompanied by an increase in Peter's age.[30] In Barrie's early text *Peter Pan in Kensington Gardens* (1906), he was just a baby, while the 1911 novel described him as a boy. On stage—and similarly in the silent film—Peter was mostly played by adult actresses, but in the most recent films, by male teenagers. These shifts corresponded with an ever stronger emphasis on adolescence, on developing a grown-up sexuality, and on Peter and Wendy as a romantic teenage couple.[31] By the early twenty-first century, Peter had acquired the ability to fall in love, something he was incapable of back in 1911.

This maturation and eroticizing of the bond between Peter and Wendy also triggered a re-evaluation of the circumstances within which Barrie had created these characters. The author dedicated his play 'to the five', the sons of Arthur and Sylvia Llewelyn Davies.[32] His relationship with these boys—after the death of their parents Barrie acted as the children's guardian—has attracted increasing public attention since the 1970s and was viewed with growing suspicion as potentially involving paedophile dimensions.[33] This indicates shifting assessments of intergenerational bonds that were also mirrored in advice literature. Around 1900, manuals appreciated affectionate relations between, for example, masters and disciples or 'erotic bonds of love towards an adored older person' as conducive to adolescents.[34] Some British manuals added that in 'primitive societies', elders customarily initiated adolescents into the mysteries of sex.[35] While several books continued to approve of intergenerational bonds,[36] the warnings against false and overly intimate relations intensified.[37] These growing fears regarding paedophile advances within and outside the family contributed to shifting emphasis from bonds between children and adults to amorous relationships among peers.

A similar development occurred in children's literature. In the nineteenth and early twentieth centuries, literary heroes were often orphans and abandoned children. Such books mostly ended happily with the original family being restored or a loving foster family being found. Thus, the stories revolved around the affectionate relationship between children and parents or other parental figures, even if the latter happened to be absent for a considerable part of the narrative.[38] In *The Secret Garden* (1911), the absence of parents and the lack of parental love even impaired the young protagonists' ability to establish any other kind of interpersonal relationship. One might conclude that if children failed to receive an appropriate education about love within intergenerational settings, they would later be unable to form any other kind of attachment. While this reading highlights the bonds between children and parents, *The Secret Garden* also allows for another interpretation, as it is ultimately within their mutual friendship that Colin and Mary learn to establish affectionate relationships with others.[39] Thus the novel also portrays peer groups as potential platforms for amorous education.

The notion that relationships among peers were best suited for youngsters to learn how to love gained currency during the twentieth century. Earlier books, like those about orphans, had often marked the absence of parents as a problem. Later children's books depicted the—mostly temporary—remoteness of parents as an opportunity for children to explore and learn among themselves without supervision.[40] In Enid Blyton's series, the *Famous Five* (1942–62), the initially withdrawn and unfriendly George/Georgina learnt to engage with others in a kind and affectionate way during a summer she spent with her cousins. Thereby she realized that '[t]alking about things to other people does help a lot.'[41] Only after experiencing this with her peers could she re-establish a loving relationship with her father.[42] This emphasis on peer relationships also informed British boarding school novels. *Tom Brown's School Days* (1857) had already highlighted the advantages—and the horrors—of boarding schools in the mid-nineteenth century. The German series *Burg Schreckenstein* ('Shiverstone castle', 1959–88) took the idealization of the secluded peer-group setting even further. Teachers and other adults remained marginal in the narrative and served either as a negative contrast to the young protagonists or as benevolent observers who encouraged the pupils to develop their own code of conduct—mainly chivalry and loyalty—and to enforce these rules among themselves.[43]

That homogenerational spaces like boarding schools figured much more prominently in British than in German novels, especially before the mid-twentieth century, is strongly connected with the different educational paths that children were supposed to follow in the two countries. German advice books located love chiefly in two strictly separated settings: between children and parents and between spouses. The transition of love from the first to the second stage happened somewhat abruptly. According to a 1913 manual, an exemplary girl when not at school or work, should spend most of her time at home with her closest family. Only occasional visits to a relative and decent and short encounters with young men were deemed acceptable.[44] This advice was intimately intertwined with strict gender boundaries dictating that girls should maintain a protective barrier around them and defining the household as their appropriate habitat.[45] These restrictions ultimately applied to obedient girls and dutiful wives alike. Thus, young women accepted their bridal obligations after a childhood that taught them to comply with other people's expectations.[46]

This trajectory for German girls leading directly from the parental to the marital home differed clearly from the paths sketched out by British manuals for boys, who were to go through an additional intermediary phase. This disparity was, first of all, based on gender. Yet it was also closely linked to boarding schools being much more common in Britain than in Germany. Thus, British manuals were intensely concerned with how boys should learn to love after having left their parents and before starting their own families.[47] Accordingly, friendships among same-sex peers gained importance. As one manual advised, a boy should decide carefully before he 'gives up his heart and mind to his friend's keeping', because with passion and jealousy he would thereafter elevate his friend to 'the pedestal of his adoration'.[48]

As the twentieth century progressed, German advice books followed their British counterparts in highlighting adolescence as a decisive phase of education about love between the ever-decreasing age of sexual maturation and the simultaneously increasing marital age.[49] In doing so, some argued against an 'artificial separation' of female and male youth and recommended more heterosocial interaction, yet within strictly regulated boundaries, for example, in dancing classes.[50] Other manuals emphasized homosocial bonds, claiming that adolescents should direct their attention to persons of the opposite sex only from the age of sixteen or seventeen.[51] National socialist publications of *Bund Deutscher Mädel* ('League of German Girls') and *Hitlerjugend* ('Hitler Youth') remained largely silent on these issues and only stressed the crucial experience of acting independently from adults within a collective of peers.[52] In the 1960s, the developmental process was further compartmentalized, leading then from filial love to homosocial friendship in the early teen years and on to early asexual love relationships between male and female adolescents, and finally to marriage.[53] Intergenerational bonds were thus relegated to a short initial phase, while peer relationships gained increasing importance.

This shift also triggered ever finer differentiations between affectionate expressions that were deemed appropriate only for particular constellations. Early manuals often blended love within families, friendships, and marriages. Gestures could cross these boundaries—friends walking 'hand in hand' and sons exchanging 'kisses' with their mothers. Metaphors could cross these boundaries as well—describing a friend as 'the other half' and claiming that a young boy should grant his mother 'the courteous attention which the true gentleman shows ever to "the weaker sex" '.[54] Later advice books drew sharper distinctions and asserted that one could kiss his mother's cheek, but not the cheek of a football team mate, while only spouses were to exchange the most intimate gestures of affection.[55] Additional graduations marked different phases in the evolvement of romantic partnerships. These escalated from dating to kissing and holding hands to petting, and 'finally touching one another's sex organs'.[56]

Some manuals welcomed the marginalization of intergenerational bonds, the growing relevance of peer relationships, and the accompanying diversification of affectionate practices, as these processes opened large playgrounds for amorous experiments during adolescence.[57] Others lamented the alienation between children and parents. They highlighted the potential dangers of a youth culture that allegedly generated enormous internal pressure to conform and that turned the young into incomprehensible aliens to grown-up outsiders.[58] This was all the more problematic, as mutual understanding and successful communication simultaneously gained crucial relevance for loving relationships.

'BABY, TELL ME DOES SHE LOVE YOU'— COMMUNICATION, NEGOTIATION, AND THERAPEUTIC CULTURE

While in earlier times lovers used to remain silent in awe, from the mid-twentieth century onwards they were expected to talk endlessly.[59] This urge for communication resulted primarily from the ideal of equality within relationships. Partners had to acknowledge each other's characters, opinions, and wishes. Talking about these things and about mutual problems was vital for achieving equality within couples, yet also between friends, or between children and parents. Interestingly, such communicative exchanges were frequently compared to parliamentary nego-tiations between the government and the opposition. Curfew hours for teenagers, for example, were not to be imposed 'dictatorially'.[60] And lovers should 'peacefully and democratically' reach a compromise, when they happened to have different plans for the weekend.[61] In terms of sex, this was linked to ethics of negotiation that gradually replaced older, more rigid moral standards. The new code held that everything was acceptable as long as all participants consented. Accordingly, part-ners were expected to voice clearly their sexual preferences and disinclinations.[62]

In this way, romantic love increasingly lost its sublime aura, and instead entered the mundane. Loving relationships should now enable both partners—almost in a therapeutic fashion—to talk about, and to deal with, their quotidian problems.[63] From the 1960s, therapeutic culture influenced love in several ways. As young people were increasingly expected to decide by themselves, regardless of their social background, whom they should love, and in which way, they needed, first, to acquire and maintain the requisite level of self-assuredness. Lack of autonomy and shyness were accordingly identified as major issues.[64] Manuals advised ado-lescents suffering from such 'problems' either to solve them on their own through self-evaluation and self-improvement,[65] or to seek professional support.[66] Second, young people needed to find sources of information on which they could base their autonomous decisions and, therefore, turned to advice literature. Although some authors frankly admitted the impossibility of ascertaining whether someone was genuinely in love, numerous youth magazines promised such certainty by enquir-ing, for example, about the alleged couple's conversation topics.[67] Manuals also took part in such redistributions and adaptations of psychological knowledge, for example, by advising readers to combine emotion and reason when making amo-rous choices.[68] Even Peter Pan entered the domain of therapeutic know-how in the 1980s, when men who confused the love of female partners with motherly love were deemed to be suffering from 'Peter Pan syndrome'.[69]

An increasing emphasis on communication also characterizes works of fiction. In the late nineteenth century, juvenile protagonists like Tom Sawyer considered love as just one among many possible adventures. Therefore, these characters usu-ally fell in and out of love rather abruptly and without much ado. When Tom sees the 'lovely little blue-eyed' Becky for the first time, he immediately focuses on this new challenge, while his hitherto beloved—'in one instant of time'—leaves 'his heart like a casual stranger'.[70] Tom neither feels guilty, nor does he think of love as a complicated issue. This is altogether different in books that were addressed to female readers, such as in the German *Backfischliteratur*, which gained currency from the late nineteenth century.[71] These works often hid their moral messages underneath entertaining surfaces.[72] They were addressed to bourgeois adolescents and typically described the *éducation sentimentale* of non-conforming, rebellious girls into well-educated, decent wives.[73] As these works narrated complete bio-graphies, they thoroughly discussed falling in love, marrying, and starting a family, either in conversations among female friends or in elaborate love letters. In *Taming a Tomboy* (1898; Ger. orig. *Der Trotzkopf*, 1885), the first love talk between the main heroine Fanny and her bridegroom-to-be Leo is triggered by a letter from Fanny's friend Nellie, in which the latter discloses her amorous relationship with a teacher. Fanny's defiance of rules and decorum threatens to sever the emerging bonds of love between her and Leo. An exemplary story about Lucy proves decisive in overcoming this obstacle. Lucy ruined her prospects of marital bliss by being sullen, presumptuous, and unwilling to apologize.[74] This has a deterrent impact on Fanny, who learns to approach her lover in an appropriate way and, thus, finally wins the bridal myrtle crown.[75]

These examples from the late nineteenth century demonstrate that amorous communications were clearly shaped by gendered asymmetries. If protagonists talked at all in any detail about affectionate feelings, this task was primarily assigned to female characters. In the late twentieth century, however, children's books began to identify communication about love as a means of reaching mutual agreement. In *Ben Loves Anna* (1990; Ger. orig. *Ben liebt Anna*, 1979), two children around the age of seven explore romantic love. The author explicitly rejects the claim that children could not yet experience love in all its adult complexity. Accordingly, the book elaborately describes the exchange of first tender touches and kisses, the writing of love letters, the bodily sensations connected with falling in love and being lovesick, as well as the implications of the crucial question: 'Will you be my girlfriend?'[76] The teacher, Mr Zimmerman, delivers the ultimate statements about love. Upon seeing the phrase 'Ben loves Anna' written on the blackboard, he adds: 'Anna loves Ben' and tells his pupils that 'love takes two people, you see'.[77]

The motif of children negotiating among themselves and carving their own path through the labyrinth of love is even more pronounced in *Leonie ist verknallt* ('Leonie has a crush', 1997). The book once more employs love letters as crucial media for articulating affectionate feelings. In her first letter, Leonie asks Florian: 'Do you want to date me?'[78] When Florian frankly admits his lack of experience, both children decide—without asking their parents for advice—to embark on a shared experimental journey towards discovering their amorous potential.[79] This example also demonstrates how the task of talking about and finding wholesome formats of affectionate bonding had become (almost) equally distributed between boys and girls by the end of the twentieth century.

'EV'RYBODY PLAY THE GAME OF LOVE'—FLEXIBLE PATTERNS OF AFFECTION

The appropriate patterns of love were increasingly described as negotiable. This stemmed partly from the gradual dissolution of gender stereotypes, as the transition from the *Backfisch* Fanny to the more open-ended femininities of Anna and Leonie illustrates. Admittedly, the German *Backfisch*—like the Anglophone 'tomboy'—had already rebelled against gendered expectations in the nineteenth century. Yet, at least until the 1960s, the genre had its heroines marry and settle down in respectful domesticity, after a phase of adolescent turbulence. Only in later decades did gender non-conformity start to be considered a potentially more sustainable option.[80]

Furthermore, it became increasingly unclear how one should love, because marriage as a stable framework for romantic bonds was gradually replaced by a variety of options. In contrast to Astrid Lindgren's *Confidences of Britt-Mari Hagström* (2005; Swe. orig. *Britt-Mari lättar sitt hjärta*, 1944),[81] for example, the fourteen-year-old Gretchen Sackmeier in Christine Nöstlinger's trilogy (1981–88) does not consider falling in love as the first step towards marriage, but rather as an entry into a vast experimental field. Until the end of the narrative Gretchen remains undecided whether she should choose the handsome heart-throb Florian or the reliable Hinzel.[82]

The wide terrain of love did not only force decisions upon its inhabitants, but was also quite perilous, as the marital conflicts between Gretchen's parents illustrated. Such representations of problematic or unstable family constellations generally gained currency in books for children and youth toward the end of the twentieth century. Earlier narratives usually underscored rather narrow notions of familial life by finally establishing or restoring a proper nuclear family with a male breadwinner.[83] From the 1970s, however, alternative patterns proliferated and single-parent households or blended families were no longer portrayed as failures; they were legitimate constellations that children should learn to handle (Fig. 6.2).[84]

Simultaneously, the heteronormative foundations of romantic love crumbled. Around the turn of the twenty-first century, a slowly growing number of children's

Fig. 6.2 The Traditional Family Model and One of its More Flexible Versions.[85]

books began to portray same-sex love, thereby following different strategies. Some stories highlighted the normality of same-sex partnerships by placing them in an everyday environment. The child protagonist in *Mini Mia and her Darling Uncle* (2007; Swe. orig. *Lill-Zlatan och morbror raring*, 2006), for example, loves her uncle, but has problems accepting his male partner Fergus. These tensions only subside when Mia realizes that Fergus is much better at playing football than her uncle.[86] *Heather Has Two Mommies* (1989) revolves around the daughter of a lesbian couple. When Heather laments the fact that she is lacking a father, one of her mothers explains to her that all families are different. The most important thing is that family members love each other.[87] In a similar vein, *Daddy's Roommate* (1990) depicts a boy whose father moves in with his male partner Frank after getting divorced. The boy's initial unease with the situation vanishes when his mother tells him that his dad and Frank are gay and that that is just another form of love.[88]

Other books employ more fantasy-based narratives, drawing on well-established traditions within children's literature. In the fairy tale setting of *King & King* (2002; Dut. orig. *Koning en Koning*, 2000), a queen wants to find a bride for her son, yet he likes none of the princesses. One candidate is accompanied by her brother, though, and the prince immediately falls in love with him and henceforth they happily rule the kingdom together.[89] A third example, such as *Hello, Sailor* (2002; Dut. orig. *Wachten op Matroos*, 2000), adds symbolic meanings and fantastic potentials to seemingly mundane constellations, thereby hinting at the possibility of same-sex love rather than explicitly representing it. Matt has waited for Sailor for a long time, before the latter returns and makes Matt's heart beat faster. The two men laugh, cry, and sort of dance together, and finally embark on a journey to somewhere.[90] This narrative asks its readers to decide to which degree the bond between Matt and Sailor is based on friendship, erotic attraction, romantic feelings, or on any combination of the three.

While these children's books tended to cast a positive light on homosexual relationships, novels for teenagers and young adults such as *I'll Get There* (1969) or *The Center of the World* (2005; Ger. orig. *Die Mitte der Welt*, 1998) described their protagonists' male-to-male experiences as one problem among several usually associated with growing up. The differences between these two novels indicate that homosexuality was considered less exceptional in the late 1990s than three decades earlier. Accordingly, the protagonist's struggle with his sexual identity attracted significantly less attention in the later book.[91] This implies a normalization of homosexuality that was closely intertwined with its decriminalization in the late 1960s. These processes shifted emphasis from the question whether one was gay or not to the question whether one proved up to the challenge and managed to handle the non-conforming dimensions of one's personality in a positive way. Against this background, it is pointless to ask which books were more subversive and which threatened to reproduce the heteronormative structures of the family and the couple.[92] The representation of alternative models necessarily tied in with pre-existing patterns. Overcoming traditional moral restrictions thus not only remained incomplete, but also exposed individuals to new challenges and responsibilities.

An examination of advice literature further supports this argument. The patterns of love offered therein grew more diverse from the mid-twentieth century, partly influenced by earlier notions, for instance 'free love'. Yet one should not misinterpret this simply as liberation from all moral rules. The new sexual liberties were instead accompanied by new responsibilities.[93] Lovers were portrayed as active navigators who had to carve their own path through an ever more varied landscape of possibilities. The most obvious effect of this challenging increase in flexibility was that marriage was no longer the undisputed harbour for all romantic liaisons. Simultaneously, the heterosexual outcome of amorous learning lost the unquestioned authority it had hitherto enjoyed. Thus, it is useful to scrutinize the growing relevance and changing meanings of the homo-hetero divide within advice literature in more detail.

Most manuals from around 1900 took the heterosexual norm largely for granted, hardly referring to homosexuality, while they explicitly warned against 'vices' like masturbation or extra-marital sex.[94] Only in later decades did authors straightforwardly and specifically condemn male same-sex desire.[95] That the heterosexual standard was increasingly destabilized can also be inferred from proposals to allow for more intimate contacts between unmarried young men and women. Such suggestions were intermittently voiced from the 1920s and indicate the intentions to strengthen the orientation towards the opposite sex.[96] After the mid-twentieth century, advice manuals struggled to define appropriate heterosexual behaviours among seemingly countless options using what they held to be deterrent examples, such as homosexual love, as well as sexual practices beyond vaginal penetration and long-term partnerships.[97]

At the same time, the previously cherished friendships among same-sex adolescents became suspicious. Some manuals defined them as purely spiritual and characterized them in opposition to 'homosexual practices'.[98] Others conceded their sexual dimensions, but highlighted their transitional character as 'training' for heterosexual partnerships.[99] While some authors claimed that the continuation of this homoerotic 'phase' should be tolerated when homosexuality was inborn,[100] others warned against getting 'stuck too early with the idea [that] you are "homosexual"' and recommended trying heterosexual intercourse instead.[101] This idea fits the experimentation-orientated 1970s, as do arguments about the relative normality of homosexuality or the notion that everybody harboured same- as well as opposite-sex desires.[102]

In the 1980s, advice books addressing teenage and young adult gay readers considered such generalizing configurations of the homo-hetero divide as homophobic. They recommended 'coming out' early instead, and committing oneself to an exclusively gay identity.[103] Instead of self-deceptively engaging in heterosexual experiments, these manuals prompted readers to overcome their shame and anxiety and to openly embrace their same-sex desire. This was considered an indispensable prerequisite for gays and lesbians to establish beneficial love relationships.[104] Some authors even argued that their chances of success after 'coming out' would exceed those of heterosexuals because of the communicative skills they had thereby acquired.[105] During the 1990s, this focus on self-confidently demonstrating a distinct gay identity partly yielded to more nuanced configurations of the homo-hetero divide, as transgender and queer critiques of identity politics further diversified non-heteronormative sexualities.[106] Simultaneously, manuals started to recommend more caution and flexibility in displaying one's sexuality—such as by avoiding same-sex kisses in front of one's father—and maintaining varied affectionate relationships with partners, relatives, and friends.[107]

These reconfigurations of the homo-hetero divide also deprived Peter Pan of his hitherto self-evident heterosexuality. Although Disney wanted the boy to lack any 'sissy'-like traits,[108] he still acquired iconic status within gay popular culture.[109] Reinterpretations of Peter Pan inspired by queer studies have furthermore highlighted his—or her—androgynous character and the intricate relations between Peter and Hook.[110] While the fact that Hook and Mr Darling were often performed by the same actor suggested oedipal features, other perspectives emphasized Hook's desire for eternal youth, his campness, and the homophile patterns of intergenerational love—ambiguously oscillating between repulsion and attraction—that shaped the bond between Hook and Peter.[111] This bond sometimes even threatened to push Peter's relationship with Wendy from centre stage.

* * *

By scrutinizing books and advice manuals for children and youth, this chapter has identified three major shifts in learning how to love. These were, of course, closely intertwined with the history of love, in general.[112] First, one may observe a gradual levelling of gender, age, and other hierarchies within loving relationships. These equalizing tendencies gained particular thrust in the early twentieth century with the concept of companionate marriage and educational reform, and in the 1970s with second-wave feminism and anti-authoritarian pedagogy. Second, communication became increasingly important during the second half of the twentieth century, when relationships came to be considered problems that required constant work and discussion either in therapeutic settings or within fair negotiations between both partners. Third, less formal and more flexible amorous models gained currency and burdened lovers with new responsibilities, as marriage and the family lost their power to unambiguously structure affectionate relationships. This process may be linked to the increasing commercialization of love, to reconfigurations of the homo-hetero divide, and to the gradual disassociation of love, sexuality, and reproduction. Children's literature sometimes lagged behind these developments, especially with regard to the display of non-heteronormative forms of attachment, and sometimes prefigured them, for example by describing romantic love among children quite early. Advice manuals even promoted some of these changes, especially the post-1960s establishment of subjectivities that combined strategies of self-management with external guidance. Together, both genres impacted decisively on the shifting ways in which children learnt to love.

NOTES

1. Barrie, *Peter and Wendy*, 259–60, 267.
2. Barrie, 158.
3. This notion of playful domesticity is particularly highlighted by Derwent, *Story of Peter Pan*, 43, 58.
4. Barrie, *Peter and Wendy*, 159.
5. Barrie, 159–60.
6. For a particularly explicit representation of this kind of love in the so-called mermaid scene, see Loisel, *Peter Pan*, 55–6.
7. This chapter is based on the close reading of over 120 advice manuals and children's books, primarily published in Germany, Britain, and the United States, and on more than a dozen movies about Peter Pan.
8. The distinction between humans and non-humans is also crucial here, see chapter 5, 'Doctor Dolittle's Empathy'.
9. On a similar shift in terms of shaming practices, see chapter 7, 'Piggy's Shame', and in terms of inflicting pain, see chapter 8, 'Lebrac's Pain'.
10. Kincaid, *Child-Loving*, 6.
11. See Moskowitz, *In Therapy We Trust*, 70–99, 218–44. For similar tendencies in the perception of homesickness, see chapter 11, 'Heidi's Homesickness'.
12. Maasen, 'Das beratene Selbst: Perspektivierung', 8–9. See also Rose, *Inventing Our Selves*. On this ambiguity of emancipation and subjectification, see also the introduction to this volume.
13. See the inscription in Benno Gammerl's private copy of Lepper, *Liebes und Leides für heranwachsende Mädchen* (all translations by the authors).
14. For mothers thanking an author for warning their sons against the dangers of love, see Stall, *What a Young Man Ought to Know*, xxvi. On how manuals being marketed directly to young readers and staging their advice as colloquial conversations impacted education about love, see Martin, 'No One Will Ever Know Your Secret!', 149; Sauerteig, 'Wie soll ich es nur anstellen'.
15. See Bradford, 'Children's Literature in a Global Age'. On the influence of American books after 1950, see Nelson and Martin, 'Introduction', 4.
16. Hodann, *Bub und Mädel*.
17. See chapter 11, 'Heidi's Homesickness'.
18. Barrie, *Peter and Wendy*; Derwent, *Story of Peter Pan*; O'Connor, *Story of Peter Pan*; see Hollindale, 'Hundred Years of Peter Pan', 198.
19. Barrie, *Little White Bird*; *Peter Pan*, Herbert Brenon, dir. (Paramount, 1924) [silent film].
20. Erich Kästner's translation of the play remained largely unknown. See J. M. Barrie, *Peter Pan oder Das Märchen vom Jungen, der nicht groß werden wollte* ([c.1950]). For the first full translation of Barrie's novels, see J. M. Barrie, *Peter Pan* (1964). See also Petzold, 'Rezeption klassischer englischsprachiger Kinderbücher in Deutschland', 84; Müller, 'Barrie, Sir James Matthew'. On Disney films as 'children's literature on screen', see Sammond, 'Dumbo, Disney, and Difference', 150, 162.
21. *Hook*, Steven Spielberg, dir. (Amblin Entertainment, 1991) [film]; *Return to Never Land*, Robin Budd and Donovan Cook, dirs. (Disney, 2002) [animation film]; *Peter Pan*, P. J. Hogan, dir. (Universal Pictures, 2003) [film].
22. For the growing popularity of Tinker Bell, see Disney's general line of merchandise featuring her, and Tinker Bell as the inspiration for Kylie Minogue's performance

as a green absinthe fairy in *Moulin Rouge*, Baz Luhrmann, dir. (20th Century Fox, 2001) [film].

23. Barrie, *Peter Pan; or The Boy Who Wouldn't Grow Up*.
24. Barrie, *Peter and Wendy*, 41, 47; Barrie, *Peter Pan; or The Boy Who Wouldn't Grow Up*.
25. Barrie, *Peter Pan in Kensington Gardens*, 111–12; Barrie, *Peter and Wendy*, 41. On how Mrs Darling could take on the role of Peter's mother by kissing him softly on the lips, see the silent film *Peter Pan*, Herbert Brenon, dir. (Paramount, 1924) [silent film], 01:39:45.
26. Barrie, *Peter and Wendy*, 107–8.
27. Ohmer, 'Disney's Peter Pan', 161; see also 153, 162, 166–7.
28. Daniel O'Connor, *Story of Peter Pan* (1914), 16; J. M. Barrie, *Peter Pan* (1964), 69, courtesy of Ricarda Lemke; *Peter Pan*, P. J. Hogan, dir. (Universal Pictures, 2003) [film], 01:26:55, courtesy of Columbia Pictures.
29. Morse, 'The Kiss'.
30. Munns, 'Gay, Innocent, and Heartless', 229–32; Ohmer, 'Disney's Peter Pan', 175.
31. Hollindale, 'Hundred Years of Peter Pan', 213.
32. Barrie, *Peter Pan; or The Boy Who Wouldn't Grow Up*, v–xxxiii; Hollindale, 'Hundred Years of Peter Pan', 204.
33. *The Lost Boys*, Rodney Bennett, dir. (BBC, 1978) [docudrama mini-series]; *Finding Neverland*, Marc Forster, dir. (Miramax, 2004) [film]. See also Birkin, *J. M. Barrie and the Lost Boys*. For arguments against the rumours about the paedophile inclinations of Barrie, see Hollindale, 'Hundred Years of Peter Pan', 205.
34. Hodann, *Bub und Mädel*, 108. See also *Boys and their Ways*, 64; Slaughter, *The Adolescent*, 37–8.
35. Storr, *Growing Up*, 74. See also Slaughter, *The Adolescent*, 2.
36. Comfort and Comfort, *Facts of Love*, 105; Powledge, *You'll Survive*, 36, 79–80.
37. Slaughter, *The Adolescent*, 37; Lepper, *Liebes und Leides für heranwachsende Mädchen*, 19; Hilliard, *Problems of Adolescence*, 13; Fischer, *Nicht Sex sondern Liebe*, 191; Seelmann, *Zwischen 15 und 19*, 191; Brückner and Blauschmidt, *Denkst Du schon an Liebe*, 53; Comfort and Comfort, *Facts of Love*, 108.
38. A number of classics count among these books: Charles Dickens, *Oliver Twist* (1838); Johanna Spyri, *Heidi* (1884/1885; Ger. orig. *Heidi's Lehr- und Wanderjahre*, 1880 and *Heidi kann brauchen, was es gelernt hat*, 1881); Mark Twain, *The Adventures of Tom Sawyer* (1876); L. M. Montgomery, *Anne of Green Gables* (1908).
39. Burnett, *Secret Garden*. On this novel, see chapter 2, 'Dickon's Trust'; chapter 8, 'Lebrac's Pain'; chapter 9, 'Jim Button's Fear'.
40. *Alfred Hitchcock and The Three Investigators* (1964–90) by Robert Arthur and others would be just one prominent example. See the first volume, Robert Arthur, *The Secret of Terror Castle* (1964).
41. Blyton, *Five on A Treasure Island*, 112.
42. Blyton, 186–90.
43. See the first volume, Oliver Hassencamp, *Die Jungens von Burg Schreckenstein* (1959; Eng. *The Gang from Shiverstone Castle*, 2004). On *Tom Brown's School Days*, see Munns, 'Gay, Innocent, and Heartless', 226.
44. Lepper, *Liebes und Leides für heranwachsende Mädchen*, 18, 38. See also Meyer, *Vom Mädchen zur Frau*, 44–5.
45. Lepper, 11, 21.
46. Lepper, 42. See also Meyer, *Vom Mädchen zur Frau*, 109. On similar gender-specific advice in a South-Asian context, see chapter 3, 'Asghari's Piety'.

47. On the impact of the boarding school experience on contemporary notions of adolescence, see Vanden Bossche, 'Moving Out', 84, 86.

48. *Boys and their Ways*, 78, 131. See also Slaughter, *The Adolescent*, 38. For warnings against 'bad companionships' among peers, see Stall, *What a Young Man Ought to Know*, 57; Baden-Powell, *Rovering to Success*, 106.

49. Fischer, *Nicht Sex sondern Liebe*, 115; Seelmann, *Zwischen 15 und 19*, 273; Brückner and Blauschmidt, *Denkst Du schon an Liebe*, 30.

50. Foerster, *Lebensführung*, 158. See also Bovet, *Von Mann zu Mann*, 32. On Friedrich Wilhelm Foerster see chapter 1, 'Mrs Gaskell's Anxiety'.

51. Hodann, *Bub und Mädel*, 114.

52. Munske, *Das bunte Jungmädelbuch*; Reichsjugendführung, *Pimpf im Dienst.*

53. Fischer, *Nicht Sex sondern Liebe*, 20–1, 85, 97. See also Brückner and Blauschmidt, *Denkst Du schon an Liebe*, 32.

54. *Boys and their Ways*, quotations 13–14, 78, 124. For an early warning against confusing different expressions of love, see Slaughter, *The Adolescent*, 36.

55. Härtter, *Warum lieben sich Mann und Frau*, 14–15.

56. Comfort and Comfort, *Facts of Love*, 52. See also Brückner and Blauschmidt, *Denkst Du schon an Liebe*, 71–2.

57. Seelmann, *Zwischen 15 und 19*, 26, 220; Storr, *Growing Up*, 77–8, 91–5; Comfort and Comfort, *Facts of Love*, 119.

58. Chamberlain, *Adolescence to Maturity*, 37; Hilliard, *Problems of Adolescence*, 13; Powledge, *You'll Survive*, 39, 81; Koch and Koch, *Bloss nicht wie die Alten*, 30–1; Farman, *Keep Out of the Reach of Parents*, 15–34, 52–70. See also Simpson, 'Advice in the Teen Magazines', 51.

59. See Chamberlain, *Adolescence to Maturity*, 45–6; Seelmann, *Zwischen 15 und 19*, 208, 214–15, 282; Brückner and Blauschmidt, *Denkst Du schon an Liebe*, 82; Molter and Billerbeck, *Verstehst Du mich*; Comfort and Comfort, *Facts of Love*, 11, 31–2, 54.

60. Hilliard, *Problems of Adolescence*, 16. See also Seelmann, *Zwischen 15 und 19*, 225; Storr, *Growing Up*, 13.

61. Seelmann, *Zwischen 15 und 19*, 215–16. See also Verheyen, *Diskussionslust*, 289–90.

62. Comfort and Comfort, *Facts of Love*, 54, 130; Joachim Braun, *Schwul und dann*, 109. See also Simpson, 'Advice in the Teen Magazines', 27. For a slightly different view recommending experimentation and practice instead of talking about sexual difficulties, see Storr, *Growing Up*, 105.

63. Seelmann, *Zwischen 15 und 19*, 214; Hanswille, *Liebe und Sexualität*, 97.

64. Chamberlain, *Adolescence to Maturity*, 25; Simpson, 'Advice in the Teen Magazines', 29; Comfort and Comfort, *Facts of Love*, 10; Powledge, *You'll Survive*, 55–6.

65. Seelmann, *Zwischen 15 und 19*, 12.

66. Storr, *Growing Up*, 96; Comfort and Comfort, *Facts of Love*, 140–2; Siems, *Coming Out*, 101–3; Powledge, *You'll Survive*, 71–84; Koch and Koch, *Bloss nicht wie die Alten*, 32, 210–18. On partnership counselling, see Elberfeld, 'Subjekt/Beziehung'.

67. Simpson, 'Advice in the Teen Magazines', 19; Brückner and Blauschmidt, *Denkst Du schon an Liebe*, 41; Koch and Koch, *Bloss nicht wie die Alten*, 74. On the popularity of such tests, see Sauerteig, 'Wie soll ich es nur anstellen'.

68. Seelmann, *Zwischen 15 und 19*, 219, Brückner and Blauschmidt, *Denkst Du schon an Liebe*, 81.

69. Kiley, *Peter Pan Syndrome*.

70. Twain, *Adventures of Tom Sawyer*, 36.

71. Barth, *Mädchenlektüren*.

72. See Schilcher, *Geschlechterrollen, Familie, Freundschaft und Liebe*, 249–92.
73. See also the *Pucki* series (12 vols, 1935–41) by Magda Trott, *Försters Pucki* (1935) up to and including, *Puckis Lebenssommer* (1941).
74. Rhoden, *Taming a Tomboy*, 107–18. The sequels to *Trotzkopf*, one of the most famous *Backfisch* series, by Rhoden's daughter, Else Wildhagen, cover the girl's complete biography: *Trotzkopfs Brautzeit* (1892); *Aus Trotzkopfs Ehe* (1895); *Trotzkopfs Nachkommen* (1930).
75. Rhoden, *Taming a Tomboy*, 233–4.
76. Härtling, *Ben Loves Anna*, 43; see also 25–7.
77. Härtling, 90.
78. Mai, *Leonie ist verknallt*, 39.
79. Mai, 43, 91.
80. Nelson, 'Jade and the Tomboy Tradition'. On gender non-conformity in the 1990s, see Vallone, 'Grrrls and Dolls'.
81. Lindgren, *Confidences of Britt-Mari Hagström*.
82. Trilogy by Nöstlinger: *Gretchen Sackmeier* (1981); *Gretchen hat Hänschen-Kummer* (1983); *Gretchen, mein Mädchen* (1988).
83. See also the ten *Nesthäkchen* books (1913–25) by Else Ury starting with *Nesthäkchen und ihre Puppen* (1913), up to and including *Nesthäkchen im weißen Haar* (1925).
84. In addition to Nöstlinger's trilogy, see also Donovan, *I'll Get There*; Willhoite, *Daddy's Roommate* and the latter's sequel *Daddy's Wedding*. For divorced or single parents and other non-normative family constellations in manuals, see Seelmann, *Woher kommen die kleinen Buben und Mädchen*, 88–93; Storr, *Growing Up*, 97, Brückner and Blauschmidt, *Denkst Du schon an Liebe*, 120–2; Comfort and Comfort, *Facts of Love*, 138; Powledge, *You'll Survive*, 79; Hanswille, *Liebe und Sexualität*, 94–5; Farman, *Keep Out of the Reach of Parents*, 96–7.
85. Magda Trott, *Pucki als junge Hausfrau* (1950), cover; Pija Lindenbaum, *Mini Mia and her Darling Uncle* (2007), not paginated.
86. Lindenbaum, *Mini Mia and Her Darling Uncle*.
87. Newman, *Heather Has Two Mommies*.
88. Willhoite, *Daddy's Roommate*.
89. Haan, *King & King*. For a similar story in which a little penguin and two penguin fathers formed a family, see Richardson and Parnell, *And Tango Makes Three*.
90. Godon and Sollie, *Hello, Sailor*.
91. Donovan, *I'll Get There*; Steinhöfel, *Center of the World*. For another young adult novel negotiating same-sex experience (Ravera and Lombardo-Radice, *Pigs Have Wings*), see chapter 12, 'Ingrid's Boredom'.
92. Such arguments are supported by Nelson and Martin, 'Introduction', 8–9; Salas, 'Power and Repression'.
93. Chamberlain, *Adolescence to Maturity*, 43; Hilliard, *Problems of Adolescence*, 18; Storr, *Growing Up*, 99; Comfort and Comfort, *Facts of Love*, 102, 129–30.
94. Stall, *What a Young Man Ought to Know*, 33, 55, 135; Slaughter, *The Adolescent*, 75; Foerster, *Lebensführung*. For an early argument against discriminating against homosexuals, see Hodann, *Bub und Mädel*, 12.
95. Bundesen, *Toward Manhood*; Lindstroem, *Zauber der ersten Liebe*, 95 claimed that acquired homosexuality could be cured.
96. Foerster, *Lebensführung*, 158–9; Bovet, *Von Mann zu Mann*, 37.

97. Fischer, *Nicht Sex sondern Liebe*, 31–2; Seelmann, *Zwischen 15 und 19*, 272; Brückner and Blauschmidt, *Denkst Du schon an Liebe*, 124.

98. Fischer, *Nicht Sex sondern Liebe*, 21.

99. Seelmann, *Zwischen 15 und 19*, 184. See also Storr, *Growing Up*, 44–5, 77, 91–2; Brückner and Blauschmidt, *Denkst Du schon an Liebe*, 203. On the paradox that children 'are encouraged to engage in homosocial relationships but then presumed to develop into heterosexuality', see Pugh, *Innocence, Heterosexuality, and the Queerness of Children's Literature*, 5.

100. Hodann, *Bub und Mädel*, 129; Lindstroem, *Zauber der ersten Liebe*, 94; Siems, *Coming Out*, 31.

101. Comfort and Comfort, *Facts of Love*, 86.

102. Storr, *Growing Up*, 80–1; Brückner and Blauschmidt, *Denkst Du schon an Liebe*, 201; Hanswille, *Liebe und Sexualität*, 79. See also Salas, *Power and Repression*, 128. For an earlier example, see Hodann, *Bub und Mädel*, 130.

103. Siems, *Coming Out*, 12, 30; Grossmann, *Schwul—na und?*, 12, 32, 64–72, 104–5. See also Hanswille, *Liebe und Sexualität*, 80–1.

104. Grossmann, *Schwul—na und?*, 17, 63, 66; Braun, *Schwul und dann*, 84.

105. Braun, 98.

106. Geißler and Przyklenk, *Ich mach mir nichts aus Mädchen*, 19, 22.

107. Geißler and Przyklenk, 35, 39, 50. For a young adult novel exemplifying this shift from 'coming out' and gay identity to more diverse landscapes of love surrounding adolescent same-sex couples, see Steinhöfel, *Center of the World*.

108. Ohmer, 'Disney's Peter Pan', 162.

109. Munns, 'Gay, Innocent, and Heartless', 219.

110. On androgeneity and the customary assignment of Peter's part to actresses, see Gubar, 'Peter Pan as Children's Theater', 487; Ohmer, 'Disney's Peter Pan', 156; Rose, *Case of Peter Pan*, xiii.

111. On Hook's effeminacy and attempts to eliminate it, see Ohmer, 'Disney's Peter Pan', 162, 173; Rose, *Case of Peter Pan*, xiii, 126. On Peter and Hook, see Holmes, 'Peter Pan and the Possibilities of Child Literature', 141; Kincaid, *Child-Loving*, 285. On the potential risks of reading the story with present-day understandings of sexuality in mind, see Munns, 'Gay, Innocent, and Heartless', 220.

112. Spector, Puff, and Herzog, *After the History of Sexuality*; Bänziger et al., *Fragen Sie Dr. Sex*; Illouz, *Consuming the Romantic Utopia*.

7

Piggy's Shame

Ute Frevert

What's in a name? In Piggy's case, everything. Piggy—his proper name is never mentioned—is so named because his looks and manners resemble those of a little pig. In William Golding's bestselling book *Lord of the Flies*, published in 1954, Piggy enters the island community of child survivors of a plane wreck somewhat scarred. Earlier in his twelve-year life, he had acquired the nickname that had caused him humiliation and pain. He now longs for a new beginning and confides in Ralph as a loyal companion. But Ralph, trying to befriend a powerful rival, Jack, betrays and ridicules Piggy in public. The 'storm of laughter' following the exposure results in 'a closed circuit of sympathy with Piggy outside'. Once again, Piggy is humiliated: 'he went very pink, bowed his head and cleaned his glasses'. Nevertheless, he remains loyal to Ralph. When Ralph betrays him a second time, Piggy confronts him, his glasses misted 'with humiliation'. Ralph suddenly understands that Piggy 'was hurt and crushed' and offers an apology: 'I'm sorry if you feel like that.' Piggy accepts it, and 'the rose of indignation faded slowly from his cheeks'. Jack, however, continues to deride Piggy while himself becoming invulnerable behind a mask of paint, 'liberated from shame and self-consciousness'. Only when he loses the contest for the group's leadership does he feel 'shame': 'Slowly the red [of anger] drained from Jack's cheeks, then came back with a painful rush. He licked his lips and turned his head at an angle, so that his gaze avoided the embarrassment of linking with another's eye.' A moment later, '[t]he humiliating tears were running from the corner of each eye.'[1]

SHAME AS A SOCIAL EMOTION

In Golding's novel, shame and shaming prove to be central points of social interaction and conflict. The author uses them generously to trace the children's road to perdition. The further they move away from civilization and its rules of sensible conduct, the more they use masks that enable them to resort to sheer, unmitigated violence. For the narrator, shame serves a moral purpose by curbing evil acts or causing regret in their aftermath. But this emotion also requires a certain degree of self-awareness and honest introspection. Those blinded by their own masks cannot experience it. Attempting to shame them only fuels their rage and violence—until a superior power forces them back into their rightful place. Shaming, in general, is practised by those who hold or assume authority over others. Ralph and Jack who compete for leadership both shame Piggy. Unlike Jack, Ralph realizes what he has done to Piggy and his feelings approach shame and remorse. The moral of the story is that a good leader should refrain from shaming others, and, if he does, he should apologize, while victims of malicious shaming should speak up instead of silently accepting and enduring it.

In this vein, Golding's readers received a full introduction into the phenomenology of shame and shaming, as well as a lesson on their social functions, both good and ill. Who were those readers? Originally, Golding had not meant to write his first novel as a children's book. Even though the boys described in it were between six and twelve years old, the readers were supposed to be adults, captivated by the major theme of tracing 'the defects of society back to the defects of human nature'. This is how Golding phrased it in a questionnaire he completed for his American publishers. Departing from the pure adventure genre with famous forerunners such as Daniel Defoe's *Robinson Crusoe* (1719), Robert Michael Ballantyne's *The Coral Island* (1858), and Robert Louis Stevenson's *Treasure Island* (1883), ironically alluded to by the boys themselves, *Lord of the Flies* was conceived of as a symbolic investigation of the 'ethical nature of the individual'. This direction, however, failed to impress adult readers in the mid-1950s. In the United States, the book only sold a few thousand copies and soon went out of print. Only when it was selected as required school reading did it become a great commercial success both in the United States and in Great Britain (more than in continental Europe).[2]

Golding's story was far from being the only one to acquaint readers with the positive and negative sides of shame. Shame figured prominently in children's literature, explicitly or implicitly.[3] As the semantic field expands to encompass embarrassment, bashfulness, humiliation, mortification, or feeling ridiculous as 'variants of the shame family', shame's presence and salience become all the more emphasized.[4] In general, shame was presented as a social emotion occurring within and through human interaction and the negotiation of social norms and expectations. Failure to meet demands might lead to shaming processes within asymmetric power relations. While in most cases directed from top to bottom, the order might be reversed and shame be brought down on the powerful. This depended on a person's level of self-awareness and the extent to which they respected the norms that they, intentionally or unintentionally, had violated.

The fact that children's books and advice manuals are brimming with references about shame reflects its importance in real life. Shame, as the work of twentieth-century psychologists confirms, 'strikes deepest into the heart of man' and appears 'in many guises'. It can be linked to early trauma and pathological suffering, and may lead to aggression and violence.[5] Even those who consider it as innately patterned allow for sources and gestures of shame 'which are learned'.[6] Shame is seen as hinging on cognitive abilities that emerge later in life. Most notably, it requires 'a clear recognition of the self as separate from others... as well as a set of standards against which the self is evaluated'.[7] Contemporary European children usually enter this stage of individuation around the age of two.[8]

The sense of shame develops during childhood and adolescence. Gradually, children learn about social habits and moral rules, and become aware of the importance of those rules to their environment and the consequences of their violation. They learn to read into others' reactions to what they do, and to care about those reactions, usually through experiences of pleasure or pain, reward or punishment. Learning how to feel and 'do' shame works both openly and in more subtle ways, and as children's literature and advice manuals highlight, direct or indirect instigations of shame have been ubiquitous. Expressions such as 'shame on you' are constantly present in everyday communication between adults and children. They also occur during peer interaction and at an increasing rate. Moreover, shaming practices cover a wide range, from excluding the culprit from social interaction to singling her out for public exposure and disdain.

TRUE VERSUS FALSE SHAME

Among children's literature recommended by doctors, teachers, and clergymen throughout the nineteenth century, Maria Edgeworth's stories, early lessons, and moral and popular tales figured prominently.[9] Edgeworth, who started publishing around 1800, and whose tales appeared in schoolbooks and magazines, was widely popular in Britain, the United States, and Germany and her books were translated into French and Italian as well.

The 'passion of shame', as she called it, played a major role in the 'practical education' that her stories offered to children and adolescents. As a general rule, shame that 'affects the mind with surprising force', should be 'very sparingly used; and the hope and possibility of recovering esteem must always be kept alive'.[10] The moral compass was not what 'the world' would say, but how a well-educated boy or girl should think.[11] Still, there were social norms to be observed. Little Rosamond was taught to be careful about her needlework and consequently felt 'ashamed' after losing four needles in one week.[12] Her six-year-old brother Frank was told a story about a boy who was 'ashamed' of being scared. Feeling shame helped him to conquer his fear and meet the expectations of being courageous, as all boys should be.[13] Shame accompanying 'wrong or foolish' acts could thus prove constructive in improving moral conduct. The same held true for corporal punishment, which caused pain but, more importantly, shame. As Edgeworth argued, physical pain was quickly forgotten. The 'dread of shame', however, if 'kept alive in the minds of children' served as a 'more powerful motive' for children to behave properly.[14]

As much as Edgeworth's tales sought to make young readers aware of shame's close connection to virtue, they also warned children against 'false shame'. Shame was false when it resulted from social pretensions or peer pressure ignoring the moral code, which, according to Edgeworth and many others, was strongly based on religious feelings and teachings. Contemporary society seemed to undermine these foundations. In 1834, the evangelical Protestant *Sunday-School Journal* in the United States published a letter whose author bitterly complained about 'false shame'. He explicitly referred to his earlier reading of Edgeworth's stories and 'a maxim which has remained in my memory ever since... *No one will ever become great who is afraid of being laughed at.*' This held mostly true for religious people who had unfortunately been overwhelmed by false shame: 'One young man is ashamed to become a Sunday-school teacher; people will take notice of it, and he will be laughed at! Another young man is afraid to own that he has religious feelings.' As a remedy against this 'mental disease', the author advised his 'younger brother' to '[b]e firm, be manly; have right opinions, and hold them fast. The dread of idle laughter is the meanest sort of cowardice... A proper regard for the opinion of others is surely desirable; but as a rational, an accountable, an immortal being, do not suffer yourself to be in servitude to other minds.'[15]

This letter is a testament to how 'maxims' described in children's literature might remain ingrained in readers' memories until their adult years. It also acknowledged the huge impact of shame on moulding people's behaviour in a positive or negative sense. Distinguishing 'false shame' from 'true shame', therefore, became a major issue of 'practical education'. On the one hand, children had to be raised to be 'firm', adhere to the 'right opinions' and, as the author of the letter recommended, 'despise ignorant ridicule' instead of dreading it. On the other hand, readers were encouraged to appreciate 'true' shame as a sign of a 'love of virtue' and accept being shamed for behaving improperly.[16]

As Edgeworth's stories about Rosamond and Frank indicate, the standards of proper behaviour differed according to gender. They also differed over time. What was deemed appropriate in the early nineteenth century, when Edgeworth first published her work, or in the 1870s, 1880s, and 1890s, when doctors still recommended it as excellent reading for girls, gradually became obsolete during the twentieth century. This referred mainly to rules of decency and modesty as they applied to the books' heroines. It also included the ways in which children were supposed to treat each other and their guardians, parents, relatives, or teachers. As an overall trend, changes to these rules gathered pace around 1900 and accelerated notably in the 1940s.

Did shame eventually also lose its prevalence? This question can only be answered sketchily by the sources chosen for this project. It may be argued that not only those who felt shame, but also those inflicting it, changed. For children, the primary agents of shame were usually adult family members, mainly mothers and fathers. Later on in life, more adults were added in the guise of clergymen and teachers. They held the power to set norms and rules, and could sanction a child's non-compliance by shaming her, either individually or in front of others (thereby increasing the effect). It was generally understood, at least in the latter part of the nineteenth century and into the 1940s, that adults were in a position to inflict 'true' shame; as the guardians of virtues and moral conventions, they knew right from wrong and passed this knowledge on to young children.

Other agents also inflicted shame, namely older children, as well as children of the same age, who figured as peers, siblings, classmates, and playmates. Like adults, they also acted as guardians of norms and rules (at times different from those prevailing in the adult world) and had the power to shame those who did not conform. As a typical feature of group dynamics, this kind of shaming practice was performed in public, which rendered it far more painful. At the same time, power structures in peer groups were not as stable as in families or teacher-student relations; they were subject to fierce competition and could be contested. New alliances might form at any time offering protection and support to those who had been 'falsely' shamed, by shaming others in return.

Resulting from social and demographic changes, the shaming power of peers and peer groups increased during the twentieth century. In the company of peers, children increasingly risked being subjected to 'false' shaming by those holding or striving for power. As families decreased in size, siblings lost their dual role as both peers and members of the family's moral universe. In turn, non-family peers became more important. This development was clearly reflected in children's literature, which began to focus more on same-age peer groups as well as conflicts outside the family. Gradually children's books addressed the perceived deficiencies within the nuclear family, which undermined its authority to set and sanction norms. Children raised in so-called 'incomplete' families, or by parents who neglected their child-rearing tasks, were portrayed as more dependent than others on peers and their 'feeling rules'. At times, the latter might prove superior, spurning the 'false' practices encountered among adults. 'True' and 'false' shame was no longer defined by adult authority, rather it was determined more and more by children themselves.

Since there were similar developments regarding changes in family structures, demographic patterns, and schooling in many Western countries, it is not surprising that children's and advice literature addressed practices such as shame and shaming in a rather uniform way. Occasional differences stemmed from institutional particularities. British books, for example, were the first to address the influence of peer groups as shaming agents, because of the nation's educational system of privileged boarding schools (especially, but not exclusively, for upper- and middle-class boys, and later for girls). Similarly, in the archetypical public school novel, teachers figured more prominently than fathers or mothers.

The extreme popularity of this genre not only in Anglo-Saxon countries, but also in continental Europe indicates the transnational appeal of children's literature. In the second half of the twentieth century, British author Enid Blyton's books, The Famous Five among others, found ardent readers among West German children, who, although they did not share the boarding-school experience, were nevertheless susceptible to the charms of an environment that seemed to offer children a great deal of self-sufficiency, including the power to shame each other. At the same time, though, it invited self-criticism and reflection on the power of shaming, empathy, and redressing the harms inflicted through 'false' shame.

GENDERED SHAME

'True' shame, as it was defined in nineteenth- and early twentieth-century novels, was reserved for acts that violated the moral rules of conduct. In Elizabeth

Wetherell's highly popular 1850 novel *The Wide, Wide World*, young Ellen strug-gles hard to lead a 'Christian' life against all odds, guided by her beloved mother's rigid principles: '[I]f you ever go an hour with a hole in your stocking, or a tear in your dress, or a string off your petticoat, I hope the sight of your work-box will make you blush.'[17] The title page of Heinrich Hoffmann's *Struwwelpeter* (1845; Eng. *Slovenly Peter*, 1850), of which one hundred editions were published over thirty years, depicted Slovenly Peter placed on a pedestal, with long fingernails and wild hair, to attract readers' outright contempt. A few pages in, starting with the 1858 edition, the same illustration was accompanied by a rhyme beginning with the exclamation: 'Look, here he stands. Ugh! Disgusting!' (Fig. 7.1). The picture evoked a classical shaming situation known from earlier times: people who had violated social norms were put on public display for finger-pointing and disdain.[18]

Sieh einmal, hier steht er,
Pfui! der STRUWWELPETER!
An den Händen beiden
Ließ er sich nicht schneiden
Seine Nägel fast ein Jahr;
Kämmen ließ er nicht sein Haar.
Pfui! ruft da ein jeder:
Garst'ger STRUWWELPETER!

Fig. 7.1 Depiction of Slovenly Peter placed on a pedestal in Heinrich Hoffmann, *Der Struwwelpeter oder Lustige Geschichten und drollige Bilder* (100th edn, Frankfurt am Main: Literarische Anstalt, 1876), [5] not paginated.

Although the cause of their shame is the same, Ellen and Peter experience shame quite differently. While Ellen has completely internalized her mother's moral lessons, 'colour[s] a good deal'[19] and successfully learns to be pious and 'humble', Peter stubbornly rejects his parents' advice and is thus forced to suffer public shaming. In his case, shaming is used as a punishment meant to improve his scandalous conduct. In terms of how shame was introduced in these stories it is no coincidence that Ellen was a girl and Peter a boy. On the one hand, boys were usually depicted as more unruly and defiant than girls. Their will had to be broken, by force if necessary, and public shaming was considered a convenient instrument. On the other hand, girls appeared more malleable, less inclined to offer resistance and more dependent on their mothers' or teachers' sympathy. Fear of losing that emotional support prompted them to immediately correct their behaviour in accordance with adults' wishes.

Nineteenth-century authors attributed the adjustable 'female character' (Rousseau) to women's nature, which allegedly equipped girls with more delicacy, patience, empathy, and self-denial. At the same time, though, they took great care to thoroughly educate girls so that they would conform to nature's 'original' plan. Advice manuals and children's literature in particular stressed the importance of girls' modesty (*Schamhaftigkeit*), generally considered to be a pivotal character trait. Modesty referred by and large to the chastity that formed the cornerstone of female honour. In this vein, Christian journals published stories and poems extolling virtue as 'the modest blush, | Maiden cheeks suffusing, | When pure thoughts indignant rush, | Sin and shame refusing'.[20] Elizabeth Blackwell, counselling parents on the moral education of their children, embarked on a crusade for '[m]orality in sex' and chastity, which was strongly linked to notions of shame, decency, and disgust for 'licentiousness'.[21]

Girls, however, were not the only recipients of this message. Boys, too, were instructed to refrain from sexually shameful behaviour. The instruction started with recommending physical work and exercise to quell lusty drives, and warned against alcohol, socializing with shameless womenfolk, and watching dubious theatre plays. Adolescent boys should refrain from reading indecent novels that filled their imagination with immoral thoughts and passions. Eugène Sue was thus deemed just as inappropriate as Charles Dickens, Alexandre Dumas, George Sand, or Emile Zola.[22]

As children's literature (initially literature for boys) began to focus more on entertainment and adventure and less on moral lessons, the theme of chastity and order became less prominent. Nevertheless, it still played a role as late as 1935, in Carol Ryrie Brink's acclaimed *Caddie Woodlawn,* in which the heroine is strongly reprimanded by her mother for bad behaviour. Although her brother Tom is equally rude, the mother only accuses Caddie: '[T]hat a *daughter* of mine should...be such a hoyden as to neglect her proper duties as a lady! Shame to her! Shame!

No punishment that I can invent would be sufficient for her.' Caddie finds this extremely unfair and plans to run away. It is only after her beloved and supportive father talks her into accepting her feminine 'responsibility' as 'a beautiful and precious one' that she relents. Even prior to this, she experiences some doubts about her own tendency to act like a 'wild Indian'.[23] When her well-mannered cousin from Boston sends a very polite letter Caddie is emotionally torn:

> It sounded like a story from *The Mother's Assistant* or *The Young Ladies' [sic] Friend*—those tiresome stories which were so much less interesting than Hans Andersen's or Tom's . . . No, Caddie Woodlawn would never write a letter like that. Couldn't she or wouldn't she? She honestly did not know, but it made her a little ashamed and apprehensive to think about it.[24]

Fifty years earlier, Emmy von Rhoden's tomboy protagonist Fanny had undergone a similar conversion. After deliberately submitting a flawed piece of knitting at school, Fanny is publicly criticized by the principal ('[y]ou ought to be ashamed of yourself') and laughed at by the other girls. Instead of demurely accepting the shame, as little Rosamond would have done, she revolts and dashes the stocking 'against the door with a violence that scattered the needles in all directions'. When the principal tells her to pick it up again, she refuses. Eventually, however, following the advice of an understanding tutor, she apologizes in a state of 'shame, if not repentance'.[25]

PUBLIC SHAMING AND PERSONAL PRIDE

In fact, public shaming practices were a common feature of the fictional classroom, from Fanny's posh boarding school in *Taming a Tomboy* (1898) to Thomas Hughes's Rugby School in *Tom Brown's School Days* (1857), or Frederic Farrar's Roslyn School in *Eric, or Little by Little* (1858). Punishments frequently included making unruly pupils stand in the corner, having them flogged in public, or forcing them to wear silly masks, thus attracting attention and ridicule of their peers.[26] Such shame-causing sanctions caused a lot of concern and controversy among contemporary pedagogues. On the one hand, such practices were advocated as a potent means of education and character formation. Echoing Edgeworth's earlier assertions, it was thought that shaming children often proved more effective than 'rebuke, admonition, threat and corporal punishment'. Shame went 'deeper' and was not easily forgotten, since it directly affected the child's self-esteem and moral agency. At the same time, shame sanctions had to be applied carefully and with restraint. Excessive shaming might cause severe damage and destroy the sense of honour that was deemed crucial for both genders. Authors of advice manuals and pedagogical tracts increasingly warned against the perils of flogging and slapping which might diminish children's self-respect and their ambition to be treated respectfully by others.[27]

The fact that shame sanctions were generally administered in front of onlookers and peers was likewise criticized. It was now argued that children should neither be shamed in the presence of their siblings, nor be punished in the presence of their classmates, which only served to incite *Schadenfreude* among their fellow pupils.[28] This opinion, voiced by more liberal-minded and reform-oriented experts, opposed what had hitherto been the essence of shaming, namely, forcing a child to feel the contempt and disdain of others or, more precisely, of a community of others who, albeit temporarily, excluded her from their company and sympathy. In this instance shaming fulfilled a genuinely social function. Not only did it demonstrate to the wrong-doers that their actions were reprehensible, but simultaneously confirmed and reinforced the validity of collectively binding norms and values.

But how could the demands of the collective—group, institution, society—be reconciled with the task of protecting a person's pride and dignity? How much humiliation could a child endure without being seriously harmed? And how much denigration should children experience in order to become reliable and trustworthy members of a given community? The heroes and heroines of nineteenth-century children's books were all somehow confronted with these questions that stood at the core of modern society's understandings of the self, and failed to find easy answers. Short stories that were read aloud to young boys and girls in order to 'educate their heart and develop their moral concepts' portrayed children as constantly blushing and lowering their gaze when reprimanded by adults. Although public exposure was hurtful, 'true' shame eventually helped to convince them that they should improve and change their naughty behaviour.[29]

But there were also cases in which juvenile protagonists revolted against humiliation inflicted by adults. One famous example can be found in Lucy Maud Montgomery's 1908 novel *Anne of Green Gables*. This book, which sold about fifty million copies during the twentieth century and has been translated into twenty languages, focused much more on shaming than on feeling ashamed. The eleven-year-old protagonist Anne is extremely sensitive about what she perceives as insults and a lack of respect, both from adults and peers. Whenever her feelings are hurt, she pays back in kind. When a teacher has her stand on the platform in front of the blackboard, Anne's

> sensitive spirit quiver[s] as from a whiplash. With a white, set face she obeyed. Mr. Phillipps took a chalk crayon and wrote on the blackboard above her head. 'Ann Shirley has a very bad temper. Ann Shirley must learn to control her temper', and then read it out loud so that even the primer class, who couldn't read writing, should understand it. Anne stood there the rest of the afternoon with that legend above her. She did not cry or hang her head. Anger was still too hot in her heart for that and it sustained her amid all her agony of humiliation.[30]

What were readers supposed to feel and think? Did they side with Anne and detest the teacher for trying to shame her? Did they admire her for standing up to adult authority and defending her sense of dignity and self-esteem? Or did they frown upon Anne's 'passionate indignation'[31] and refusal to accept shame? We cannot know, since readers' reactions were usually not recorded or monitored.

Nevertheless, there are some subtle indications. Overall, the narrator introduces her heroine as a positive character, bright, quick, joyful, and imaginative. Moreover, Anne usually reacts in defence of her honour being assaulted by third persons. Still, in terms of the message conveyed to readers, controlling one's temper was surely not a bad thing, even if it seemed less salient in Montgomery's book than in Rhoden's *Taming a Tomboy* (1898; Ger. orig. *Der Trotzkopf,* 1886). Growing older and more mature, Anne herself realizes that an unforgiving attitude is problematic and successfully seeks to alter it.

Here, another major theme of shame came to the fore: the feelings of pride, self-love, and arrogance. Though Anne's classmate quickly apologizes for making fun of her, she refuses to forget: 'Gilbert Blythe has hurt my feelings *excruciat-ingly.*'[32] But apologies usually had to be accepted since they indicated regret on the part of the perpetrator. Time and again, this message was spread through religious and educational tracts, as well as in children's literature. Religious overtones were paramount. Just as God forgave sinners once they repented, children, too, should forgive. Turning down a sincere apology was rude and conveyed a sense of arrogance that could itself become a cause of shame.

Pride, arrogance, and self-pity played a crucial role when children's books dealt with shame and shaming. Frederick Marryat's enduringly popular *Masterman Ready* (3 vols, 1841–2) told the story of six-year-old Tommy who always feels sorry for himself whenever he is reprimanded or punished. He shields himself from remorse and only later learns the lesson that feeling ashamed and repenting is the first step towards salvation.[33] Very often in children's books, pride stood in shame's way. Toad, in Kenneth Grahame's *The Wind in the Willows* (1908), never really feels ashamed for things that he does wrong, even if he is generally quick to apologize 'with that frank self-surrender which always disarmed his friends' criticism and won them back to his side'. Only at the very end of the story does he become convinced that he had better stop his 'conceit and boasting and vanity' of which Badger says he should be 'ashamed', and shift his attitude from one of 'self-praise' to one of 'modest' pleasantry.[34] An honest apology was hard, as tomboy Fanny painfully found out. It took Mark Twain's unruly Huckleberry Finn fifteen minutes to bring himself to apologize to his friend Jim whom he gravely offends. The fact that Jim is a 'nigger' and a former slave makes matters worse, but eventually Huck does apologize, and he 'warn't ever sorry for it afterwards, neither'.[35]

Owning up to one's mistakes, taking responsibility for failures and misdeeds, and apologizing to those hurt were essential parts of a moral upbringing and maturation. This was never easy, especially for those children who had developed a strong sense of pride. Pride was not altogether contemptible. Children obviously needed some degree of self-assertion in order to develop the kind of autonomous and independent personality that was increasingly considered healthy and desirable.[36] At the same time, they had to contemplate the impact of their pride on others. When twelve-year-old Pauline, in Noel Streatfeild's 1937 novel *Ballet Shoes* treats the supporting cast arrogantly during her first ballet engagement, the director dismisses her. First she feels sorry for herself, but gradually learns her lesson. Deep inside, she knows that out of self-love and pride she has been impolite and haughty to them, 'and she was ashamed, and though she was quite alone she turned red'.[37]

Whenever pride opposed civic morality and harmed another person it had to be fought and subdued. While Huck struggled against the racial pride that initially prevented him from acknowledging his misbehaviour, Senator Bird's wife in Harriet Beecher-Stowe's *Uncle Tom's Cabin* (1852) shames her husband for voting in favour of a law to forbid helping escaped slaves: 'You ought to be ashamed, John!... It's a shameful, wicked, abominable law.'[38] Similarly, in Hoffmann's *Slovenly Peter*, the mighty Nicolas shames Ludwig, Kaspar, and William who scream and laugh at the Moor because he is 'black as ink'.[39] And in Maria Edgeworth's *Popular Tales*, civilized and well-mannered people should be 'ashamed' for holding anti-Irish prejudices and sharing a misled national or ethnic pride.[40] They should also refrain from social or class pride rather than considering 'tradesmen and manufacturers as a cast, disgraceful to polite society'.[41]

The message in all these books was that social arrogance was to be considered a source of shame, not honour. Those who displayed arrogance had to be taught a lesson and be made to feel ashamed. This was precisely the case in a story by Theodor Dielitz about an English aristocrat who, after treating an alpine guide with utter condescension, is shamed when the guide saves the haughty man's daughter.[42] In a similar vein, in a story by Ottilie Wildermuth, Karl, a proud, rich man's son, suffers 'harsh humiliation' when he has to borrow money from a poor old man.[43] Poverty as such was not deemed shameful as long as it did not result from personal vice or laziness. Children who were ashamed to be seen with poorer relatives learnt to understand that their own behaviour was itself shameful and they were taught to refrain from hurting the pride of poor people.[44] 'Poverty is no disgrace. We should honour honest Poverty', asserts Dora Bastable in Edith Nesbit's *The Story of the Treasure Seekers* (1899). 'And we all agreed that that was so.'[45]

False pride, however, was also an issue when someone reacted out of proportion. Lewis Carroll's Alice in *Alice's Adventures in Wonderland* (1865) did not mind apologizing when she had hurt an animal's feelings by asking silly questions. She does lose her patience, though, with those who are too easily offended. The mouse, for example, always feels insulted, withdraws immediately, and has to be begged many times to come back. Such behaviour was deemed just as inappropriate as when a child was too easily upset by her playmates' banter.[46] As a general rule, children were not to be overly sensitive when teased or challenged by peers. They were supposed to either laugh it off, as Dorothy and the scarecrow do at the latter's mishap in *The Wonderful Wizard of Oz* (1900),[47] or they were supposed to stay calm, like Briant in Jules Verne's *Adrift in the Pacific* (1889; Fre. orig. *Deux ans de vacances*, 1888). Briant does not accept Donagan's challenge to a fist fight, which he considers unfair and aggressively provocative. It is only when his antagonist calls him a coward and treats him with contempt that he is forced to relent. Cowardice for boys was the worst and most shameful insult they could imagine, and was to be avoided at all costs.[48]

Cowardice was a recurring theme in an endless variety of plots and stories that were told and re-told in children's literature throughout the nineteenth and twentieth centuries. A particularly striking example was given in Louis Pergaud's 1912 novel *The War of the Buttons* (1968; Fre. orig. *La guerre des boutons*, 1912) which was published in more than thirty editions and, after being turned into several films, became even more popular among French, German, and English-speaking audiences. In the story, boys from two neighbouring villages engage in a ritual of collective fighting. They first insult each other by exchanging the most abominable (and sometimes misunderstood) slurs and invectives. The insults must then be rebuffed by force to avoid being accused of dishonourable cowardice. Humiliation after humiliation, attack after attack, the ritualized conflicts eventually spin out of control. The ultimate stage of shame and denigration is reached when one group cuts off the other's buttons, buckles, and clasps, leaving them with their pants down and their underwear exposed, and as for Lebrac '[a] new flush of shame or rage purpled his brow.'[49]

SHIFTING AUTHORITIES

What was apparent in Pergaud's book was how shaming practices had begun to shift. In much of nineteenth-century children's literature, shaming was performed vertically, from top to bottom. Disobedience both at home and at school was a major source of shame, as authors from Maria Edgeworth to Heinrich Hoffmann, from Thomas Hughes to Emmy von Rhoden, told their readers, with parents, relatives, and teachers inflicting shame on children to remind them of their weaknesses and to curb their feelings of pride and self-assertiveness.

This pattern, however, changed in the course of the twentieth century. Shame was now increasingly inflicted and experienced horizontally, among peers. Shaming in Pergaud's novel takes place among the boys themselves who prove extremely inventive in devising new words and practices of humiliation. Likewise, in Erich Kästner's *The Flying Classroom* (1933; Ger. orig. *Das fliegende Klassenzimmer*, 1933), adults are not involved in such practices and play only a small part in the plot. Uli, ashamed of his fear and lack of courage in the eyes of his classmates, jumps from a high ladder as a dare. He is so upset about the other boys not trusting him to meet a challenge that he takes this risk and nearly kills himself. This leaves his friends in shock and awe and they begin to discuss the benefits of shame among each other. Clever Sebastian confesses that he also feels a lack of courage but has instead tried to conceal it: 'My timidity does not trouble me much. I'm not ashamed of it, because, you see, I have some common sense. I know that everyone has his own faults and failings and the main thing is simply to prevent people noticing them.' An older pupil objects: 'I think it's better to feel ashamed of it', and Sebastian silently agrees.[50]

This debate invited readers to consider the dual nature of shame. As much as it was an instrument of power in the hands of those who could inflict shame on others, it also testified to one's honest feelings and sincere aspirations. It could bring out the best in a person and lead to acts of impressive willpower. But it could also result in foolish and self-destructive behaviour. At least, in Uli's case, it served the good end of prompting the boys to talk openly about emotions such as fear, which were commonly hidden behind the mask of the so-called masculine bearing.[51] In this respect, *The Flying Classroom* clearly went beyond the usual boarding school novel. In 1857, Hughes's Tom Brown had initially dreaded the shame of being ridiculed by other boys for openly saying his prayers. But eventually he followed little Arthur's example, knelt by his bed, and then 'rose from his knees comforted and humbled, and ready to face the whole world'. Tom thus learnt to adhere to his own principles instead of adopting the dominant attitude through fear of shame.[52] With Uli, there is no such conflict between 'me' and 'them'. His own fear shames him and he seeks to overcome it with a courageous, if foolhardy, jump.

Shame had thus become internal instead of being externally enforced. This reflected the growing power of friends and peers, with whom one identified, whose approval one sought, and whose principles one intentionally and wholeheartedly shared. Under these circumstances, the heroes in these stories felt shame as a personal and self-inflicted state once their actions and attitudes veered away from accepted group norms. This was the case in Streatfeild's novel *The Circus is Coming* (1938), in which the protagonists Peter and Santa '[sink] to depths of humiliation' when they discover themselves to be 'appallingly backward' compared to what the circus children are able to accomplish.[53] In Enid Blyton's *The Twins at St. Clare's* (1941), lower-class student Sheila tries to hide her 'feelings of inferiority' behind a haughty 'smoke-screen' and is shamefully exposed by outspoken Janet.[54] Similarly, in Blyton's *Five on a Treasure Island* (1942), George/Georgina blushes when she confesses to her cousins that she would rather be like them: kind, supportive, and relaxed, instead of lonely, deficient, and unpopular.[55]

Many books also made clear that the shaming power of peers could be contested and negotiated. Even if one desperately wanted to be accepted in a group, there were limits to what some protagonists would put up with. In Blyton's *Five on a Treasure Island*, Anne, the youngest cousin, refuses to be humiliated when the older children insultingly call her a baby who still plays with dolls. Even though she is hurt, she does not accept the shame since playing with dolls is something she loves and enjoys. She is self-confident enough to defend her interests and passions against group expectations, which eventually earns her the respect of the others.[56] In contrast, in Judy Blume's *Blubber* (1974), Linda loses respect by not standing up to the constant bullying perpetrated by her classmates. Even Jill, who eventually speaks out against their cruel behaviour, cannot bring herself to sympathize with Linda: 'There are some people who just make you want to see how far you can go.' Letting 'other people decide what's going to happen' and allowing 'everybody [to] walk all over her' makes Linda unappealing and charmless. Jill, on the other hand, after being shunned by her former clique, fights back and successfully finds new friends.[57]

The message here was unequivocal: Although peer groups were of primary importance for children and held enormous power of inclusion and exclusion, they were not everything. Instead of fully complying with a group's rules and standards, children could voice their dissent—or, if this failed, distance themselves. Those who accepted bullying and shame, offering no resistance, brought true shame on themselves. It is in this vein that Piggy confronts Ralph about shaming him in front of the other children. Ralph, too, does the right thing when he apologizes (though somewhat nonchalantly).

Twentieth-century children's literature thus sought to empower children to follow their own trajectory and resist 'false shame' by speaking up against other people's demands and expectations. As much as the books' heroes and heroines were portrayed as vulnerable to peer pressure and shaming, they were also encouraged not to hide their feelings but to negotiate them within the group. At the same time, they were advised against being overly sensitive, like Alice's mouse or Alberta Rommel's Marianne from *Der goldene Schleier* ('The golden veil', 1955). Marianne is portrayed as being continually ashamed, and she blushes constantly, which eventually leads her friend (and future lover) to burst out in exasperation: 'Are you insulted? Jesus, girl, don't be so touchy!'[58] Social interaction obviously could not work without a certain degree of mutual tolerance. One person's hypersensitivity triggered another's insecurity, which in turn rendered communication awkward and difficult. As numerous books suggested, it often helped to laugh off insults or embarrassment instead of taking them too seriously, blowing them out of proportion.[59]

Another interesting trend to be observed is how shame and shaming gradually entered the adult sphere. An early example is the Earl of Dorincourt in Frances Burnett's classic novel *Little Lord Fauntleroy* (1886). The haughty aristocrat is deeply shamed by his grandson's kindness and trust: '[A] dull red crept up under his withered skin, and he suddenly turned his eyes away.' Shamed by Cedric's love and gentleness, he reflects on his former self and finally 'make[s] it all right'.[60] In Kästner's *Annaluise and Anton* (1932; Ger. orig. *Pünktchen und Anton*, 1930), Anton shames a gentleman who arrogantly scolds him for selling matches and shoelaces at night: ' "You ought to be in bed, not standing there" said a man. Anton glared at him. "But begging is such fun," he muttered. The man was a little ashamed.... "Don't be angry." And he gave him a coin.'[61] The shift was even more evident in Kurt Held's *The Outsiders of Uskoken Castle* (1967; Ger. orig. *Die Rote Zora und ihre Bande*, 1941). Set in Croatia during the 1930s, the novel follows red-headed Zora and her orphan friends surviving gracefully and courageously in a hostile environment, playing tricks on complacent townspeople and confronting them about their shameful fear and cowardice. The children also bring home the message, voiced by the old fisherman Gorian, that the repeated conflicts between the children and the town folk are the fault of the adults, who shamelessly look the other way and refuse to take care of the orphans in their community.[62]

Other books taking a similar approach were Kästner's *Lisa and Lottie* (1950; Ger. orig. *Das doppelte Lottchen*, 1949) and, more than any others, *The Animals' Conference* (1949; Ger. orig. *Die Konferenz der Tiere*, 1949), in which government officials are shamed by smart animals and forced to negotiate a world without war, hunger, or ecological destruction. In Blyton's *The Six Bad Boys* (1951), parents are also shamed for mistreating their children in a thoughtless and selfish manner. Such incidents occurred more frequently in post-war children's literature, for example in Christine Nöstlinger's acclaimed novels *The Cucumber King* (1975; Ger. orig. *Wir pfeifen auf den Gurkenkönig,* 1972) and *Conrad* (1976; Ger. orig. *Konrad,* 1975). In this period, adults were increasingly portrayed as inadequate, lacking primary social skills including empathy, introspection, and the ability to acknowledge their shortcomings and apologize. They were no longer the immaculate role models they had once been, capable of teaching children essential moral lessons.

More and more, however, parents and adults were absent altogether, and child protagonists were left on their own. This sometimes ended in the collapse of morality, as in Golding's *Lord of the Flies,* where shaming Piggy was the first step on the road to disaster. The absence of adults might, however, also lead children to invent their own codes of solidarity and honour, as in Held's *The Outsiders of Uskoken Castle,* who take great care not to hurt and shame each other and their friends. Alternatively, it might be embodied in a figure like Astrid Lindgren's orphaned Pippi Longstocking, whose deceased mother was an angel and deceased father was a skipper. Left all alone, nine-year-old Pippi is free to establish her own rules of conduct. When they clash with what ordinary people deem appropriate, Pippi is saddened, but only briefly. She never feels ashamed because she does not understand or accept why others (mostly adults) exclude her for what they see as bad behaviour. At the same time, Pippi is highly sensitive about weaker children or adults being shamed, and, thanks to her physical and moral strength, unflinchingly intervenes on their behalf. In a crucial scene, she rebels and lets shame boomerang against Miss Rosenblom, a wealthy old lady who has initiated a ritual of selectively rewarding school children whom she considers worthy of her generosity. Twice a year, the children must stand in line and be assessed. Those who cannot answer Miss Rosenblom's questions are sent to stand in a corner before returning home empty-handed and shamed. When Pippi fails the test she refuses to be shamed. Instead, she alters the ritual by posing her own twenty questions and manages to restore the children's self-esteem, rewarding them with presents which make them feel happy and proud (Fig. 7.2). Although, or rather because, she often violates the standard moral codes, Pippi is deeply admired by her co-protagonists Tommy and Annika, who have been raised as ordinary, well-mannered children.[63]

As a literary character, then, Pippi served as a new role model, especially for girls who had traditionally been brought up to strictly obey the rules of decency and modesty. This was certainly not the first time that children's literature had described heroines who defied expectations. Strong, independent, and acting more out of anger, however, the character of Pippi went far beyond the Fannys, Annes, and Caddies of former times. Lindgren used this fearless young protagonist to condemn shaming practices in schools which had come under increasing criticism as humiliating and undermining a person's dignity. As the moral superiority and authority of adults were called into question, children were invited to develop their own moral codes and experiment with feelings that did not conform to adult wishes.

At the same time, these codes and feelings were challenged by peer groups. Self-assertion might clash with other children's sense of pride. Even if it was considered important to shield children from too much shame (defined as 'hatred of the self' and 'acute self-denigration'), they should not indulge in what twentieth-century psychology identified as narcissism.[64] Abundant self-love at the

Fig. 7.2 Astrid Lindgren, *Pippi in the South Seas* (New York: Viking, 1959), 47.

expense of others was held to be just as harmful to the self as a complete lack of self-love. It would produce a 'shameless society' which, in the 1970s, was actually diagnosed as a dangerous trait of contemporary Western life. Confronted with individuals who increasingly wished and managed to free themselves of shame's 'paralyzing shackles', civilization was seen to be in decline. The 'loss of shame' would ultimately threaten 'our survival as a civilized society' in which 'moral standards' should be sustained to the benefit of all.[65]

* * *

This analysis (and warning) seemed to resonate well with Norbert Elias's arguments about how the 'civilizing process' had, since the early modern period, depended on increasing thresholds of shame, embarrassment, and repugnance. Emanating from court society and state agencies like the military and civil service, new standards of self-restraint had gradually been popularized through social institutions like the family, school, church, and private associations. The more restraint people were expected to show in social manners and interaction, the more shame they were expected to feel in the event that they did not meet those norms and expectations. In this vein, shame, both internalized and inflicted by external agents, worked as a powerful mechanism of socialization and pacification.[66]

From early on, children's literature and advice books generously supported this kind of civilizing process on an ontogenetic level. They introduced readers to a number of moral rules that were to be, under all circumstances, observed and followed. Adults were presented as potent and legitimate guardians who had the responsibility and authority to enforce those morals and inflict shame on children if they chose to disobey. Shaming could take the form of corporal punishment, but it could also come about, and increasingly did, as more symbolic violence. Withdrawing emotional support, reprimanding someone sternly and reproachfully, or ridiculing her in front of others was thought to make an even stronger impact on a child's psyche and compliance. Girls, who by nature seemed more sensitive and gentle, were seen as prime targets of emotional shaming strategies, while strong-willed and defiant boys more often than not deserved to be given the stick as the strongest form of honour-related punishment.

Over the course of time, both sets of practices and their underlying assumptions were increasingly called into question. First, corporal punishment disappeared from children's books altogether as it was seen to violate children's right to dignity and undermine their sense of self. As much as societies came to value the concept of dignity and inscribe it into systems of education, law, and welfare, children were sheltered from degrading and derogatory treatment. If adults still resorted to physical violence, their behaviour was depicted as lacking legitimacy and public recognition. Second, and similarly, emotional shaming practices came under severe criticism especially when performed in public. Debasing a child in front of her peers, and thus inviting others to sneer at her, was no longer something authority figures should and might be allowed to do.

At the same time, those adult figures of (moral) authority were subject to sceptical inquiry as well. While many nineteenth-century books had emphasized the importance of obeying parents' or teachers' advice or else enduring shame, later authors stressed the merits of self-assertion.[67] They encouraged children to rebel against being shamed and to question rules whose violation was intended to cause shame. They showed how shame burdened children and lowered their self-esteem. This was particularly apparent in the way that shame was gendered. Whereas nineteenth-century literature was keen on stressing girls' natural modesty and boys' innate courage, twentieth-century narrators told a somewhat different story. They invented confident, risk-loving girls who deviated from earlier traditional roles. Instead of being obsessed by and ashamed of their bodies, girls were invited to embrace and expand the range of possibilities that life offered them. Authors even depicted their heroines feeling compassion for boys who were, as it seemed, trapped far longer in the normative cage of shame. For them, shame was, and remained, associated with acts of alleged unmanliness, such as crying or admitting to being scared. In Virginia Sorensen's *Miracles on Maple Hill* (1956), for example, Marly did not mind that her friend Joe had shown fear and pitied him for experiencing such strong feelings of shame: 'For the millionth time, she was glad she wasn't a boy.... if anybody caught Joe asking a dumb question or even thought he was the littlest bit scared, he went red and purple and white. Daddy was even something like that, as old as he was.'[68]

Turning red and purple (out of shame) and white (out of rage) was not something, however, that children's books came to totally discard. In one-on-one relationships, between friends or classmates, shame could at times be important and helpful since it was seen as paving the way to repentance and redress. Even as societies and social institutions became increasingly liberal and democratic, they did not let go of certain codes and models of behaviour. Rather than being enforced by authority figures, those codes and models were now tested and negotiated by citizens themselves, including children and youth. The latter were then free to introduce their own proper rules and styles, and create shaming practices and rituals of their own. Children's books were very much aware of this development and discussed it in a variety of ways. While addressing the fear of being shamed and exposed to the scorn of others, they encouraged children to stand up against it. Reflecting children's (growing) need to be members of peer groups, the books alerted them to the internal power dynamics that involved the power to shame others. But shame was not a predetermined fate that had to be passively endured. On the contrary, one should embrace it as a necessary means of self-correction, or, more often than not, resist against it.

This implied empathizing with those who suffered shame, and consequently refraining from inflicting it on others. Children's literature tried to educate young readers to free themselves of social shame attached to styles and attitudes that diverged from what conventional or peer-group power considered appropriate. Children should laugh off disapproval and ridicule instead of feeling hurt, offended, and ashamed. The difficulty of putting this into practice was a recurrent theme. Still, it seemed crucial in order to protect what was deemed more and more important: a sense of dignity, pride, and self-worth.

Nevertheless, setting a premium on personal pride did not altogether rule out shame. As an individual emotion, shame remained a staple in the stories told by children's books in the latter half of the twentieth century. Navigating personal shame, however, proved by no means easier than fending off social shame. It implied both a strong sense of oneself and a complex appraisal of one's environment. And it called for a flexible personality and the ability to smoothly adjust one's feelings and behaviour to ever-changing circumstances, while maintaining a core perception of oneself as morally decent and upright. How this could be achieved in the absence of powerful institutions and adult guardians was open to debate. Golding, in his 1954 *Lord of the Flies*, had taken a clear stance. Without institutions and guardianship, civil order would soon break down, and shame, as its main buttress, would be eradicated. As Ralph, Jack, and Simon are about to kill their first piglet they suddenly become aware of the 'place of terror' and 'laugh ashamedly'. Later, though, shame disappears and violence breakes out, claiming Piggy—and, within a hair's breadth, Ralph—as victim.[69]

NOTES

1. Golding, *Lord of the Flies*, 29, 33, 80, 157–8.
2. Epstein, 'Afterword', 203–8, quotations 204. As to the novel's literary pretexts and how they were reversed and interrogated, see Stephens and McCallum, *Retelling Stories, Framing Culture*, 270–8, 291. In English-speaking countries today, it often features on reading lists around the ninth year of school.
3. This chapter is based on a close reading of more than a hundred children's books published between the early nineteenth century and the 1970s, in Britain, the United States, France, and Germany. In addition, around forty advice manuals and journals from the same countries and same period have been chosen as major informants on educational norms and discourses.
4. Lewis, 'Shame and the Narcissistic Personality', 110.
5. Tomkins, *Affect, Imagery, Consciousness*, 118; Wurmser, *Mask of Shame*, 3, 97; Scheff and Retzinger, *Emotions and Violence*; Braithwaite, *Crime, Shame, and Reintegration*; Deonna, Rogno, and Teroni, *In Defense of Shame*. For philosophical approaches to shame, see Williams, *Shame and Necessity*; Demmerling and Landweer, *Philosophie der Gefühle*, 219–44.
6. Tomkins, 120, 123, 185.
7. Tangney, 'Self-Conscious Emotions', 542.
8. Donald L. Nathanson ('A Timetable for Shame') tends to set the date somewhat earlier. As to older children (aged five to thirteen), see Ferguson, Stegge, and Damhuis, 'Children's Understanding of Guilt and Shame'.
9. Recommendations came from American Methodists, such as William C. Brown's journal *The Mother's Assistant and Young Lady's Friend* (see, for example, 'Scene from Real Life', 74), as well as from German doctors, such as Hermann Klencke, *Die Mutter als Erzieherin ihrer Töchter und Söhne*, 433.
10. Edgeworth and Edgeworth, *Practical Education*, i, 246, 248.
11. Edgeworth, 'Angelina', 215.
12. Edgeworth, 'Rosamond', 19.
13. Edgeworth, 'Frank', 69, 157. The story about fear and cowardice was identical to the one Emile's teacher told from his own adolescence in Rousseau's 1762 'collection of reflections and observations', which is generally judged to be the first modern educational tract; Rousseau, *Emile, or, On Education*, 157 [Preface], 276–7.
14. Edgeworth and Edgeworth, *Practical Education*, i, 253.
15. 'Letters to a Younger Brother', 88 (emphasis in original).
16. Maria Edgeworth, 'The Bracelets', 28. On these stories and their appeal to child and adolescent readers (including the future Queen Victoria), see Vallone, *Becoming Victoria*, 195–8.
17. Wetherell, *Wide, Wide World*, 28. The book written by US author Susan Bogert Warner (under her pen name Elizabeth Wetherell) underwent fourteen editions within two years and was well received in Germany (first German translation in 1853 as *Die*

weite, weite Welt); it was recommended as appropriate reading for girls by Klencke, *Die Mutter als Erzieherin ihrer Töchter und Söhne*, 67, 510, for similar advice, 532; Foerster, *Lebenskunde*, 120: 'And whoever is not ashamed of their own dirty hands and nails will feel no shame about their dirty talk, and eventually choose dirty thoughts in their daily dealings' (all translations by the author). As to the equivalence of (female) cleanliness and sexual purity, see Vallone, 'True Meaning of Dirt'.

18. Hoffmann, *Der Struwwelpeter*, 2. This was how the German rhyme began. The English version was slightly milder, ending with the more courteous declaration that 'See this frowsy "cratur" | Pah! It's Struwwelpeter!'; Hoffmann, *Slovenly Peter*, 2. The book was translated into several languages and remained popular well into the twentieth century. On public shaming, see Nash and Kilday, *Cultures of Shame*, chapter 2.
19. Wetherell, *Wide, Wide World*, 67.
20. Dyer, 'Virtue'.
21. Blackwell, *Counsel to Parents*, 2, 23. For more evidence, see Klencke, *Die Mutter als Erzieherin ihrer Töchter und Söhne*, 535–6; Foerster, *Lebensführung*, 149.
22. 'Scene from Real Life', 82; Blackwell, *Counsel to Parents*, 18–22, 36–8. Blackwell actually held men more responsible for the spread of vice and licentiousness than women. Klencke, *Die Mutter als Erzieherin ihrer Söhne und Töchter*, 571; Matthias, *Wie erziehen wir unsern Sohn Benjamin*, 198–203; Faßbinder, *Am Wege des Kindes*, 292.
23. Brink, *Caddie Woodlawn*, 240, 246, 14 (emphasis in original). The book won the Newbery Medal in 1936 and the Lewis Carroll Shelf Award in 1958, and was translated into several languages.
24. Brink, 216.
25. Rhoden, *Taming a Tomboy*, 100–21, quotations 101, 102, 119.
26. In chapter 8 of Hughes's *Tom Brown's School Days*, bullies' names are 'written up on the walls with every insulting epithet'; in Farrar's *Eric, or Little by Little*, Eric feels deep shame and profound anger as he is flogged by the headmaster, 61–2, 113. In Ottilie Wildermuth's popular stories, *Aus Nord und Süd*, 128, a boy has to wear a grey paper cap with huge donkey ears. This 'shameful punishment from old times' generates laughter among his fellow students, which in turn mortifies him 'much more than the most painful correction would have done'. In a spelling competition at school in Brink's *Caddie Woodlawn*, 72: 'The best spellers were promptly snapped up, and the worst ones left simmering in their shame until the end of the choosing'.
27. Klencke, *Die Mutter als Erzieherin ihrer Töchter und Söhne*, 531–2, 555–6. See also the articles in the periodical *Mother's Assistant and Young Lady's Friend*, esp. Newcomb, 'For Maternal Associations'; Newcomb, 'Rewards and Punishments', 30–31; Ackermann, *Häusliche Erziehung*, 184–5; Schreiber, *Das Buch vom Kinde*, i, part II, 194–5; Schnell, *Ich und meine Jungens*, 137–8. Throughout the nineteenth and early twentieth centuries, shaming was discussed in pedagogical encyclopaedias under its own headword, which demonstrates its valence and ubiquity. See, for example, Reuter, *Pädagogisches Real-Lexicon*, 11–13; *Encyklopädie der Pädagogik*, i, 60; Lindner, *Encyklopädisches Handbuch der Erziehungskunde*, 110; Monroe, *Cyclopedia of Education*, 89–91.
28. Kooistra, *Sittliche Erziehung*, 78; Matthias, *Wie erziehen wir unsern Sohn Benjamin*, 103.
29. Weber, 'Marie und die beiden Sperlinge', 12; 'Kirschenmütterchen', 28; Sautier, 'Ein Unglückstag', 59; Schwahn, 'Die kleinen Freundinnen', 73; Petzel, 'Wie Hänschen das Lesen lernt', 93; Gockel, 'Warum', 37.
30. Montgomery, *Anne of Green Gables*, 157–8.
31. Montgomery, 92.
32. Montgomery, 159.

33. Marryat, *Masterman Ready*. The first German translation appeared the very same year and sold well into the twentieth century.
34. Grahame, *Wind in the Willows*, 259, 295, 265, 295, 299.
35. Twain, *Adventures of Huckleberry Finn*, 133.
36. See Hetzer, *Seelische Hygiene*, 53; Haarer, *Unsere kleinen Kinder*, 240.
37. Streatfeild, *Ballet Shoes*, 174.
38. Beecher-Stowe, *Uncle Tom's Cabin*, i, 121.
39. Hoffmann, 'Tale of the Young Black Chap' in *Slovenly Peter*, not paginated.
40. Edgeworth, 'Rosanna', 172.
41. Edgeworth, 'The Manufacturers', 284.
42. Dielitz, 'Alpen-Wanderung', 83.
43. Wildermuth, *Aus Nord und Süd*, 73.
44. Edgeworth, 'Rosanna', 126; A., 'Julia Litchfield and Helen May', 42–6.
45. Nesbit, *Story of the Treasure Seekers*, 268. See also Nesbit, *Railway Children*, 187.
46. Carroll, *Alice's Adventures in Wonderland*, 38, 68, 142. See also Klencke, *Die Mutter als Erzieherin ihrer Töchter und Söhne*, 491.
47. Baum, *Wonderful Wizard of Oz*, 43.
48. Verne, *Adrift in the Pacific*, 120–1.
49. Pergaud, *War of the Buttons*, 50. See chapter 8, 'Lebrac's Pain'.
50. Kästner, *Flying Classroom*, 112–13. See also Sperry, *Call it Courage*.
51. See chapter 9, 'Jim Button's Fear'.
52. Hughes, *Tom Brown's School Days*, 252. Tom also learnt to stand up against 'this bullying, persecuting spirit, so common in all schools', which was criticized as 'the most hateful trait in the character of many schoolboys' by Edward Huntingford, *Advice to School-Boys*, 123; see also *Boys and their Ways*, 111–18.
53. Streatfeild, *Circus is Coming*, 129.
54. Blyton, *Twins at St. Clare's*, 152–3.
55. Blyton, *Five on a Treasure Island*, 113.
56. Blyton, 19–20.
57. Blume, *Blubber*, 89, 148, 62.
58. Rommel, *Der goldene Schleier*, 194; praised as the 'most beautiful book for girls' in 1956.
59. See, for example, Blume, *Blubber*, 62; Wölfel, *Tim Fireshoe*, 5.
60. Burnett, *Little Lord Fauntleroy*, 109, 139.
61. Kästner, *Annaluise and Anton*, 95–6.
62. Held, *Outsiders of Uskoken Castle*.
63. Lindgren, *Pippi in the South Seas*, 40–52.
64. Lewis, 'Shame and the Narcissistic Personality', 95–6.
65. Lowenfeld, 'Notes on Shamelessness', 69; see also Hoffer, 'Long Live Shame'.
66. Norbert Elias, *Civilizing Process*, i.
67. Advice manuals similarly changed gears, with the exception of Johanna Haarer's highly influential books, which deliberately contradicted early twentieth century tendencies to 'question the principle of absolute and unconditional obedience'; Haarer, *Unsere kleinen Kinder*, 236; see also Haarer, *Deutsche Mutter und ihr erstes Kind*, 259–60.
68. Sorensen, *Miracles on Maple Hill*, 99.
69. Golding, *Lord of the Flies*, 40.

8

Lebrac's Pain

Anja Laukötter

The War of the Buttons (1968; Fre. orig. *La guerre des boutons*, 1912), by Louis Pergaud, describes the adventures of young Lebrac and his gang, the Longevernes. The novel recounts in detail the numerous pain-inflicting fights between the Longevernes and their rival gang from the neighbouring school, the Velrans. In one of these scuffles, the protagonist falls into the hands of his opponents:

> He didn't even have time to say 'Ouf!' Before he could rise to his knees twelve of them had pinned him down, and wham! bing! bang! pow! they grabbed all four limbs while somebody else went through his pockets and confiscated his knife. Then, using his own handkerchief, they gagged him.... Since Lebrac wasn't the kind of man to take things lying down, his buttocks were soon beaten so black and blue that he had no choice but to lie still.... and Lebrac, vanquished, stripped, and whipped, was set free in the same pitiful condition that Big-Assed Squinty had been five days earlier.[1]

The fights between these gangs of youths take place without any intervention or even knowledge on the part of the adults. The educational efforts by their naïve parents are limited to doling out similarly painful beatings, a prospect of which Lebrac is certain even before arriving home:

> When he was put together as well as could be expected, he inspected his accouter-ments [*sic*] with a melancholy eye, mentally estimating the number of kicks in the behind that his appearance would cost him. Then he summed up his apprehensions in a laconic phrase that wrenched the very heartstrings of his men: "Christ! What a shellacking I'm going to get at home!"[2]

At home on this occasion, Lebrac is in fact so heavily beaten by his father that he writhes in pain, screaming so loudly that the windows vibrate. Pondering all his pain and misery, he remains sleepless for a long while.[3]

LEARNING HOW TO FEEL PAIN

The feeling of pain is central in *The War of the Buttons*, as it was in many other children's books from the late nineteenth century to the end of the twentieth century.

The term 'war' in the book's title ironically implies that this pain is not caused by disease, but is meted out in physical confrontations, defined as injury-inflicting acts perpetrated by one body on another, and occurring between both individuals and groups. It is assumed that the sensation of pain can, in principle, arise not only from injuries to the body, but also to the mind. Loss, longing, and shame in front of another person can, for example, be perceived as painful experiences. This broadening of the concept of pain corresponds to new approaches in both the history of emotions and in medicine, and the focus on pain related to physical confrontations in this chapter is therefore merely a pragmatic decision.[4] The conflict scene between the Longevernes and the Velrans described above offers an example of the diverse manifestations of the feeling of pain in such confrontations and thus highlights the key points of this chapter.[5]

In *The War of the Buttons*, pain appears in two kinds of relationships, each with a different meaning, namely relationships between children and parents or teachers, and peer-relationships among children. When Lebrac's father beats him yet again because his clothes are soiled after all his fighting, the narrative creates an association between pain and pedagogical incompetence, lack of educational principles, and superfluous comments on the part of the father.[6] In line with the etymological origins of the word 'pain'—*peine* in French, *Pein* in German, and *poena* in Latin, meaning punishment—pain is used here as a form of penalty or reprimand.[7] Lebrac's parents' method of education, based on pain and aimed at raising obedient, modest, trustful, and ambitious children, appears doomed to fail. However, in the story, Lebrac's friends do not simply suffer helplessly at the hands of their parents. Rather, they defy their guardians by keeping their actual daytime pursuits within the confines of a secret double life. Although they frequently feel severe pain, the children do not disclose their peer-group activities, thus reversing the asymmetrical power relationship between themselves and adults. Despite their aches and agonies, they are the 'winners' in this situation, while their parents remain oblivious.

On the whole, the children's relationships with adults (parents and teachers) play only a minor role in the narrative. The story focuses instead on the fights between the Longeverne and the Velran gangs, both consisting of boys around the same age.[8] These peer-group relationships are described in a rather ambivalent manner in terms of the emotions involved, including the feeling of pain. It becomes especially obvious here that pain does not appear as a singular emotion in these conflicts. Rather, the emotions accompanying pain are dependent on the situation and the agents involved, and can range from fear to anger and despair. Moreover, the boundary between 'perpetrators' and 'victims' is less than clear: at one point Lebrac experiences tremendous physical pain as a prisoner of the Velrans, but is desensitized to it because of his anger, contempt, and hatred for them. On another occasion, the Longevernes capture Big-Assed Squinty, a member of the Velrans, in revenge and subject him to painful blows that he is forced to bear while sobbing and moaning. But it is the anticipated pain generated by the threat to cut off an ear which eventually has maximum effect and makes Big-Assed Squinty tremble with fear.[9] The boundary between attackers and attacked is blurred in these fights, because a fight for honour dictates retaliation after a painful blow. In addition to the numerous expletives, the regularity, severity, and seriousness of the fights are astonishing: choking, biting, pulling out hair, nose bleeds, and the like, are commonplace.[10] However, as the narrative progresses it becomes evident that these fights occur within certain commonly accepted limits. The experience of pain is described as a process of negotiation between these rival groups and is, therefore, an important part of their learning process.

Moreover, the possibility for pain itself to be heterogeneously interpreted is evident. Nineteenth-century discourses often highlighted the close relation between pain and pleasure. According to present-day interpretations, pain resulting from fights is discussed in connection with bullying, among other things whereas in the intense, strategic fights of the Longevernes described in *The War of the Buttons*, the emphasis is on pleasure.[11] Pain is not exclusively associated with suffering produced by fighting, but pain is also a prerequisite for perceiving the situation as pleasurable. In this context, the experience of pain is an important part of the boys' group identity and in-group feeling, and may also have a community-building function as part of an initiation rite or courage test. Pain is understood here not only as an intense subjective experience,[12] but also as an inter-subjective reality through its expression.[13] It is thus a reciprocal process between an inner emotional state and a performed act.[14] This latter element, including gestures, attitudes, and expressions, is what enables us to observe and evaluate pain as an emotion.[15] It is formed by a social reality and shaped by cultural factors such as gender, social class, and religion. In this sense the emotion of pain and its relative meaning is something that has to be learnt.[16]

In investigating the manner in which we learn how to feel pain, children's books and advice manuals are an important source in the process of constructing meaning in Western societies. *The War of the Buttons* and many other children's books not only describe how pain can variously occur in the context of physical confrontations, these books also provide knowledge on the different expressions of the emotion pain in particular situations, and the meanings ascribed to them. Furthermore, they provide a repertoire of semantic descriptions of pain through the use of 'as though' phrases and metaphors, such as when protagonist Lebrac screams so loudly in pain that the windows rattle.[17] These books offer practical knowledge as to how physical confrontations are experienced and with which attendant feelings—namely, they offer knowledge on the meanings of pain and how pain may be understood, which renders them an important tool for mimetic learning. Likewise, advice manuals for parents on children's development are a useful source for this investigation as they are not only strongly normative, but are also oriented toward imparting clear guidelines for social *practice*. Advice manuals aimed to clarify whether, and in what manner and intensity, pain should be a part of children's education.[18]

Pergaud's novel was first published in France in 1912, and quickly became a success with over thirty editions printed. Eventually, after a delay of half a century, its success also extended beyond French borders.[19] In light of this, the children's books and advice manuals from the mid-nineteenth century to the late twentieth century examined here have been used to explore multiple dimensions of pain as an emotion within a transnational context, incorporating Germany, France, and the English-speaking world.

This chapter will investigate in what manner and in which situations pain is described and how it is experienced, perceived, and handled. Addressing inter-generational relationships first, and then peer groups, it will analyse when and why pain is interpreted as a threat, as a method of disciplining, or as a liberating or group-forming instrument. Furthermore, it will explore how and why these different concepts of pain changed over time from the mid-nineteenth century to the late twentieth century. It will examine in which relationships the approach of a pain-free education appears and whether this occurred as part of a vision of a humane society or as a result of humanitarian activism.[20]

PAIN IN INTERGENERATIONAL RELATIONSHIPS— FROM EDUCATIONAL PRACTICE TO PERCEIVED THREAT

A central motive connected with the feeling of pain in intergenerational rela-tionships is the education of the unruly and disobedient child who sometimes causes other people or even animals pain. One form of the emotional assessment of 'pain-causing children' is paradigmatically introduced in *Slovenly Peter* (1850; Ger. orig. *Struwwelpeter*, 1845). This book not only had multiple editions and translations, but also provoked many adaptations, even in local dialects, and var-ied narratives well into the twentieth century, including narrative adjustments to the political system, and alternative concepts of education and gender to cater to different readership interests.[21] In the original version with protagonists Frederick and Konrad, the way in which deviant behaviour is physically sanctioned is explic-itly described and obviously exaggerated.[22] While the stubborn Frederick suffers from a pain in his leg, a consequence of his mistreatment of animals, the dis-obedient Konrad loses his thumb which results in tears and great sadness. In his world-famous picture book *Max and Maurice* (1871; Ger. orig. *Max und Moritz*, 1865), Wilhelm Busch provides a more complex narrative. He too poses the idea of pain (and even death) as an answer for disobedience.[23] The bourgeois adults, whose attitude is described in a sarcastic tone, fear the anarchic power of the parent-less protagonists. Moreover, the protagonists' evil tricks against both animals and human beings have painful consequences for the victims (strong grief, near drown-ing, and exploded bodies). This leads to an aggressive counter-strike by the farmer and the miller designed to restore the adults' authority: the bodies of the chil-dren are taken apart in a mill (see Fig. 8.1). The message here is that pain-causing actions bear even more painful consequences, and the book's illustrations reveal that the adults' actions are governed by intense feelings of revenge and pleasure. In an obviously hierarchical structure, pain serves the enforcement of obedience and discipline in such stories. It is an educational tool controlled by the parent or educator, and thus directly connected with the learning process of children.

Fig. 8.1 Wilhelm Busch, *Max and Maurice* (1871), 54.

Uncle Tom's Cabin (1852) by Harriet Beecher-Stowe is also set in an extremely violent world. This plea against racism and slavery continued to be widely read throughout the twentieth century. Its impact on readers was even discussed by Sigmund Freud, who argued that the multitude of abuse incidents described in the book compounded fantasies of being beaten in children.[24] As far as children's education is concerned, the use of violence in *Uncle Tom's Cabin* is prominent mainly in a scene involving Topsy, a maltreated slave girl, and her adoptive guardian, the Christian, bourgeois, and childless Miss Ophelia.[25] In line with the regulation of emotions outlined in Christian advice literature, Miss Ophelia follows distinct rules in educating the girl: she is to obey and, mainly, to learn the catechism, and if she lies, then the process has failed. These educational norms are eventually put to the test. When Miss Ophelia discovers that Topsy not only tells lies, but even steals, Topsy demands to be beaten, the same punishment she had witnessed being meted out to her slave parents. Miss Ophelia, doubting that corporal punishment is the appropriate tool for Topsy's tutelage, is perplexed: 'What is to be done with her, then?'[26] Her nephew reminds her that she will have to beat the child hard if she wants to make an impression on her. Finally, and in exasperation, she strikes Topsy, but not very hard. Miss Ophelia's doubts about the effectiveness of pain as an educational tool are embedded into the book's overall criticism of violence, which focuses on the maltreatment of slaves who are deprived of all rights. The book describes how they are humiliated, beaten (even to death), exploited, sold, separated from their partners and children, and regarded as inferior, non-human beings. The descriptions extend to their reactions to this vicious cycle of fear and pain, including escape, counter-violence, alcoholism, and suicide. Beecher-Stowe's novel has therefore been described as a critical voice against pain-inflicting practices in former colonies.[27]

Miss Ophelia's doubts about her actions reflected a broader debate on the adequacy of pain as an educational tool in countries such as the United States, Britain, France, and Germany, which lasted throughout the late nineteenth century and into the early twentieth century. The debate found its institutional expression in the establishment of the New York Society for the Prevention of Cruelty to Children in 1875. This newly founded society had broad international appeal and inspired similar foundations in several other countries.[28] Furthermore, advice manuals by renowned authors such as Ellen Key's *The Century of the Child* (1909; Swe. orig. *Barnets århundrade*, 1900) and Heinrich Lhotzky's *The Soul of Your Child* (1924; Ger. orig. *Die Seele Deines Kindes*, 1909), or Félix Hément's *Petit traité des punitions et des récompenses* ('A short treaty on punishment and reward', 1890), all denounced cruelty to children and advocated the abandonment of corporal punishment, which was still popular at the time.[29] Children were now to be regarded as equal to adults and inflicting pain on them was therefore a deplorable practice that undermined their personality.[30] These authors favoured trust in the self-regulatory processes of children instead.[31]

This approach can be seen in children's books such as Selma Lagerlöf's adventure story *The Wonderful Adventures of Nils* (1907; Swe. orig. *Nils Holgerssons underbara resa genom Sverige*, 1906/1907).[32] As with *Slovenly Peter* and *Max and Maurice*, the main character here is a moody and self-centred child who willfully inflicts pain on everyone around him. Nils is transformed, not through the strictness and pain-inflicting actions of the parents, but through sharing experiences with others. His maltreatment of animals and his disobedient behaviour towards his parents has certain physical consequences as, by magic, he shrinks and becomes tiny. Nils embarks on a journey with wild geese and by living with animals is able to experience friendship and the feeling of trust. He learns to empathize with others and in doing so is able to overcome his own aggressive tendencies.[33] In the end, he is rewarded by being returned to his normal size and by the prospect of a happy life. In a similar way, the protagonist Mary, in Frances Hodgson Burnett's *The Secret Garden* (1911), has to learn to keep her anger under control and not 'slap' the new service personnel as she used to do.[34] By living with the house staff, and through their excursions in the countryside, she outgrows her aggressive behaviour and loneliness, acquiring a new zest for life, at the same time helping her cousin achieve a similar change in his personality. Both novels thus demonstrate in a didactic manner how mastering one's own deviant, pain-inducing attitude and feelings can lead to a successful life. In this sense, it is not the experience of feeling pain, but rather overcoming the practice of causing pain that is the effective starting point for a positive personality change.

This new interpretation of pain based on the work of prominent advice authors was not met with exclusively positive responses. Opponents were of the opinion that adults administering punishments that caused pain to children were an appropriate and necessary means for combating obstinacy, disobedience, and dishonesty in children from a very early age.[35] Drawing on Christian traditions, they argued that pain inflicted by parents was an educational tool based on the intimate relation between body and soul, and in this way it was constructed as an integral part

Fig. 8.2 Louis Pergaud, *Der Krieg der Knöpfe*, trans. Gerda von Uslar (Hamburg: Dressler, 1997) [Fre. orig. *La guerre des boutons* (1912)], 71.

of pedagogy.[36] Hence the French proverb 'he who loves well, chastises well' was well known not only in France, but also in Germany, and across the English-speaking world.[37] The actions of Lebrac's father in *The War of the Buttons* adhere to this tradition (see Fig. 8.2). In addition to Ellen Key, other authors highlighted the effects of 'tyrannical' corporal punishment. Parents should be able to control their own passions, especially rage, and act in a level-headed manner.[38] The theme of enraged parents is also central with regard to pain in children's books. In Mark Twain's *The Adventures of Huckleberry Finn*, first published in 1884 and shortly thereafter translated into German and French, it is implied that the widow with whom Huck lives at that time beats him for skipping school.[39] The story, however, focuses more on the educational methods of Huck's father, described as aggressive, violent, and completely unable to control his emotions, who forces Huck to accompany him, and beats him for going to school, failing to give him money, or simply for no reason at all. Huck faces him with cunning and usually manages to avoid physical confrontation, but when his father locks him in a cabin for three days in a row, he formulates a clever plan to escape, and eventually goes on to experience numerous adventures with his companion Jim. The violence in the story highlights the father's incompetence as a parent and guardian. Advice literature of the time explicitly addressed this lack of control over one's emotions. For Huck Finn, though, the pain he has endured is the main catalyst for his escape to freedom and adventure. In other words, pain disqualifies the father as a parent and activates the protagonist, who has to endure not only pain, but also fear and shame, to become a hero and to pave the way for a better life.[40]

Along the same lines, and similar to the *Pucki* series (1935–41),[41] but this time with a prominent Nazi background, is the story of *Der Hitlerjunge Quex* ('Hitler Youth Quex', 1932).[42] This explicitly political conversion narrative tells the story of Heini, who very often experiences physical pain, accompanied by fear and rage, at the hands of his unemployed, alcoholic, and communist father. In this desperate situation, and in search of friendship and a feeling of belonging, he becomes a member of the Hitler Youth, where he experiences comradeship and security before dying a martyr's death.[43] Although the book was made into a film in Nazi Germany it was never translated into any other language.[44] *Der Hitlerjunge Quex* and *The Adventures of Huckleberry Finn* share a narrative structure, albeit from opposite political perspectives, in which the parental failure and the experience of pain become the main catalysts for the protagonist's actions.

Such books written within a realist frame of reference stand in sharp contrast to the fantasy worlds created by writers like Erich Kästner and Antoine de Saint-Exupéry, which defy hierarchical structures and create a kind of parallel world. In *The 35th of May* (1933; Ger. orig. *Der 35. Mai*, 1933), a book that quickly became popular not only in Germany, but also in the United States, Britain, and France, Kästner similarly describes a father who uses painful punishments to make his son more resilient.[45] When the father, a butcher, lands in a kind of juvenile paradise where children reign, his actions are punished with painful blows to the head. Thus, the principle exhibited in *Max and Maurice*, that pain brings on more pain, is transferred and expanded into the adult world. The goal of this inversion is to educate parents on the basis of their own physical experience, to learn emphatically what pain-inflicting actions feel like. This 'school for parents' was thus designed to help prevent future violence and pain. Maurice Druon's *Tistou of the Green Fingers* (1958; Fre. orig. *Tistou les pouces verts*, 1957), inspired by the internationally famous *The Little Prince* (1943; Fre. orig. *Le petit prince*, 1943) by Antoine de Saint-Exupéry, also takes place in a fantasy world, in which the relationships between adults and children and the role of pain are reinterpreted.[46] Here, the protagonist Tistou is able to survive painful wars unscathed, just as the lion is able to kill the witch in *The Lion, the Witch and the Wardrobe* (1950).[47]

In his widely read advice manual, *The Common Sense Book of Baby and Child Care* (1946) Benjamin Spock introduced his perspective on the use of pain in education.[48] Although he allowed for exceptions ('no parent...is always happy and reasonable'), he condemned physical pain in general as it saddens and weakens children, often provoking even worse behaviour. If punishment in any form is replaced by love, respect, and trust, it will not only prevent children from stealing and lying, but it will also teach them in general to do the right thing. According to Spock, children learn to control their own feelings.[49] Less tolerant than Spock of lapses in respectful parenting was A. S. Neill's *Summerhill*, published in 1960 and widely translated in subsequent years, which strongly supported an 'education without fear' approach.[50] Parents had to create an atmosphere of love and respect for children, whereas discipline and punishment generated fear that, in turn, generated hostility.[51] Hence, the use of pain as an educational and disciplinary tool was, in Neill's view, an act of hate.[52] He described cruelty as perverted love, and extreme sadism as perverted sexuality.[53] Although advice manuals that favoured pain as a last resort were still on the market, both Spock's and Neill's educational models inspired new school concepts, the most famous being Summerhill, an English school based on freedom and self-governance by children. These new ideas and institutions were quite influential, strengthening demands for the abolition of corporal punishment.[54] What implications did this have for children's books? Did the use of pain in intergenerational relationships disappear in the second half of the twentieth century?

At first glance, children's books such as *Strawberry Girl* (1945) by Lois Lenski seem to build on familiar narratives.[55] The story describes the confrontations between two American farm families. Envy and resentment mark their relationship, fuelled by social and economic inequalities, leading to clashes with numerous physical altercations. As with *The Adventures of Huckleberry Finn*, these conflicts are aggravated by the alcoholism of Sam Slater, the father of the poorer family, who suffers from uncontrollable emotional outbursts, which seem to cause the pain-inducing scraps between the families to escalate. Only an illness leads to a crisis and to the ensuing change that resolves the conflict. Unlike *The Wonderful Adventures of Nils* or *The Secret Garden*, it is not just children who must learn to change and control their behaviour and emotions, but also the parents. A positive outcome in *Strawberry Girl* can only be obtained through the characters' emotional work on themselves. Moreover, pain obtains a new dimension here with respect to how it is described in the narrative. Although pain-inflicting attacks pervade the story, they are implied within depictions of specific social practices rather than being described directly in detail. In other words, the performative part of how to feel pain is removed from the field of direct mimesis and transferred into the realm of the readers' imagination.

In Russell Hoban's *Bedtime for Frances* (1960), pain is likewise discussed as part of the social reality, but with a different nuance. This bedtime book for younger children introduces the badger parents and their daughter, Frances, who procrastinates to avoid going to bed with several requests (for kisses, milk, comfort against her fears of tigers, etc.). At first, all her needs are accommodated very gently, until she wakes her father up because she is scared of the moving curtain. Her father explains that 'everybody has a job to do' and must act accordingly, otherwise they will lose their job. Frances's job is to sleep,

> "And if you do not go to sleep now, do you know what will happen to you?"
> "I will be out of a job?" said Frances.
> "No", said Father.
> "I will get a spanking?" said Frances.
> "Right!" said Father.[56]

In other words, the possibilities to indulge one's emotions have limits. When it comes to fulfilling duties Frances is expected and required to manage her own emotions (in this case fear), otherwise she will be confronted with pain. She accordingly overcomes her fear and sleeps through until morning.[57] It must be emphasized that although corporal punishment never actually takes place in the book, it is certainly introduced as a threat and as such it is still part of Frances's social reality, yet the threat can only be effective when linked to the very real prospect of an actual beating. Such a threat in the air is also present in Astrid Lindgren's *Emil of Lönneberga* series (7 vols, 1970–86; Swe. orig. *Emil i Lönneberga* series, 12 vols, 1963–97) where the protagonist frequently has to flee to avoid getting spanked by his extremely enraged father.[58] With the exception of one scene, in which his father hurts Emil by forcefully grasping his arm and shaking him, physical pain is never actually inflicted.[59]

Even though pain proves to be effective as an unrealized threat in both *Emil of Lönneberga* and *Bedtime for Frances*, the two books differ regarding the moral outcomes they present. Whereas for Frances, the threat of being beaten by her father helps her to overcome her fear, no such emotional advancement occurs for Emil, who is continually forced to evade his desperate and overstrained father. Nevertheless, he is compensated for his troubles when the wooden figures he carves at his place of refuge later help him to become famous in his village.[60]

While Emil's character is depicted as somewhat vulnerable, next to him the heroine of Astrid Lindgren's *Pippi Longstocking* (1945; Swe. orig. *Pippi Långstrump*, 1945) seems untouchable.[61] In Pippi's world the experience of pain seems to be no danger at all, due to her own physical strength and cunning both in escaping any attempts at her 'proper' upbringing and defending herself in conflicts with adults. She is able to evade the childcare worker, win a fight in an amusement park, and even stop burglars. One could argue that pain is always present precisely through its negation, yet it also becomes superfluous for Pippi's emotional education. In this sense, Lindgren created Pippi Longstocking as a character that not only transcended contemporary gender models and educational institutions (family and school), but also the use of pain in learning how to feel in intergenerational relationships.

This does not mean that pain disappeared altogether. In some children's books, such as René Goscinny's *Young Nicolas* (1961; Fre. orig. *Le petit Nicolas*, 1960), as well as *The War of the Buttons* translated into both German and English in the 1960s, pain is still presented as a common practice in the educational process (by parents and teachers).[62] In these books, however, pain as an educational tool tends to play a marginal role, whereas pain in physical confrontations among peer groups is in the foreground.

PAIN IN PEER GROUPS—FROM SUFFERING TO PLEASURE

In general, physical altercations among peer groups in children's books usually take place in two specific settings: either in boarding schools or among 'free' gangs that operate largely independently of adults, but often have a reference to school. Until the twentieth century, schools were portrayed as institutions in which discipline prevailed through violence. Thus teachers inflicting pain on students in these books are not uncommon, but nor are they in the foreground. While gang formation is usually temporary in nature, schoolboy fiction includes a longer-term perspective, namely the transition from a public school boyhood toward manhood, in which the questions and problems of growing up are addressed.[63] In both cases the composition of the group is usually dictated by the age and sex of the children.[64]

Thomas Hughes's *Tom Brown's School Days* (1857) is paradigmatic of typical British schoolboy fiction, but was very quickly translated into many other languages and became very popular in Germany and France in particular.[65] *Eric, or, Little by Little* (1858), Frederic W. Farrar's strongly religious novel, also belongs to this genre, and enjoyed great popularity in England.[66] In terms of pain, these novels also describe teachers causing pain, but the primary focus is on peer-group practices of bullying. In *Tom Brown's School Days* these include daily humiliation and pain inflicted by the older boys on younger, more devoted students.[67] Tom, the main character, initially feels helpless when confronted by the practice of 'tossing', but is later glorified because he overcomes the trial without showing fear: '[He] took his three tosses without a kick or a cry, and was called a young trump for his pains.'[68] Even before starting school, Tom's father had warned him about the 'great many cruel blackguard things' that may confront him there and advised him that he should neither have nor express any fear.[69] Despite following this advice, the fighting escalates. During a bullying ritual of 'toasting' boys by fire, Tom even loses consciousness. And when Tom and his friend Harry refuse to give in to the demands of an older student, more painful altercations follow. But Tom triumphs again, as he does not cry and even strikes back.[70] He eventually undergoes a change when he becomes the mentor of George Arthur Arnold, an intimidated Christian classmate, with whom he develops a deep friendship and love.[71] When his protégé is attacked by another rough pupil, Tom challenges the antagonist to a boxing match. Despite bloodied lips and lumps on his face, Tom defends the fight as one for honour and virtue.[72] His hurting, pain-riddled body thus becomes a vehicle for morality. The principle that moral discipline can, if necessary, be enforced through physical discipline reflected the concomitant educational ideas of the second half of the nineteenth century.[73] Thus, in Part Two of his novel, and in a manner reminiscent of an advice manual, Thomas Hughes writes that battles for honour and justice should be fought without fear of physical pain. Boys could indeed refuse to fight, but they should state clearly the reasons for their refusal:

> It's a proof of the highest courage, if done from true Christian motives. It's quite right and justifiable, if done from a simple aversion to physical pain and danger. But don't say 'No' because you fear a licking, and say or think it's because you fear God, for that's neither Christian nor honest.[74]

In Rudyard Kipling's *Stalky & Co.* (1899) fear of pain plays a more marginal role. Physical confrontations and shaming practices in the fight for honour are also commonplace among the boys, but unlike Tom in *Tom Brown's School Days*, the main character Stalky (like the title character in *Eric, or Little by Little*) is not the ideal noble hero. Rather, he fights gleefully, employing cunningly deceptive tricks. The confrontations reach a climax as Stalky and his friends avenge a younger classmate, Clewer, who has been bullied by the older students. They use the same bullying practices as their opponents, resorting to physical violence, shaming and fear tactics, as well as a kind of interrogation in which they demand answers to various questions. Eventually, their victims capitulate in sheer desperation.[75] Like *Tom Brown's School Days*, *Stalky & Co.* also contains descriptions of an intense application of pain, which knows few limits. Moreover, these actions are viewed positively by adults, in this case by the Reverend, who claims that such painful experiences are much more effective in children's education than the efforts of adults.[76] This position is in line with the advice book *Youth* (1906) by G. Stanley Hall which declared that 'An able-bodied young man, who can not fight physically, can hardly have a high and true sense of honor, and is generally a milk-sop, a lady-boy, or a sneak. He lacks virility, his masculinity does not ring true, his honesty can not be sound to the core.'[77] This corresponded to popular notions regarding the education of boys, whose fights were described by another advice manual author, John Willis Slaughter, as a form of 'healthy locking of horns' in the sense of Aristotelian catharsis: 'the few bruises received are a small price to pay for the moral benefits involved'.[78] Explicitly described pain, as with *Tom Brown's School Days*, is constructed as a necessary part of growing up and especially as an important self-regulatory process among children.

While not explicitly named as such, bullying practices among groups of boys also feature strongly in Pergaud's *The War of the Buttons*. Here the fights are likewise about honour, and, in a sense, justice. Yet, unlike the schoolboy fiction discussed above that takes place in an adult-dominated educational environment with boundaries set by adults, the painful attacks in Lebrac's adult-free world have limits silently agreed upon by the boys themselves. Moreover, Lebrac and his peers' time and distance from adults is especially emphasized. It is not the violent parents and teachers who educate the children, but the children themselves. Acting out emotions (including pain) during the fights is not only a form of self-regulation, but also constitutes (the only) 'free' space in their violent educational environment. It is also understood that the pain occurring in fights between the Longevernes and the Velrans can be interpreted mainly as a kind of pleasure in its function for group-identity formation.

The question of free space for children and young people (or the power of parents' intervention) became an important educational issue at the end of the nineteenth century in France, Germany, and Britain.[79] A negative portrayal of this adult-free time was put forward in the internationally popular French novel *Adrift in the Pacific* (1889; Fre. orig. *Deux ans de vacances*, 1888) by Jules Verne, about students from a liberal boarding school who get stranded on a deserted island and attempt to organize their lives without adults. A looming brawl is averted by the leader, who stresses the destabilizing effect of pain-inflicting clashes, and appeals to the aggressor's sense of responsibility by advising him to channel his anger differently.[80] In this context, pain is offset by the children themselves.

Erich Kästner's *The Flying Classroom* (1934; Ger. orig. *Das fliegende Klassenzimmer*, 1933) offers another view on the connection between children's environments, their behaviour, and their emotions. This boarding school story, with its trusty and friendly character of the teacher Bökh, takes place in a liberal environment where the struggle for the greater good finds support.[81] Interestingly, in addition to feelings of courage, rage, and pleasure, fear is also addressed in relation to a pain-causing duel with the protagonist Uli. Through Uli's friendship with the strongest and bravest boy, Matthias, fear acquires a positive connotation. While in *Tom Brown's School Days* the fear of pain performs a primarily dramatic function, *The Flying Classroom* explores not only the conquering of fear, but also the legitimacy of feeling it when confronted with pain.[82] The narrative allows for pain to be felt individually in a supportive and understanding environment: it presents, in other words, options for the experience of feelings. Kurt Held's *The Outsiders of Uskoken Castle* (1967; Ger. orig. *Die Rote Zora und ihre Bande*, 1941) follows a similar model. In this widely read book, Held describes the anarchic life of a clique of five children which, like Enid Blyton's *Five on a Treasure Island* (1942), includes several boys and one girl. As with Kästner's *The Flying Classroom*, the clique never uses pain for selfish or mean reasons, but only in self-defence or where they must fight for the rights of their friends (both children and adults) and against the ruling (violent) system—in other words, pain is only used in the interests of freedom and justice. It is not the children's physical conflicts that are inherently violent, but rather the system that determines the children's behaviour, leaving them no other option.[83] For this reason *The Outsiders of Uskoken* prefigures Benjamin Spock's approach.

Spock holds parents explicitly responsible for ensuring the non-violent behaviour of children. For him parents must provide a friendly environment that enables children to be willing to do the right thing.[84] According to Spock, a child does not simply *have* 'aggressive' or 'violent feelings', but can also learn to control them 'through the unfolding of his own nature and the good relationship he has with his parents'.[85] In 1938, in the preface of his novel *The Last Man Alive* (1938), A. S. Neill had already touched on the importance of acting out emotions in children's own development: 'One could argue that if children can live out their aggressive fantasies at nine they will be unlikely to be aggressive at 40.'[86] Furthermore, he argued, children know their limits in a suitable environment. Neill asserted (perhaps in reference to *Adrift in the Pacific*) that 'any group of free children would never kill each other when wrecked on an island'.[87] Accordingly, the 'violent feelings' which manifest in pain resulting from peer-group fights form an important component of a specific phase in a child's development. 'Suppression' of these feelings might lead to exacerbation, and acting them out was therefore a vital prerequisite for overcoming them.[88] This argument positing the developmental necessity of 'violent feelings' and self-awareness was also supported by liberal educators in the context of youth conflicts in the 1950s, but was expanded to include a therapeutic nuance: attacks to inflict pain were now interpreted as an expression of boredom, frustration, and anger on the part of individuals in the 'emotional crisis of adolescence'.[89]

In this respect, the novel *Lord of the Flies* (1954) can be read as a kind of antithesis to Benjamin Spock's trust in the self-control of violent feelings. Again the story revolves around children stranded on a desert island, but while the main character and leader Ralph tries to establish a new world within a framework of rules, rights, obedience, and self-discipline, he is challenged by his antagonist Jack, who starts a vicious cycle of attacks that even result in two killings. Although Ralph is not involved in the killings, the book describes how 'contagious' the lust for violence can be, even for him.[90] Here, unlike *Adrift in the Pacific*, a world absent of adult regulation does not lead to pain-free self-organization and management of emotions by child protagonists, but devolves instead into a hell of unleashed violence and terror. Ralph flees fearing for his life and is rescued with the help of adults on a warship. Originally not written as a children's book, the novel is an exception in its phenomenology of pain.

This exception aside, in fact two other models of children's novels dominated the book market in the second half of the twentieth century: those in which peer groups have no conflicts (or disagreements are resolved peacefully) and those in which pain is introduced in the form of a game. The first model is exemplified in books like *Alfred Hitchcock and The Three Investigators* (1964–90) by Robert Arthur and the little band in Astrid Lindgren's *Ronia, the Robber's Daughter* (1983; Swe. orig. *Ronja Rövardotter*, 1981), both of which belong to a narrative tradition that includes earlier works such as *Emil and the Detectives* (1930; Ger. orig. *Emil und die Detektive*, 1929) and *Five on a Treasure Island*.[91] In all of these books, painful experiences do not feature in the repertoire of learning how to feel. The second model is epitomized in books such as Goscinny's *Young Nicolas*. Here, practices of boxing, punches, kicks, and slaps are daily occurrences among the members of the group headed by Nicolas and are described in the context of school situations (see Fig. 8.3). It seems that every conflict ends in pain, but in contrast to books like *Tom Brown's School Days* or *Stalky & Co* the endless fights in *Young Nicolas* do not concern larger questions of honour or justice. Their aim is not to shame others, and, importantly, no one seems to *suffer* under pain in this story. Rather, these playful physical altercations seem to be the only form of communication among the children. Nicolas describes the pleasure he feels especially in these mutual pain-inflicting actions, and seen through his eyes, the stories have a humorous character. This underlines the harmless and frolicsome nature that is attached to the feeling of pain. Similarly, the highly successful novel *The Best Christmas Pageant Ever* (1972) by Barbara Robinson describes the Herdmanns' very violent children (boys

Fig. 8.3 René Goscinny, *Der kleine Nick und seine Bande*, trans. Hans Georg Lenzen (Zürich: Diogenes, 2001) [Fre. orig. *Le petit Nicolas* (1960)], 68.

and girls) in a humorous manner.[92] At the same time, their unpredictable and often very painful attacks on other children are explained as a product of parental neglect. Accordingly, receiving the appropriate attention from adults within their environment produces a change in the children's behaviour. In the end, they are described as peaceful children, capable of empathy. These socially critical aspects of the story appeal to an understanding that incorporates not only the results of, but also the reasons for certain actions within the process of learning how to feel. Moreover, the narrative can be read as a class critique addressed to the expected bourgeois readers.

* * *

The transnational dimension of this chapter highlights two complementary perspectives on the emotion of pain. While pain was still considered an integral part of the educational practice at the end of the nineteenth century, this approach changed gradually over the course of the twentieth century. Breakthroughs in medicine (such as the development of anaesthesia, the use of pharmaceuticals, and so on), the emergence of new scientific disciplines (such as experimental psychology and educational science), and the creation of humanitarian institutions contributed to a new evaluation of pain with the aim of reducing suffering.[93] In a society increasingly assumed to be humane, the use of pain in parent-child relationships was also decreasingly seen as a legitimate practice, without, however, disappearing entirely. The fact that pain was used as a threat even in the second half of the twentieth century symbolizes and marks a transition which has been described as a change from a command-oriented family to a negotiation-oriented family.[94]

From the mid-nineteenth century and into the twentieth century, pain in peer-group relationships was described not only as a legitimate, but also a necessary part of the communication and self-regulation process. In contrast to intergenerational relationships, the gender-specific component of peer groups is especially significant here. While girls only occasionally appeared in groups involved in physical confrontations, for boys, experiencing and inflicting pain were described as constituting a central component both of male identity and development, and the group-bonding process.[95] A change took place, however, in the level of intensity of pain that was regarded as legitimate (ranging, for example, from a black eye to unconsciousness) and in the tendency toward the differentiation and individualization of how to feel it. As the experience of the heroes of Lebrac's gang in *The War of the Buttons* show, pain may be increasingly felt as a form of suffering, and it is also closely associated with feelings of pleasure and freedom. These 'feeling options', along with the paradigm of 'acting out feelings', were based on a new understanding of childhood and education, which demonstrates the importance of pain in the process of learning how to feel from the end of the nineteenth century and throughout the twentieth century.

NOTES

1. Pergaud, *War of the Buttons*, 37–8. In the original French edition, Big-Assed Squinty's name is Migue-la-Lune.
2. Pergaud, 43.
3. Pergaud, 48.
4. See Biro, 'Is There Such a Thing as Psychological Pain'; Morris, *Cultures of Pain*, 9. For a definition of violent physical confrontations, see also Trotha, 'Violence', 5194.
5. Reimer, 'Introduction', 104; Lindenberger and Lüdtke, 'Einleitung', 7. On aspects of 'structural violence' (privileges, social forces, limitations of chances, etc.), see Bourdieu, *Logic of Practice*.
6. Pergaud, *War of the Buttons*, 44–5.
7. Scarry, *Body in Pain*, 31; Morris, *Cultures of Pain*, 15.
8. Heywood, *History of Childhood*, 110.
9. Pergaud, *War of the Buttons*, 28–9.
10. Pergaud.
11. In particular, Dumont, *Théorie scientifique de la sensibilité* (1875) hints at the relationship between pleasure and pain. For a contemporary approach, see, for example, MacDonald and Jensen-Campbell, *Social Pain*.
12. Arendt, *Human Condition*; Scarry, *Body in Pain*. See also Biro, *Listening to Pain*; Le Breton, *Anthropologie de la douleur*.
13. Moscoso, *Pain*, 7–8.
14. Reddy, *Navigation of Feeling*; Scheer, 'Are Emotions a Kind of Practice'.
15. The first effort to visually depict the multiplicity of the expression of pain was Mantegazza, *L'Atlante delle espressioni del dolore* (1876).
16. Scarry, *Body in Pain*, 89–90; Moscoso, *Pain*, 5, 9; Biro, *Listening to Pain*, 89–90; Morris, *Cultures of Pain*, 20.
17. Scarry, *Body in Pain*, 14; Biro, *Listening to Pain*, 89.
18. Höffer-Mehlmer, 'Erziehungsratgeber', 671. This chapter is based on a corpus of approximately one hundred children's books and forty advice manuals.

19. An important reason for this was probably Yves Robert's 1961 film adaptation of the novel. Aside from the 1968 English edition, it was also published in German in 1964 as *Der Krieg der Knöpfe*. There are additional translations in Czech, Italian, Catalan, Esperanto, Japanese, Korean, Slovenian, Spanish, Serbian, and Vietnamese.

20. Abruzzo, *Polemical Pain*, 2; Jakob Tanner, 'Körpererfahrung, Schmerz und die Konstruktion des Kulturellen'.

21. Among others, see, for example, *Struwwelliese* (c.1890); Robert and Philip Spence, *Struwwelhitler* (c.1941); Hansgeorg Stengel and Karl Schrader, *So ein Struwwelpeter* (1970); Friedrich Karl Waechter, *Der Anti-Struwwelpeter* (1970). See also Freeman, 'Heinrich Hoffmann's Struwwelpeter'.

22. Hoffmann, *Slovenly Peter*, not paginated.

23. Busch, *Max and Maurice*. See Jones and Brown, 'Wilhelm Busch's Merry Thoughts', 167.

24. Freud, 'Child Is Being Beaten'.

25. Beecher-Stowe, *Uncle Tom's Cabin*, ii, chapter 20.

26. Beecher-Stowe, ii, 45.

27. Moscoso, *Pain*, 81.

28. See Flegel, *Conceptualizing Cruelty to Children*; Cunningham, *Children and Childhood in Western Society since 1500*.

29. Key, *Century of the Child*; Lhotzky, *Soul of Your Child*; Hément, *Petit traité des punitions et des récompenses*; Höffer-Mehlmer, 'Sozialisation und Erziehungsratschlag'.

30. Lhotzky, 49–52.

31. See Borchardt, *Wie sollen wir unsere Kinder ohne Prügel erziehen*, esp. chapter 2 on trust.

32. Lagerlöf, *Wonderful Adventures of Nils*.

33. See chapter 5, 'Doctor Dolittle's Empathy'.

34. Burnett, *Secret Garden*, 31–2.

35. Pollock, *Forgotten Children*, esp. chapter 5; Pleck, *Domestic Tyranny*; Matthias, *Wie erziehen wir unsern Sohn Benjamin*.

36. Heitefuß, *Mutter und Kind*, 44.

37. Heywood, *Growing Up in France*, 164; 'Pädagogische Schläge sind Schläge des Liebhabers'; Heitefuß, *Mutter und Kind*, 21.

38. Vallès, *The Child*; Matthias, *Wie erziehen wir unsern Sohn Benjamin*; Schreiber, *Kindesmißhandlung*, 72–3.

39. Twain, *Adventures of Huckleberry Finn*, 34.

40. Kokorski, 'Invisible Threat', 201. See chapter 7, 'Piggy's Shame'.

41. Besides others in this series, see, for example, Trott, *Puckis erster Schritt ins Leben* (1937).

42. Schenzinger, *Der Hitlerjunge Quex*.

43. This particular book, with its explicit political convictions, is an exception among the children's books used for this chapter. See Lyons, *History of Reading and Writing*.

44. *Hitlerjunge Quex: Ein Film vom Opfergeist der deutschen Jugend*, Hans Steinhoff, dir. (UFA, 1933, banned) [film].

45. Kästner, *35th of May*.

46. Druon, *Tistou of the Green Fingers*; Saint-Exupéry, *Little Prince*.

47. Lewis, *Lion, the Witch and the Wardrobe*.

48. Spock, *Common Sense Book of Baby and Child Care*. See also Gebhardt, 'Haarer Meets Spock'.

49. Spock, 269–72, quotation 270.

50. Gebhardt, 'Haarer Meets Spock', 94.

51. Neill, *Summerhill*, xiii.

52. Neill, 157.

53. Neill, 269. In line with Spock, see, among others, Petri and Lauterbach, *Gewalt in der Erziehung*.
54. See, for example, Haarer, *Deutsche Mutter und ihr erstes Kind*, 260. See also: Brockhaus, 'Lockung und Drohung'.
55. Lenski, *Strawberry Girl*.
56. Hoban, *Bedtime for Frances*, not paginated.
57. Hoban, not paginated.
58. See, for example, Lindgren, *Emil in the Soup Tureen*.
59. Lindgren, 56.
60. See chapter 9, 'Jim Button's Fear'.
61. Lindgren, *Pippi Longstocking*.
62. Goscinny, *Young Nicolas*.
63. This setting also inspired literature for adults, such as Musil's novel *Young Törleß*.
64. Heywood, *History of Childhood*.
65. First French translation in 1875 as *Tom Brown: Scènes de la vie de collége en Angleterre*; in German in 1867 as *Tom Brown's Schuljahre*.
66. Farrar, *Eric*.
67. Martin, 'Boys Who Will Be Men', 488.
68. Hughes, *Tom Brown's School Days*, 148.
69. Hughes, 78.
70. Hughes, 194.
71. Nelson, 'Sex and the Single Boy', 538.
72. Hughes, *Tom Brown's School Days*, 347.
73. Galbraith, *Reading Lives*, 95.
74. Hughes, *Tom Brown's School Days*, 334.
75. Kipling, *Stalky & Co.*, esp. chapter 'The Moral Reformers'.
76. Kipling, 157.
77. Hall, *Youth*, 94. See chapter 1, 'Mrs Gaskell's Anxiety'.
78. Slaughter, *The Adolescent*, 75.
79. Giloi, 'Socialization and the City', 99.
80. Verne, *Adrift in the Pacific*, 120–1.
81. Kokorski, 'Invisible Threat', 201.
82. Kästner, *Flying Classroom*, 115.
83. Held, *Outsiders of Uskoken Castle*, 331.
84. Spock, *Common Sense Book of Baby and Child Care*, 270.
85. Spock, 252.
86. Neill, *Last Man Alive*, 5.
87. Neill, 191.
88. Neill, *Summerhill*, 271.
89. Schumann, 'School Violence and its Control', 242; Kurme, *Halbstarke*. See chapter 12, 'Ingrid's Boredom'.
90. Golding, *Lord of the Flies*, 142.
91. Arthur and others, *Alfred Hitchcock and The Three Investigators*; Lindgren, *Ronia, the Robber's Daughter*; Kästner, *Emil and the Detectives*; Blyton, *Five on a Treasure Island*.
92. Robinson, *Best Christmas Pageant Ever*.
93. Moscoso, *Pain*, 82–4, 194.
94. Höffer-Mehlmer, 'Sozialisation und Erziehungsratschlag', 79.
95. On the topic of manhood and emotions, see, among others, Borutta and Verheyen, *Präsenz der Gefühle*.

9

Jim Button's Fear

Bettina Hitzer

In 1960 one of the most successful West German children's books of the post-war era was published: *Jim Button and Luke the Engine Driver* (1963; Ger. orig. *Jim Knopf und Lukas der Lokomotivführer*, 1960) by Michael Ende. At a crucial moment in this story, the two heroes come across a giant. Jim, a boy about eight years old, shakes with fear. But his friend, the grown-up Luke, decides to confront the giant while explaining to Jim: 'Fear doesn't get you anywhere. If you are afraid things usually look a lot worse than they really are.' When approaching the giant, both find out that he gets smaller and smaller until he reaches normal size when faced directly. He is what is called a *Scheinriese* (a make-believe giant). Once aware of this, Jim vows to himself never to be afraid again before taking a closer look at the object of his anxieties.[1]

In the same year, another post-war classic was published: *Summerhill: A Radical Approach to Child Rearing* (1960), a bestselling compilation of older texts written by A. S. Neill that revived interest in 1920s reform pedagogy in Britain, the United States, and West Germany. This book wholeheartedly disapproved of fear: 'Fear can be a terrible thing in a child's life. Fear must be entirely eliminated—fear of adults, fear of punishment, fear of disapproval, fear of God. Only hate can flourish in an atmosphere of fear.'[2]

These two texts testify to a major, but short-lived, shift in conceptualizing fear in the world of the child during the modern era. By the 1960s, fear had come to be regarded by child psychologists, education experts, and philosophers as something fundamentally problematic—it was seen as deceitful and irrational on the one hand, and potentially harmful and debilitating to the child's fragile soul on the other. Learning how to deal with fear was no longer regarded an essential part of a challenging, but for the most part eventually successful, process of character-building. On the contrary, at the end of the post-war period, fear itself appeared to be a much more complex feeling. The problem children encountered when it came to fear was as much about determining how to face it as about how to define and feel it. Within the realm of children's books, this process of problematizing and contesting the emotion of fear eventually brought to fruition what had been initiated more than half a century earlier. It freed fear unequivocally from its long-standing association with shame and moral vilification.[3] One thing was clear: fear was nothing to be ashamed of any more.

How does this specific moment register within a longer history of learning how to be afraid? To date, only a few historians have drawn particular attention to childhood as a possible formative period in education around fear, and even then, they have primarily focused on advice literature intended for parents without going into much detail when analysing children's literature.[4] There has thus been relatively little investigation into the models, settings, and conceptualizations of fear to which children have been exposed over the past 150 years through reading and listening to children's stories.[5]

This chapter focuses on children's literature from the late nineteenth century to the late twentieth century in (West) Germany and in Britain.[6] It examines what these books presented to child readers as inspiring fear along with what they suggested about how one should deal with fear and on whom one could lean when afraid. Although fear education clearly was (and to a certain degree still is) gendered, this perspective is not systematically explored within this chapter. Rather, it devotes itself to analysing the multi-faceted relationship between *fearful* and *fearless* heroes. Nevertheless, the issue of gender is touched upon at certain points, given that one of the overall assertions here is that there is a distinct trend toward a de-gendering of fear models in this period. This chapter does not systematically approach the question of whether the stories themselves aimed at deliberately inspiring fear within young readers. Even though this question is related to the childhood process of learning emotions, as well as to adult considerations about the value and use of specific feelings such as fear in educating or shaping children, the question of intent is part of a different conceptual framework.[7] By contrast, this chapter is based on the assumption that children learn how to feel at least partially through a process of mimetic reading. They use what they have read as 'material' to play with—either literally or only in their imaginations—and may 'test' what a certain role causes within them in terms of emotions.[8]

Two principal characters will be starring in this chapter. The first and longer section is dedicated to a figure who prevailed throughout most of the twentieth century: the faint-hearted, scared, or terrified hero. The last part explores the destiny of a character who excelled in the nineteenth century, but was gradually sidelined during the twentieth: the fearless hero.

FAINT-HEARTED, SCARED, TERRIFIED— CHILDREN'S NEW HEROES IN THE EARLY TWENTIETH CENTURY

Toward the end of the nineteenth century, fear crept into the stories of children capturing part of the heroes' hearts and gaining influence within the narrative. Earlier heroes did have to face fear, but they were not haunted by it, nor did they really have difficulty in mastering it.[9] Mastering fear through emotional restraint had hitherto been part of a boy's everyday moral education and, as depicted in the stories, mastering fear should present no major challenges to the boy, leaving no room for the possibility of failing. Self-control was equally at stake for girls, but not in terms of mastering fear. For the girls, feeling and expressing fear was more acceptable. Toward the end of the nineteenth century, however, another character was to enter the stage, and would not depart for the duration of the twentieth century: the fearful, but 'positive' and most often male, hero who would, however, live through the manifold changes this period would bring with it.

One of the first appearances of the fearful hero is the Cowardly Lion in L. Frank Baum's long-selling classic *The Wonderful Wizard of Oz*, first published in 1900. While not presented as the most praiseworthy role model, the lion is far from being ridiculed despite being named a 'coward'. He is one of the most reliable friends of the story's heroine Dorothy, never deserting her when dangers arise. Of course, the deliberate irony of this is the fact that the most powerful animal in the story while inspiring fear in almost every other character at first sight, is himself very scared. Cowardly Lion is partly aware of this paradox, since he is deeply ashamed of not living up to his image and vocation as king of the beasts. Standard education programmes both in the United States and in European countries promoted mastering fear as one of the principal characteristics of being a boy—in this respect, boy readers could perceive the lion as a role model for themselves when struggling to master fear.[10] The Cowardly Lion never completely manages to master his anxieties and fear stays with him until the moment he drinks the wizard's liquid, which he has been led to believe is magic. Despite his lasting anxieties, his heart racing in fright, the lion never *acts* in a cowardly manner. As the great wizard Oz explains to him toward the end of the story, 'There is no living thing that is not afraid when it faces danger. True courage is in facing danger when you are afraid, and that kind of courage you have in plenty.'[11] For the lion, however, this realization is insufficient to calm his worries and he declares, 'I shall really be very unhappy unless you give me the sort of courage that makes one forget he is afraid.'[12]

The Cowardly Lion is thus one of the first heroes of his time to lend himself as a role model to boys, in particular to those who did not easily overcome their fears and were prone to suffering anxiety, even when acting courageously. This model did not 'lower' moral standards for boys since it never contested the idea that one should be brave, but sought merely to portray in more detail the struggle to achieve this aim. It conceded that some assistance might be necessary and destabilized the assumption that fear was something to be ashamed of, provided one did not act in a cowardly manner. As such, the Cowardly Lion testifies to a growing awareness in late nineteenth-century society that childish or juvenile anxieties were no simple matter, that fear could be haunting and debilitating to children, and that their anxieties should be handled in a sensible and sympathetic way.[13] Accordingly, some popular advice manuals encouraged parents not to exert pressure on their child, not to test his (or her) courage on purpose by putting him (or more seldom, her) into fearful situations simply in order to compel him to face his anxieties.[14]

While nineteenth-century children's stories did not generally delve deeply into fear, often reserving only one or two sentences to describe the state of being scared in order to demonstrate the successful mastering of anxiety, by the turn of the century children could encounter more powerful descriptions of fear and panic. Childhood fears were no longer regarded as something simple or unproblematic, but as something that could verge on terror and—in extreme cases—endanger the psyche and lifelong happiness of the child.[15] In Kenneth Grahame's very popular novel *The Wind in the Willows* (1908) child readers witnessed, in a long and enthralling paragraph, the growing terror felt by Mole, one of the story's four animal protagonists, while walking through the Wild Wood. Without directly conveying or naming Mole's inner feelings his increasing panic is portrayed in two ways. On the one hand, readers read about what Mole himself hears, sees, senses—an ever-accelerating series of threatening sounds, sights, and physical sensations. On the other hand, Grahame gives a detailed account of what fear does to Mole's body, how it makes him run, stumble, lose control, tremble, and shed tears. Through the vivid narration, both parts of the story could easily convey Mole's fear experience as a corporeal experience to child readers. After eventually seeking shelter in a hollow Mole becomes aware of what was most terrible in what he just experienced: not the danger itself, but 'that dread thing which other little dwellers in field and hedgerow had...known as their darkest moment...the Terror of the Wild Wood!'[16]

In contrast to the Cowardly Lion, who is constantly afraid but always acts courageously, Mole panics and in the end it is not even clear if the creatures of the Wild Wood were really threatening him or if it was all just in his imagination. Nevertheless, the Wild Wood's menace is described and conveyed to the reader in a very imposing way, and at the moment when his friend, Rat, appears at his side fully armed with pistols and a club, courage immediately prevails in Mole's heart. Thus, contrary to being depicted as a 'sissy', he is presented as someone who faces a dangerous situation alone, without being properly prepared or well-equipped to fight back. Young readers could learn that they need not be ashamed of feeling panic. Rather, it was simply a question of realizing the surrounding dangers, meaning that they should avoid foolhardiness and prepare themselves to face dangers appropriately. In a way, this corresponded to the anxieties felt by one of Mole's contemporaries in another book: the protagonist Colin from Frances Hodgson Burnett's *The Secret Garden* (1911), who is haunted by the conviction that he is destined to become a hunchback and that this will be the cause of his premature death. His anxieties completely shut him off from life because he does not dare embrace it. When he learns from his cousin Mary that his fears are more the stuff of imagination (or 'hysteria' as Mary puts it) than reality, Colin ultimately turns to life and learns to be more courageous.[17]

While stories like *The Wonderful Wizard of Oz*, *The Wind in the Willows*, or *The Secret Garden* provided their child readers with a sense that fear could potentially be embarrassing or even debilitating, they also presented them with rather unproblematic ways to escape or resolve this state of anxiety or panic. Young German readers in the early 1930s, by contrast, were presented with a somewhat harsher stance toward handling perpetual fear. In Erich Kästner's *The Flying Classroom* (1934; Ger. orig. *Das fliegende Klassenzimmer*, 1933), a novel widely read in Germany, child readers came to know Uli, a boarding school pupil.[18] Bright, cautious, frail, and homesick, he resembles a type described by German child psychologists as especially prone to sheepishness.[19] Unlike the Cowardly Lion, his American counterpart from thirty years earlier, he not only suffers from faint-heartedness, but from behaving accordingly. Despite this, he is still depicted as likeable and he and his worries are not described in a condescending tone. Child readers were therefore able to identify with him. The only remedy for fear that Uli's strong, brave, but less intellectually gifted friend Matthias recommends is doing something audacious. The underlying logic, reminiscent of *The Wonderful Wizard of Oz* and its Cowardly Lion, was that it was not bravery itself that a faint-hearted person lacked, but self-confidence. While Cowardly Lion grew self-confident by swallowing a 'magic' potion, Uli is advised to gain self-confidence by undertaking a daring act. Desperate, he chooses to jump off a high ladder using an umbrella as a kind of parachute. Even though Uli is severely (but not mortally) injured, the headmaster approves of his action when he learns why Uli decided to jump. Leading a life paralysed by fear seems far more grave to the headmaster than being injured by an audacious or even foolhardy act that might have maimed Uli or even cost him his life. This existential quality of overcoming fearfulness was specific to Germany in defining fear as an obstacle to life's happiness and above all to a person's usefulness within society. From this perspective, the most problematic factor was not that a child was haunted by his personal fears, as American child psychologists of this era would have defined it, but that he suffered from being aware of his faint-heartedness, from lacking courage, and the child therefore lacked the ability to confront unknown and dangerous situations.[20]

In the 1920s, another character defined by fear emerged in Germany who was different from the protagonists with which American or British novels presented their juvenile public. These 'new' German novels did not portray the struggle their protagonists undertook to master, face, or overcome anxieties and fear or to develop a more secure, morally grounded, emotional character having acted courageously. These stories did not explore the triangular relationship of fear, bravery, and cowardice at all. Instead, they were preoccupied with fear itself as a general feeling towards a menacing world: it marked the whole body and could be seen in the eyes, which revealed 'a world full of fright'.[21] This emergence of fear that possesses the body and shows itself palpably despite the heroes' will undermined broader trends in emotional cultures that might have been more obvious in the United States. This fear could not be matched with 'cool conduct', nor with the trend toward 'anti-intensity', nor with the outward callousness of the 'post-bourgeois white-collar subject' that other historians have described when analysing the 1920s.[22] This trend, however, is more consistent with what has been said about the mobilization of feelings such as fear in the first half of the twentieth century, implied in violent rows and ethnic killings.[23] It would seem that these children's stories were closer to the day-to-day experience of violence in the streets than to the realm of adult employment, which might have more closely resembled 'cool conduct'.[24]

While this generalized feeling of fear was initially portrayed as a character trait of the poor, weak, subordinate, or powerless arising from experiences of humiliation, violence, and distress as well as from sheer desperation,[25] children encountered a series of frightened heroes within right-wing literature in the late Weimar Republic and in early National Socialism. Heini, the protagonist of Schenzinger's *Der Hitlerjunge Quex* ('Hitler Youth Quex', 1932) adapted as the first Nazi propaganda film in 1933, popular among both middle- and working-class children, repeatedly experienced a very deep-seated fear which took hold of his body to the point that it was difficult to control its outward signs. He was constantly afraid of his violent father and scared to the core by his father's communist friend Stoppel, who threatened Heini with violence if he did not stay with the communists. Fear, threats, and violence were part of Heini's everyday experience. This kind of fear was very different from what the Cowardly Lion, Mole, or Uli had experienced. Heini did not suffer from being cowardly or acting in a faint-hearted manner, he suffered from the destructive force of his enduring anxieties. The gruelling nature of this constant fear on a weaker character could be seen in Heini's mother who, desperate to escape from her fear, eventually committed suicide.[26] Juvenile protagonists like Heini could not overcome this fear on their own. Alone they would end up like Heini's mother. To be sheltered from the worst of their fear, they were offered the chance to join the youth organizations of the National Socialist party—even though the party comrades could not completely protect them from the communist threat, as Heini's eventual murder by communists demonstrated.[27] When National Socialism was established in reality, these terrified heroes disappeared from the narrative repertoire.

ESSENTIALLY HUMAN—FEAR AND THE FEELING OF VULNERABILITY

In the meantime another type of hero came into being, one found primarily in a certain branch of British fiction. While this chapter has so far outlined the evolution of fearful characters such as animals, children, or adolescents, numerous stories for older children also recounted the deeds of adult men. In the nineteenth and early twentieth centuries these men were mostly characterized by manliness, which implied a certain form of fearlessness and bravery. Starting in the late nineteenth century, some of these men did mention fear when telling their adventures retrospectively. But since they usually did not go into much detail, these descriptions generally served merely as illustrations for the great dangers they faced.[28] Nevertheless, they attested to an integration of the transitory feeling of fear into the concept of manliness.[29] The same was true for references to fear in the countless popular adventure, detective, or (boarding) school stories featuring male or female child heroes. Fear functioned there more as an enhancement to the sense of excitement and suspense intended for the reader than as a representation of an individual feeling or as an in any way serious feeling.[30]

Fantasy stories published from the 1930s onwards shared a different tale. In 1934, the hobbit Bilbo Baggins was introduced to a juvenile and adult public. The story begins with him being asked by the wizard Gandalf and some dwarves to help them reclaim their treasure from a dangerous dragon. Formerly, a manly hero would have embraced this adventurous quest without showing any signs of fear—not Bilbo. As soon as the flames of a wood-fire bring to his mind dragons, his curiosity and adventurous spirit fade away quickly and he tries to hide. With no possibility for evasion left, he panics, shrieking, his whole body shaking. This sudden panic appears rather ridiculous—to the dwarves and probably also to readers. What makes the hobbit recover his supposed fierce and brave spirit is the dwarf Gloin's assumption that Bilbo might be so frightened that he will not live up to their expectations.[31] Shame and anger thus prevail over Bilbo's fear. But *The Hobbit* (1934) is not only the story of a diminutive man-like creature overcoming his 'natural' fear by being reminded of an ideal of manliness. His inclination to succumb to fear is also presented as a kind of prerequisite for accomplishing what he is meant to undertake. It was not only bravery, but the ability to have pity for an abominable and menacing creature like Gollum, the guardian of the ring, and his incapacity to act with 'cold' bravery, that was necessary to retrieve both the treasure from the dragon and the powerful ring which would take centre stage in Tolkien's later three-volume novel *The Lord of the Rings* (1954–5).[32]

Stories like that of Bilbo Baggins brought about a fundamental change in course regarding what fear meant in adventure novels for older readers. Fear no longer represented an exclusively unfortunate, problematic, and disturbing part of human nature that had to be mastered in order to act courageously. It was conceived of as something essentially human, a necessary precondition to counterbalance sheer, and possibly brutal, bravery with a feeling of one's own as well as another's vulnerability. But for those boy (and later, girl) heroes encountered in popular stories, both feeling and facing fear remained an important moral challenge, even though the meaning of fear had changed. This contradicts the commonly held assumption that children's books from the 1920s onwards tended to portray either 'fear-free' environments or fearless heroes (as in science fiction stories).[33] In this respect, many stories written for children clearly did not follow the advice given to parents to avoid situations that could instil fear. Instead, juvenile fiction was deeply concerned with war and the political struggles which all children experienced in some way or another during this time.

This element was renewed and increased after the Second World War. In 1954, Tolkien created a successor to Bilbo, his nephew Frodo, whom he sent on a much more challenging quest to save Middle-earth from the evil forces of the Dark Lord Sauron. While Frodo differed from Bilbo in many respects, he resembled him insofar as he experiences time and again that intense fear which qualifies him both as a compassionate and, in a way, humble creature who seeks no fame or power, and at the same time as someone who is not afraid of fear.[34] Unlike Bilbo, however, he overcomes his fear not only by being reminded of his task and the ideals of manliness, but by the force of utter desperation.[35]

It was not only Tolkien who portrayed fear as something deeply human. Readers were able to encounter a similar conception of fear in the other great fantasy epic of the British post-war period, C. S. Lewis's *The Chronicles of Narnia* (1950–6), even though the link between fear and the capacity to feel compassion, or act in a human way, was much less visible.[36] In *Narnia*, as in *The Lord of the Rings* or a bit later in Madeleine L'Engle's *A Wrinkle in Time* (1962), the mastery of fear becomes detached from a simple notion of bravery. It is a very existential form of desperation, a deep-rooted physical knowledge that there is no way out of complete subjugation or death other than fighting back, which enabled boys or men (and later on girls and women) to overcome fear and to react.[37]

FROM THE FEARFUL PROTAGONIST TO FEAR *AS* PROTAGONIST

While fear was an important element of a hero's character in these stories, it was not a central element in the narratives themselves in British fantasy epics of the 1950s. In West Germany, one children's fantasy novel in which fear did feature centrally received the *Deutscher Jugendbuchpreis* (in the bonus category) in 1956. Astrid Lindgren's *Mio, My Son* (1956; Swe. orig. *Mio, min Mio*, 1954) focused precisely on the problem that *The Lord of the Rings* and *The Chronicles of Narnia* had touched upon.[38] Fear was the leitmotiv of this story, repeated time and again in a kind of invocation as being 'afraid, terribly afraid'. Like in *The Lord of the Rings* and *Narnia*, Mio's idyllic world, the kingdom of his beloved father, is endangered by an evil knight, Sir Kato, who abducts the kingdom's children to turn them into captive birds in his shadowy land. When Mio learns that he is the only person in a position to free them, he becomes scared and desperate, fearful and trembling, convinced that he cannot do it. In a powerful scene, he fully embraces his fear, realizing that he has to face his fears all by himself, without relying on his father and his best friend Pompoo. Eventually, the profound grief of those who have lost someone to Kato inspires him with a kind of tranquil anger which gives him the power to set out on his quest despite the fear that never really leaves him until the end of the story.[39] Mio has to overcome feelings of feebleness and fear several times until he is ultimately able to fight Kato, sword in hand—in this moment Mio at last turns into the proverbial knight in shining armour.[40]

Mio's story was not a stunning success in terms of sales figures. The hero's repeated avowal of being 'afraid, terribly afraid' conflicted with an emotional culture in post-war Germany (and Britain) which demanded a public denial that one's political acts were motivated—partly or wholly—by fear.[41] But the fact that *Mio* was awarded the prestigious *Deutscher Jugendbuchpreis* points to the latent fear present in public discourse that would soon become a much debated individual and political emotion. One might read Mio's story as a kind of *emotional refuge* opening up a discussion of previous war-time fear as well as of post-war fear that was difficult to formulate in other, more adult public arenas.[42] To this extent, Mio's fearful struggle against Sir Kato can be understood as a kind of prelude to the centrality that fear was to acquire in subsequent decades.

During the 1960s and 1970s, child readers encountered a multitude of narratives relating to fear. Three different, but at times intertwined, dimensions of fear dominated during these two decades. The first of these retold, and to a substantial degree removed the gender of, the story of the fearful, essentially human, and compassionate hero. This hero's ultimately insurmountable power derived from being unafraid of anxiety as well as from a form of desperate and empathetic rage based on acknowledging his or (now) her emotional openness and vulnerability. According to this representation, fear did not separate humans, but was as fundamental to uniting them as compassion and love—two emotions that were to be intimately connected with fear.[43] In Otfried Preußler's *The Satanic Mill* (1972; Ger. orig. *Krabat*, 1971), Krabat, a journeyman in a bewitched mill, succeeds together with his beloved Kantorka in breaking the evil and deadly spell, because she is able to recognize the enchanted Krabat by his intense feeling of fear for her life.[44] Karl, the younger brother in Astrid Lindgren's *The Brothers Lionheart* (1975; Swe. orig. *Bröderna Lejonhjärta*, 1973), is constantly afraid, but soothed by his adored elder brother's imagination and courage. But his fear does not prevent him from fighting when his brother's life is in danger. In the end, it is he who must save both their lives by jumping off a cliff, admitting: 'No, . . . yes, I am afraid! But anyhow I will do it!'[45] Momo, the female heroine from German author Michael Ende's *The Grey Gentlemen* (1974; Ger. orig. *Momo*, 1973), like Karl, acknowledged her fear openly when encountering the grey men who rob humans of their time, their humanity, and their happiness by tricking them into becoming time-effective. Unlike those who fall prey to the grey men, Momo feels fear because she senses their inner coldness. Fear serves as a kind of heuristic instrument for what is essentially human, as well as serving as a rational instrument to help Momo recognize life's dangers. This depiction of fear echoed that of Richard Adams's influential novel *Watership Down* (1972), which recounts the quest of a group of rabbits to find a new safe place after their warren is destroyed.[46] This conception of fear continues to be essential to some of the most popular children's stories told from the 1980s to the present day, seen for instance in heroes like Bastian Balthazar Bux, protagonist of Michael Ende's *The Neverending Story* (1983; Ger. orig. *Die unendliche Gechichte*, 1979) or various characters in J. K. Rowling's *Harry Potter* series (1997–2007).[47]

THE FUNDAMENTAL AMBIVALENCE OF FEAR AND HOW TO FACE IT

The Grey Gentlemen points to a second dimension of fear which was delineated with increasing urgency in children's literature of the 1970s: the capacity of fear to blind people to what was really at stake.[48] At first, this seems to contradict what has just been said about fear's heuristic capacity. Yet the significance of fear had obviously radically changed compared to how it had been understood in the first half of the twentieth century. The depiction of fear in 1960s and 1970s children's literature no longer concerned itself with the question of to what extent fear was 'natural' and, above all, an impediment to bravery. Fear was no longer represented in opposition to courage at all. On the contrary, it came to be perceived as a double-edged phenomenon. The positive side of fear was characterized by the fact that it was an essential component of a sensible and empathetic creature aware of his or her own and of others' vulnerability. Without this awareness there could be no love or friendship. Feeling fear was therefore construed as a necessary step towards genuine and very human bravery. Fear's negative side was defined by its degradation into irrationality, which prepared the ground for manipulation, emotional isolation, or even hatred. Jim Button's encounter with the make-believe giant, mentioned at the beginning of this chapter, bears witness to this flipside of fear. Jim's fear is based on a misperception whereby his awe at the giant's size obscures all other indications of his friendly character, which the adult Luke, unaffected by fear, could easily decipher.[49] Jim's story was thus not about mastering fear, but about the necessity to look at the world and at others more closely, in an unbiased manner, and to not shy away from even those events or people that inspire fear at first.

This new 'even-handed' stance towards fear also manifested itself in the subjects in children's stories and thus presented a third dimension of fear. Some of the new stories for older children presented a hostile world imbued with fear, yet in contrast to the stories of the 1920s in which fear was similarly omnipresent, these stories were not about being afraid of something 'simple' and tangible like everyday violence. Children could now learn about heroes for whom fear was part of their attitude towards life with only a little space left for hope and definitely no place to be secure. These sinister worlds were either overshadowed by nuclear war or by a generalized feeling of teen angst that called into question all human contact and where adults for the most part could neither offer a feeling of security nor a role model to turn to for guidance, since adults were equally haunted by fear or personal crises.[50] Fear in these narratives transcended, and eventually blurred, the boundary between the internal and external world, and the individual was increasingly represented as fully permeable.[51]

Even when the world seemed dark and daunting, children's stories in this period left no doubt that one should not shy away from fear. The only hope for all protagonists lay in taking on their fears at face value, and in examining their anxieties rather than fighting back against them. This conviction was articulated by a great many novels for children and juvenile readers and it reflected a more general turn towards exploring emotions psychologically and making them accessible to diverse therapeutic interventions. This is characteristic of both West Germany and Britain in the 1970s.[52] Being straightforward and using one's imagination were two different ways in which protagonists chose to cope with their anxieties. Straightforwardness was applied to a theme that was new to children's literature in such an explicit form: the death of a beloved person. Though earlier children's books occasionally recounted the death of a parent or child, this death was either part of a bygone era with few emotional repercussions in the present or the story narrated how the dying person faced death.[53] From the 1970s onwards, children and juveniles would encounter the subject of death much more often in stories written explicitly for them, usually via descriptions of the feelings of those who were losing a loved one. Fear was the predominant emotion here, not only fear of the actual fact of death, but even more so the fear of merely speaking about the impending death. Confronting the fear of even speaking about the approaching death by talking about it in a straightforward manner was presented as emotionally the most bearable way to cope.[54]

Around the same time, other stories were more explicit in their indications of how children and young adults could come to terms with fear. Fantasy played a very important role in this handling of fear: as a nightmare, as a symbol, or eventually as a means to overcome anxieties. While fear had been hitherto described in terms of bodily gestures or expressions, the 1970s witnessed a turn towards symbols of fear in children's and young adult's stories, with birds being one of the most powerful. While the bird in Felice Holman's *Slake's Limbo* (1974) is a lasting symbol for fear's oppressiveness, the birds in Norwegian author Tormod Haugen's novel *The Night Birds* (1985; Nor. orig. *Nattfuglene*, 1975) are both a symbol of and the means for handling fear. The recurring nightmare the protagonist Joachim lives through every night, in which the birds swoop out of his wardrobe to tear chunks out of him, opens up an opportunity for him to speak to his parents and to do something about his otherwise scarcely tangible anxieties. However, when his parents prove incapable of offering him an emotionally stable home, he ultimately creates an imaginary friend who, though not a bird, seems to help him through his difficulties.[55] Stories for younger children approached scary fantasies and nightmares as if they were 'real'. Whether Irina Korschunow's little Adam drew himself a dragon to gain self-confidence in order to overcome his shy and faint-hearted character[56] or whether Kirsten Boie's Juli was afraid of the monster in the toilet,[57] the message was the same: it was only through taking these fantasies seriously and addressing them as if they really existed that fear could be made to dissipate.

FEARLESS HEROES—A DIVERSION TO TWENTIETH-CENTURY CHILDREN'S LITERATURE

While children throughout the twentieth century became acquainted with numerous fearful or faint-hearted heroes they could also come across several undaunted or foolhardy ones. Some of these stemmed directly from young adult or adult literature of the nineteenth century, a distinction that was not clearly drawn then. These were stories which continued to be re-edited and shortened for adolescents during the twentieth century and were sold in great numbers. Their protagonists were either situated in the Wild West or would travel the world as explorers and inventors.

One of the most popular of these long-term bestsellers was *Leatherstocking Tales* (1823–41) by James Fenimore Cooper. The protagonist Natty Bumppo and to a lesser extent his Native American friend, the chief Chingachgook, are both invested with what could be called manliness in the muscular Christianity sense.[58] According to this ideal, men have to be brave, but not brutal; they do not kill to prove their bravery; they are in complete control of their emotions; and never act out of passion, even when blamed for cowardice.[59] Even when threatened, Bumppo does not show any sign of being afraid, not even sweating or trembling. Moreover, readers are never given even the slightest hint as to whether he is feeling fear, nor of how he manages to remain apparently fearless without being emotionless. Bumppo never has to struggle to overcome anxiety; he simply seems to feel no fear at all. Readers could only presume that the education he got from the Native American tribe is responsible for him having mastered fear once and for all. The same is true for other late nineteenth-century heroes from the 'Wild West', the Native American chief Winnetou and his German friend Old Shatterhand, who continued to enjoy immense popularity in Germany until fairly recently—even among young readers from the lower classes who were much less likely to read stories like *The Flying Classroom* or *The Wonderful Wizard of Oz*.[60] But unlike Bumppo, Winnetou, a later creation, appears to be less robust, more sensitive, and does not shy away from talking about his feelings, even though he never explicitly shows or speaks of fear. In a telling scene, he reveals to Old Shatterhand his foreboding of his own imminent death. For the first time, he appears to be less secure, full of sorrow, and the reader wonders whether he is afraid, although this speculation is never uttered either by the narrator or his friend. But when Old Shatterhand advises him to stay away from an impending fight, Winnetou turns the advice down, since he would feel himself a coward regardless of what anyone else thought.[61]

Winnetou's successors in twentieth-century children's books continued to adhere to an ideal of physical and moral bravery, but the protagonists ceased to be fearless. Over eight volumes, published in the 1930s, German author Fritz Steuben creatively narrated the biography of the Native American chief Tecumseh. In contrast to Bumppo and Winnetou, Steuben's hero was marked time and again by unspeakable fear, 'but his will was stronger than the fear in his soul, stronger than his body, which trembled and shook'.[62] Fear had crept into the hearts of fictional Native Americans, as it had into the souls of hobbits, but no longer ruled out bravery.

A different, but equally fearless, emotional character was presented to children and juvenile readers in numerous stories of explorers and inventors that likewise continued a storyline that had been started in the nineteenth century. The French author Jules Verne's novels were a kind of prototype for this genre and were sold in great numbers throughout the twentieth century not only in France, but in Britain and Germany as well. With Phileas Fogg, the protagonist in *Around the World in Eighty Days* (1873; Fre. orig. *Le Tour du Monde en Quatre-Vingts Jours*, 1873), readers got to know a slightly eccentric Briton completely committed to his venture—travelling round the world in eighty days—and thereby seemed to see no dangers nor feel any fear. But in contrast to Bumppo and Winnetou, it was not his heroic manliness that prevented him from being afraid. On the contrary, he was modelled on the ideal of a British gentleman who did not show any sign of passionate emotion, let alone fear, except for a kind of detached empathy. Moreover, he was driven by his quasi-scientific devotion to his mission which did not allow fear to arise. This 'fear-free' attitude went along with a somewhat dispassionate character which made even love look rather 'unemotional'.[63] Some fifty years later his compatriot Doctor Dolittle, loved by generations of British and later German children, set sail for Africa, while never losing his calm. Much like Phileas Fogg, he seemed to ignore danger and to be exempt from fear most of the time. He acted out of a resolute feeling of empathy towards animals, even though this feeling never gets close to a passion that might creep beyond the proper emotional restraint of a gentleman.[64] Throughout the twentieth century, there were some popular successors to Phileas Fogg and Doctor Dolittle but these later fearless heroes played more of a supporting role in children's and young adult literature.[65] These findings modify older assumptions about a fading of fear in children's literature during the mid-twentieth century in favour of 'high-action adventure without emotional strings'. This misplaced assumption is based almost exclusively on the reading of science fiction stories which, in Germany and Britain at least, did not represent the bulk of children's literature from the 1920s onwards, and totally neglects the role of fantasy epics like *The Chronicles of Narnia* as well as other novels with 'real-world' heroes.[66]

Other empathetic *and* 'fear-free' heroes re-emerged after 1945 in such a different guise that the similarities can easily escape detection at first. These heroes are neither British gentleman, nor are they heading to other worlds, but in a way they are also non-conformists. And—rather surprisingly—these new fearless characters were mainly female. One can wonder whether male 'fear-free' heroes would have been conceivable, let alone morally acceptable, after the atrocities of the Second World War, which saw men in roles both as 'perpetrators' of extreme violence and as 'victims' experiencing feelings of powerlessness, desperation, and humiliation. Astrid Lindgren's *Pippi Longstocking* (1945; Swe. orig. *Pippi Långstrump*, 1945) is one of the first and to date most popular heroines of this type in Germany, and since 1957, Otfried Preußler's *Little Witch* (1961; Ger. orig. *Die kleine Hexe*, 1957) has kept her company.[67] Both protagonists completely ignore fear: they do not have to master or overcome it, and they simply do not feel it, albeit for slightly different reasons. While Pippi has superhuman physical strength at her disposal and is accustomed to relying on herself alone, the little Witch counts on her witty and inventive mind, even though she—like Pippi—has no one to rely upon in her quarrel with the adult witches over performing magic exclusively to a good end.

Even though these two heroines are loved and re-enacted by (mostly German) children to this very day, they are in a way characters from a bygone world. First, because both—without adults to lean on—reflect a model of psychological thinking that later came to be viewed as outdated. According to this model, fear in children was for the most part not inherent but acquired through misconceived education by ill-advised mothers (or parents) who pampered their children. Second, novels of this kind may have been part of a utopian project that envisioned creating a world without fear by means of education. That is what A. S. Neill, for instance, intended when founding his Summerhill School, mentioned above. Hope, not fear, was the feeling that dominated this utopian project. As Ernst Bloch (*The Principle of Hope*, 1954–9) put it, hope was hegemonic when it came to leftist thinking in the 1950s

and early 1960s.[68] *Jim Button*, whose story opened this historical investigation into
fear, is a telling example of such an approach towards fear's demystification. Yet this
'disrespect' of fear represented only a brief moment in history.

* * *

Fear, often described as universally stable and, in principle, unaltered since ancient
times—in short: *the* basic emotion per se—has made an astonishingly vicissitu-
dinous career in children's literature from the late nineteenth century to the late
twentieth century. Describing this process as the shift from a more or less optimistic nineteenth century, harbouring only some concrete anxieties, to an angst-driven
twentieth century captures only a fraction of what children encountered and learnt
about fear when reading books during these hundred or so years.[69]

Fear was not a major issue within children's books in the mid- to late nineteenth
century. While reading, children followed the deeds of mostly male, essentially
fearless, heroes. Even though these heroes had to face manifold dangers and were
frequently afraid they did not have any fundamental difficulty in mastering fear,
due to their long-standing training in emotional restraint and self-control, while
heroines rarely, if ever, had to face dangerous, fear-inducing situations. This kind
of 'character-building' narrative went largely unchallenged—children's souls were
said to be emotionally robust.[70] Beginning in the late nineteenth century and gaining momentum after the First World War, a much more complex and problematic
stance toward fear took hold of children's literature. Being afraid, panicking, or
becoming paralysed with fear was now described at length, which was possibly
both haunting and enthralling for young readers. During the 1920s, some books
presented adolescent readers with a world imbued with fear, desperation, and violence. An increased awareness of fear's hold on the human soul—a soul which
could not once and for all be made resistant against fear and its destructive force—
and a clear admission of the emotional vulnerability of both children and adults
found their way into books for children and adolescents. Nevertheless, being fearless remained the moral goal, and being afraid did not cease to invoke shame.

This only started to shift in the late 1930s with the genre of British fantasy epics,
which seemed to be the most important break in twentieth-century fear education.
Being afraid now increasingly implied self-awareness on the part of heroes, and
with growing frequency heroines, in relation to human vulnerability. Fear now
went along with a sense of one's own limits and was thus equated with humbleness
and compassion. In this respect, it kept the heroes from becoming cold and brutal.
But compassion and desperation also operated as important antagonists to fear
since they provided storybook heroes with a sense of urgency, empowering them
to fight despite being afraid.

This change may have been linked to some other major processes: the shift
from character-building to personality development to happiness becoming the
major trajectory of a successful childhood, or the changes that occurred in family
structure and size, as well as new findings within the emerging disciplines of (child)
psychology, psychoanalysis, and psychosomatic medicine.

Post-war literature witnessed an ambivalent assessment of fear, which lingered at the threshold between the rational and the irrational, the essentially human and the potentially inhuman, as *Jim Button* aptly demonstrated. However, the conceptualization of fear which prevailed during the 1950s and early 1960s is best understood as transitional, since the period from the 1970s onwards was characterized by an increasing internalization of fear and a more positive evaluation of it. Fear came to be understood as an important and non-irrational incitement to a critical and anticipatory attitude towards mainstream society and its ills.[71] In the children's books of the 1980s, being afraid, along with facing disease, death, and environmental dangers became a crucial issue for boys and girls alike. That one should acknowledge one's fear and talk about it was by then beyond question. Nevertheless, mimetic learning models on how to deal with, master, overcome, or live with one's fear are far less obvious in stories that are preoccupied with the role of fear and the never-ending fearfulness of human existence.

NOTES

1. Ende, *Jim Button and Luke the Engine Driver*, 116–22, quotation 121.
2. Neill, *Summerhill*, 124.
3. For a detailed discussion of shame in children's literature, see chapter 7, 'Piggy's Shame'.
4. Stearns and Haggerty, 'Role of Fear', 89; Bakker, 'Meaning of Fear'.
5. There are few exceptions, notably Stallcup, 'Power, Fear, and Children's Picture Books'.
6. This chapter is based on the reading of roughly eighty children's novels published in (West) Germany (i.e. Germany up to the Second World War and West Germany afterwards) and Britain. All were either written in or translated into German and/or English, with publication dates distributed more or less evenly over the one hundred years focused on here. In addition, fifteen parental advice books that were considered influential in Britain and (West) Germany are also included. It has frequently been argued that modern German culture, especially after 1945, was particularly prone to fear—to the point of speaking of a *German angst*. Investigating how fear was learnt by German children thus promises important insights. To encompass a broader perspective, British children's literature has been added to the analysis. While constituting a distinct corpus, it nevertheless has more in common with the German literary tradition than, for instance, American children's literature. This choice allows for delineating more general tendencies that are true for both countries while highlighting significant differences at certain points.
7. See, for example, Watanabe-O'Kelly, 'Angstapparat aus Kalkül'.
8. For a more detailed discussion of the concept of mimesis, see the introduction to this volume.
9. Stearns and Haggerty, 'Role of Fear', 70–2. More specifically on Britain, Roper, 'Between Manliness and Masculinity', 347; Boyd, *Manliness and the Boys' Story Paper in Britain*.
10. Stearns and Haggerty, 70. On the learning of courage and fear in early twentieth-century Russia, see chapter 10, 'Ivan's Bravery'.
11. Baum, *Wonderful Wizard of Oz*, 189–90.
12. Baum, 190.

13. Stearns and Haggerty, 'Role of Fear', 71. Vivid depictions of childhood terrors can be found in some of the best-known Victorian novels written for adults, e.g. Charlotte Brontë's *Jane Eyre* (1847). See also, Shuttleworth, *Mind of the Child*, 42–59.

14. Faßbinder, *Am Wege des Kindes*, 205–14; on the general trend, Dekker and Rölling, 'Fear', 355.

15. Stearns and Haggerty, 'Role of Fear', 77.

16. Grahame, *Wind in the Willows*, 55.

17. Burnett, *Secret Garden*.

18. Kästner, *Flying Classroom*. On Kästner in Nazi Germany, see Doderer, *Erich Kästner*, 77–91.

19. See Hetzer, *Seelische Hygiene*, 31. For more on Uli's homesickness and homesickness in general, see chapter 11, 'Heidi's Homesickness'.

20. Haarer, *Unsere kleinen Kinder*, 186.

21. Kurt Faber, *Rund um die Erde*, 213 (all translations by the author).

22. Lethen, *Cool Conduct*; Stearns, *American Cool*; Reckwitz, *Das hybride Subjekt*, 416–19.

23. Peterson, *Understanding Ethnic Violence*. See also Biess, 'Feelings in the Aftermath', 31–2.

24. The relationship between physical violence and pain is discussed in chapter 8, 'Lebrac's Pain'.

25. See, for example, Werner Chomton, *Weltbrand von Morgen* (1934).

26. Schenzinger, *Der Hitlerjunge Quex*, 124–8.

27. See also Weidenmann, *Jungzug 2*.

28. Kloss, *In der wilden Klamm*.

29. Tosh, *Manliness and Masculinities in Nineteenth-Century Britain*; Roper, 'Between Manliness and Masculinity'; Levsen, *Elite, Männlichkeit und Krieg*.

30. See, for example, Wolf Durian, *Kai aus der Kiste* (1926); Franklin W. Dixon, *The Tower Treasure* (1927); Karin Michaelis, *Bibi und die Verschworenen* (1932; Dan. orig., *Bibi og de Sammensvorne*, 1932); Enid Blyton, *The Twins at St. Clare's* (1941); Enid Blyton, *Five on a Treasure Island* (1942).

31. Tolkien, *The Hobbit*, 15–17.

32. Tolkien, *The Hobbit*, 82; Tolkien, *Lord of the Rings*.

33. Stearns and Haggerty, 'Role of Fear', 88–91.

34. In a similar vein, L'Engle, *Wrinkle in Time*, 40.

35. Tolkien, *Fellowship of the Ring*, 185. In 2003, a BBC survey asked 750,000 readers in the UK to name their best-loved novel of all time. *The Lord of the Rings* was ranked no. 1, *The Lion, the Witch and the Wardrobe* no. 9, and *The Hobbit* no. 25 on the list. *The Lion, the Witch and the Wardrobe* also featured on a list of the best children's books ever (ten per age group) published in *The Guardian* in 2010 as well as on 'The 25 best children's books' list published the same year by *The Telegraph* (together with *The Lord of the Rings*). In 2004, a German list, 'Unsere Besten', compiled by television broadcaster ZDF and based on the votes of 250,000 readers, ranked *The Lord of the Rings* as the best book ever.

36. Lewis, *Lion, the Witch and the Wardrobe*, 122–3.

37. In *A Wrinkle in Time* it was a female heroine, Meg, who chose to fight despite of her fear. This book received several awards in the US (*John Newbery Medal* 1963, *Lewis Carroll Shelf Award* 1964, and *Sequoyah Children's Book Award* 1964).

38. Lindgren, *Mio, My Son*.

39. Lindgren, 80–3. In the Swedish original, the character Pompoo was called Jum-Jum.

40. Lindgren, 156.

41. Nehring, 'British and West German Protests against Nuclear Weapons'.

42. The term 'emotional refuge' was coined by Reddy, *Navigation of Feeling*, 129. See also Biess, 'Feelings in the Aftermath', 38–9.

43. See chapters 5, 'Doctor Dolittle's Empathy' and 6, 'Wendy's Love'.

44. Preußler, *Satanic Mill*, 261–2. In its year of publication this book was ranked no. 31 in the German Libri-Index based on actual sales of all books. A year later, it was awarded the *Deutscher Jugendbuchpreis* and in 1973 the Dutch *Silberner Griffel*. In 2004 it was ranked no. 58 on broadcaster ZDF's 'Unsere Besten' list.

45. Lindgren, *Brothers Lionheart*, 238. It won the German *Wilhelm-Hauff-Preis* in 1979 and the Dutch *Silberner Griffel* in 1975.

46. Ende, *Grey Gentlemen*, 83–5. The German original won the *Deutscher Jugendbuchpreis* in 1974, and in 2004, was ranked no. 53 on broadcaster ZDF's 'Unsere Besten' list. Richard Adams's *Watership Down* was first translated into German in 1975, and in 2004 the twenty-fifth German edition was published. The English edition received the *Carnegie Medal* in 1972 and the *Guardian Children's Fiction Prize* in 1973.

47. Ende, *Neverending Story*; Rowling, *Harry Potter* series.

48. Ende, *Grey Gentlemen*, 142.

49. Ende, *Jim Button and Luke the Engine Driver*, 126–7. This book won the *Deutscher Jugendbuchpreis* in 1961.

50. See, for example, Bruckner, *Day of the Bomb*; Pausewang, *Last Children*; Coerr, *Sadako and the Thousand Paper Cranes*, Holman, *Slake's Limbo*; Haugen, *Night Birds*.

51. This is in contrast to Biess, 'Sensibilisierung des Subjekts', who argued that fear shifted from external anxieties to internal angst during the 1970s.

52. This trend toward therapy started earlier in the United States, but only gained importance in West Germany in the 1970s. See Herrman, *Romance of American Psychology*; Moskowitz, *In Therapy We Trust*. For West Germany, see Maasen et al., *Das beratene Selbst*.

53. See, for example, Held, *Outsiders of Uskoken Castle*; Lindgren, *Pippi Longstocking*. For the death of a protagonist, see Spyri, *Gritli's Children* or May, *Winnetou III*. From the 1920s to the early 1960s, children's stories rarely portrayed the death of 'good' protagonists. Some exceptions could be found in young adult literature dealing with war, e.g. Westecker, *Grita wächst heran*. An early example of a post-1945 emergence of death was White, *Charlotte's Web*.

54. See, for example, Elfie Donnelly, *So long, Grandpa* (1980; Ger. orig. *Servus Opa, sagte ich leise*, 1977) which won the *Deutscher Jugendbuchpreis* and the *Hans-im-Glück-Preis* in 1978, Gudrun Mebs, *Birgit* (1982), and Susan Varley, *Badger's Parting Gifts* (1984). For further discussion of the 1970s' emphasis on talking about feelings see chapter 12, 'Ingrid's Boredom'.

55. Haugen, *The Night Birds*.

56. Korschunow, *Adam Draws Himself a Dragon*.

57. Boie, *Juli und das Monster*.

58. Roper, 'Between Manliness and Masculinity', 347. For a discussion of the interface between muscular Christianity and trust, see chapter 2, 'Dickon's Trust'.

59. Cooper, *The Deerslayer*, 6–7. It was translated into German in 1841. Cooper's *Leatherstocking Tales* was among the most read books by German youth in the nineteenth century. See Budde, *Auf dem Weg ins Bürgerleben*. In 1961, a re-adaptation of *The Deerslayer* won the German *Deutscher Jugendbuchpreis*.

60. There are numerous documents that support the assumption that May's stories were immensely popular among both (male) adolescents and adults from the lower classes. In 1928, a collection of data showed that his books were purchased by large numbers

of adolescents (40.05%) and adult workers as well as craftsmen (14.95%), see Volck, 'Begleiterscheinungen zur Absatzstatistik'. In 1930, a public library employee— libraries usually being frequented by the lower classes—complained about the 'epi- demical demand' to borrow May's books, see Prüfer and Schmid, 'Karl May in den Volksbüchereien', 340. On the longstanding German fascination with Karl May's novels, see Michaels, 'Fantasies of Native Americans'. For May's significance in the colonial context, see chapter 4, 'Ralph's Compassion'.

61. May, *Winnetou III*, 260–2.
62. Steuben, *Der Sohn des Manitu*, 297.
63. Verne, *Around the World in Eighty Days*, 53–4. The English and German translations were published in the same year as the French original.
64. Lofting, *Story of Doctor Dolittle*.
65. Professor Habakuk Tibatong, a protagonist from Max Kruse's *Urmel* series, closely resembled Doctor Dolittle. *Urmel* enjoyed great popularity with the German children's public when staged and telecast as a puppet-play by the Augsburger Puppenkiste. The first and best-known volume was *Urmel aus dem Eis* (1969).
66. See Stearns and Haggerty, 'Role of Fear', 90.
67. Preußler, *Little Witch*. The English edition of *Pippi Longstocking* was published in 1945, the same year as the Swedish original, and the German translation in 1949. It also appeared on a 'One Hundred Best Books for Children' list in *The Sunday Times* in 1958. It was ranked no. 1 on the 1971 German *Libri-Index*, with *Little Witch* at no. 18. In 2004, *Pippi Longstocking* still appeared in broadcaster ZDF's 'Unsere Besten' list.
68. Bloch, *Principle of Hope*. See also Gaddis, *Cold War*.
69. See Bourke, *Fear*; Stearns, *American Fear*.
70. Stearns and Haggerty, 'Role of Fear'; Bakker, 'Meaning of Fear'.
71. Biess, 'Sensibilisierung des Subjekts', 54, 62–7.

10

Ivan's Bravery

Jan Plamper

Sergei Auslender's *Dni boevye* ('Fighting days', 1926), a children's novella set during the Russian Civil War of 1918–21, is a story about a ten-year-old boy, Ivan Kartuzov, who joins the Bolshevik underground in a city dominated by monarchist forces, and helps the Reds achieve victory.[1] *Dni boevye* is a story providing several models: it tells a tale about how to choose the right side in an epic struggle between reactionary and progressive forces, how to sacrifice individual interests (and individuals) for the sake of the collective, how to become a manly Bolshevik, and, fundamentally, a man. It is also a story teaching young readers how to feel like a quintessential Bolshevik, and here no feeling plays a greater role than bravery.

The novella begins with the description of a bomb shelter in which the inhabitants of a house, all of various social backgrounds, congregate during the shelling of their city by the Reds. In this shelter we encounter Ivan with his mother. Neither of the two is scared by the shelling, but both worry that the father, Aleksei Kartuzov, a leftist worker, has not arrived home safely from the factory. Ivan is the only one who dares to venture outside for a bucket of water. By contrast, the pro-tsarist retired general, who is described as 'cowardly', gets on his knees and hides in a corner at the first sound of an exploded shell. As soon as the shelling stops, the general 'immediately waxes in gravity and bravery and shouts at everyone' and a little later he is described as 'walking [the courtyard], leaning on his cane, with his chest decorated with medals and crosses and epaulettes shining on his shoulders, as though he were the main hero and conqueror of the town'.[2]

Subsequently Ivan gets enlisted into the Reds by a clandestine Bolshevik and participates in the robbery and assassination of the general. He joins the underground movement, but gets caught during a surprise visit to his mother during the night. Both are arrested and Ivan again proves exceptionally courageous. Ivan's mother dies in prison while he is being interrogated. Ivan is then freed by a detachment of the Reds and reunited with his father, who, it turns out, is an influential Bolshevik and the leader of the Red detachment. They join forces and, together, they reconquer the town. The Red victory is soon threatened by an impending White attack, and Aleksei Kartuzov, instead of attacking first, fearlessly sets out to talk to the simple White soldiers in the hope that they will fraternize. Indeed he manages to win over the soldiers, most of whom are workers and peasants, and to arrest the bourgeois officers. The novella ends with a speech by Kartuzov the Elder in the town's main square during the solemn burial of those who have fallen for the Reds, including his wife, Ivan's mother: 'We won't cry. We can survive this misfortune. We can survive anything, for we know that the tears and blood were not shed in vain.'[3]

Auslender's *Dni boevye* invites many interpretations. One might, for instance, point to the thinly veiled elements of a Christian sacrifice narrative, in which individual suffering acquires a higher meaning through the redemption of a larger collective.[4] Or one might identify bravery as the dividing line between Self and Other, on a matrix in which Self is synonymous with bravery and the Reds, while Other signifies fear and is associated with the Whites. Alternatively, one might ask more broadly how children's literature such as this early Soviet novella functioned in the process of emotional learning, in general, and in the production of future brave soldiers, in particular. It is this question that will occupy centre stage in this chapter. First, pre-revolutionary instruction manuals for teachers on what (and how) to read will be examined, followed by children's literature proper, and, finally, a case study of how a combination of narratology, Extended Mind Theory, and Paul Virilio's writings on media technology might allow for a more generalized model producing bravery in children. The focus is on early Soviet Russia with a prelude in the late Tsarist period from the mid-nineteenth century onwards.

TEACHERS LEARN TO TEACH BRAVERY: INSTRUCTION MANUALS ON CHILDREN'S READING

Several handbooks and instruction manuals on what to read appeared in the late Tsarist era.[5] Partly digests of previously published reviews of children's reading, partly original texts, these manuals serve as a window into the logic governing reading as it was organized, overseen, or instigated by teachers in settings both in and out of school. They also provide more general clues about reading practices and, as in the case of 'the novel *Cleg Kelly* by S. R. Crockett, one of those books that children read several times', valuable information (here about repeated, habitual reading) with consequences for emotional learning.[6]

The 1900 manual *Chto chitat' detiam?* ('What should children read?') is a collection of excerpts from children's literature reviews that appeared in pedagogical or general literary-cultural journals (the so-called 'thick journals'). Targeted at regular teachers engaged in educating large numbers of children, it is structured around age groups and features literature recommended for children of 'the young age', 'middle age', and, finally, 'oldest age'. By contrast, the 1913 *Ukazatel' knig dlia vospitatel'skogo chteniia kadetam* ('Manual of educational reading for the cadet corps'), the cadet corps being an elite institution that trained high-ranking military officers and was a stronghold of conservatism, is geared more directly toward the

instrumental purpose of grooming efficient soldiers. It moves forward chronologi-
cally by grades, from first to seventh, and for each grade includes such sections
as 'On the devotion and love to the Emperor and the Motherland', 'Everyday
Military Life and Service', 'Religiosity', but also the 'Sympathetic treatment of
animals'.[7] In every section it discusses prose and poetry, more specifically, the 'short
synopsis' of a text and a suggested topic for a classroom discussion connected with
it. At the end it lists 'Teachers' Comments'.

All manuals were united by the fact that they were suffused with a language of
feeling, even if feeling at the turn of the century still had a wider range of meanings and encompassed morality, religious beliefs, and behaviour deemed right or
wrong; it was only over the next two decades that the semantics of feeling were
gradually reduced to the more scientifically understood 'emotion' as a response to
an outside stimulus.[8] The introduction of the manual for cadets expresses a hope
that the manual will be of help to teachers whose task is—and here it cites a legal
document (an Imperial 'Instruction')—to promote 'those well-founded ideas and
ambitions that serve as a firm grounding for genuine dedication to the throne, for
the subservience to the state and the law, and the feelings of honour, goodness, and
truthfulness'.[9] The individual reviews of children's texts, too, are awash with emotion words. Thus 'the fairy tales and stories by Mr Zasodimskii' are said to be 'suffused with warm feeling of love both towards people and the surrounding world'.[10]

As for the breakdown of emotions, bravery is by far the most prevalent, while
fear is conspicuously absent from the spectrum of feeling. This absence actually signifies presence because in fact most emotions discussed implicitly revolve around
the single most dangerous soldierly emotion—fear. Thus in the 'Teachers' comments' rubric of Fedor Tiutchev's *Tovarishch* ('Comrade', 1888), a story recommended for first-graders, it is mentioned that 'the cadets listened to the story with
great interest and praised the bravery and self-sacrifice of the main character'.[11]
Teachers were also advised to read Ivan Shcheglov's (Ivan L. Leont'ev's) 1881 story
Pervoe srazhenie ('The first battle'), 'an exemplary portrayal of the mental state of
a young officer before and during his first battle, which is likely to raise a number
of questions among the students'. What is more, 'if the class is in a somewhat pessimistic mood, omit pages 26–28'—because this section of the story focuses on
the officer's first-time experience in combat, including the sight of a corpse and
such thoughts as 'I am going to die soon' and feelings of 'cowardice', 'shame', and
'desperation'.[12]

The question of change over time is as important as it is difficult to answer due
to the absence of post-1917 teacher instruction manuals. And yet, extrapolating
from post-revolutionary children's literature, it is the role of religion that changed
most dramatically after the Revolution. The 1913 manual for cadets introduces
O. I. Shmidt's *Galia* (1886) as 'a children's story from the times of pagan Rus''
about 'the sacrificial heroic deeds and sufferings of the deeply believing Christians
Galia and Annushka'. Its moral is that 'deep faith gives great strength for the com-
pletion of heroic deeds' and 'many cadets were moved to tears when listening to
this story'.[13] All kinds of transmutations and rechannelling of religion notwith-
standing, it was unthinkable to perceive Russian Orthodoxy as the main source of

courageous behaviour after the establishment of the first socialist state. To be sure, some elements of the new role of religion were present before 1917. *Chto chitat' detiam?*, for instance, the manual for regular teachers, not those teaching cadets, who were known to sympathize with liberalism and who, by and large, hoped for civil liberties, legality, and a republic or at least a constitutional monarchy, recommended a book of animal stories for children, translated from English. This book was worth reading because its 'author propagates the idea that nature has also endowed animals with intelligence, and from this it follows that animals are naturally resourceful, brave, thankful, and so on'.[14] In other words, the review praises the fact that the English children's book traces positively connoted emotions, such as bravery, back to reason rather than a metaphysical entity, such as God.[15]

CHILDREN LEARN BRAVERY THROUGH LITERATURE

Bravery in children's literature is rarely encountered on its own as a stand-alone emotion. It is usually part of a field that includes other emotions, first and foremost fear and cowardice, but also hatred, rage, and shame. At its most basic level, bravery is conquered fear. Hatred, rage, and shame are auxiliary emotions in overcoming fear and attaining bravery. The field of bravery in children's literature came in a variety of shapes and forms that changed over time. The following pages will examine some of these forms across the late Tsarist period into the early Soviet period.

Readers (or listeners) were generally expected to emulate a hero, be it one from history (for example, General Suvorov from the War of 1812), from the world of pure fantasy (for example, a knight [*bogatyr'*], or the invented Boyar Iurii Miloslavskii from the Polish-Muscovite War of 1605–18), or any anonymous person (for example, 'the little soldier', *soldatik*).[16] It is the hero's deeds, his bravery, his experiencing no fear or his overcoming of fear that had to be learnt.

One of the variants included a young protagonist who did not have to traverse a path to bravery, but was inherently courageous. Before the Revolution, this sometimes took a form that could be termed phantasmagoric estrangement. One example is 'The fearless soldier' from a collection of *Soldatskie skazki* ('Soldier's fairy tales') published in 1915, during the First World War.[17] In the story, a soldier who 'never knew fear', having served his twenty-five years in the army, goes off 'to roam the world in search of fear' (in an inversion of the original Grimm brothers' fairy tale *The Story of a Boy Who Went Forth to Learn Fear* our Russian hero never finds fear). After a long day, he and a fellow soldier chance upon a lonely hut in the woods to sleep, but it turns out that a coffin containing a corpse is in the room. The other soldier is horrified and wants to run away, but the constitutionally brave one convinces him to stay. In the middle of the night the corpse awakens and tries to pull the fearless soldier into the coffin; he gets angry and fends off the (un)dead man, driving him out of the hut. The two soldiers then resume walking through the woods with the dead man, until they encounter a group of robbers, who are gathered around a fire, eating. The soldiers overpower the robbers and prepare to cut the leg off one of the robbers—which scares the robbers and prompts them to run away.[18] In this story, the fear of the second soldier, who accompanies the fearless main protagonist, is inverted and turned into a strange, alien object. The corpse that comes to life, the march through the woods with the corpse, and the severing of a robber's leg like a piece of meat cut from livestock, all border on the absurd and fantastic. Fear is thus separated from the soldierly Self through the literary technique of phantasmagoric estrangement. This is one example of fear management.

In an example from Soviet times, A. Gromov's Pet'ka in the 1926 novella *Za 'obchee delo'* ('For the common cause') is also a hero for whom bravery was a state of being rather than a goal to achieve.[19] Set during the Civil War (1918–21) in Siberia, the novella revolves around a small unit of partisans engaged in fighting a detachment led by Admiral Kolchak of the White Army. Pet'ka joins the partisans on his own initiative and has to overcome their distrust because of his young age. ' "I want to be a partisan." Stepchuk laughs out loud: "You? Ha...Ha..." Pet'ka seemed all too small and even pitiful to him. "Don't laugh, comrade commander! I repeat seriously...," says the boy sombrely, "I want to fight the White Guards." ' Asked why, Pet'ka explains that his father, an engineer and a Bolshevik, has been killed by the Whites, and that his mother has been arrested. 'If [only] you knew how passionately I hate the Whites.'[20]

It is hatred that has made Pet'ka fearless. And it is a Christian-turned-Communist sacrifice pattern—see also Auslender's *Dni boevye* and many other children's texts— that endows with meaning Pet'ka's brave willingness to give up his individual life for the common good. When Pet'ka proposes a ruse to infiltrate the White detachment and lead it into an ambush, his Partisan commander asks how he will react if exposed:

> 'I'll die,' replies Pet'ka simply and without thinking. Heavy silence follows. 'Comrades, come on, don't worry about me. You are also always prepared to die, right?...And am I not a partisan like you? Am I worse than you? Why can't I also die for the common cause?...We live in a time when we all, young and old, have to work together to break Kolchak's neck as soon as possible. But if we start thinking for too long, nothing good will come of it!'[21]

Pet'ka then sets out for the village where the White detachment is causing mayhem, burning huts, and killing women and children (here the function of the graphic descriptions seems to be to ignite the readers' anger). Pet'ka manages to infiltrate the detachment and to convince them to go into the woods to fight the partisans, whose hiding place Pet'ka pretends to give away. As Pet'ka leads the White detachment into the ambush, mounting tension is created through descriptions of how the horses get scared—'frightening...the horses snuffled in a frightened manner'—but never Pet'ka. As the Whites start suspecting that they have been tricked, they start hitting Pet'ka, who bleeds and loses some teeth, but hardly moans and shows almost superhuman courage. 'Will they kill me? I don't give a damn.'[22]

In a final, cathartic scene, the Whites are trapped in the high grass and bushes and get shot at by the Reds, while Pet'ka lies down and escapes the shooting. It is here, at the very end and when the danger has passed, that the first fear word surfaces in Pet'ka's narrative: 'Pet'ka lay down sneering. "Alright, you White devils, now you can shoot as much as you like. I'm not scared... Now... Ouch!" ' The last lines of the novella are a song that Pet'ka sings in this situation. Hatred towards a clearly identifiable enemy, voluntarism, actionism, and the sublimation of individual suffering for a higher, collective good is the particular mix that keeps fear at bay and presents a childhood hero who does not show any sign of fear.[23]

Much more often than these two variants of constitutional courage, we encounter protagonists for whom bravery is a matter of becoming rather than being. This goes for both the late Tsarist and early Soviet periods, although pre-revolutionary writers—likely due to their liberal bias—played down the ultimate telos of bravery to such an extent that their protagonists became fearful heroes.[24]

To be sure, there were also the pre-revolutionary liberals who questioned the ethics of bravery. These authors all wrote in the wake of Leo Tolstoy's *Sevastopol' Sketches* (1887; Rus. orig. *Sevastopol'skie rasskazy*, 1855), widely considered the first realistic Russian account of the combat experience, including the experience of fear, and a blueprint for *War and Peace*. One of these liberals was Vsevolod Garshin, whose *Four Days* (1959; Rus. orig. *Chetyre dnia*, 1877) features a first-time soldier, Private Ivanov, who courageously kills a fearful Turk, but when lying wounded for three and a half days next to the Turk's dead body, he is beset by moral doubts. 'Before me lies a man that I have killed. Why did I kill him?' asks first-person narrator Ivanov. He ends up asking larger moral questions about the purpose of war and individual guilt that begin with humanizing the Turk:

> Why did Fate drive him here? Who is he? Perhaps, like me, he has an old mother? For a long time she will sit at the door of her poor mud hut, gazing northward, waiting: is her darling, her support, her breadwinner coming?... My bayonet pierced his heart. There is a big, black hole in his chest, and all around it is blood. *I did that.*[25]

Private Ivanov is depicted as fearless, although the basis of his fearlessness is unclear. He is not characterized as fearless by nature and descriptions of his excruciating pain from his injury figure prominently in the story. As a matter of fact, in the genre of late nineteenth-century Russian psychological realist fiction, and in the wake of Leo Tolstoy's and others' graphic accounts of the soldierly fear experience, including its physical symptoms, Private Ivanov's bravery appears somewhat naïve or even hard to believe. This bravery is juxtaposed against the fear of his enemy, the Turkish soldier:

> He was a big, fat Turk, but I ran straight at him though I was thin and puny.... But, with a cry of terror, he tried to press back into the bush. He might have gone round it, but he was so frightened that he forgot everything and thrust himself into the thorny branches.[26]

Later in the story when lying next to the Turkish soldier he has killed, Ivanov again puts himself in the enemy's place:

He was ordered to go [to the Russo-Turkish War of 1877–8], and he went. Had he refused to go, he would have been beaten with sticks or shot by a bullet from some pasha's revolver. He had made long, difficult marches from Stamboul to Rustchuk. We attacked, they defended themselves. But seeing that we, horrible people, were unafraid of his patent English Peabody and Martini gun, seeing that we continued to advance, he became terrified. When he wanted to run away, a small man, whom he could have killed with one blow of his black fist, sprang towards him and plunged a bayonet into his heart.[27]

Is it possible that Garshin expected readers to displace some of the fear descriptions of the Turk onto Ivanov? Might the humanization of the Other, the enemy Turk, have also spelled the infection of the Self, Ivanov, by the emotion of fear? Do soldierly Self and enemy Other merge in *Four Days*?

At the very end of the story there is the amputation of Ivanov's leg (and the doctor's comment 'Well, you may thank God for your luck. You will live. We've had to take one [leg] away, but that's nothing. Can you talk?'), which may be read as the metaphoric and final separation of the soldierly Self from superhuman courage.[28] By losing one of his legs, Ivanov becomes, one could argue, emotionally whole.

Much more often than its pre-revolutionary precedents, Soviet children's literature conforms to the genre of *Bildungsroman* and features narratives of moving to new, higher stages of personhood, in which bravery plays a key role. First, there is the example of Arkady Gaidar, perhaps the Communist Bloc's most famous author for children, and his 1936 children's novella *Chetvertyi blindazh* ('The fourth shelter', 1936).[29] In *Chetvertyi blindazh* a group of children in a dacha settlement are observing from afar how a Red Army commander prepares a cannon for firing. The children are frightened by the surprising sound and there is a full page devoted to denying having been scared.[30] It turns out that the firing has to do with military manoeuvres and that the Red Army soldiers are shelling a model village—but the children do not know this. While venturing into the model village some of them get trapped in a cellar when the shelling starts again. While shells are exploding above them, the children experience fear of death. ' "Kol'ka [a boy]," sighed Niurka [a girl], searching for his hand in the dark, "stay where you are, or I'll get even more afraid." "I myself am afraid," admitted Kol'ka and fell silent.'[31] The girl Niurka is indispensable in this economy of bravery: it is through her that the boys wax courageous. To cure her fear they start joking and next suggest singing a canon-like tune with different voices. Both devices work, especially the singing, in which their voices become increasingly self-assured.

The children then get discovered by the Red Army soldiers and are brought to the commander. It turns out that this shelter, the fourth shelter, was indeed singled out for shelling on that particular day. Upon their release one of the children gets to keep a part of a shell as a token of remembrance. As soon as they return to the dacha settlement, another boy, Isaika, starts telling them about the Red Army soldiers, but the children only laugh at Isaika's silly, 'childish' banter. Having been shelled in the cellar has set them apart from other children; it has in fact allowed them to prepare their passage from childhood to adulthood. Acquiring bravery is synonymous with becoming an adult. It might be argued that the shelling also prefigures actual shelling in times of war. It is a kind of early drill for the bomb shelter.

EMBODIED READING AND THE 'COGAFFECTIVE' PRODUCTION OF BRAVERY

There were numerous instances in which children's literature actively involved the body in the reading process. In Gaidar's novel *R.V.S.* ('Revolutionary Military Council', 1926), the male hero Dimka 'plays bravery' and thus provides children with an example of how to act courageously via mimetic role play. In *Shkola muzhestva* ('The school of bravery', 1954), the later film version of *R.V.S.* with its revealing title, one group of children beats another group in a battle on the river with a boat tellingly named *SMELYI* ('The brave one').[32] Apart from mimetic play, the characters of various children's books are shown to be singing to strengthen their bodies against physiological fear reactions: for example, the children in the cellar in Gaidar's *Chetvertyi blindazh* or Pet'ka, the hero of *Za 'obchee delo'*, who sings a song while bullets whistle through the air above his head.

In expanding these examples, the question may be asked as to how reading, if perceived as a physical practice that imparts 'practical knowledge' which can later be 'constitutive of social ... action', figures in the making of potentially brave future soldiers.[33] In other words, how can reading in one's youth produce courage in adult soldiers? Let us illustrate with a close reading of a text.

Konstantin Bozhenko's *Prikliuchenie malen'kogo trubacha* ('The adventure of the little trumpeter', 1927) is a nineteen-page story with six full pages of illustrations.[34] Published in 1927 in the *Library of the pupil* series in paperback and in a first edition of 10,000 copies, it was typical of the mass children's literature generated during the New Economic Policy (NEP), the period between the end of the Civil War (1918), and Stalin's First Five-Year Plan (1928) when the Bolsheviks experimented with elements of a market economy. The story revolves around twelve-year-old Kesha Rudykh, a farmer's son, who lives in a solitary hut with his parents in a clearing in the forested taiga (the story is aimed at children from other parts of the Soviet Union, as can be seen from explanations of local Siberian words in the body of the text and in three footnotes). Kesha attends a vocational school in a nearby village and is a passionate trumpeter, a hobby that he has inherited from his father, who played the trumpet in his regiment's orchestra during his time in the army.

The reader or listener is subtly prepared for a later link between the trumpet and a dangerous feature of the taiga, namely wolves, at the story's very beginning, in lines 7–9: 'There were all kinds of animals in the taiga: bears, wild boars, lynxes, and especially a lot of wolves. Kesha was a good trumpet player.'[35] These early hints are crucial because developing the fantasy, imagining something horrible having to do with Kesha and the wolves, takes time to build up.

The story then continues by describing how Kesha inherited the talent of trumpet-playing (and a trumpet) from his father. It next describes the preparation of the October Revolution festivities for which Kesha is going to perform in a concert with other children who play instruments. During the daily practice concerts, Kesha does not go home to his parents' hut. Instead he stays in the village with his grandfather and uncle who live together there. He only comes home once just before the celebration of the October Revolution in order to put on his freshly washed best clothes. As he is about to leave for the village and the actual concert, his father tells him: '"Don't even think of walking home after the concert! There are an awful lot of wolves out there. Last night about twenty sat around our hut. They only ran away when I shot one of them." "Alright, I will sleep over at grandpa's," Kesha promised.'[36]

The concert at the October Revolution celebration is a resounding success. Late into the night ('high above the village the full moon shone') Kesha leaves the school with a group of other children, they play music, there is dancing and merry-making, but suddenly Kesha realizes that he has gone far past his grandfather's house and the village. Because of the merry company, he has taken the habitual way home to his parents' hut. By this point readers have been cued several times about the presence of wolves in the woods. First, sentences such as 'Far from the village it suddenly dawned upon Kesha: "Where am I going? I have to go back. I have to return. Father was adamant that I not walk home during the night"' create mounting suspense. The suspense is further enhanced with the classical literary strategy of slowing down time as the unknowing protagonist moves toward the source of danger: Kesha forgets about his resolution as soon as the girls in the group start begging, 'Play, Kesha, please play your trumpet for us! You play so well.'[37] And so he plays, 'moving further and further away from the village, but with a heavy heart, constantly thinking: "It's not right for me to walk home. Papa told me not to do this. What if there are really…wolves?"'[38]

But the night is so bright with the full moon and the mood so good with the merry company that Kesha brushes aside his doubts: 'What is there to be afraid of? It's bright. And we're so many; we're an entire gang. We're so loud, the wolves will run away.'[39] He decides to stay with the group until a point towards the end, where his way will have to part with that of the group, and he will have to run the final distance to his parents' hut. Kesha's interior monologue, or rather, dialogue, or yet more apt, a tug-of-war between two voices, is revealed. It is hard to avoid siding with the voice of reason, the voice that urges Kesha to stop and go back to his grandfather's in the village, for by this time the reader knows more than Kesha and has all the bits of information warning of an impending disaster. Kesha plays *The Internationale* one last time, parts with the group, and runs off in the direction of his parents' place.

Here the story is interrupted, followed by a new section before which most people reading aloud for others would probably have paused to take a deep breath, further building the suspense. This third part's first sentences read, 'Kesha was a brave boy and a good runner. He ran fast and gave the wolves little thought, but he did occasionally look to the side.' By calling Kesha 'brave' in this moment the reader is alerted to the fact that his bravery will soon be tested. The story then turns to onomatopoetic means to create a sense of Kesha's isolation as he is running in the middle of a clear night in the snow-covered Siberian woods: 'There was silence in the taiga. The only sound was the snow under Kesha's boots: crack, crack, crack, crack (*khrup, khrup, khrup, khrup*).' Kesha runs and gets closer and closer to home, giving the reader a sense of hope that he will make it after all.[40]

'Suddenly ahead of him and very close by a wolf let out a loud, drawn-out, and wailing howl: Uh-u-u … uh-u-u … u-uh-u-u … hu-u-u!' Kesha freezes and his heart beats fiercely. He is encircled by other wolves and there is a rising sense of terror, amplified by descriptions of the wolves' howling and eyes, which 'burned like two green lights, like two glow-worms'. He tries to scare the wolves away by

> screaming: 'Go away! I'll get you!' But it didn't work. Kesha's voice trembled and broke; the wolf in front of him only lifted his ears, bared his teeth, and snarled. The wolf behind him kept howling and the sound got closer and closer…Now Kesha got really scared. Out of fear he dropped his trumpet and it fell to his feet.

The paralysis, the trembling voice, and the unintended action (dropping the trumpet) indicate the physical symptoms of fear; in addition, the explicit fear-related phrases 'got really scared' (*stalo sovsem strashno*) and 'out of fear' (*so strakhu*) occur for the first time. All of this is complemented by a potent full-page illustration (see Fig. 10.1).[41]

Dropping the trumpet gives Kesha the idea to start playing, and so he does, which is initially very effective at scaring off the wolves. He varies his marches and, while still playing, he moves toward one of his grandfather's nearby hunter's huts. It is small and empty but is only fifty steps away. The author has quite jarringly introduced this safe haven right before Kesha was first surprised by the wolves' howling. The improbable appearance of this hut out of the blue shows that place and distance in this story serve the emotional narrative rather than geographical purposes: they function as devices that relax or amplify the fear experience.

Kesha's trumpet-playing works for a while, but then loses its fear-inducing, protective power. 'Kesha became even more frightened [*ispugalsia*] than before but did not lose his mind.' He moved toward the hut and got on top of the snow-covered roof, continually playing the trumpet. Seven wolves surround the hut, 'lit by the moon and with their furry tails laid out across the snow. They stared at the moon-lit little trumpeter with eager, hungry eyes, snapped their teeth, and periodically howled.' And Kesha? Kesha stands on the roof, playing the trumpet for his life, literally, and regrets having disobeyed his father. 'For his foolishness and disobedience Kesha cursed himself as a "jackass" and "idiot." He shook from fear and with tears in his eyes incessantly played cheerful marches for the wolves, *The Russian* and *The Internationale*…The moon sank fast.'[42]

At this point in the narrative there is another pause before the final section. As it turns out, Kesha's parents' hut is so near that his father, who wakes up early to get ready for a long day of work, hears the sound of the trumpet playing, interrupted by the howling of the wolves from a distance. He immediately understands what is going on, grabs his hunting gear, runs out toward the hunter's hut, and shouts to his son, 'Kesha, don't be afraid, it's me!'[43] He shoots one of the wolves whereupon the others run away in shock (see Fig. 10.2).

Fig. 10.1 Konstantin Bozhenko, *Prikliuchenie malen'kogo trubacha* (1927), 13.

Fig. 10.2 Konstantin Bozhenko, *Prikliuchenie malen'kogo trubacha* (1927), 17.

Fig. 10.3 Konstantin Bozhenko, *Prikliuchenie malen'kogo trubacha* (1927), 19.

'Happily Kesha played *The Russian* once more, and he played it so cheerfully that his father laughed out and did not scold him. Dmitry Petrovich [Kesha's father] figured that his son was punished enough for his carelessness and that this adventure with the wolves would be a good lesson for him.'[44] Here the story ends with a picture with 'THE END' written in Russian over a dead wolf (see Fig. 10.3).

Part morality tale, part adventure story, part lesson in Soviet regional geography, *Prikliuchenie malen'kogo trubacha* may also be interpreted as an exercise in bravery training for the future soldier within the child. First, readers or listeners can share Kesha's experience of fear and bravery. The descriptions of Kesha's courageous running through the snow-covered taiga after parting with the group and of his bodily symptoms of fear (the paralysis upon encountering the wolves, the fast heartbeat) allow for the mimetic experience of similar sensations. At the same time, readers may experience fear and bravery beyond reliving the protagonist's emotions. The narrative provides more knowledge about the future than is available to Kesha, and this information enables the development of emotional imagination, for example, by picturing after the early cue in lines 7–9 of the story a horrifying link between the trumpet and the wolves or by picturing oneself as behaving more courageously than Kesha (e.g. single-handedly fighting off the wolves with one's fists). There are also numerous literary conventions readers or listeners are privy to, which Kesha ignores. For instance, a child having read or heard similar children's stories will know that most end happily and that it is hardly likely that Kesha will be torn to pieces by the wolves. Kesha, by contrast, does not know this and fears for his life in an existential manner.

By living through these emotions while reading or listening to a story, practical knowledge is provided that can later be recalled. This practical knowledge is enhanced through repetition, as many children's texts were read (aloud) multiple times. (Just how emotional recall works is a question beyond the confines of this chapter. Suffice it to say that it is likely not a one-to-one reproduction, rather it is a continual overwriting and rewriting—consider merely the possible effects of knowing the outcome of the story. What we are dealing with, then, is precisely the difference and polyvalence associated with 'trying emotion'.)[45]

The reading and listening processes are not exclusively cognitive, but are a mixture of cognition and bodily affect, a proposition requiring an explanation that expands on the theoretical-methodological grid laid out in the introduction to this book. Two hypotheses are particularly relevant here. Both break down the barrier between aspects of reading that are considered cognitive and thus more interiorized (in 'the soul', in 'the mind', or in 'the brain') and those that are deemed affective and thus more outwardly corporeal. One concerns the Extended Mind Theory (EMT), according to which, cognition takes place in peripheral parts of the body as well as in the mind. Alva Noë, for instance, writes

> that there's no principled reason even to think that our bodies stop where we think they do. Parts of me—tools—can be spatially discontinuous with me: What makes them me, what makes them part of my body, is the way my actions take them up. And insofar as I act in, and feel with, my extended body, my mind is extended too.[46]

The other relevant hypothesis is provided by the media philosopher Paul Virilio's musings on 'tactile telepresence', that is the disappearance of distance between the fingers that touch the screen and the naked body that is shown on the screen in cybersex; the disappearance of distance between the fingers that touch a screen and the virtual world of the computer war game; or, one might add, the fingers that move a joystick controlling a drone that is targetting individuals thousands of miles away.[47] In essence, tactile telepresence is the collapsing of simulation into reality, and, although Virilio refers to our own age of smartphones, touchscreens, and the like, his thought may also be applied to children's literature in a different age. For it is not at all clear that the effects of printed children's literature as a medium are categorically different from the effects of more modern media technologies. Consider, for example, lavishly illustrated children's books of the 1920s that entered peasant households in the Soviet countryside. These homes were dominated by oral tradition, with no rivalling audio (or visual) media such as radios or televisions, and whose children had just become literate, while their parents, especially their mothers, were still largely illiterate. In this scenario, it becomes easier to fathom the power and reach of children's literature. Combining this with such reading techniques as reading out loud, moving the finger across the page, touching illustrations (or not touching them—such as a picture of a snake—out of fear), moving various body parts during reading, one approaches the realm of Virilio's tactile telepresence.

It now becomes plausible to consider reading done by children not as some kind of passive or exclusively cognitive action, but rather as a wholly embodied and indeed 'cogaffective' practice. This term, introduced here, is more appropriate than Barnett and Ratner's 'cogmotive' because the stem 'affective' captures the less intentional, less signified, and less conscious aspects of the reading experience.[48] Bodies move during and are moved by reading with signs including palpitation, galvanic skin response, breathing, but also a foot that twitches out of boredom, a mouth involuntarily left gaping, or a drawing interrupted during a particularly suspenseful moment in the narrative. This cogaffective reading/listening experience can get stored as practical knowledge that is also simultaneously cognitive and corporeal, and this practical knowledge can be recalled—this is the contention of this chapter—in different circumstances, including those of warfare. A reader/listener of *Prikliuchenie malen'kogo trubacha* could then, when faced with an external threat in a later real-life combat situation, recall the experience of fear and its management and thus act more bravely than he might otherwise have acted. Good readers, one could suggest, are better, more courageous soldiers, who can better deal with the business of war—killing and dying.

The fact that the foregoing is cast in tentative terms—'*can* share', '*may* experience fear', '*can* get stored', '*could* recall'—is related to a number of factors that account for causal connections that are less straightforward than in some other areas of history-writing. To mention but two, there is often, though not categorically, a gap between fear and bravery in real-life environments and fictional faux fear and faux bravery.[49] Actually encountering a hungry wolf in the Siberian taiga need not be a priori, but it is quite different from reading about a hero who is faced with the same threat in a work of children's fiction. Second, there is, once again, the issue of 'trying emotion'. The emotional processes associated with reading are just as open-ended and subject to variation and failure as emotional processes in real life.

And yet the case is made here for the elements that can be extrapolated and applied generally of the cogaffective fear experience in reading. If the retelling of Kesha's story recreated some of the sensations in the reader of this chapter, there is a first argument in favour of elements that can be universalized. What is more, any scepticism as to what reading has to do with the production of brave soldiers will seem less justified when zooming forward in the century from the Soviet 1920s and 1930s. Starting with the Second World War in the United States, for instance, films were used in combat training 'to desensitize recruits to the noise and bloody gore of battle'.[50] War movies for the general public were thought to have similar effects. Today, computer games, especially with first-person shooters, are employed for the training of soldiers and it has in fact become commonplace to remark on how porous the borders between games designed for the market and games designed for the military have become.

* * *

Ivan, the protagonist of Sergei Auslender's *Dni boevye,* is actually called 'Van'ka' throughout the novella, a diminutive used mainly for children (see Fig. 10.4). Young 'Van'ka' becomes adult 'Ivan' after showing signs of fear that his recently reconquered town might fall back into the hands of the Whites. 'Van'ka hid in the corner of the sofa and thought, "is it possible that we will experience another defeat, that we will have to run again and be taken prisoner?"' Enter Van'ka's

Fig. 10.4 Sergei Auslender, *Dni boevye* (1926), 167.

father, Aleksei Kartuzov, the leader of the Red detachment: 'Van'ka thought hard about this, he even winced a bit, when a loud voice suddenly resounded: "Ivan!" '[51] The father's first-time designation of his son as 'Ivan' rather than 'Van'ka' marks not just a progression from childhood to adulthood (and thus to a higher stage of personhood) in the *Bildungsroman* mode, but it is also an emotional growth narrative, a narrative always aligned with the grand historical and inexorable move from the stage of capitalism to socialism. Ultimately, the name 'Ivan' represents a cipher and the endpoint of a utopian time: it encapsulates what it takes to *become*—a Bolshevik, a man, a collective, and a socialist society. No bravery—no Ivan. No socialization of feelings—no socialism. These, in the final analysis, are the heights to which the stakes in emotional learning can be raised.

NOTES

1. See Auslender, *Dni boevye*.
2. Auslender, 36, 13, 14 (all translations by the author).
3. Auslender, 167.
4. On these Christian overtones see Halfin, 'From Darkness to Light'.
5. I found Kurnin, *Chto chitat' detiam?* ('What should children read?', 1900); Flerov, *Ukazatel' knig dlia detskogo chteniia* (1905); Zotov, *Ukazatel' knig dlia vospitatel'skogo chteniia kadetam* (1913). No such manuals have surfaced for the Soviet period. As for the sample of children's literature, it consists of thirty-eight texts that may be classified as pre-revolutionary (with an emphasis on the 1870s–1910s) and fifty-six as post-revolutionary (predominantly from the 1920s–30s). Fairy tales and picture books are excluded.
6. Kurnin, *Chto chitat' detiam?*, 130.

7. On 'military-patriotic education' (*voenno-patrioticheskoe vospitanie*) for all children (not just a group, such as cadets) in Soviet schools, see Aspatore, 'Military-Patriotic Theme in Soviet Textbooks and Children's Literature'. On empathy with animals, see chapter 5, 'Doctor Dolittle's Empathy'.

8. On this general shift see Frevert et al., *Emotional Lexicons*.

9. Zotov, *Ukazatel' knig dlia vospitatel'skogo chteniia kadetam*, viii.

10. Review of P. V. Zasodimskii's *Dedushkiny rasskazy i skazki*.

11. Zotov, *Ukazatel' knig dlia vospitatel'skogo chteniia kadetam*, 14.

12. Zotov, 66. Shcheglov, 'Pervoe srazhenie', 94, 96. In recommending to 'omit pages 26–28', the manual must be citing a different edition of the story from the original journal publication in *Novoe obozrenie* (1881). I surmise the manual had in mind the passage I have quoted because (a) pp. 94–6 conform to pp. 26–8 in the story and (b) because this is the first passage that is less upbeat and treats the demoralizing aspects of the combat experience.

13. Zotov, 27.

14. Review of *Sto rasskazov iz zhizni zhivotnykh*, 53. In a similar vein, see chapter 5, 'Doctor Dolittle's Empathy'.

15. See also chapter 3, 'Asghari's Piety'.

16. See, for example, Pogoskii, *Aleksandr Vasil'evich Suvorov, Generalissimus russkikh voisk*; Furman, *Aleksandr Vasil'evich Suvorov*; Zagoskin, *Iurii Miroslavskii ili Russkie v 1612 godu*.

17. On children as soldiers in the First World War, see Kelly, *Children's World*, 11. On children combatants in the Second World War, see Kucherenko, *Little Soldiers*.

18. Kozyrev, *Soldatskie skazki*, 204–5.

19. See Gromov, *Za 'obchee delo'*.

20. Gromov, 6.

21. Gromov, 10–11.

22. Gromov, 14, 22, 27.

23. In other cases constitutional, inherent bravery in a hero is derived from character configurations, such as family ties that are presented as natural and instinctual. In Dorokhov's *Syn bol'shevika* ('The son of a Bolshevik', 1928), also set in Siberia during the Civil War, young Misha, whose father is in the Bolshevik underground, defends his mother whose honour is verbally offended by one of the Whites during an apartment search. It is a 'natural' defence mechanism that leads him to take his father's place in courageously defending his mother; Dorokhov, 4, 7.

24. See also chapter 9, 'Jim Button's Fear.'

25. Garshin, *Four Days*, 480 (emphasis in original).

26. Garshin, 476. Earlier on the same page Ivanov describes the terror of seeing a dying soldier from his own detachment: 'I remember how we ran through the wood, how the bullets whistled, how the broken branches fell, how we pushed through the haw-thorn bushes.... Sidorov, of the first company...suddenly squatted on the ground and looked at me with big, frightened eyes. A stream of blood poured from his mouth. Yes, I remember it all perfectly.'

27. Garshin, 481.

28. Garshin, 489 (the substitution of 'leg' for 'foot' is my own; while the Russian *noga* signifies both 'leg' and 'foot', the context within the story and general knowledge about military surgery at the time suggest that the leg was amputated, not only the foot).

29. Autobiographical reasons might account for why Gaidar returned to the theme of fear/bravery time and again. During the Civil War he was diagnosed with traumatic

neurosis, the Russian version of shell shock, and was treated in a psychiatric hospital. See his grandson's memoir, Gaidar, *Days of Defeat and Victory*, 4. See also chapter 11, 'Heidi's Homesickness'.

30. Gaidar, *Chetvertyi blindazh*, 8.
31. Gaidar, 22.
32. *Shkola muzhestva*, Vladimir Basov and Mstislav Korchagin, dirs. (Mosfilm, 1954) [film].
33. See Wulf, 'Mimetic Learning', 56.
34. Bozhenko, *Prikliuchenie malen'kogo trubacha*.
35. Bozhenko, 3.
36. Bozhenko, 6.
37. Bozhenko, 6, 8. On this strategy, see narratology, for example, Shklovsky, *Theory of Prose*, 101–16; Carroll, *Theorizing the Moving Image*, 94–117; Ricoeur, *Ricoeur Reader*, 99–116.
38. Bozhenko, 10.
39. Bozhenko, 10.
40. Bozhenko, 10, 11.
41. Bozhenko, 11, 12.
42. Bozhenko, 16, 18.
43. Bozhenko, 19.
44. Bozhenko, 19.
45. See the introduction to this volume; Eitler and Scheer, 'Emotionengeschichte als Körpergeschichte'; Reddy, *Navigation of Feeling*, 32, 322.
46. Noë, *Out of Our Heads*, 80. Also see Scheer, 'Are Emotions a Kind of Practice'.
47. See Virilio, *Open Sky*, 105 (the context of 'tactile telepresence' here is indeed cyber sexuality).
48. 'Cogmotive' is derived from 'cogmotion' in Barnett and Ratner, 'Organization and Integration of Cognition and Emotion in Development'. On 'affective', see Leys' characterization of affects as 'independent of, and in an important sense prior to, ideology—that is, prior to intentions, meanings, reasons, and beliefs—because they are nonsignifying, autonomic processes that take place below the threshold of conscious awareness and meaning'. Leys, 'Turn to Affect', 437.
49. I borrow 'faux fear' from Mieszkowski, 'Fear of a Safe Place', 102.
50. Bourke, *Intimate History of Killing*, 96. See also Bourke, *Fear*, chapter 7.
51. Auslender, *Dni boevye*, 151.

11

Heidi's Homesickness

Juliane Brauer

Heidi, the young, innocent, scarcely educated heroine in Johanna Spyri's classic, *Heidi* (1884/1885; Ger. orig. *Heidis Lehr- und Wanderjahre*, 1880 and *Heidi kann brauchen, was es gelernt hat*, 1881), who has grown up close to nature in the Swiss Alps, suffers from dreadful homesickness. After being forced to leave her beloved mountains for Frankfurt, she displays all the pathological symptoms of the so-called Swiss illness, otherwise known as nostalgia.[1] Heidi talks incessantly and nostalgically to her friend Clara about life in the Alps, 'till her longing grew so great that she added: "I have to go home now. I must go tomorrow"'. The normally cheerful, rose-cheeked child becomes pale, emaciated, and 'quiet as a mouse'. Insomnia, dreams about her home, and secret tears are all symptoms of her illness, which the doctor, a family friend, rightly diagnoses as 'homesickness'.[2] Characterized as a longing for a certain place that is bound to the feelings of familiarity, of being protected and cared for, of happiness, belonging,[3] and identity, homesickness can also evidently cause severe physical pain. Heidi is completely helpless and overwhelmed by her feelings and only her return home to the Alps rescues her from impending death. Her ailment is simultaneously essential in fostering her trust in God as well as in encouraging her to learn to read.[4] With the skills that she has acquired in faraway Frankfurt, her well-established sense of belonging and identity, and her unwavering faith in God, Heidi uses what she has learnt and becomes a moral authority in the book's sequel, *Heidi kann brauchen, was es gelernt hat* (1881).[5] She reads religious verses and songs to Peter's blind grandmother and thus helps her endure the dark winter. The doctor, trapped in his immense sadness after the death of his daughter, learns from Heidi to resign himself to God's will and to trust the healing power of the mountains. In Frankfurt, pale, wheelchair-bound Clara longs for Heidi, the goats, and the healing effects of Heidi's Swiss Alps. Her longing is characterized by her search for happiness and satisfaction, feelings which the fragile girl expects to find on the Alps. Finally she is allowed to visit her bosom friend in the mountains and as the summer ends Clara overcomes her illness with Heidi's help. The experience of homesickness has transformed Heidi from an ignorant and overwhelmed girl into a mature child of sound moral convictions.

Heidi, having sold nearly fifty million copies worldwide in over fifty languages, and with around twenty adaptations for movie and television, offers an excellent starting point for examining conjunctures and continuities of learning how to feel and cope with homesickness, as well as wanderlust, in nineteenth- and twentieth-century German, British, and North American children's literature.[6]

In *Heidi* and in another story published in the same year, *Daheim und wieder draußen* (1880; Eng. *Renz and Margritli*, 1931),[7] Spyri described a typical medical case of homesickness as a potentially fatal disease. She thus introduced the paradigm of the homesick child into the realm of children's literature, albeit with some delay compared to the medical literature.[8] Twenty to thirty years earlier, discourses about homesickness had shifted from medical to psychological literature. Homesickness was increasingly interpreted as representing emotional suffering linked to the pain of separation, sadness, and loneliness. According to contemporary advice manuals, it could cause serious mental illness, such as depression, and could lead to crimes committed out of sheer desperation.[9]

However, as indicated above, Heidi's homesickness emerges not only as potentially dangerous, but also as potentially positive. The story highlights the educational efforts to cultivate this pure and under-educated child, with her primitive and helpless reactions in situations of emotional overload, on the basis of Spyri's own interpretation of popular psychology literature. Heidi's story therefore served as a lesson that the phenomenon of homesickness was a legitimate and essential stage in children's socialization which, as the first section of this chapter will examine in more detail, could be managed through the right educational environment. The second section will then analyse examples of one typical situation of separation and homesickness in predominantly British school stories. Whereas homesickness appeared over many decades as a female emotion, wanderlust was a topic of mainly boys' adventure books. Characteristically, it was regarded in a positive sense as a necessary phase in boys' development and therefore linked to 'male' attributes such as courage, self-reliance, fortitude, and restlessness. In a different way, Clara's story in *Heidi*'s second volume about longing for a faraway friend, the Alps, and physical healing, indicates that homesickness and wanderlust share one common characteristic: the yearning for a place of belonging, of familiarity, and is combined with feelings of happiness, protection, trust, and love.[10] The longing for this one real or imagined place—collectively called home, or *Heimat*[11]—in which a person is born, for which they have feelings of connectedness, and in which they have lived through their formative experiences of socialization marks the particularity of this longing. The entanglement and complementary natures of wanderlust and homesickness are examined in the third section.

While wanderlust retained its legitimacy throughout the twentieth century, homesickness disappeared from children's literature in Germany around 1950. The fourth and final section argues that this emotion in fact re-emerges with different meanings and in different contexts in the socio-critical children's books of the 1970s. Moreover, the gender boundaries traditionally delineating homesickness as female and wanderlust as male become blurred around 1970, after which both boys and girls are depicted as experiencing homesickness and longing for adventure as critical reactions to the sense of alienation they face as a negative by-product of modernity.

EDUCATIONAL TAMING—HOMESICKNESS IN POPULAR GIRLS' FICTION[12]

As *Heidi* demonstrates, when homesickness was recognized as a legitimate problem for children, narratives that described it as a disease declined. In the worst cases it was thought to cause physical ailments, while the only cure that could save the heroines from their impending death would be to return home.[13] The narrative suggesting the healing power of the homeland originated in medical discourse during the seventeenth and eighteenth centuries. Even soldiers were sent home to escape the certain death caused by homesickness, a treatment that was widely accepted before 1900, wholly eliminating the idea that they might be considered weak or cowardly.[14]

With few exceptions, this narrative of homesickness as a physically overwhelming emotion with medical consequences was soon replaced by a more psychological notion of it as a serious adjustment problem in children, to be handled through appropriate educational methods. As advice literature for parents around the turn of the century shows, homesickness was redefined as a deadly threat not simply to the body, but to legitimate transitional emotions in the process of children's development. Advice books offered opinions to pedagogues and parents as well as practical measures for supporting children in coping with homesickness. Most of the guidance focused on both preventive and curative aspects, while prioritizing the former:

> Prevention is indeed better than the curative effect of education...it increases the pupil's strength of character and morality so that a sense of home, this individual form of love for nature and man, is held in check through reason and its growth to a psychopathic phenomenon is thus prevented.[15]

Educational measures should focus on 'targeting the homesick child's circle of thoughts' to divert attention from the 'one-sidedness of the imagination and emotional life', aiming to contribute to the 'development of new useful fresh ideas and emotional circles',[16] for which educators needed love and patience.[17]

Educational discourse permeated popular girls' fiction. Very widely read novels frequently described the transition—through education—of so-called 'tomboys' as they matured from orphaned, boyish, wild, untamed, spontaneous, emotionally explosive girls into women, wives, and mothers. Around the turn of the century, the intermediate stage in the socialization process of young girls between childhood and womanhood was referred to in Germany as the *Backfisch* phase and in England as 'the awkward age'.[18] This developmental phase was addressed in what has become known as *Backfischliteratur*.[19]

Many girls' books were published as a longer series of books. The readers could thus follow their fictional heroines as they matured, identifying their own stages of development in various volumes over several years. This extended affinity over time meant that readers became very familiar with the heroines, their families and friends, and their way of thinking and acting. Young readers could experience emotions together with their beloved heroine in an imitative and adaptive way by imagining themselves in the stories. Numerous narratives offered readers a wide scope for learning by trying, reproducing, or echoing emotional stages together with or alongside these heroines. In consideration of reading habits, the circulation of books among peer groups, and numerous personal notes and inscriptions in books, literature experts assume that girl readers probably developed a strong emotional bond to these books and stories.[20] In principle, the series format provided ideal conditions for engaged young readers to be taught the appropriate emotions affiliated to particular stages of growing up, and to learn how to recognize their feelings and how to deal with those emotions. The overwhelming feelings with which readers were confronted in their 'awkward age' found some expression and explanation in the story. It can be assumed that this kind of popular girls' fiction was successful because it expressed the interests as well as the psychological and emotional needs of the 'new girl' generation that emerged around 1900.[21]

Four commonly occurring narrative settings may be identified in which protagonists feel a longing for familiarity, belonging, and identity, and which correspond loosely to four different life-changing events: death of a parent, early separation from parents by entering a sanatorium or visiting far away relatives, attendance at a girls' boarding school, and, finally, entry into the workforce.

In the story 'Bei der Patin' ('At godmother's', 1904) by Agnes Sapper, one of the most important authors of her time for German-speaking children, little Klara mourns the death of her parents.[22] Her guardian takes her to her godmother's, thus separating Klara from her two older brothers, her last links to the family. Despite the godmother's very caring attitude, the nanny charged with looking after the girl talks Klara into feeling homesick and uncomfortable in order to get rid of the child and absolve herself of any responsibility. Klara's refusal to get used to the new circumstances and to accept her new 'mother' is subsequently construed as ingratitude and obstinacy. Eventually, however, the nanny is dismissed, and Klara is then able to develop feelings of gratitude and happiness at finding a new place of familiarity, protection, and love, and in which she opens her mind and heart and looks forward once again to a protected life. A similar narrative structure is present in *Fata Morganas alte und neue Heimat* ('Fata Morgana's old and new home', 1922) by Frieda Henning, in which the endearing young Morgele loses both parents within a short span of time.[23] To make matters worse, her guardian puts up for auction not only the small, shabby house where Morgele lived, but even the girl herself. Unlike Klara, who finds support in her godmother, almost no one cares about Morgele's well-being. Now homeless and orphaned, she is driven by a yearning for belonging and security, and she eventually finds a goat who helps her overcome her grief and loneliness.[24] As a lovable girl, she is able to win the heart of a lonely Baroness who lives nearby and, after observing Morgele with the goat several times, finally adopts her. These magical twists in the fates of orphaned and impoverished girls taught young readers that homesickness hindered potential positive developments and had to be overcome.

A more ordinary situation involved the heroine's temporary separation from home and family. The manner in which these situations are introduced in books varies depending on the age of the girls. Typically the heroine experiences a short separation in early childhood, like Bärbel in Magda Trott's series *Goldköpfchen* ('Little golden head', 1928–53), who at the age of five visits her grandparents in the city. Her homesickness comes as no surprise, but since she is unable to independently overcome her woes, she has to have help, and her aunt soon returns her to her native village.[25] In the later volumes, the readers find out that Bärbel benefits as an adolescent from this and other early childhood experiences. She grows up to be a confident young woman of strong character, who never suffers from homesickness again.

This was not the case for Annemarie in the third volume of Else Ury's *Nesthäkchen* ('Youngest child' or 'Family pet') series, *Nesthäkchen im Kinderheim* ('Nesthäckchen at the children's home', 1915),[26] in which the ten-year-old Annemarie is separated from her parents for the first time. In this case, however, homesickness is linked more with boredom. The lively, upbeat, and lovable Annemarie has to stay at a children's home on the North Sea island of Amrum for a year to recover from scarlet fever. In order to prevent the dreaded homesickness, she is first accompanied by her mother who is described by the narrator as the symbol of home: 'Children's tears dry quickly…especially when they sit next to their mother who takes them in her arms and consoles them. Then no child feels they are going into the unknown, as their home, their mother is indeed with them.'[27] Following the relevant contemporary parenting advice, Annemarie's parents appeal to the ten-year-old's reason and rely on a distraction strategy. A suitcase packed with new things, especially a new swimsuit, helps her to cope with the first pangs of sorrow, just as playing with other children does. In addition to homesickness, boredom, and loneliness are also thus prevented. Sooner than expected, Annemarie begins to feel at home at this sanatorium called, significantly, *Villa Daheim* ('At-Home Villa'), and in the end, she leaves the place with great regret. *Nesthäkchen im Kinderheim* reflects the educational optimism of the time. Parents as well as young readers learnt that Annemarie's homesickness is not an unresolvable problem, and certainly not a dreaded 'mental illness', but can be helped by avoiding boredom and loneliness.[28]

Boarding school stories featured prominently in girls' books, as in Emmy von Rhoden's famous German novel *Taming a Tomboy* (1898; Ger. orig. *Der Trotzkopf*, 1885).[29] The fifteen-year-old Fanny is described as a wild, boyish girl who grows up without a mother, but is adored by her father. On the advice of her stepmother, Fanny is sent to a boarding school for girls to be tamed and socialized: 'The school's strict regulations are adverse to her unbridled nature; fortunately for her, she will learn to conform, shed her ferocity and be a sweet-natured girl.'[30] Due to her immaturity, Fanny lacks the strength of character and morality identified by pedagogue Gustav Siegert as the key preventive means of combating homesickness.[31] The homesickness of which she writes in her first letters to her beloved father is mingled with self-pity, and she expresses anger at having been deprived of her former life of freedom. The stepmother is proved right in her opinion that over-coming homesickness is an important step in the girl's maturing process.

In complete accordance with the parents' expectations, Fanny learns the neces-sary skills and virtues. Hence, although destined to suffer from homesickness due to an initially weak character, Fanny is eventually able to overcome it by taking on a greater level of responsibility. A mere five years after *Heidi*, this understanding of homesickness is devoid of all physical, disease-related implications, and is merely considered an educational challenge. Homesickness, like immaturity, was now regarded as a *moral* shortcoming that had to be overcome. Through Fanny's exam-ple readers might realize that it is better to tame homesickness as well as anger. At the end of the story, the now well-adjusted Fanny meets her future husband.

The heroine of *Kari* (1931; Nor. orig. *Kari Kveldsmat*, 1913) by Gabriel Scott may be viewed as the opposite of tomboy Fanny. Kari is facing the challenge of moving to a nearby city in order to get a better education. The decision to go away is difficult for her. Like Heidi, she has a physical bond to the familiar landscape of her home. But Kari is older than Heidi and, unlike Fanny, possesses the required maturity and strength of character to confront the challenge alone. From the very first evening at boarding school she feels 'light-hearted' and at home in her new surroundings, in line with contemporary educational narratives which posited that homesickness could be overcome in the right environment. Kari's curiosity and love of life facilitate her adjustment and she quickly feels quite at home in the big city, but in the end she is also happy to return home. The story ends with a declaration of love for home as a place of identity and belonging: 'Down in the meadow the creek was churning around....It was homelike and confident....At times when Kari came to the creek she thought of many queer things, for the creek represented her own life. It was her wheel of fortune.'[32] Living in boarding schools is thus a particularly prominent theme in these stories and has its counterpart in British school stories which will be addressed later.[33]

The separation of adolescent girls from their family home in order to earn a living was one of the last steps in the socialization process of young girls. In German books for girls of the 1930s, heroines frequently leave home, opting for professional training or to start a new job. While in service, they undergo the fin-ishing touches of their education. Only a few heroines still feel homesick during this transition phase, most having already dealt with homesickness in previous years and thus they have already formed a mature and strong character. Hedi, dubbed 'Pucki' in the Magda Trott series of the same name, is one exception. Her nickname refers to the mischievous mythological sprite Puck, because Hedi herself is childish and immature.[34] In *Puckis erster Schritt ins Leben* ('Pucki's first foray into life', 1937), she leaves her home for the first time looking for a job as a domestic worker and nanny. Primarily motivated by wanderlust, she dreams of spending the first money she earns on a trip to Italy. Although the separation from her parents is not easy, she bravely tries to be cheerful and optimistic. In the alien household of an artisan family in Eisenach she feels very lonely and lost, overwhelmed by her duties as a nanny, but 'bravely she fought the longing she felt for her home'.[35] Her biggest fear is of failing and having to return home too soon. In the end, she arrives home no longer as Pucki, but as a resilient and mature woman, a master of her own destiny.

In North American children's literature, too, homesickness serves as a measure of maturity.[36] Up until the 1970s, children were systematically confronted with separation situations in order to learn from the experience of homesickness. Summer camps were particularly suited for the purpose,[37] and fictional literature as well as picture books supported juvenile readers in their learning process. Based on the example of the protagonists, children learnt to identify homesickness, like Victoria in *The Secret Language* (1960) as the 'worst nightmare ever'.[38] Narratives with intensely emotional descriptions of the heroine's grief and loneliness engaged readers' empathy. But the stories also offered strategies for dealing with these overwhelming feelings of isolation and anxiety. Victoria, for example, befriends another unhappy girl and together they dream of their ideal imaginary place. In *Katie Goes to Camp* (1968) little Katie chooses another way to cope. She takes her doll Corrie with her to summer camp and at first will not let go, because the doll vicariously suffers from homesickness on Katie's behalf. Over the course of the first day the doll, that is, Katie, learns to see the camp as an opportunity to make friends and overcomes her anxiety.[39]

Fictional literature for girls illustrates a variety of ways to cope with homesickness, considered to be a transitional emotion in the process of separation from parents and towards maturation. The seriousness of homesickness depends on the reasons, on the expected duration of the separation, and on the linked emotions. Boredom, anger, and anxiety are predictable emotions in situations of 'necessary' separation in order to educate children in becoming independent. It is easy to deal with such feelings in advance, and the younger the child, the more responsible parents and educators are for the success of the adaptation process. Feelings of loneliness, grief, and desperation in children that accompany the irreversible loss of their home requires far more intensive emotional work in order to re-establish trust, faith, and happiness as well as feelings of familiarity and belonging. The stories explored here show that the main characters are able to learn to deal successfully with homesickness, albeit in different ways. The heroines emerge from their homesickness crisis as responsible young women of strong character, who can continue their journey independently, in pursuit of success and happiness.

By 1950, homesickness had lost its meaning as a transitional emotion in girls' books. Nevertheless, mild homesickness remained acceptable as a natural sense of longing and as the marker of a close relationship with parents. Homesickness that is tamed by means of education is short-lived and of bearable intensity, or as Erich Kästner personifies it in *Lisa and Lottie* (1950; Ger. orig. *Das doppelte Lottchen*, 1949), 'sometimes of an evening... the gray dwarf Homesickness sits by the beds in the dormitories, takes from his pocket his gray notebook and his gray pencil, and with a glum face counts up the tears around him, those shed and those unshed'.[40]

HOMESICKNESS IN BRITISH SCHOOL STORIES

The genre of British school stories is particularly suitable for examining how boys and girls were viewed in separation situations. From the mid-nineteenth century onwards no other kind of school has been more frequently represented in English children's literature than public boarding schools.[41] Children's books in Germany featured stories set in boarding schools for girls more often than those for boys.[42]

The school stories paint an attractive picture of public schools, marked by life among peers, experimentation with new things, rebellion against authority, and the charm of dabbling in mischief and escaping unnoticed. Authors of stories set in boarding schools often describe the conditions of daily life fairly realistically, drawing on personal experience. Through the process of mimetic learning, young readers—usually the same age as the characters—can experience the feelings associated with living at a boarding school, making friends, or dealing with unpleasant classmates. They can emotionally simulate how it might be to leave their parents and settle in a new environment, and how curiosity and love of adventure might clash with a desire to be at home. Given the repetition of similar narratives within the genre, school stories offered excellent opportunities for conveying perceptions of appropriate behaviour and feelings to young readers, as Frederick Willis recalled in his memoirs: 'We were great readers of school stories, from which we learnt that boys of the higher class boarding-schools were courageous, honourable, and chivalrous...We tried to mould our lives on this formula.'[43]

The earliest nineteenth-century British school stories about boys, such as *Tom Brown's School Days* (1857), are the most important and influential.[44] It is striking that although situations highlighting separation were a constitutive part of these stories, homesickness played only a minor role. In *Tom Brown's School Days* the shy and gentle Arthur, who comes later to school and feels lost, embodies the boys' homesickness. Tom takes the fragile Arthur, who is still mourning his recently deceased father, under his wing. He warns Arthur first of all against letting the other boys know of his homesickness and grief 'or they'll call you home-sick, or mama's darling'.[45] The attribute 'mama's darling' suggests that homesickness was considered a weakness to be punished by peers with humiliation and exclusion. It is interesting that, more often than not in these stories it is the 'anxious heroes'[46] who are most likely to suffer from homesickness, such as Uli in *The Flying Classroom* (1934; Ger. orig. *Das fliegende Klassenzimmer*, 1933). His classmates scorn him for his lack of courage and claim that he is homesick, which he admits ashamedly. However, both Arthur and Uli, despite their anxiety, become the unsung heroes, Arthur with his religious and moral beliefs and Uli, through his ill-fated test of courage that helps him win the affection of his classmates and become the bravest boy.

Stephen is also ashamed of his homesickness and tries to play it down in *The Fifth Form at St. Dominic's* (1887). He comes as a novice to boarding school. Parting from his mother at the train station is hard for him, but he 'want[s] to figure as a hero', so he quickly overcomes his moment of weakness and focuses instead on his future plans. Writing a letter to his mother, however, he is even more overwhelmed with homesickness: 'As he wrote, and his thoughts flew back to the home and the mother he had left only yesterday, his spirits fell, and the home-sickness came over him worse than ever. What would he not give to change places with this very letter, and go back home!'[47] Boredom and loneliness are present here too and feed into his homesickness. The ridicule of his classmates who brand him a 'blub-baby' who just left 'mammy', spurs Stephen to overcome his homesickness, and two weeks later he has not only settled in, but has also won the respect and recognition of his classmates by engaging in more daring and nonconformist behaviour.

The clear message transmitted in these stories, then, was that homesickness was something of which boys were or should be ashamed and for which they were scorned.[48] It seemed to be attributed to weakness and timidity, but protagonists could compensate for these weaknesses if they showed other strengths. These ideas correspond with the relevant contemporary advice literature which posited discipline, activity, and courage as desirable masculine virtues.[49] Homesickness, in contrast, had disturbing, blocking effects. It was an emotion with no place in the socialization process of boys, and was more suited to marking an anxious, hesitant, and inactive character. These stories taught the reading public how important it was to overcome homesickness and quickly transform it into spiritual superiority, courage, and bravery, for who would wish to be exposed to the mockery of his classmates as an outsider?

The first British school stories for girls appeared around 1880.[50] This trend may be viewed within the context of a change in approach to girls' education in the late Victorian and Edwardian era. This change saw new efforts to cultivate the 'modern girl', that is, to deploy the notion of 'unconventional femininity' in educating girls who would escape the domestic realm and would be strong and independent, and thus useful subjects of the Empire.[51] In accordance with the 'modern girl' narrative, heroines in these school stories are only required to conform to traditional femininity for a time, and either do not suffer from homesickness at all, or overcome such feelings and blend quickly into the community of students, as does Hester in *A World of Girls* (1886). Like many other heroines, Hester has lost her mother and is 'a child of the strongest feelings'. Her father sends her to a public school to become a 'good girl' and to 'curb...wild spirits'. Parting with her younger sister Nan is more difficult than anything else for Hester, and on the train she can hardly hold back her tears. Like her German counterpart Fanny in *Taming a Tomboy*, she feels that her life at boarding school will be like imprisonment compared to her previous freedoms. But upon her arrival at Lavender House, she realizes how wrong her prejudices were and that she will have 'the sweetest, brightest episodes in her existence' there.[52]

Enid Blyton's *St. Clare's* series (1941–45), as well as her *Malory Towers* series (1946–51), were two of the most successful twentieth-century British book series for girls in Germany.[53] In addition to the translations of the original English editions, numerous spin-off books based on these same heroines and written in Enid Blyton's style were published in German.[54] It is striking that in the original books written by Enid Blyton homesickness hardly features at all. In fact, the protagonists Darrell and twin sisters Patricia and Isabel cannot wait to get to Malory Towers or to St Clare's. These British upper-middle-class girls are strong, confident, and witty individuals, who face boarding school with an open and adventurous spirit. Only secondary characters in the series suffer from homesickness, and even then only rarely, such as Gwendoline in *First Term at Malory Towers* (1946), for example, whom Darrell and her friends find unpleasant even at the station on the way to school. Gwendoline, 'clinging to her mother and wailing', could not be separated from her mother and vice versa: 'The mother was almost as bad as the girl.' The girls comment on her behaviour mockingly ('[p]oor little mother's darling') and hold the mother responsible for making a 'fool' of her daughter.[55] But Gwendoline is not just homesick—she is also portrayed as a spoiled, obstinate, and mollycoddled child who fails to integrate into the boarding school community and is often made a laughing stock.

The message of this narrative is twofold. First, using the example of the protagonists, it is evident that leaving the family home is not only a natural step in the process of growing up, but is also desirable and not necessarily painful, promising a life of friendships, variety, and adventure. Second, it is asserted that homesick children have suffered from a poor and inadequate upbringing. As was obvious in the school stories for boys, the insults 'mama's darling' or 'blub-baby' reflect popular assumptions about excessive maternal love, attention, and mollycoddling as the 'really pernicious evil', as John B. and Rosalie Watson had warned in their popular advice book.[56]

In the subsequent spin-off books for German readers written in Enid Blyton's style, homesickness is mentioned on occasion, but in contrast to Gwendoline's case, it was depicted as a legitimate and normal feeling. As newcomers to Lindenhof (as the school is called in the German editions), Grit, the Philippine governor's daughter in *Hanni und Nanni in tausend Nöten* ('Hanni and Nanni in a pickle', 1974), and Gina Garribaldi, an Italian girl in *Hanni und Nanni gründen einen Klub* ('Hanni and Nanni start a club', 1971), suffer as outsiders who miss their homes. Although their homesickness is only one of the reasons for the girls' difficulties in adapting, the central thread in these stories is the notion that in such cases, the thoughtfulness, concern, and friendship of the twins helps the new girls to overcome their longing for home. A striking difference between German and English school stories for girls is that homesickness is regarded far more obviously as illegitimate and as an indication of poor upbringing in English stories, while in the German stories it is afforded a certain legitimacy as a transitional emotion.

Indulging in school stories full of adventures, experiences, and emotions, young readers compensate for an emotionless daily life.[57] Through the prism of school-based stories readers were supposed to learn to enjoy the pleasures of boarding school life, sharing the joy and happiness of their classmates. In these stories, happiness, curiosity, courage, openness, and, at the same time, diligence and obedience were the foundations of a successful personality, and were qualities that had to be acquired mainly in childhood.[58] Curiosity, interest, and openness, and in general the desire for emotions and adventures motivated both boys and girls to leave home in order to learn to be independent. As the next section shows, however, a desire to travel was initially a predominantly masculine emotion.

ENTANGLED FEELINGS—WANDERLUST
AND HOMESICKNESS

One of the most widely read Robinsonades (the literary genre taking its name from *Robinson Crusoe*) was *The Coral Island* (1858) about three boys shipwrecked on an island in the Pacific. The story starts with a passionate description of roving, which can be interpreted as a declaration of love for the feeling of wanderlust.

> Roving has always been, and still is, my ruling passion, the joy of my heart, the very sunshine of my existence. In childhood, in boyhood, and in man's estate, I have been a rover; not a mere rambler among the woody glens and upon the hill-tops of my own native land, but an enthusiastic rover throughout the length and breadth of the wide, wide world.[59]

Jim, too, in *Treasure Island* (1883) is 'full of sea-dreams and the most charming anticipations of strange islands and adventures'.[60] Despite the many Robinsonades for girls of the late Victorian era reaffirming the 'modern girl' type,[61] the most famous adventure books, having been established in direct proportion to the spread of the British Empire in the nineteenth century, have predominantly male protagonists. Unlike homesickness, wanderlust does not appear as a feeling to be tamed and rechannelled. On the contrary, wanderlust and the longing for adventure seem 'natural', even *essential* for the overwhelmingly male adolescent protagonists in the adventure book genre. Boys were not only allowed, but actually encouraged to feel swept away by wanderlust and to give in to their 'runaway tendenc[ies]'.[62] Following in the footsteps of the restless Robinson Crusoe, who rarely, if ever, felt homesick, wanderlust is the engine that drives young heroes in these books towards adventure, making them strong and independent. It is therefore transmitted as a highly suitable emotion for a modern society demanding ever-increasing mobility.

Many classic adventure books do not mention homesickness at all. On the contrary, the stories tell of heroes, who, dissatisfied with their lives, are inspired to leave their old homes in search of faraway places, which they then define as their new homes. In fantasy books for children both the male and female protagonists are spurred by the same impulses, but in contrast to the strong male heroes of the adventure books, the stories oscillate between wanderlust and homesickness, as seen in *Golden Island* (1966; Ger. orig. *Delphinensommer*, 1963).[63] In this award-winning book, Andrula grows up lacking a father, isolated from other children, and living with her hardworking mother in poverty-stricken conditions on a small Greek island. Andrula escapes with a dolphin to a nearby island, Hyria, where she feels welcome, wanted, and happy. Mythical creatures are her new family, and Hyria, the legendary island that gives everyone what they desire, becomes her new home. At the end of the summer, with the start of school, she cannot bear to leave this fantasy island that she already desperately misses and to which she can never return. In other words, she suffers from homesickness for Hyria. The reader learns together with Andrula that the only way for her to escape this longing and desperation is to change her real life and to redevelop a feeling of belonging in her true home and she finally succeeds in doing so.

The island Hyria, the raft in *The Adventures of Huckleberry Finn* (1884), the land of Neverland in *Peter and Wendy* (1911), the garden in *The Secret Garden* (1911), or Villa Villekulla in *Pippi Longstocking* (1945; Swe. orig. *Pippi Långstrump*, 1945) are all new homes, depicted as spaces of refuge and linked with feelings of security, happiness, and familiarity. The child characters all find new friends there with whom they can bond. These stories each describe how strong the heroes are both physically and emotionally, as strength is a positive quality associated with their new home. They also contain descriptions of imaginative efforts by protagonists to turn these refuges into new homes, the associated processes of emotional bonding to these homes, troubles arising from or in the home, and finally the protagonists' longing for these new homes. Throughout the narratives the heroes learn about themselves, processing and reframing their own identity, which is in turn mirrored in their newly constructed home.

Homesickness and wanderlust are similarly entangled in the story *The Adventures of Maya the Bee* (1922; Ger. orig. *Die Biene Maja und ihre Abenteuer*, 1912) and the book's plot is primarily guided by these two emotions. In the beginning, Maya is motivated by restlessness, impatience, and curiosity.[64] She decides to indulge her curiosity and craving to see the world, but after many adventures, her curiosity and desire for the new is replaced by a sudden feeling of sadness and loneliness. In a dramatic twist at the end of the story, just as her old beehive is about to be attacked by hornets, Maya is seized by a feeling of responsibility to, and longing for, her old home and family. Both Maya's wanderlust and her homesickness are important and necessary elements in the plot, for it is only through her adventures that Maya acquires the knowledge, courage, and wisdom required to save her hive, the place to which her homesickness leads her.

Similar narratives about wanderlust, homesickness, and the rediscovery of an old homeland are central themes in several other award-winning books, such as *The Trip to Panama* (1978; Ger. orig. *Oh, wie schön ist Panama*, 1978) by Janosch. From a banana box labelled 'Panama' emanates the tempting aroma of an exotic place, little Bear's and little Tiger's dreamland. The two set out to search of this wonderland, but, without realizing it, what they find is their own hut, their own river, and their own home, all identical to their imaginary dreamland. In Kenneth Grahame's *The Wind in the Willows* (1908), the shy and introverted Mole likewise initially flees his home to escape his tedious spring cleaning, and joins the curious and enterprising Ratty. With Ratty he comes to meet new animals and areas of the forest and river. But one day, as they pass nearby his home, he remembers his home and is overcome by a strong longing for the place: 'Home! That was what they meant, those caressing appeals, those soft touches wafted through the air, those invisible little hands pulling and tugging, all one way!'[65] Only through his experience of 'escape' does Mole become painfully aware of what he has left behind: the smell of familiarity, the intimacy of untidy chaos, the strong conviction of belonging. At the same time, these feelings of belonging give Mole the courage to leave home once again for another adventure.

In the prize-winning *Secrets of the Andes* (1952) by Anne Nolan Clark, Cusik, an Inca boy, is raised in a hidden valley with a secret about his birth which engenders in him insecurity and the yearning for belonging and familiarity. His mentor gives in to the boy's wishes and allows him to move to the next town, but Cusik soon misses his old valley high up in the mountains. His longing leads him back there, and he recognizes that his mentor, Chuto, is for him both home and family. He promises to never again seek faraway places and to dedicate his life to the rituals and traditions of the people in the hidden valley. Thus, Cusik's wanderlust on the one hand and homesickness on the other are both necessary for him to internalize his given home as a *felt* home. Similar emotions guide young Cordula in *Cordulas erste Reise* ('Cordula's first journey', 1867)[66] and nine-year-old Pino in *Nimm mich mit, Kapitän* ('Take me with you, captain', 1970; Dut. orig. *O, die Pino*, 1961), who muses, 'Maybe there really is such a thing as wanderlust—a wanderlust that can make people sick, and drive them to act beyond prudence and reason.'[67] Cordula and Pino both long for remote places, far away from their villages. Curious and adventurous, each embarks on a journey and, driven by homesickness, returns home with the knowledge of 'how wonderful it is to own a home, a place where you belong'.[68]

Young readers could learn from these literary heroes that wanderlust is an essential and normal desire. The heroes develop and strengthen important character traits such as courage, self-reliance, and fortitude. While they are away they learn the meaning of home as a place of belonging and identity, and can grow to love it. Through imaginary experiences, readers could satisfy their own longing for adventure by joining these heroes in their fantasies, but also share their ambivalent feelings and their relief to be back home again. In an extraordinary way Bastian Balthazar Bux in Michael Ende's *The Neverending Story* (1983; Ger. orig. *Die unendliche Geschichte*, 1979) not only escaped from his sad daily life through his imagination by reading a book, but he also became the hero of the story, acting out his longing to be carried far away in the book. The story highlights the emotional power of reading, through which children learn in a mimetic, imitative, and adaptive way.

CRITIQUE OF MODERNITY—HOMESICKNESS IN POST-WAR GERMANY

By the 1950s, the notions of childhood homesickness as an educational problem had almost disappeared from the conscious socialization process. Most young fictional heroes, such as the five-year-old Monika in Hans Hempe's *Pitzelchen hat kein Heimweh,* ('Pitzelchen is not homesick', 1969), now ignored the feeling, in contrast to their parents who were still anxious about the homesickness they expected their offspring to feel. An entry on the topic last appeared in a German educational manual in 1952.[69]

Around 1970, however, homesickness re-emerged in different contexts and with different meanings. Following the flight, displacement, and homelessness brought on by the Second World War, homesickness began to reappear in children's books written about the era of National Socialism, as seen in Lisa Tetzner's so-called *Kinderodyssee* ('Children's odyssey') series. Between 1932 and 1949, while in exile in Switzerland with her husband Kurt Held, Tetzner wrote this series of nine books about the fate of three children from Berlin who had grown up together in the back courtyard of apartment block no. 67. The series only became widely known in German in the 1970s, following a socio-critical turn in children's literature in Germany.[70] Tetzner's young wandering heroes have the experience of displacement and homelessness in common. But what truly unites them is their mutual longing for house no. 67 in Berlin where they all grew up together. Erwin is the most homesick of all, torn from a happy childhood after his escape from Paris to Lapland with his father. He misses his mother dearly and, in a letter to her, he writes: 'This long night is also within me, because mother is not here…Perhaps this darkness is everywhere where you are alone and abandoned, because then even the sun cannot help.'[71]

In times of war, therefore, home is no longer a fixed place, but located in the family, and particularly the mother that the young heroes miss or who cures their homesickness. In Judith Kerr's multi-award-winning *When Hitler Stole Pink Rabbit* (1971), siblings Anna and Max do not feel homesick as they flee through Europe with their parents. Anna acknowledges the fact that she can only withstand the flight as long as she is with her parents: 'If you haven't got a home you've got to be with your people.'[72] Longing for their mother, the brothers Achim and Werner Adamek in Gudrun Pausewang's *Auf einem langen Weg* ('On a long journey', 1978) endure their flight to the West in the last months of the war. Their home town, including the house they grew up in, has been lost and yet they are not sad about it. Their only home now is their mother, from whom they were separated during a bombing raid and whom they now set out to find: 'Yes, we're going home…to our mother.'[73] Thomas in Peter Härtling's *Crutches* (1988; Ger. orig. *Krücke*, 1986) is also looking for his mother, lost during their escape from the Russian Army. During his quest, he meets a war invalid who calls himself 'Crutches', and with him finds a new sense of familiarity, security, and home. Crutches takes care of Thomas like a father, but the boy still misses his mother. Home functions as the reference point in post-war literature about the displaced. The meaning of homesickness had shifted, however, to become more of a nostalgic yearning for the home lost in war, but was no longer connected to a desire for return.[74] In these children's books, then, young heroes are driven by a longing for their mother and not for a lost place. A similar narrative about homelessness and the search for a parent who represented 'home' underpins the Russian story about Boris in *School* (1967; Rus. orig. *Shkola*, 1930) which was compulsory reading in East German (GDR) schools.[75]

In early GDR children's literature, likewise, homesickness rarely featured in the plot. It may be assumed that in the aftermath of war, exile, displacement, and destruction, and against the backdrop of Nazi ideology, the concept of homeland needed to be redefined. In Anneliese Jahnke's *Neue Heimat* ('New home', 1949), for example, a book for early childhood readers approved for German-language lessons, Uli and Rita, arrive in the village of Rinow with their mother and their belongings. There is no mention of a father, nor where the family came from, nor why they had to find a new home. The story sought to help young GDR pupils understand that both the children and their mother could be easily integrated into the village collective, feeling happy and confident about the future.

The dominant narrative in socialist children's literature of the 1950s and 1960s identified the collective as a home.[76] Feelings of homesickness or wanderlust were rarely addressed in socialist children's books until the 1970s. The young heroes in the two most influential books, *Tinko* (1954) by Erwin Strittmatter and *Kaule* (1962) by Alfred Wellm, were children searching for belonging and identity after the loss of a parent or their home. 'Heimat' here was a beleaguered concept, offering no clear sense of belonging or identity to the young heroes. Negotiating their way through various conflicts, the protagonists eventually adopt the modern idea of the collective as a home, integrating themselves into their school classes and becoming members of the Pioneers, the socialist youth organization.

In the 1970s, the children's book genre underwent a significant change in Germany. Authors in both East and West Germany individualized their main protagonists, attributing to them particular desires, hopes, and problems. Families were no longer synonymous with feelings of happiness, belonging, and security and instead were often insecure places, harbouring problems with siblings, parents' separations, and even family violence. Heroes and heroines, albeit seldom and hesitatingly, began to question the standard idea of family as a home. Wanderlust became the desire to trade the unloved home with another place anywhere else. Heroes such as the East German Moritz in *Moritz in der Litfaßsäule* ('Moritz in the morris column', 1980) by Christa Kozik or the West German Theo in *Theo Runs Away* (1978; Ger. orig. *Theo haut ab*, 1977) by Peter Härtling lacked a sense of belonging and identity, feeling instead unfamiliarity and rejection.

Another change in the genre in the 1970s was that gender boundaries become blurred: both boy and girl protagonists experienced homesickness and longing for adventure, but in different ways. Furthermore, homesickness as a critique of modernity emerged in the well-known children's books of East German writer Peter Brock, including *Ich bin die Nele* ('I am Nele', 1975) and *Bine und die Parkoma* ('Bine and Parkoma', 1978), along with *Insel der Schwäne* ('Island of swans', 1980) by Benno Pludra. These stories all begin with the family moving into an unfamiliar city. All three protagonists, Nele, Sabine, and Stephan, disagree with their parents' decision to abandon the familiar childhood home for the modern comforts of a city apartment close to work. They miss the grandparents or friends they have left behind, and refuse to settle down in the anonymity of their new housing blocks: 'It reaches all the way to the sky, smooth like a steep bedrock... Hundreds of windows, a thousand windows, nobody can count them. And the children stare up, both stone silent.'[77] The contrast between their happy and fulfilling former lives in rural areas and what is felt as the alienating, cold, and boring city is the central preoccupation of these books,[78] especially *Insel der Schwäne*, one of the most important children's books in East Germany in the last decade before reunification. When Stephan moves with his parents from rural Oderbruch to Berlin, he begins missing his best friend, grandparents, and the countryside.

His criticism of his father for the family's so-called progress is unforgiving, and the coldness of the city reflects his feelings of desolation and loneliness. The parents in these stories are too busy to find time for their children, and the homesickness of the main characters is given a new legitimacy. It is no longer considered a transitional emotion, but a legitimate criticism expressed by children about an environment into which they have been dragged and against parents who leave them feeling isolated. At the same time, this criticism also signifies greater independence on behalf of the children: agency of their own. The solution offered in these books is an autonomous children's space with new friendships that spell the end of isolation and loneliness. The heroes, together with their new friends, look for analogues to the homes they have abandoned: they discover the river, the parks, and through a slow and trouble-filled process, they make these new spaces their home.

* * *

Like Heidi nearly a hundred years earlier, the heroes of 1970s children's literature are driven by a longing for their childhood locales, consisting of the natural landscape together with a small community of familiar people. These books posit that children need nothing more and nothing less than the particular place with which they can form or already have formed this intense bond, in order to be happy. It turns out that the tendency within *Heidi* to connect feelings and perceptions of home with countryside, nature, and rural life, and to define city life as alienating returns in a new form. In the 1970s especially, the urban environment, perceived as inhospitable, cold, and anonymous, alienates children from this close relationship, this certainty of belonging and identity.

Yet many things had also changed: Heidi was allowed to return home. Stephan, Bine, and Nele had to learn to keep up with the mobility requirements of a modern society. Whereas the homesick heroines in earlier children's books had been helpless and overwhelmed by their emotions, and early heroes had given in to their natural longing for faraway places, homesickness and wanderlust in the 1970s appear to have been relevant to more confident, autonomous children struggling to cope with the requirements of the modern era, and to define their own agency.

Homesickness in earlier children's books highlighted the immaturity of the protagonists, and their dependence on family structures, from which they had difficulty parting. As emotional objects, they had to become accustomed to separation situations, learning to recognize homesickness as disturbing and unnecessary and, accordingly, to suppress it. A little nostalgia for home was still permitted, however, since the family home served as a measure of the emotional quality of the parent-child relationship. The perspectives of children's homesickness therefore underwent significant shifts. In later children's fiction, heroes were not only longing for a place of belonging and identity; their emotions also reflected a criticism of their living conditions. The young heroes acted out these emotions, making them useful in articulating their protest against the parents and the requirements of modernity. Thus homesickness and wanderlust marked a new independence and emotional strength of the protagonists. Homesickness, even more than wanderlust, now referred to a process of empowerment. Fictional characters outgrew the stage in which they were considered as mere educational objects to become emotional subjects with inherent rights and strengths. What indicated their maturity was no longer their successful adaptation to new living conditions, but their ability to stand up for their own well-being and to use wanderlust and homesickness for this purpose, thus enhancing and strengthening their own feelings of belonging, familiarity, and identity.

NOTES

1. First described by the Swiss doctor Hofer, *Dissertatio medica de nostalgia*. See further Bunke, *Heimweh*, 14 n. 1, 25–44; Matt, 'You Can't Go Home Again'.
2. Spyri, *Heidi*, 123–4, 127, 163.
3. On the concept of belonging, see Pfaff-Czarnecka, *Multiple Belonging and the Challenges to Biographic Navigation*, 13: 'Belonging is an emotionally charged, ever dynamic social location—that is: a position in social structure, experienced through identification, embeddedness, connectedness, and attachments'.
4. See chapter 2, 'Dickon's Trust'.
5. Both the original novel and its sequel were published in English as one combined volume.
6. This chapter is based on a corpus of nearly 150 children's books, nearly sixty of which have been directly cited. Additionally, contemporary advice manuals and encyclopaedias have been taken into consideration.
7. In Spyri's *Renz and Margritli* orphan boy Renz suffers desperately from longing for a particular place. In the 1930s, German editors republished the story and changed the title, significantly, to 'Heimweh' ('Homesickness').
8. Bunke, *Heimweh*, 572.
9. For detailed descriptions of crimes committed due to homesickness among maids, see Jaspers, *Heimweh und Verbrechen*.
10. See Duyvendak, *Politics of Home*, 38–42.
11. In German-speaking countries, *Heimat* is a complex and challenging term with highly individual and emotional associations. See Blickle, *Heimat*; Applegate, *Nation of Provincials*. The concept of *Heimat* has been especially well-researched in literary studies. See, for example, Heinze, Quadflieg, and Bührig, *Utopie Heimat*; Gunther, Geisler, and Schröter, *Heimat*.
12. See Grenz, 'Zeitgenössische Mädchenliteratur', 243; Bilston, *Awkward Age in Women's Popular Fiction*; see also chapter 6, 'Wendy's Love'.
13. The same narrative can be seen in the modern *Heidi* adaptation by Hassebrauk, *Heimweh nach dem Rosenhof* (1962).
14. Matt, *Homesickness*, 92–101.
15. Siegert, 'Heimweh', 186 (all translations by the author).
16. Siegert, 185–6.
17. Widmann, 'Heimweh', 705.
18. James, *Awkward Age*; Bilston, *Awkward Age in Women's Popular Fiction*.
19. Grenz, 'Das eine sein'.
20. Romalov, 'Unearthing the Historical Reader', 93: 'young females indeed showed a penchant not only for relating life to fiction but also for behaving like fictional characters'.
21. Mitchell, *New Girl*.

22. Sapper, 'Bei der Patin'.
23. Henning, *Fata Morganas alte und neue Heimat*.
24. For a discussion of animal-child relationships, see chapter 5, 'Doctor Dolittle's Empathy'.
25. See Trott, *Goldköpfchen*.
26. See Redmann, 'Nostalgia and Optimism in Else Ury's Nesthäkchen Books'.
27. Ury, *Nesthäkchen im Kinderheim*, chapter 'Nesthäkchens Seereise'.
28. For a modern adaptation of the *Nesthäkchen* story, see Hildegard Diessel, *Resi hat Heimweh* (1971).
29. Rhoden, *Taming a Tomboy*. See also Grenz, 'Der Trotzkopf: Bestseller'.
30. Rhoden, *Der Trotzkopf*, 71 [this paragraph is missing from the Oswald translation].
31. Siegert, 'Heimweh', 185.
32. Scott, *Kari*, 241.
33. See chapter 2, 'Dickon's Trust'.
34. The volumes of this series were written in the 1930s, and by the 1980s, some volumes had reached their fortieth edition.
35. Trott, *Puckis erster Schritt ins Leben*, 30.
36. Matt, *Homesickness*, 6: 'those unable to adapt to a new environment and stricken with nostalgia were doomed to fail in life and business, perhaps even to perish'.
37. Matt, *Homesickness*, 198–9.
38. Nordstrom, *Secret Language*, 15.
39. Schick, *Katie Goes to Camp*. See also Marilyn Sachs, *Laura's Luck* (1965); Marc Brown, *Arthur Goes to Camp* (1982); David McPhail, *Pig Goes to Camp* (1983).
40. Kästner, *Lisa and Lottie*, 3–4.
41. See Richards, *Happiest Days*, 3. See also Kirkpatrick, *Encyclopaedia of Boys' School Stories*.
42. Nevertheless, these combine adolescent crises with experiences at boarding school, albeit for an adult readership. See Hesse, *The Prodigy* or Musil, *Young Törless*, 3. It was mainly Törless who 'suffered from frightful, agonising homesickness' that would burst forth in 'an obstinately rising sob'. See also chapter 2, 'Dickon's Trust'; chapter 7, 'Piggy's Shame'.
43. Willis, *Book of London Yesterdays*, 49.
44. See Richards, *Happiest Days*, 18.
45. Hughes, *Tom Brown's School Days*, 246. See chapter 2, 'Dickon's Trust'.
46. See chapter 9, 'Jim Button's Fear'.
47. Reed, *Fifth Form at St. Dominic's*, 22, 30.
48. See chapter 7, 'Piggy's Shame'.
49. Baden-Powell, *Rovering to Success*.
50. See Humphrey, *English Girls' School Story*; Sims and Clare, *Encyclopaedia of Girl's School Stories*; Mitchell, *New Girl*.
51. Smith, *Empire in British Girls' Literature and Culture*, 2–3, 15.
52. Meade, *World of Girls*, 7, 5, 20.
53. The *St. Clare's* series was published in German as *Hanni und Nanni* and the *Malory Towers* series as *Dolly*.
54. The two series were originally published in six volumes each. By contrast, the German *Dolly* series spanned eighteen volumes, while the *Hanni und Nanni* series spanned twenty-four volumes. See also, Rudd, *Enid Blyton and The Mystery of Children's Literature*; Prieger, *Werk Enid Blytons*.
55. Blyton, *First Term at Malory Towers*, 5.

56. Watson and Watson, *Psychological Care of the Infant and Child*, 76. See chapter 1, 'Mrs Gaskell's Anxiety'.
57. See Mitchell, *New Girl*, 139–40.
58. Stearns, 'Defining Happy Childhoods', 171.
59. Ballantyne, *Coral Island*, 1. The 1965 German translation is more explicit: 'As far as I can remember, I was drawn with irresistible force into the distance. To travel, to see distant lands, was my passion, my one true joy, the content of my existence'; Ballantyne, *Im Banne der Koralleninsel*, 7.
60. Stevenson, *Treasure Island*, 54. See also Butts, 'Birth of the Boys' Stories'.
61. Smith, *Empire in British Girls' Literature and Culture*, 84–106.
62. Tebbutt, *Being Boys*, 245.
63. Allfrey, *Golden Island*. Methuen published the same English translation under the title *On a Dolphin's Back* in 1967.
64. Bonsels, *Adventures of Maya the Bee*, 3–4. From 1912 to 1938, 770,000 copies were sold in Germany; Adam, *Lesen unter Hitler*, 52. Because of his contacts and activity during the Third Reich, the author Waldemar Bonsels was temporarily banned from publishing in the post-war period.
65. Grahame, *Wind in the Willows*, 98.
66. Wildermuth, *Cordulas erste Reise*. The story was first published in 1867 in Wildermuth's collection *Jugendgabe: Erzählungen für die Jugend*. An adaptation was published in 1954.
67. Marcke, *Nimm mich mit, Kapitän*, 64.
68. Wildermuth, *Cordulas erste Reise*, 23.
69. Müller, 'Heimweh'. It also occurs in the unchanged editions up until 1964. The term *Heimweh* appears in no other German encyclopedia after the 1950s, checked against a sample of around thirty texts.
70. See Bolius, *Lisa Tetzner*, 187–222; Ernst, 'World is my Country'.
71. Tetzner, *Die Kinder aus Nr. 67*, 82.
72. Kerr, *When Hitler Stole Pink Rabbit*, 179.
73. Pausewang, *Auf einem langen Weg*, 126.
74. Faehndrich, *Eine endliche Geschichte*.
75. Gaidar, *School*; see chapter 10, 'Ivan's Bravery'.
76. Nelke, *Kind im Buch*, 21.
77. Pludra, *Insel der Schwäne*, 12.
78. See chapter 12, 'Ingrid's Boredom'.

12

Ingrid's Boredom

Joachim C. Häberlen

Ingrid Völker, the sixteen-year-old protagonist of Irene Rodrian's youth novel *Viel Glück, mein Kind* ('Good luck, my child', 1975), had gone through an exciting and complicated year. For the first time in her life, she had fallen in love. Her boyfriend, Norbert, an older school mate, had promptly impregnated her, but then had turned into a boring square, who dreams of a petty-bourgeois family life with himself in the role of fatherly protector, which is why the left-leaning Ingrid soon breaks up with him. Her equally leftist parents convince Ingrid to fly to London with Norbert to have an abortion, even though Ingrid herself wants to keep the baby. Arriving in London, she turns her back on the increasingly protective Norbert, and soon meets two other Germans, Rudi and Wolf, with whom she eventually falls in love. Back in Munich, she moves to Wolf's communal apartment, and finally seems happy. But problems persist. Ingrid is expelled from school, and then when child services threaten to take her, she is forced to move back with her parents. Only at the end of the novel does Ingrid reflect on the fact that through it all, she had been searching for something. 'But', she admits to her boyfriend Wolf, 'I didn't know what it was, only that I didn't find it'. 'Love?' offers Wolf,

> but she shakes her head. 'Not just love. The way it's always used, that's just a term....Anyways, that was not enough for me. I think that's why I figured I really wanted to have a baby. I thought, that's where I might find it. *Touching. Tenderness. Feeling.*...That's what I've always been looking for. But not with a child. With another human being. With a partner.'...Then she puts her head into his arms and says: 'I'm afraid.'[1]

Finding emotions—feelings which included love, but also, as the back cover of Rodrian's novel stated, 'animosity' and 'affects' in general—was a key theme in many books written for children and adolescents during the 1970s and 1980s, especially, but by no means only, in those books that were written within the context of the New Left.[2] Such a 'search for emotions' was necessary because the world of urban capitalism was deeply boring and frustrating. On the surface, these books tried to teach their readers how they might overcome this boredom.[3] At the same time, they also created and imparted practical knowledge about what boredom was, how it felt, and what its sources were. The chapter will thus focus on the knowledge that the book created rather than on the author's intentions. While authors probably assumed that their readers would be familiar with such feelings, the books effectively told children and teenagers when and how to feel bored, as the first section of this chapter will show. Overcoming this boredom was possible, though difficult. There were just as many 'false' ways to 'find' feelings, as the second section will show, as there were successful ways, which will be discussed in the final section. On one level, the stories were quite explicitly instructive, telling their readers precisely what to do to overcome boredom. But by doing so, the books also explained, though less explicitly, what emotions were and how they 'functioned'. Finally, the chapter will analyse these 'alternatives to boredom', moving beyond boredom and frustration as such.

In contrast to the other chapters of this book, this chapter focuses on a rather narrow time period, predominantly the 1970s, and primarily on West Germany geographically. What are the reasons for and benefits of this approach? While it would be an overstatement to claim that New Leftists were the very first to criticize capitalist society for the allegedly negative feelings it produced, it was only during the 1970s that the theme of boredom in capitalism gained such prominence from a distinctly leftist perspective.[4] Children's books written in the context of the 'old' left, namely the working-class movement in Germany from the late nineteenth century to the mid-twentieth century, developed their social critique around issues of oppression or social justice, rather than on emotional grounds.[5] Even reform-oriented pedagogues, such as A. S. Neill in Britain, who became influential among German New Leftists during the 1960s and 1970s, were mostly concerned with the fear adults instilled in children, but less so with boredom or frustration.[6] Furthermore, the focus on the 1970s will highlight how ambivalent the process of empowerment and democratization was, as already described in several other chapters. On the one hand, children were encouraged to openly accept and embrace fear, to be free of social shame, or to accept homesickness as a legitimate feeling.[7] At the same time, however, as the introduction has stressed, this process of emotional empowerment also put new and heavy burdens of responsibility on children and teenagers.[8] In the 1970s, children and teenagers reading the books analysed here would not only learn that life in modern cities was boring and frustrating, but also that overcoming boredom was a difficult and challenging, although ultimately possible, task.

Concern with the boredom of modern urban life was most prominent in West German books published within the context of the New Left, which is why this chapter will pay particular attention to these books.[9] Most of the books were published by small left-wing publishers, most notably Weismann in Munich. Some of them reached only a limited readership. Others went through several editions and reached tens of thousands of readers within a few years, but have since been forgotten. Numerous other books were published by the more popular Rowohlt Verlag in its *rororo Rotfuchs* series for young readers. The single most popular book that addressed the themes discussed in this chapter was probably Michael Ende's *The Grey Gentlemen* (1974; Ger. orig. *Momo*, 1973).[10] The success of this book suggests that the boredom of life in modern cities was a broad concern that reached beyond the limits of a narrow political milieu.[11] The narrower focus of this chapter thus allows a more detailed exploration of the political and socio-cultural context in which these books were produced and generated their meaning.

The focus on a relatively limited period means that the analysis will not trace change over time. Rather, the chapter will explore in detail the knowledge that was created and conveyed in these books about boredom and related feelings during this period. It will analyse the practices and issues the stories presented as feeling boring, frustrating, or dull, as well as various practices these stories offered to children and teenagers as means to overcome boredom. Two general features of these books are relevant with regard to the process of mimetically learning how to feel. First, most books told somewhat realistic stories of 'ordinary' teenagers, though some of them, like *The Grey Gentlemen*, also contain fantastic elements. This narrative strategy would allow teenage readers to imagine themselves in the situation of the protagonists and to empathize with their feelings. At times, authors and publishers even made an effort to include teenage readers in the publication process to ensure that the story was plausible. The editors of Rodrian's novel, for example, noted that they had shown the book to several teenagers before deciding to publish it and asked them whether they liked the book and considered Ingrid's story realistic. Girls for the most part liked the book, the editors claimed, while boys were divided. But all of them believed the story could have happened.[12] Such anecdotal evidence suggests that at least the books did not fall on utterly deaf ears, but found an audience interested in the knowledge that they provided. Second, many of the stories described what might be called an 'emotional transformation': while the teenage protagonists at the beginning of the story were bored and frustrated, they somehow managed to 'find' the feelings they were looking for and succeeded in overcoming boredom. Since these narrative details, as well as the specific practices described in these books—both those that were supposed to feel boring and dull and those that would yield intense emotions—are relevant for understanding the emotional knowledge the books created and imparted, the chapter will focus on a select number of books, though similar topics were addressed, albeit less explicitly, in numerous other New Left children's books.[13]

THE BOREDOM OF URBAN LIFE IN CAPITALISM

While the obvious goal of most books was to instruct readers on how to overcome boredom, they also created knowledge about boredom itself. Scrutinizing this knowledge about boredom is not only necessary to make sense of the suggestions these books made for how to escape from boredom, to be discussed later in this chapter, but also because it will enable an understanding of what children and teenagers learnt about how it felt to be bored and what the sources of boredom were.

In short, feeling bored was, according to these books, characterized above all by the absence of any other 'intense' feelings. This is why Ingrid, for example, was searching for *any* feelings, not only love. Michael Ende's *The Grey Gentlemen* provides a similar perspective on boredom. Grey Gentlemen, 'thieves of time', easily decipherable symbols of capitalism, use their mathematical skills to fool people into giving them their time. The result is a uniform and efficient, but boring, world that has no place for feelings. In this reading, mathematical rationality is anti-emotional and hence boring.[14] Gerd-Gustl Müller's novel *Der Job* ('The job', 1977) describes a similar emotional void as frustration, rather than boredom. When Manne, the book's main teenage protagonist, for example, accidentally walks in on his girlfriend Biene and his friend Sieke having sex, he just turns around and leaves. 'He waited for the pain, disappointment, or anger. But there was nothing', only 'frustration'. Afterwards, Manne does not take any action, for example confronting either of them, nor do he and Biene ever talk about what happened. Only once does Sieke mention 'carelessly' how he had 'fucked' her.[15] The problem of boredom and frustration was, as these examples suggest, a general emotional emptiness. This was, to be sure, not a fundamental reinterpretation of what boredom was. What is striking, however, is that a sense of time and its painfully slow passing, which plays a crucial role in other literary and philosophical treatments of boredom, played no explicit role in these stories.

To further understand the *practical* knowledge the books conveyed about boredom, it is necessary to analyse those practices that were described as feeling boring. A first practice to be considered is dwelling in modern cities, which highlights the importance of the built environment for feelings. Typically, the urban spaces that formed the setting of the stories were described as monotone and uniform. The fictional city that is the setting of *The Grey Gentlemen*, for example, begins to change once the Grey Gentlemen take over. Old neighbourhoods are torn down and replaced by new buildings that look all the same—'a desert of order'. Dwelling in these buildings makes their inhabitants 'colder', and their lives become just as monotonous as the buildings.[16] The unnamed West Berlin neighbourhood in which Manne from *Der Job* lives is rapidly changing in a similar direction. 'Old houses, decorated with stucco' were turned into 'piles of rubbish within minutes'.[17] The cities described in Irene Rodrian's novels look and feel the same. Ingrid, for example, observes Munich's 'grey cement blocks with small light gaps. "Awful, if you have to live there"', she comments.[18] One reading of these stories would be that the built environment of modern cities *generated* boredom and frustration. Read through a praxeological lens, however, the stories conveyed a slightly different kind of knowledge: it was the practice of living in such a place that felt deeply boring.

A similar argument can be made with regard to other practices in which children and teenagers typically engaged, such as playing, working, or attending school. In *The Grey Gentlemen*, for example, time-saving parents have no space left in their schedules to play with their children and thus they compensate by buying them expensive toys. Yet, these automatically moving robots and trucks are so perfectly designed that 'there was absolutely nothing left to the imagination'. Children are left only staring at these toys, 'mesmerised yet bored'.[19] Nevertheless, the children in the story prove immune to the Grey Gentlemen's efforts to steal their time and make them efficient, which is why they are eventually banned from playing in the streets and parks and brought to 'Child Depots', where they are only permitted to play games that teach them something useful. But 'they were also forgetting something at the same time—how to be happy, how to care about anything, how to dream.... Sulky, bored and hostile they did as they were told'.[20] The story provided children, quite conspicuously, with a certain kind of knowledge about what felt boring: playing with expensive and perfect toys, or simply following rules. But Ende's novel also informed young readers about what 'doing' boredom meant: *not* being imaginative, *not* being excited, *not* dreaming.[21]

Working was another everyday practice for teenagers that was depicted as a source of boredom. Again, the important question is precisely what made working such a boring experience. Manne, who was to stand in 'for the countless youths that stand aside, that sag and have no job', as a line at the beginning of Müller's novel notes,[22] provides a good example. After several weeks of unemployment he manages to find a job, albeit only for a short while, at a small company producing handles for cupboards or towel rails. But the job is utterly boring. 'Even a brain amputee could do this job', Manne complains. 'Arse, stomach, noggin, cock, and feet—none of that was necessary. Ready to be amputated. All you needed was your thumb and two fingers.'[23] The crucial point here is that Manne's labour neither requires his full bodily involvement, nor his mental attention.

In Gudrun Pausewang's novel *Etwas lässt sich doch bewirken: Ein Roman aus der Friedensbewegung* ('Something can be done: A novel from the peace movement', 1984), work is likewise characterized as boring. The main protagonist Robert has just finished high school. Given the immense 'frustration and stress' and the pressure to perform well during his school years, he longs for the freedom that will come with graduation. Yet, once school is over, all he feels is a 'big emptiness', due in part to the lack of prospects he has for the future. His parents want him to enter his father's painting business, but he does not want to 'suffocate amidst paint, varnish, and wall papers.... Balance sheets, gains, and losses. No, not such a life.'[24] Readers of this story, too, would learn that 'frustration' was above all a feeling that was characterized by the absence of any other feelings. His description of the work awaiting him at his father's business furthermore suggested that (mathematical) rationality and lack of diversity were responsible for his lack of feelings.[25]

Adult figures, mostly parents, represented in this literature a capitalist rationality against which children had to struggle to 'find' their feelings.[26] The most prominent example of a young protagonist struggling against rationality is young Momo, who defeats the Grey Gentlemen and thereby restores joy and happiness to a grey, monotone, and boring world. Other books described teenagers' parents as merely concerned with rational arguments and at times even hostile to feelings. Robert's father, for example, is at first incapable of understanding his son's desire to feel. After a violent altercation with a peace activist, Robert goes to a nearby peace camp where he hopes to escape his frustration. When his parents come to visit, Robert explains to them why he enjoys being there. 'Here, you may show your feelings.' His father replies: 'You lacked nothing at home', meaning nothing material, and he should be happy that he did not have to suffer like they had after the war. But Robert reproaches them for creating a 'different sort of misery', that is, a world in which only 'utility, security, representation' mattered, and by implication, emotions had no place and were irrelevant.[27] The father of Paula, one of the main characters of Helma Fehrmann and Peter Weismann's popular love story *Und plötzlich willste mehr* ('And suddenly you want more', 1979), also urges his daughter to 'think realistically' when discussing the news that large amounts of cauliflower had been thrown into the ocean. While his daughter argues that the cauliflower could have been given to the needy, her father explains the capitalist logic behind this: 'If they throw too much cauliflower on the market, the price falls....If they didn't do this, it would have consequences for foreign markets, the stock market, and the currency. These are significant considerations.'[28] From the perspective of capitalist rationality, only efficiency and profits mattered, but not the (physical) feelings of the needy—and neither did Paula's emotions. Even Ingrid's left-wing and generally supportive parents appeal to her rationality when they try to convince her to have an abortion.[29]

These stories, then, explained to children and teenagers what boredom was and how it felt. Most importantly, boredom was characterized by a variety of deficiencies and absences. Feeling bored or frustrated meant *not* feeling anything at all—feeling 'empty', as many books put it. Practices were described as boring because they lacked certain qualities, such as diversity, imagination, physical or sensual experiences, or a relation to teenage protagonists' own lives. Readers were not only told what boredom was, but also informed about its social sources, which gave these books a critical edge. It was the way that modern cities were built, the organization of labour in capitalism, and, most significantly, the logic of capitalist rationality itself that caused the feelings of boredom and frustration. Indeed, the emotional deficiencies that characterized boredom and frustration, the books claimed, also defined the mathematical and efficiency-oriented rationality of capitalism, which was hence portrayed as inherently anti-emotional and deeply boring.

Reading about boring games with expensive toys or the frustrating work Manne had to do, child and teenage readers would also learn which activities would or should feel boring in their own lives. It was, in other words, by no means a *natural* reaction to feel bored when studying the history of the Napoleonic wars, as Paul from *Und plötzlich willste mehr* did; boredom was learnt. This, however, meant that the books, while they aimed at criticizing capitalist boredom, might in fact have participated in the very production of this feeling, precisely by creating and imparting knowledge regarding which practices in capitalist society felt boring.

TRYING AND FAILING—HOW NOT TO ESCAPE FROM BOREDOM

Living in a boring world, fictional teenage protagonists try to find ways to escape from this boredom. But not all attempts to move beyond boredom were described as viable and successful. Describing such 'failed' attempts to escape from boredom, children's books conveyed further knowledge both about boredom and frustration, and about feelings more generally. First, children's books critically addressed what might be called the promise of happiness and excitement offered by a capitalist consumer society. Neither expensive toys, as *The Grey Gentlemen* claimed, nor extensively using cosmetic products, as the story of Marlene in *Und plötzlich will-ste mehr* suggested, would yield the feelings they promised.[30] The same was true for the glamorous world of pop stars, as the play *Bravo, Girl!* (1975) pointed out. This play, based on a true story, portrayed the young textile worker Inge who spends her days reading the fictional teenage magazine *Hallo*, easily identifiable as popular and real *Bravo*, and dreaming about the world of stars and consumption the maga-zine glamourizes. Hoping to gain access to this world, Inge participates in a *Hallo* beauty contest, which she wins with the help of her boss, who wants to use her to promote his business. As a prize, she tours America, where she must endlessly model her company's fashion. Soon enough, the supposedly exciting trip turns into a nightmare for Inge. When she starts complaining, the photographer just tells her: 'Your job is to smile.' The real emotions felt by Inge and her colleagues, the stress and frustration at the textile factory, were, by contrast, of no interest to the magazine, she is told.[31] It is probably not surprising that New Leftists criticized consumerism. More interesting are the reasons the play criticized consumerism, and what children would thus learn about feelings: the world of consumption and stars would not provide joyful and exciting feelings, precisely because it ignored *genuine* feelings, be it the uncomfortable physical feeling of how a piece of cloth felt, as Inge complains, or frustration and stress in the workplace.

According to leftist books, looking for excitement in the world of consumer-ism was a vain pursuit because it produced only images of feelings, but no real or authentic emotions. Even some of those practices that would lead to genuine intense feelings were problematic. Since boredom was above all characterized by the absence of such intense emotions, any feeling that went beyond the monotony of everyday life was a way out of boredom. This included even supposedly 'negative' feelings such as physical pain or the excitement of fear, as Irene Rodrian's popular *Blöd, wenn der Typ draufgeht* ('Too bad, when the guy bites the dust', 1976) sug-gests. After observing a burglary committed by a gang of teenagers from the neigh-bourhood, the book's main character, Bert, confronts the teenagers and is badly beaten. But Bert, who is desperately looking for friends, urges them to let him join their gang. Impressed by his courage, they agree. The next day he is in terrible pain, but it gives him 'the feeling of being alive'. Looking out the window, he can see details he has never noticed before. There is a 'new intensity', both emotional and sensual, that he feels. But the feeling of being alive soon disappears as he joins the gang and becomes involved in its criminal activities, which result in the death of a guard when they burgle an electronics shop. While Bert feels remorse, his fellow gang members—whom he refuses to call friends—feel nothing.[32] Violence and criminality might offer brief moments that transcend boredom, but, the novel implied, they were not viable as long-term solutions.

The most promising, but difficult way to escape from boredom and frustra-tion was engaging in love relations. Bert, for example, finds a way out of his dull life when he falls in love with Isa, though only after the deadly robbery.[33] Other books discussed the problems teenagers faced in such relationships. Loving as a practice was, in other words, described as a process of trying, failing and, some-times, succeeding.[34] Young readers of these stories could thus 'try out' these feel-ings alongside the protagonists. The key problem of many of these relations was that teenagers were incapable of communicating with each other. Consider Ingrid from the beginning of this chapter who had been searching for feelings. The first attempt to find these feelings was her brief affair with Norbert that begins with them having sex at a lake. While having sex, Norbert whispers twice 'I love you', but Ingrid can barely hear him. Lying there, she 'felt naked, alone, and lost'. Had he asked her if she had slept with him because she actually liked him, she would have had to lie, she admits to herself. But luckily, he does not ask. Instead, he just makes small talk without engaging in any genuine conversation.[35]

The story of Manne and his girlfriend Biene offered a similar lesson. Hanging out at a local youth club, the two lovers do not talk to each other. First, Biene blames Manne for being so silent, but later, when Manne wants to talk about their feelings for each other—'do you love me, or what', he asks her—she herself reacts angrily.[36] The situation does not change when Manne and his friends move into an abandoned house with other squatters. 'They did not come closer', the author wrote. Even their break up happens without a word. Later on in the novel, Manne goes to a disco and hits on a girl from West Germany. But their 'conversation did not get going', and when Manne tries to kiss her, she rejects him.[37] Being incap-able of communicating, young readers would learn, was one way of being bored and frustrated, or at least one reason why they could not transcend such feelings. Communication, as the final section will show, would then be key to generating emotions beyond boredom.

Sexuality, too, is portrayed as ultimately boring without communication, as shown in the love story of Rocco and Antonia, who are the main fifteen- or sixteen-year-old protagonists of *Pigs Have Wings* (1976). Only for a brief moment does the couple find something like love, for which communication is crucial. Antonia especially enjoys intimate moments when they talk about future family plans.[38] But soon enough, their affair is reduced to Rocco having sex with her in a humiliating way. The situation escalates when Rocco has anal intercourse with her, which she passively endures.[39] Afterwards, Antonia is ready to break up. 'It can't go on this way', she tells Rocco, 'it gets boring after a while, it doesn't give me the sen-sation of being alive but only of doing gym lessons and chalking up orgasms'. At the beginning, it had been different, she says, when 'every kiss came with words—a thousand words'.[40] Sex that lacked diversity and imagination would become as boring as any other practice lacking these characteristics, readers might learn.

Quite obviously, these books encouraged young readers to talk about their feel-ings and thus to change their behaviour. But they also informed them about at least one social source for their incapability to talk: their parents, who in most cases failed to teach their children how to openly communicate. The implication was that one emotional practice—*not* talking—was itself learnt from role models like parents, but that children and teenagers could overcome it once they understood where they had learnt it. The parents of Paul and Paula provide the best example for this. Paul's parents always told their son that he could talk about everything with them. But when Paul confronts his father about cheating on and generally mistreating his mother, his father just yells at him, saying it was a matter between him and Paul's mother and none of Paul's concern.[41] Paula's parents are even less willing to talk with their daughter, but simply tell her what to do. Paula, on the other hand, yearns to talk to her mother, in particular about her sexuality. But her mother does not even name her 'fanny', merely referring to it as 'down there', a part of the body that was supposed to remain clean and was useful for having children, but not a source of pleasure.[42] After Paula finally had sex with Paul, she would have liked to say: 'Mum, I've fucked [him].' But of course, she cannot.[43] Other parents act similarly. Robert's father, who misses his son dearly when he is away camping with the peace activists, only comments that he could smell his son's return. Knowing that his father is happy to see him, but unable to express his feelings, Robert just says to himself: 'Well, that's how Father is. Don't show emotions.'[44] Manne's father constantly yells at his son after the latter has lost his apprenticeship and proves unable to find any other work for a long time, but the father is not able to talk to his son about his frustrations.[45]

TRYING AND SUCCEEDING—HOW TO ESCAPE FROM BOREDOM

Escaping from boredom and finding feelings was, for the stories' protagonists, a difficult and challenging process that required effort and could fail. But it was also possible to succeed, as most stories ended with children and teenagers over-coming their boredom, frustration, and general emotional emptiness. Instructing readers on how to achieve this was probably the books' most important aim. The concluding section of this chapter will thus analyse what children and teenagers were supposed to do in order to develop better feelings—to explain how they were supposed to love and find joy and happiness in working or studying. These stories provided readers with practical knowledge about boredom's 'radical Other': not one specific emotion, but any intense feeling at all, about what it was, and how it might occur. Furthermore, the books created knowledge about the social dynamics of feelings, especially by emphasizing how communicating about feelings would itself result in experiencing feelings; how, in other words, an ability to empathize with others and their feelings, even if these were feelings of frustration and stress, was a way out of emotional emptiness.

A number of practices were suggested as a way to overcome boredom. Interestingly, and in particular with regard to the argument about mimetic learn-ing, even reading books could be exciting, as Rodrian's *Blöd, wenn der Typ drauf-geht* claimed. While Bert watches the gang of other kids burgling a store, he has a 'feeling of excitement, like one has when reading a book or watching a film'. In a way, the book thus suggested to its readers how to feel when reading it, namely, exactly as the protagonist in the book feels at that moment.[46] Other practices the books suggested constituted, in a way, responses to those boring practices that characterized urban capitalism. If living in the grey and monotone buildings of modern cities was deeply boring, frustrating, and instilled aggression in children, then going to the countryside and living in nature might encourage better feelings. Robert, for example, sitting on the bus to a peace camp in the nearby village, enjoys the 'peaceful landscape' and the picturesque villages he observes. What uniform cities lacked, nature and small villages could offer: a sensual diversity that would yield peaceful feelings.[47] More generally, activities that would require imagination or that would provide full sensual experiences were presented as ways to produce intense feelings. Paula, for example, studies her own vagina extensively. She looks at it, feels its warmth and moisture, smells it. 'That's all me', she says. In contrast to her classmate Marlene, who treats her body with all kinds of cosmetic products, Paula feels good about her body in its natural state. Paul is similarly interested in his body. Bored by reading about Emperor Wilhelm II, he masturbates and afterwards examines his semen under a microscope, which impresses him as he realizes that 'these could become human beings'.[48]

The stories of Manne and Robert, on the other hand, provide examples for how work might be emotionally fulfilling. Being unemployed, Manne spends most of his time at home, listening to music. He builds an amplifier, using several old radios, and he enjoys doing it: the brazing, 'the smell of hot tin and the fumbling with the forceps'. Later on, he repairs a set of speakers during a concert in a squatted house, proud of the skills his father taught him. Importantly, it is work that requires both his technical understanding and his physical skills, and that provides him with a full and pleasant sensory experience.[49] Robert, too, finds joy in manual labour, first carving wooden demons at the peace camp, later working with plants at a nursery.[50] His parents' reaction to the wooden demons provides a telling contrast. While his mother reacts with positive surprise, his father wonders: 'What are they good for?' 'If you think in terms of usefulness, then there is no answer', Robert replies. 'But I enjoyed the carving.'[51] Such stories provided readers not only with a certain kind of knowledge about how to avoid feeling bored, but also about how not being bored might feel. It was a diverse sensual and corporal feeling that allowed them to relate to both their own bodies and to the material objects they created and cared about. Such experiences would foster, the books suggested, intense feelings beyond boredom.

Situations that disrupted the routines of everyday life were other moments that would feel intense, as the story of Rocco and Antonia shows. The two teenagers have known each other for quite a while through their political youth collective, but have never shown any real interest in each other—until a demonstration following a young, not personally acquainted, comrade's violent death. Interestingly, Rocco thinks about this death as the radical and final end of feeling. 'The police didn't give *him* [the comrade] time...to feel good and feel bad', Rocco reasons. In a way, the violent death symbolizes most dramatically the absence of emotions, inflicted, in this case, by the state. And yet, it is the moment of commemorating this death that makes Rocco experience intense emotions. He feels enraged, and for the first time in a long while, he has a 'real urge to go to the demonstration'.[52] Not feeling bored could, as these examples show, take different forms. Joy, sadness, rage, even pain, as noted above, could feel 'not boring'—what mattered was the intensity and exceptionality of the feelings, even if they were 'negative'.

It is worthwhile to follow the story of Rocco and Antonia a bit further, because it also created knowledge about how emotions could be transformed in such intense situations. Usually, Rocco is too embarrassed to chant and sing, but on this day, he joins the crowd. It is the same with Antonia. When Rocco sees her, he recognizes that she looks different. She no longer has 'that little sad face', as if she wanted to say 'what a shit this life is, all gone. In a word, she was beautiful.' When they meet, Rocco takes Antonia's hand, a gesture she doesn't expect. 'Maybe this is how snow feels when spring comes—it just melts and flows happily down the hill.' And when she throws her arms around him and puts her head on his shoulder, her 'tears became sobs and the sobs became tremors that shook us both like an earthquake'.[53] In an exceptional situation, the episode suggests, it was possible to overcome typical isolation and show feelings, for example by chanting or taking a friend's hand. This act of transgression, the novel suggested, was then itself an (intense) emotion because it connected people. In other words, readers of the episode might learn that feeling *not bored*, was the act (rather than habitualized practice) of crossing the boundary between (two) people.

Rocco's story provides an excellent example for discussing the emotional relevance of communicating feelings. As noted above, the relationship between Rocco and Antonia soon fails due to Rocco's inability or unwillingness to talk to her. Seeing Antonia having sex with an older comrade at a party, he asks his friend Roberto to pretend to have diarrhoea, so that they can leave, an act that in turn upsets Antonia who wishes Rocco would show his anger. At home, Rocco starts talking with Roberto and has sex with him. It is this night, Rocco writes to his friend Luca, that 'I was finally able to cry, that I allowed myself to be consoled, to let myself go, all that, you know'. It was utterly different from being with a girl, he stresses.[54] Obviously, the episode implicitly encouraged readers to openly express their own feelings. But it also suggested to them that such an act of showing feelings, both verbally and non-verbally, was itself an intensely emotional act that, as in this case, could even lead to sex. Talking about feelings would, in other words, itself result in experiencing positive feelings.

Paul and Paula's love story, on the other hand, suggested that talking about negative feelings, such as fears about sexuality, was a way to overcome these feelings by creating trust and intimacy. Before Paul and Paula have sex for the first time, Paul asks her 'Are you afraid?' 'Yes', she thinks, but replies 'no'. 'Are you?'—'No', Paul says too. But when they undress each other, Paula admits that she is afraid to take off her trousers. Paul, too, is able to admit his fears when he insists on using a condom.[55] The book's final scene underlined this message. Paul is worried that Paula will break up with him because she went to a party with another male friend. But Paula tells him in the book's final line: 'I'm in love with you.'[56] Verbalizing and communicating feelings was, the episode showed, not only a way to overcome emotions like fear, but also to perform different and better emotions, namely mutual sympathy and trust.[57]

A mutual understanding of feelings might also change the emotional situation between parents and children. Somewhat in contrast to books that depicted adults as merely rational and even hostile to children's feelings, other books aimed at explaining to children how adults felt, because only if children were able to understand their parents' feelings and empathize with them, would solidarity between them be possible. In *Die Geschichte von Trummi kaputt* ('The story of Trummi in pieces', 1973), for example, children set out to explore why their working-class parents are always so angry and nervous, which is, as the children find out, due to their jobs.[58] Another book, *Mann, du bist gemein!* ('You're so mean!', 1974), is written entirely from the perspective of a single mother whose son has run away in order to make young readers understand how she feels as a mother. Quite obviously, these books tried to explain adults' feelings to children, above all their frustration due to pressure at work and their difficulties finding love. But they also suggested that this understanding would yield feelings itself, in this case a feeling of solidarity. On the other hand, teenage books also implied that feelings could be taught by teenagers once they had overcome their emotional emptiness and could then serve as role models for their parents by showing them how they, too, could escape from their boring and rational life and embrace their dreams and feelings.[59]

A particularly interesting practical attempt to teach children (how) to feel that moves beyond the focus on children's books deserves presentation and analysis in some detail: the West-Berlin-based amateur theatre company, *Rote Grütze*, and its play for elementary school children *Darüber spricht man nicht!! Ein Spiel zur Sexualerziehung* ('You don't talk about that!! A play for sexual education', 1973).[60] The play tried to put the lessons offered by leftist children's books and advice literature on stage by practically and visually teaching children how to feel. In West Berlin, though conservative politicians harshly criticized it, the play was officially recommended by the senate for elementary school classes, while Bavarian teachers were not allowed to organize trips to attend the play with their students.[61] A text version of the play that included facsimiles of children's handwritten reactions to it was published by Weismann in 1973. It was published in six editions until 1984, with a total print run of 19,000 copies, but, because it had been put on stage, it reached a much wider audience and still does today.

The play's goal was, as Norbert Burkert, consultant on sexual education at the West Berlin Pedagogical Centre, wrote in the preface, to convey that sexuality was not only a 'biological fact', but also 'an emotional, social experience'. Children, but also teachers and parents who attended the play, would realize that they lived in a 'social world lacking in or devoid of emotions', but would also 'make the experience of how nice it can be to touch each other, to fondle, how much fun it is to see how children react to this'.[62] Since feelings had, from this perspective, an essential corporeal component, the teaching of feelings also required physical practices. The play then conveyed not only knowledge about feelings in the body, but the knowledge that children were to learn *with* their bodies, both doing and trying emotions.[63]

A key part of this play was to teach children not to be ashamed of their bodies and their bodily functions. To this end, the theatre group developed a number of 'games' on stage in which both children and adults would actively participate. During these games, children would practice how to overcome shame and how to enjoy their bodies. The first step was openly talking about the body, especially the parts and functions that were usually considered shameful—like penises, vaginas, and urinating. Children would thus understand that there was no 'rational' reason to be ashamed of their bodies—after all, all human beings had to pee. To make sure that children not only heard the message, but could practically experience overcoming shame, the actors invited the children to invent names for their penises and vaginas as well as other parts of their bodies. Then they sang collectively:[64]

> I'm so ashamed, I'm so ashamed,
> I'm ashamed when I pee,
> I'm so ashamed, I'm so ashamed,
> Why am I so ashamed?
> A human being is a human being [Mensch],
> And a human being happily pees.
> So don't be ashamed, so don't be ashamed,
> So please don't be ashamed so much.

Further stanzas similarly addressed children being ashamed of sweating, their bottoms, and being naked. Singing collectively that they were not ashamed, children practised not being ashamed. Having overcome shame, as well as fears related to masturbation, children would then learn to enjoy their bodies. To this end, they played the 'rubbing box'. One of the adult actors declared: 'Touching each other and fondling is great.' Then the actors on stage started cuddling, tickled each other, and showed how much fun they had. Soon enough, the children would join the game, and ultimately they would be joined by their parents and teachers. Actively involving children on stage, the play not only imparted a practical knowledge about feelings, but allowed children to quite literally embody this knowledge by practising it.[65] Feelings, the play implied, were bodily practices. That is why they could be not only learnt, but should be practised and trained, be it by openly talking about them or by actually cuddling and fondling.

The play ended with an explicit social critique in a reversal of parent-child relations. The actors on stage impersonated two children who had attended the play and their prudish parents who want to educate their children about sex. Being incapable of talking to their children, the parent characters simply leave a conservative sex education book, for which a text by Kurt Seelmann was used as a template,[66] in the children's room. But the children have already learnt about sexuality at the play, both in terms of biological facts and the emotional pleasures it involved, and thus simply laugh about the book. Instead of reading it, they call their parents into their room and teach them a lesson. They begin by instructing their parents to act out being in bed and cuddling. Suddenly, they, the children, come in and surprise them. But instead of being shocked, their parents openly say that they were cuddling and kissing. Having done as they were told, their parents can admit how much they like physically loving each other. But these are rare moments, the actor playing the mother confessed, as they are usually too tired from work. They have only learnt how to work, she sadly says, but not 'how to better love and understand each other'. Their own parents had only induced fear about the opposite sex, both parents complain. Even though the play did not elaborate on this issue, it suggested, in line with the other children's books analysed here, that ultimately the capitalist labour regime was responsible for people's hostility towards (physical) feelings. Having been able to admit not only the unjustified fear and its sources, but also the joy they actually did experience during sex, fear is finally replaced by joy in the play's last collectively sung song.[67]

* * *

The books discussed here imparted a multifaceted practical knowledge about boredom and its 'radical Other', that is, 'intense' feelings, as well as about how emotions in general 'functioned'. Young readers learnt that they lived in a deeply boring world in which genuine feelings had no place. They learnt how it felt to be bored, which practices felt boring, and the reasons they felt that way. Above all, boredom was characterized by multiple absences: a general absence of other intense feelings, but also a lack of imagination and sensual diversity, all of which characterized (capitalist) rationality. Yet readers also learnt how they might overcome this boredom and frustration, most importantly by openly talking about feelings, which was itself a way to 'generate' feelings, and also by engaging in physical practices like meaningful work and pleasurable physical contact. On an explicit (and important) level, these books provided practical guidelines for how to find these feelings. Reading about them, children and teenagers would then also learn something about feelings in general, what they were, and how they occurred. In particular, they would learn about the social dynamic of feelings. In some of the books, finding these feelings seemed fairly easy and doable. Other novels stressed, however, as Ingrid with whom this chapter began put it, that 'we don't have a particularly good chance, not really'.[68] Finding feelings beyond boredom was, in other words, a process of trial and error, and a process that could fail. As the introduction has pointed out, feeling the right way was a difficult, complex, and contradictory task.

NOTES

1. Rodrian, *Viel Glück*, 98 (emphasis added; all translations by the author).
2. On the alternative and non-dogmatic New Left in Germany, see, with further references, Reichardt, *Authentizität und Gemeinschaft*; Reichardt and Siegfried, *Das Alternative Milieu*. More generally, see Davis, 'What's Left'. The politicized approaches to emotions in children's literature discussed in this chapter are very much in line with what the New Left argued more generally about feelings in urban, capitalist society, as would be shown by a study of New Left journals, such as *Das Blatt* (Munich), *Pflasterstrand* (Frankfurt am Main), or *Carlo Sponti* (Heidelberg).
3. Boredom has not been a particularly prominent topic for historians of emotions. An exception is Kessel, *Langeweile*. Literary scholars, psychologists and philosophers have paid more attention to the feeling, see, for example, Heidegger, *Grundbegriffe der Metaphysik*; Große, *Philosophie der Langeweile*; Goodstein, *Experience without Qualities*. This chapter will not make use of philosophical or psychological treatments

of what boredom is, but will reconstruct the knowledge about boredom imparted by children's books.

4. On boredom in different political contexts, see Kessel, *Langeweile*, 257–78. See also, with further references, Midgley, 'Los von Berlin'; Rohkrämer, *Eine andere Moderne*, especially part two.

5. See, for example, Herminia zur Mühlen, *Was Peterchens Freunde erzählen* (1921); Herminia zur Mühlen, *Ali, der Teppichweber* (1923); Alex Wedding, *Eddie and the Gypsy* (1935; Ger. orig., *Ede und Unku: Ein Roman für Jungen und Mädchen*, 1931); Walter Schönstedt, *Kämpfende Jugend* (1932). See also Leutheuser, *Freie, geführte und verführte Jugend*, 68–81; Altner, *Das proletarische Kinderbuch*.

6. See Neill, *Summerhill*. See also chapter 1, 'Mrs Gaskell's Anxiety'; chapter 8, 'Lebrac's Pain'; chapter 9, 'Jim Button's Fear'.

7. See chapter 7, 'Piggy's Shame'; chapter 9, 'Jim Button's Fear'; chapter 11, 'Heidi's Homesickness'.

8. See introduction to this volume; chapter 6, 'Wendy's Love'.

9. On New Left and 'Anti-Authoritarian' children's literature in Germany, see Leutheuser, *Freie, geführte und verführte Jugend*, 190–212; Steinlein, 'Neubeginn, Restauration, antiautoritäre Wende'; Kaminski, *Jugendliteratur und Revolte*; Dahrendorf, *Jugendliteratur und Politik*, 108–63.

10. Ende, *Grey Gentlemen*.

11. For a contemporary perspective on children and adolescents and their emotions, see the essays in Ilsemann, *Jugend zwischen Anpassung und Ausstieg*.

12. Rodrian, *Viel Glück*, 100.

13. Even though only a small number of books are discussed in this chapter, it is based on a reading of approximately seventy books. Not all books, however, addressed feelings as explicitly as those cited here. It should also be added that 'classic' themes of New Left children's books, such as oppression and exploitation in capitalism, by no means disappeared. Books like *Martin, der Mars-Mensch* ('Martin, the Martian', [1970]), sought to educate their readers about the basic principles of class relations in capitalist societies, while books like *Fünf Finger sind eine Faust* ('Five fingers make a fist', 1969), sought to instil a sense of solidarity among children.

14. Ende, *Grey Gentlemen*, 51–65.

15. Müller, *Der Job*, 36–7.

16. Ende, *Grey Gentlemen*, 64.

17. Müller, *Der Job*, 10.

18. Rodrian, *Viel Glück*, 15–17, quotation 15. See similarly Rodrian, *Blöd, wenn der Typ draufgeht*, 8, 13–14; Ludwig and Friesel, *Geschichte von Trummi kaputt*, 8. For a similar perspective in children's literature in East Germany (GDR), see Pludra, *Insel der Schwäne*. See also chapter 11, 'Heidi's Homesickness'.

19. Ende, *Grey Gentlemen*, 67–8.

20. Ende, 162–4.

21. On the practice of dreaming, see also Pausewang, *Etwas lässt sich doch bewirken*, 68–9.

22. Müller, *Der Job*, [2] (half-title verso).

23. Müller, 74.

24. Pausewang, *Etwas lässt sich doch bewirken*, 5–6.

25. For a similar point about the boredom of school, see Fehrmann and Weismann, *Und plötzlich willste mehr*, 8–9, 49, 75–6.

26. For a theoretical outline of this struggle between the adult 'party of rationality and alienation' and the children's 'party of feeling and sensuality', see Röttgen,

'Kinderrevolution'. An important reference for Röttgen was French writer Rochefort, *Encore heureux qu'on va vers l'été*.

27. Pausewang, *Etwas lässt sich doch bewirken*, 42.
28. Fehrmann and Weismann, *Und plötzlich willste mehr*, 15. The book was based on a play by the New Left theatre group 'Rote Grütze' written by Helma Fehrmann, Jürgen Flügge, and Holger Franke, *Was heisst hier Liebe?* (1977). In 1977, it won the Brüder Grimm prize in Berlin, and in 1978 was made into a film which would show, as the Munich-based journal *Das Blatt* wrote, that 'feelings' could be learnt and that these feelings, be they 'fears, inhibitions or joy' should be actively communicated. See 'Was heißt hier Liebe?'.
29. Rodrian, *Viel Glück*, 59–63.
30. Fehrmann and Weismann, *Und plötzlich willste mehr*, 26–7. On the boredom of watching TV, as well as how boredom and anger were, in general, the feelings that characterized a thirteen-year-old girl's life, see Hornschuh, *Ich bin 13*, 13, 47–50.
31. Geifrig, *Bravo, Girl!*, 46. In writing the play, Geifrig had talked to several 'Bravo Girls' about the career they were promised. Particularly helpful to him was the report of Cornelia Greiner about her experience as a 'Bravo Girl', published in the leftist trade union youth journal *ran* in September 1973, reprinted in Geifrig, 79. On the teen magazine *Bravo*, which had at the time about three million readers, see with further references Sauerteig, 'Herstellung des sexuellen und erotischen Körpers'; Archiv der Jugendkulturen, *50 Jahre BRAVO*; Nothelle, *Zwischen Pop und Politik*.
32. Rodrian, *Blöd, wenn der Typ draufgeht*, 21–35, 69–72, quotations 35.
33. Rodrian, 80–3.
34. See also chapter 6, 'Wendy's Love'.
35. Rodrain, *Viel Glück*, 22–4, 28, quotations 24.
36. Müller, *Der Job*, 13–14, 22–5, quotation 23.
37. Müller, 70–2.
38. Ravera and Lombardo-Radice, *Pigs Have Wings*, 91–3. The novel was a huge success worldwide. In Germany, where it was published as *Schweine mit Flügeln: Rocco und Antonia, Sex und Politik, Ein Tagebuch* (1977), nearly 100,000 copies were sold by the early 1980s.
39. Ravera and Lombardo-Radice, 101–9.
40. Ravera and Lombardo-Radice, 118. For a similar point, see Fehrmann and Weismann, *Und plötzlich willste mehr*, 28–9, 60–5.
41. Fehrmann and Weismann, 99–106.
42. Fehrmann and Weismann, 20–1.
43. Fehrmann and Weismann, 131.
44. Pausewang, *Etwas lässt sich doch bewirken*, 57.
45. Müller, *Der Job*, 16–17, 44–5, 60–1.
46. Rodrian, *Blöd, wenn der Typ draufgeht*, 15–16.
47. Pausewang, *Etwas lässt sich doch bewirken*, 12–13, see also 96–7, 101, 164.
48. Fehrmann and Weissmann, *Und plötzlich willste mehr*, 20–1, 49.
49. Müller, *Der Job*, 19, 33–5.
50. Pausewang, *Etwas lässt sich doch bewirken*, 79.
51. Pausewang, 43.
52. Ravera and Lombardo-Radice, *Pigs Have Wings*, 53, 55.
53. Ravera and Lombardo-Radice, 56, 60.
54. Ravera and Lombardo-Radice, 130–7, 167–71, quotation 169. Interestingly, a lesbian encounter Antonia has does not yield a similar response, 163–6.

55. Fehrmann and Weismann, *Und plötzlich willste mehr*, 124–30, quotation 126.

56. Fehrmann and Weismann, 139. On love and sexuality, see also the stories by Danish author Maria Marcus *Ein starkes Frühjahr* (1981; Dan. orig. *Alle tiders forår*, 1977), and *Das Himmelbett* (1982, Dan. orig. *Himmelsengen*, 1979). There are no English translations of the two books. See also the discussion in Dahrendorf, *Jugendliteratur und Politik*, 133–63.

57. See similarly Müller, *Der Job*, 96–104; Hornschuh, *Ich bin 13*, 56–7. For an example from advice literature, see Kunstmann, *Mädchen*, 25, 33. See also chapter 2, 'Dickon's Trust'; chapter 9, 'Jim Button's Fear'.

58. Ludwig and Friesel, *Geschichte von Trummi kaputt*, 14, 21, 24; Ladiges, *Mann, du bist gemein*, 5, 9, 15. See also the book's back cover for an explanation of its purpose.

59. See Pausewang, *Etwas lässt sich doch bewirken*, 71, 167

60. Kinder- und Jugendtheater Rote Grütze, *Darüber spricht man nicht*. This play was the precursor of Fehrmann, Flügge, and Franke, *Was heißt hier Liebe?*, see above note 28. About leftist theatres in post-1968 Germany, see Schneider, *Kindertheater nach 1968*. About sexuality, children, and anti-authoritarian education, see in general Herzog, 'Antifaschistische Körper'.

61. 'Theater Rote Grütze'; Oppodeldok, 'Theater'.

62. Kinder- und Jugendtheater Rote Grütze, *Darüber spricht man nicht*, unpaginated preface. See also the detailed advice on how to make use of the play, for example with the help of role-playing games, at the end of the text. Such advice literature, which was explicitly suggested in the play's appendix, included for example Amendt, *Sexfront*; Kunstmann, *Mädchen*; Kentler, *Sexualerziehung*.

63. With regard to the importance of the body for a history of emotions, see Eitler and Scheer, 'Emotionengeschichte als Körpergeschichte'.

64. Kinder- und Jugendtheater Rote Grütze, *Darüber spricht man nicht*, 14–21, quotation 20. See also chapter 7, 'Piggy's Shame'.

65. Kinder- und Jugendtheater Rote Grütze, 69–73, quotation 70.

66. Seelmann, *Wie soll ich mein Kind aufklären*.

67. Kinder- und Jugendtheater Rote Grütze, *Darüber spricht man nicht*, 75–89, quotation 87.

68. Rodrian, *Viel Glück*, 99.

Epilogue
Translating Books, Translating Emotions

Margrit Pernau

The preceding chapters explored a broad landscape of children's books and advice manuals. They spoke about love and fear, about shame and trust, about homesickness and empathy, to name only a few of the wide variety of emotions under investigation. The time frame stretched from the eighteenth century to nearly the present and geographically moved from the United States to India, passing through Western Europe and Russia. As mentioned in the introduction, the very concept of childhood underwent dramatic transformations, leading to changes both in the emotions learnt and the way they were learnt. The reading practices and their cultural embedding showed no less variety: until at least the middle of the twentieth century, many of the Indian stories were situated at the interstices of oral and written culture, whereas in the West, film and television had already started leaving a mark on the way children read books and stories.

Presented throughout the preceding chapters is not only the great diversity, but also the interconnectedness of the developments taking place in different countries. Advice manuals and children's books travelled not only across languages, but also across historical epochs—they were translated, adapted, and rewritten in large numbers. The epilogue will take this aspect of the learning processes further and explore the new questions it allows us to address. As explicated in the introduction, the assumption that emotions are socially constructed is the motivation behind this book. This implies that children have to learn their society's and culture's emotions. This learning process pertains not only to norms and expressions, but also to the ability to read emotions—those of other people, as well as their own—and to develop the required feelings. A central question, posed here, is if these learning processes are culturally specific, how is it that translations work so well for children? How is it possible that children are able not only to decipher more or less correctly the depiction of emotions from a different culture, but even to engage mimetically with these emotions and to feel them?

On a more general level, this leads us to the question of how to conceptualize the communication of emotions across cultures—a communication which covers a much larger field of highly complex emotions than those Paul Ekman called, 'universal basic emotions'[1]—without having to revert to the idea of a universal body into which the emotions and their expressions are already inscribed. Can emotions be both culturally embedded and also to some extent legible across cultures? What are the implications of this question for our concept of emotion and our concept of culture? Do new ways of conceiving cultural difference arise? And finally, what are the implications of these questions for overcoming the dichotomy between relativism and universalism, between nature and nurture, which has so long marked the study of emotions?[2]

CHILDREN'S BOOKS AND ADVICE MANUALS—CULTURAL EMBEDDING AND TRANSNATIONAL LEGIBILITY

Like other forms of knowledge, emotion knowledge—understanding what emotions are, how they arise, whether and how they can be evoked or controlled—travels easily. This neither implies that emotion knowledge is not culturally bound, nor that it does not encounter resistance and becomes more or less profoundly transformed in the course of its travels. While this is true for the centuries during which this knowledge was negotiated in moral philosophy and theology, the fact gains in importance with the nineteenth century movement towards medicine and psychology.[3] The universal claims of these disciplines increasingly informed pedagogy, in schools or through advice manuals, manuals helping and instructing parents on how to educate their children and manuals addressing young people directly. In a world globalized through colonialism, this knowledge spread more quickly than ever before. Namely for the colonies and semi-colonies, this new emotion knowledge was endowed with the promise of participation in progress. Education and self-education based on scientific principles would create the men and women, as well as the emotions, needed for the redemption of the society and the nation.[4] The history of reform pedagogy in the early twentieth century shows that these processes of transfer, translation, and adaptation were and became increasingly more complicated and multidirectional than can be expressed solely in the image of knowledge originating in the West and spreading to the colonies.[5]

The history of the translation of children's books starts simultaneously with the development of children's literature as a genre itself—if not before, as even earlier children had already been reading translated texts, such as Aesop's fables at school or the *One Thousand and One Nights* in chapbook editions.[6] We still lack empirical knowledge on a broad and comparative basis about which books were translated as of the nineteenth century in different countries, and moreover, what processes influenced the decision to translate one book rather than another, or to translate at all. The role of translation differs widely, even within European countries. In Great Britain only 1 to 3 per cent of all published books were translations, whereas in continental Europe the percentage of translations was as high as 70 per cent.[7]

While translations from English often include contemporary stories, transporting an image of present day life, for a long time translations into English (and to a lesser extent other European languages) from non-European languages were drawn from fairy tales and folk stories.[8] If stories were meant to introduce children to other countries, the strategy chosen was more often to write them from scratch, and thus provide a bespoke translation and commentary. Most of the juvenile imperial adventure stories belong to this category,[9] but also the genre which developed in Germany since the 1970s that depicted children's lives in the 'Third World' to sensitize young children to cultural differences. A middle ground is held by intralingual translations, that is, the adaptation of older texts, written for children or for adults, which are deemed no longer directly accessible to children, either for linguistic or for cultural reasons. *Robinson Crusoe* (1719) is a case in point for such an often re-told and translated text.[10] Depending on the strategy of the adaptation, the confrontation with emotions of a different historical epoch may lead to an experience of alterity similar to an encounter with a foreign country, or contrarily to reinforce the sense of cultural identity by projecting it onto the past.

Decisions on whether and what to translate or rewrite reflect publishers' experience of what sells and what does not. But they also reflect a social consensus of what children should be exposed to: is knowledge about other cultures, is the (reading) experience that emotions can work differently in different places and cultures something valued? Or should children instead be protected against an awareness of the possibility of divergent values coming too early, before they have been firmly socialized into their own society's values and emotions? How do global power relations influence these decisions? Are there children considered more deserving of protection from potentially destabilizing experiences of alterity than others? When and for whom, on the contrary, is emotional bi- or multilingualism considered an advantage or even a source of strength?

The answers to these questions not only decide if and when texts are translated, they also directly touch upon translation strategies. Every translation glides between the poles of domestication, that is, guiding the text toward the familiar and hiding the fact that it is a translation, and of foreignization, that is, guiding the reader through an unfamiliar text and the unknown world it describes.[11] The choice between the two strategies hinges on the status accorded the text—works considered belonging to the canon of classical literature are negotiated differently from texts that are seen primarily in relation to their pedagogical or entertainment value. The choice also depends on an evaluation of the public—adult readers from the educated middle classes are presumed to possess the intellectual and emotional resources to cope with alterity more than children. Very often, therefore, translators aim at softening the encounter of the child reader with the unfamiliar without completely erasing it. This may lead to changing the names of the protagonists and some unknown cultural markers: the Sullivan twins become Hanni and Nanni in German, their boarding school changes from St Clare to Lindenhof.[12] But it may also involve partly rewriting the text. Astrid Lindgren's *Pippi Långstrump* (1945) had an impact in France much later than in Britain and Germany,[13] and even then it was considered necessary to tone down her personality and make her slightly less anarchical and strong—instead of a horse, for example, it was enough that she was able to lift a donkey.[14] This rewriting also involved the practical knowledge on emotions offered to children through the text. Discouraging an overly tight and unhealthy emotional bond to home and family was one of the important aspects of British boarding schools. Learning to overcome homesickness was thus a topic running through many of the boarding school novels, but this was not an emotion felt to be translatable into the German context without modification.[15]

In view of these manifold transformation processes, it no longer makes sense to focus attention only on the comparison between the original and the translation, but instead to look at the multiple actors playing a role in the negotiation of emotions between two or more languages. These negotiations begin even before the text in the source language is first written, thus further destabilizing the notion of the 'original' as a starting point.[16] At least for the period under consideration in this book, an author was essentially already a translator, not necessarily of texts, but certainly of culture and of emotions.[17] The next stage of negotiation consists in the carry-over from the source language to the target language. As we have seen, this may encompass a variety of different processes—from nearly word-for-word literal translation to a creative recreation of the text and its adaptation to a new audience. What is less often taken into consideration is that the translation process does not end here. Paratexts like introductions and afterwords provide a framework for reading and interpreting the book.[18] Parents and teachers help make sense of the unfamiliar, either in a running commentary while reading a book aloud to children, or in discussions before or after the children engage with the book on their own. On a different level, this process can be seen at work in much of the missionary endeavour. Unlike his teachers, the Indian bearer Boosy is not able to directly decipher God's will, either through prayer or through reading the Bible, but needs a European Christian, even if only a little boy, to translate for him.[19]

Last but not least, children themselves play an active role in translating and adapting unknown emotions and relating them to their known universe. This translation can be linguistic, but more often it will transfer the cultural meaning of feelings depicted in the books and stories from one context into another. This translation can invoke the mimetic learning processes laid out in the introduction to this volume, thus allowing children to experimentally adopt new emotions and try out how they feel. While this potentially happens in all books, it gains importance in translated books, which depict emotions, situations, and practices more unfamiliar to children than usual. Mimesis here plays into children's *Fernweh*, their longing for the unknown and far away. But this is not the only way children can react to the unfamiliar. Rejection can take the shape of a refusal to engage with a certain text at all: Russian children's stories translated into Urdu in the 1960s, for instance, were often spurned by their intended audience, in spite of their ready and cheap availability and the favour in which they were held by leftist-minded parents.[20] But rejection can also imply re-negotiating the values ascribed to emotions as they are depicted in the book by disregarding the difference in cultural contexts. Emotions considered worthy of emulation by the author and even the translator can thus be found ridiculous by children, or inversely, feelings intended as reprehensible in their original context can be read as secretly desirable by their new audience—today's girl readers of *Der Trotzkopf* (1885, Eng. *Taming a Tomboy*, 1898), for instance, might well identify with Ilse's (Fanny in the English translation) tomboy behaviour, resent her shaming, and find her transformation into a well-behaved young lady rather boring.[21] The attempt to escape boredom through the exploration of feelings in teenage love, on the other hand, in some cultures might lead not to a critique of capitalism, but to outright condemnation of what is perceived as immoral behaviour.[22]

A first answer to the questions raised above of how an emotional communication and understanding across linguistic and cultural boundaries is possible therefore needs to consider familiarization of the text, which often occurs through translation and the explanations translators, parents, and teachers provide, as well as the possibility that at times children neither want, nor succeed in entering, into unknown emotions. Still, this leaves the large field of successful mimesis to consider and explain. For this we now turn to anthropology.

ANTHROPOLOGY AND MIMETIC PRACTICES— KNOWING HOW THE OTHER FEELS

Anthropology traditionally defined itself as the discipline investigating difference. Unlike sociology, anthropology focused on those groups who were as dissimilar from European culture as possible and ideally had no previous contact with 'the West'. Within this paradigm, research aims could differ widely. In periods when the search for universal laws was at the forefront of the discipline, comparison of empirical material from remote villages and tribes substituted for the laboratory of the natural sciences.[23] In more recent periods, the aim of anthropology was seen in its contribution to 'the enlargement of the universe of human discourse'[24] that informed the beginnings of the anthropology of emotions. This interest in difference drew together studies which otherwise differed widely in their stance on universalism or relativism. Notably, the earlier studies drew on psychological knowledge to understand the emotions they encountered in the field. Cultural difference, for them, was to be found in a different expression and interpretation of emotions, which in turn led to different behaviour, whereas emotions themselves were either seen as universal or at least as having a universal core.[25] The more radically relativist position, associated in particular with the work of Catherine Lutz and Lila Abu Lughod in the 1980s,[26] insisted that the difference went deeper and extended to the way emotions were experienced: no less than expression, experience was marked by discourse and was thus profoundly cultural. This position had political implications. On the one hand, it claimed a right to difference and thus aimed at overcoming Euro-centrism,[27] on the other hand, it was perceived as a threat to universal values, which in many cases were based on the notion of emotions shared by all humans qua their humanity.[28]

If the emotions encountered in the field are different from those the anthropologist has been socialized in, if they are not only structured by different norms, but also expressed differently, if their meaning varies and if they even feel different, how is communication in the field possible? How can the anthropologist learn to read behaviour and facial expressions for their emotional content? How can he or she move in the field without giving offence, and when does the communication break down because differences can no longer be accommodated on the one or the other side?[29] How do anthropologists get to know how a particular emotion is experienced, for instance, what makes *song* feel different from anger, to use Catherine Lutz's famous example?[30] Anthropologists often use the metaphor that in the field they lose their adult status and become like children going through a basic process of socialization. If anthropologists are like children, children reading about unfamiliar emotions may, in a way, be considered anthropologists. What, therefore, can the experience of anthropologists tell us about the learning processes of children?

Since the 1920s, the most important tool for acquiring anthropological knowledge has been participant observation. This set a premium not only on personal encounters, but also replaced interviews of selected informants with observations gathered by sharing daily life. This participation, it was hoped, would enable the anthropologist to learn the language and culture of the village or society he or she was studying. This strategy was especially important for the anthropology of emotions, as this participation encompassed the possibility not only for observing emotions, but also for mimetically engaging with them—living through the same experiences, articulating the emotions required by the situation, even copying the facial expressions would permit the anthropologist to acquire an intimate knowledge not only of how emotions worked and what they meant, but also, to a certain extent, how they felt.[31] The anthropologist's own emotions have thus become a tool of research, a methodology which needs a high degree of self-reflection in order to avoid simply equating the researcher's own emotions with the emotions he or she sets out to study.[32]

Mimesis, or what the anthropologist takes for mimesis, therefore must be tested constantly. This testing process involves (at the very least) two different translation processes. The first consists of an intersemiotic translation, in which emotional expressions and practices are linked to local emotion words, that is, a translation from a non-verbal to a verbal sign system.[33] To use Benedicte Grima's example: weeping while telling of misfortunes is a sign and indication of the presence of *gham*.[34] The second, based on this, is an interlinguistic translation from emotion words in the local language into the researcher's—translating *gham* into grief, an emotion known to the anthropologist and her readers. As with every translation, here too, equivalences are not simply given or pre-existent, but are the result of a process of trial and error. Whether emotions have been read correctly, whether the mimetic endeavour of the anthropologist is successful or not, can never be said with certainty. Failure and success are gradual: a good enough translation is one which avoids a rupture in communication. Communication, it should be kept in mind, can also be successful in the creation of power structures and the transmission of orders. Even the misreading of emotions can be a form of successful communication.[35]

How then does anthropology help us understand the reading and learning experiences of children? For anthropologists, mimesis is central both in learning about new emotions and in learning to feel them. Reading provides children with the space for an imaginary experience of the unknown, which they can both observe and participate in by identifying with the characters—whether the emotions they mimic are the same as the author imputes to his protagonists or whether their mimesis is built upon a cultural misreading. In the field, anthropologists are often helped by a local informant translating meaning and providing a running commentary. For children's books, this function is built into the narrative structure, which provides an inside perspective to the thoughts and feelings of one or more of the protagonists.[36] In the same way that actors in the field may not be forthcoming with descriptions of their inner lives and feelings, leaving the anthropologist to infer their emotions through an intersemiotic translation, not all children's books thematize emotions in so many words. This leaves children to infer the relevant knowledge from the way the characters are shown to behave and from indications of their body language, either in the text or in the illustrations.[37] As this relation of non-verbal signs to specific emotions is strongly culturally coded, some misunderstanding may occur if the children are not familiarized with the code. While anthropologists usually work in a face-to-face situation that permits them to engage in a dialogue, the book remains silent. The real test of the adequateness of translation is continued communication; as long as a child reads on, the negotiation over the meaning of unknown emotions is carried on to some extent. This process only stops once the gap becomes so wide that the child closes the book and refuses to engage further with the narrative and the emotions depicted—even more than the anthropologist, the child reader is in control and cannot be contradicted or defied in his or her creation of the Other and its emotions.

ANTHROPOLOGY AND THE HISTORY OF EMOTIONS IN A GLOBAL PERSPECTIVE

The contribution of anthropologists to the nascent field of emotion studies in the 1980s and early 1990s was massive. Through micro-studies in a variety of different places, they challenged a facile assumption that emotions were 'natural' and opened the field for cultural difference. This led them to assume the role of life sciences' opposite: if life sciences stood for nature and universalism, anthropology represented nurture and relativism. Though artificial, this dichotomy was helpful for the time being.

In recent years, however, voices claiming that it is time to move on and overcome this division are becoming increasingly heard. For life sciences, this means giving up the idea that nature and the body are universal, and instead investigating the ways cultural experiences mark the body, and more specifically the brain, from birth.[38] The implications this could have for the contribution of life sciences to emotion studies as a whole have been intensively discussed.[39] The discussion on what this move might mean for anthropology has been comparatively more muted—unnecessarily so, as the developments and transformations that anthropology as a discipline went through since the middle of the 1990s and the new studies to which it gave rise also point to new ways of thinking about culture which help to overcome this dichotomy.

The increasing globalization of the 1990s led historians to rethink the role of the nation, which had been central to their discipline since nearly its modern inception, and to focus on transnational encounters instead. For anthropologists, globalization was not only an experience, but increasingly a research topic as well. If the local had been at the core of anthropology, the new emphasis was on the translocal and on the investigation of movements. As James Clifford famously phrased it, 'routes' replaced the interest in 'roots'.[40] Increasingly, anthropologists no longer limited their research to remote villages and tribes, but moved into cities and spaces of rapid change. Encounters and mobility—of which earlier anthropologists, of course, were aware—no longer were considered marginal or even disturbing, but relocated to the core of the study.[41]

This gave rise to new studies on emotions under conditions of rapid cultural transformation: the impact of economic globalization; the new media and the rising influence of the Taliban on Pashtun emotions; the emotional regimes of urban riots; the celebration of St Valentine's Day in urban India; the schooling of nationalist passions; and the way new concepts of masculinity and male emotions were mediated through popular cinema, to name only a few recent works related to South Asia.[42] Research increasingly takes place not within cultures (if the notion of 'within' still makes sense), but between them, in what Homi Bhabha called the third space.[43] This brings to the fore a concept of culture no longer centrally premised on difference. It is no longer the work of the anthropologist that creates the first intellectual connection between cultures, but cultures, their differences, as well as their similarities, are (not exclusively, but to an important degree) the result of encounters right from the beginning.

This has far-reaching implications for the way alterity is conceived, and hence for the possibility of communicating across difference. Emotions can still be viewed as culturally constructed, but if culture hinges less on difference and more on encounter, the cross-cultural legibility of emotions no longer needs a universal body outside of and before culture—in the figure of an enculturated body, anthropology and life sciences can find a common ground.

Anthropologists are not the first to bridge the gap between cultures, and they are not the sole authority who may translate between cultures. Theirs is not only a construction of a previous construction, but also a translation of a translation, competing with earlier and simultaneous translations. This, in turn, highlights the role of the informant in a new way: translation does not consist in 'finding' equivalents, but is the result of dialogue and negotiation. Dialogue and negotiation, as colonial encounters remind us, need not take place outside of power relationships and may not necessarily be peaceful. Translation—of words, of cultures, of emotions—is a performative process which constantly creates and re-creates the equivalents it needs for communication. These equivalents are neither right nor wrong at the start; their validity lies in whether they are able to do the work for which they have been devised and permit the continuation of verbal communication and communicative action.[44]

Difference arising out of encounter is no longer the absolute and unmediated opposite of sameness. Instead of a stark dichotomy, we find gradual stages of difference: *song* is not the same as anger, *gham* is not the same as grief, but neither are the word and its translation completely unrelated.[45] We need to give up the essential and essentializing difference between the 'West and the Rest' and instead investigate what Walter Mignolo and Freya Schiwy have called the 'West in the Rest' and the 'Rest in the West'.[46] Furthermore, this implies that translation between cultures and languages is not a process radically distinct from everyday translation as much as it is mediation between differences within a culture. All communication involves the transposition of meaning from one context to another, and this allows us to view 'translation…as a dimension of all social life'.[47]

For children, too, this translation is something they encounter and learn both inside and outside of books. They bring to their reading an ability to learn about and deal with unknown emotions: they have already acquired this ability in their day-to-day life. Books, in turn, not only provide them with practical knowledge on emotions they have encountered or will encounter in the future, but perhaps even more importantly, with the ability to confront the unknown, to translate alterity. For this, mimesis, the ability to imitate and to feel along with another person, is an important strategy which has to be learnt and developed. Children thus not only draw on their mimetic abilities to learn and try out emotions depicted in books, but also make use of books to further learn mimesis and translation, and hence become able to communicate emotionally across differences. People are different but, as Jim Button shows, a little boy can understand not only a princess from Mandala, but even become friends with a make-believe giant, a half dragon, and an engine.[48] This holds even more true for the mutual empathy that is shown to be possible between children and animals.[49]

Learning to read and translate emotions across cultures is only a specific and more pointed case of what children are already faced with in many other situations. Children's books, the translations they offer, and the translations they teach, may therefore be read not only as indicators, but also as factors of a global encounter, which is not restricted to moving goods and actors, but involves emotions as well. Like globalization as a whole, the globalization of emotions, too, is more complicated than the 'happy "hybridity"'[50] of the global village, but also brings forth new boundaries and new differences. As shown above, children's books not only offer, but also prevent translations, either by not engaging with foreign literature at all, or by domesticating it in a way that dilutes the encounter with alterity; they not only teach how to empathize with and translate emotions, but also how to avoid translation and engagement with the emotions of the Other. A potential legibility of emotions across cultures, based on a multitude of pre-existing translation processes, is not necessarily conducive to actual understanding. Children's books can overcome alterity, but they can also naturalize and thus reinforce it.[51] Understanding and communicating, moreover, need not be those benign activities as they have been viewed for a long time. Communication may create empathy, cutting across power relations, but it also encompasses the transmission of orders. Learning to read other people's emotions may allow for governing them more efficiently. The ability to learn quickly how to understand and cope with different emotional rules and codes across the globe may further world peace, but it may also bolster a neoliberal global economy, premised on the possibility of shifting people from one locality and culture to another.

LEARNING TO COMMUNICATE (WITH) EMOTIONS

The legibility of emotions, as the preceding sections have shown, may well depend less on the universality of the body, held to produce at least some basic emotions and their expressions, independent of culture, and more on the possibility and the ability to translate emotions from one context into another. This translation as a rule is not perfect, but can often be good enough to prevent a rupture of communication.

Translation as an answer to alterity may take place across cultures and languages, but it is also found at an everyday level—across boundaries of gender, age, class, or origin. The thesis of this monograph throughout has been that children's books are essential for children to develop these abilities of translation. They develop them through mimesis and reflection, as well as through the acquiring of practical knowledge. In a last step, we can now proceed to historicize the category of mimesis itself. Even if it may be based on an innate faculty, mimesis has to be learnt and developed under specific historical circumstances, which may value and promote it to different extents.

Does our reading of children's books and advice literature allow us to trace some of the conditions for mimesis and for successful communication of emotions? Do all emotions lend themselves equally to mimesis and translation? Are certain emotions more translatable than others? It is tempting to argue that emotions like fear, anger, or pain are experienced by children across cultures, and that they are therefore more easily able to relate to the protagonists' feelings. The chapters in this volume have shown the extent and depth of the historical transformation of these seemingly universal emotions. A child, who has learnt from literary heroes that fear can and should be overcome, will probably find it difficult to empathize with a fearful hero.[52] Even a category so closely linked to the body as the sensation of pain, as we have seen, can be felt very differently at different times and places, but also at the individual level.[53] Translation, as we have seen above, is not the finding, but rather the creation of equivalence. This holds true even for the translation of emotions through empathy and mimesis—if we take the creativity of the child reader seriously, mimesis does not reproduce given emotions, but transforms them.[54]

Mimesis, this monograph claims, is at the centre of learning emotions through children's books. The mimetical learning of emotions, however, is by no means limited to this medium. Leaving aside the mimicking of facial expressions at a very early age, what are the cultural spaces for mimesis into which the books get inscribed? Are there practices in which mimesis is regularly enacted? It would be worthwhile to explore religious traditions and teaching in this respect: is there a link to popular Passion plays, for instance in Catholic or Shia rituals, in which participants are encouraged to physically and emotionally revive crucial scenes from the religious tradition? Do religious teachings and sermons amplify the short, and at times rather matter-of-fact, narratives from the Holy Scriptures and provide an introduction about how nevertheless to engage mimetically and supplement the missing emotions? Do such practices generate an appreciation for mimesis even outside of the rituals? And closer to children's books: how do children learn to engage with stories they either listen to or read themselves? Are they encouraged to identify with a hero, to daydream, to act out scenes from books when playing with their friends? Do these different forms of mimesis change in their relative importance over time? These questions are often left aside, as they pose a problem of finding sources. On the other hand, advice books regularly contain sections of right and wrong ways of reading,[55] and sometimes books themselves go into descriptions of play-acting other books. For instance, Tom, with Huck Finn's help, liberates Jim strictly according to the rules of adventure books, although he knew the latter was not a slave any longer.[56] It could be worthwhile to follow these indications systematically. Or are parents and teachers, on the contrary, worried that children will be drawn too deeply into the world of books, or nowadays into films and computer games? What is the role of book and film merchandizing and, for instance, the ready availability of Peter Pan or Harry Potter costumes?

Following Paul Ricoeur, we have linked mimesis to the narrative structure of children's books, holding that it was longer novels and the preponderance of a personal perspective which offered the space for children to engage with the books' personae.[57] It would need more investigation of the ways texts are actually read and assimilated at different times and places to find out if this is the only option—the already mentioned Passion plays, but also the practice of reading books again and again[58] or to quote fairy tales or exempla from moral literature in everyday conversation, all show different ways of adding context to stories and embedding them in children's day-to-day life and thus creating options for mimesis which might not have been in the original text. What is the importance of mimetic engagement given the shift from a primary emphasis on books, which always require a translation, to films, which can transport iconic images and iconic patterns of behaviour in a more direct (though not unmediated) way?[59]

And finally: if mimesis is itself a culturally and socially learnt ability, what are its historical contexts and conjunctures? We have seen that different countries translate foreign children's literature to a very different extent—is there a correlation between the willingness to engage with linguistic translation and the felt need for cultural translation and mimesis? How are power differences and cultural hegemonies played out in mimesis? Is there a clear dichotomy between mimesis targeted solely at understanding the Other for whatever reasons, ranging on the one hand from anthropologists using their emotions and empathy to gain knowledge, to colonial administrators' felt need to correctly anticipate the arousal of passions in order to retain their control, and what we might call a transformative mimesis on the other hand, where empathy would be aimed at modelling the subject's emotions on those of the Other?

* * *

It is often frowned upon for books to end with questions. But *The Neverending Story* (1983, Ger. orig. *Die unendliche Geschichte,* 1979) has shown that the adult attempt to find an answer to everything and to reduce the world to a realm of cause and effect creates dark holes of nothingness. Fantastica can only be saved if the reader is willing to forgo the safe distance which separates him from the book and to become part of the story. The adventure does not end with this last page, it is only about to begin. In its course, every reader will find his own answers and questions, creating a never-ending story of ever-new Fantasticas.

NOTES

1. Ekman, 'Basic Emotions'.
2. Central for the laying out of this dichotomy is Reddy, *Navigation of Feeling*. Critically aware of the need to overcome this division, Plamper, *Geschichte und Gefühl*, shows very convincingly how this creates a need to reread some of the basic assumptions of life sciences and draws out what their new role could be. On a much smaller scale this chapter offers some ideas on how the same process might work with reference to anthropology.
3. Frevert et al., *Emotional Lexicons*.
4. See chapter 1, 'Mrs Gaskell's Anxiety'; Pernau et al., *Civilizing Emotions*.
5. See chapter 3, 'Asghari's Piety'.
6. Lathey, *Role of Translators in Children's Literature*.
7. Goldsmith, 'Found in Translation', 88.
8. For the predominance of fairy tales and folk stories see Lathey, *Role of Translators in Children's Literature*.
9. See chapter 4, 'Ralph's Compassion'.
10. See chapter 7, 'Piggy's Shame'.
11. For a strong argument in favour of foreignization, see Venuti, *Scandals of Translation*; Venuti, *Translator's Invisibility*.
12. See chapter 11, 'Heidi's Homesickness'.
13. English translation: 1945 as *Pippi Longstocking*, German: 1949 as *Pippi Langstrumpf*, French: 1951 as *Mademoiselle Brindacier* (though the first French translation true to the original did not appear until the 1990s).
14. Lathey, *Role of Translators in Children's Literature*; Blume, *Pippi Långstrumps Verwandlung zur dame-bien-élevée*.
15. See chapter 11, 'Heidi's Homesickness'.
16. This emphasis on the original being already the product of multiple encounters and cultural translation, however, is not the same as Walter Benjamin's, which is based on a notion of 'pure language', toward which both the 'original' and the 'translation' are but steps. Benjamin, 'Task of the Translator'.
17. For a book which can be perceived as a web of translations from Hindu mythology to orientalism and self-orientalization for a Western audience without any written

original, see the reading of Dhan Gopal Mukerji's *Gay-Neck* and see chapter 3, 'Asghari's Piety'.

18. Thomson-Wohlgemuth, 'Flying High'.
19. See chapter 2, 'Dickon's Trust'.
20. Oral communications, Delhi, March 2012. This attitude contrasted with the great impact translations of Russian literature for adults had at the same time. See also Panandiker, 'Soviet Literature for Children and Youth'.
21. See chapter 7, 'Piggy's Shame'.
22. See chapter 12, 'Ingrid's Boredom'.
23. For instance, in kinship studies, which aimed to show the development from matriarchal to a patriarchal society, see Maine, *Ancient Law*; Engels, *Origin of the Family*.
24. Geertz, 'Thick Description', 14.
25. Briggs, *Never in Anger*; Lindholm, *Generosity and Jealousy*; Ewing, *Arguing Sainthood*.
26. Lutz, *Unnatural Emotions*; Abu-Lughod, *Veiled Sentiments*.
27. Lutz, 40–7.
28. Reddy, 'Against Constructivism'.
29. See the famous example of Briggs, *Never in Anger*.
30. Lutz, *Unnatural Emotions*, 155–82.
31. Wikan, 'Managing the Heart to Brighten Face and Soul'.
32. Davies and Spencer, *Emotions in the Field*. I thank Monique Scheer for this reference.
33. Munday, 'Issues in Translation Studies'.
34. Grima, *The Performance of Emotions among Paxtun Women*.
35. Fuchs, 'Soziale Pragmatik des Übersetzens'.
36. See chapter 6, 'Wendy's Love'.
37. See chapter 8, 'Lebrac's Pain'.
38. See Choudhury and Slaby, *Critical Neuroscience*.
39. See notably Plamper, *Geschichte und Gefühl*, 177–294, who takes the discussion to a new level.
40. Clifford, *Routes*. Together with Appadurai, *Modernity at Large* and Hannerz, *Transnational Connections*, the latter book marked the departure of anthropology in the direction of a new concept of culture.
41. Markovits, Pouchepadass, and Subrahmanyam, *Society and Circulation*.
42. Marsden, *Living Islam*; Blom, '2006 Anti-Danish Cartoons Riot in Lahore'; Brosius, 'Love in the Age of Valentine and Pink Underwear'; Bénéï, *Schooling Passions*; Osella and Osella, *Men and Masculinities in South India*.
43. Rutherford, 'Third Space'.
44. Fuchs, 'Übersetzen und Übersetzt-Werden'; Buzelin, 'Translation Studies, Ethnography and the Production of Knowledge'.
45. Shimada, 'Zur Asymmetrie in der Übersetzung von Kulturen'.
46. Mignolo and Schiwy, 'Double Translation'.
47. Fuchs, 'Reaching Out', 21.
48. See chapter 9, 'Jim Button's Fear'.
49. See chapter 5, 'Doctor Dolittle's Empathy'.
50. Ahuja, 'Mobility and Containment', 112.
51. For the communication between the colonizer and the colonized, see chapter 2, 'Dickon's Trust'; chapter 4, 'Ralph's Compassion'.
52. See chapter 9, 'Jim Button's Fear'.
53. See chapter 8, 'Lebrac's Pain'.

54. See chapter 5, 'Doctor Dolittle's Empathy'.
55. Bilston, 'It is Not What We Read'.
56. Twain, *Adventures of Huckleberry Finn*, 301–62.
57. See introduction to this volume; chapter 6, 'Wendy's Love'.
58. See chapter 10, 'Ivan's Bravery'.
59. See chapter 6, 'Wendy's Love'.

References

PRIMARY LITERATURE

Ackermann, Eduard, *Die häusliche Erziehung* (Langensalza: Beyer, 1888).

Adams, Richard, *Watership Down* (London: Rex Collings, 1972).

Ahmad, Shamsululuma Maulvi Nazir, *The Bride's Mirror: A Tale of Life in Delhi a Hundred Years Ago*, trans. G. E. Ward (London: Frowde, 1903) [Urd. orig., *Mirat ul arus* (1869)] <http://archive.org/details/bridesmirror030546mbp> accessed 27 May 2013.

Aldrich, Charles Anderson, and Mary M. Aldrich, *Babies are Human Beings: An Interpretation of Growth* (New York: Macmillan, 1938).

Allfrey, Katherine, *Golden Island*, trans. Edelgard von Heydekampf Bruehl (Garden City, N.Y.: Doubleday, 1966) [Ger. orig., *Delphinensommer* (1963)].

Amendt, Günter, *Sexfront* (Frankfurt am Main: März, 1970).

Anon., *Biography of a Spaniel* (London: Minerva, 1803).

Anon., *Boys and their Ways: A Book for and about Boys: By One Who Knows Them* (London: Hogg, 1880).

Anon., *Encyklopädie der Pädagogik vom gegenwärtigen Standpunkte der Wissenschaft und nach den Erfahrungen der gefeiertsten Pädagogen aller Zeit bearbeitet von einem Vereine praktischer Lehrer und Erzieher*, i (Leipzig: Schäfer, 1860).

Anon., *Fünf Finger sind eine Faust* (Berlin: Basis, 1969).

Anon., *Girls and Their Ways: A Book For and About Girls. By One Who Knows Them* (London: Hogg, 1881).

Anon., 'Kirschenmütterchen', in Gumpert, Thekla von, ed., *Herzblättchens Zeitvertreib: Unterhaltungen für kleine Knaben und Mädchen zur Herzensbildung und Entwickelung der Begriffe*, xxix (Glogau: Flemming, 1884), 26–9.

Anon., 'Letters to a Younger Brother: No. XIII', *Sunday School Journal & Advocate of Christian Education*, 4/22 (1834), 88.

Anon., *Martin, der Mars-Mensch* (Berlin: Basis, [1970]).

Anon., 'Pädagogische Schläge sind Schläge des Liebhabers (1887)', in Katharina Rutschky, ed., *Schwarze Pädagogik: Quellen zur Naturgeschichte der bürgerlichen Erziehung* (Frankfurt am Main: Ullstein, 1977), 433–7.

Anon., Review of P. V. Zasodimskii, *Dedushkiny rasskazy i skazki*, in S. V. Kurnin, *Chto chitat' detiam? Sbornik retsenzii iz zhurnalov, preimushchestvenno pedagogicheskikh: Posobie pri izuchenii detskoi literatury* (Moscow: Solntsev, 1900), 19.

Anon., Review of *Sto rasskazov iz zhizni zhivotnykh*, in S. V. Kurnin, *Chto chitat' detiam? Sbornik retsenzii iz zhurnalov, preimushchestvenno pedagogicheskikh: Posobie pri izuchenii detskoi literatury* (Moscow: Solntsev, 1900), 53.

Anon., 'A Scene from Real Life: The Book Club', *Mother's Assistant and Young Lady's Friend*, 5/4 (1844), 73–82.

Anon., *Struwwelliese* (n.p., n.d. [c.1890]), <http://www.digibib.tu-bs.de/?docid=00000576> accessed 24 May 2013.

Anon., 'Theater Rote Grütze', *Das Blatt*, 57 (1975), 19.

Anon., 'Tierschutz', in *Brockhaus' Conversations-Lexikon: Allgemeine deutsche Real-Encyklopädie*, xv (13th rev. edn, Leipzig: Brockhaus, 1886), 693.

Anon., 'Was heißt hier Liebe?', *Das Blatt*, 132 (1978), 31.

Arthur, Robert, *The Secret of Terror Castle* (New York: Random House, 1964).

Arthur, Robert, and others, *Alfred Hitchcock and The Three Investigators*, American Series, 55 vols (New York: Random House, 1964–90).

Atkinson, Eleanor, *Greyfriars Bobby* (New York: Harper, 1912).

Auslender, Sergei, *Dni boevye* (2nd edn, Moscow: Guosudarstvennoe izdatel'stvo, 1926).

Ayodhya Prasad, *Guldastah-e tahzib* (Bareilly: Matba-e Society, 1969).

Baden-Powell, Agnes, *The Handbook for Girl Guides, or, How Girls Can Help to Build Up the Empire* (London: Nelson, 1912).

Baden-Powell, Robert, *Rovering to Success: A Book of Life-Sports for Young Men* (London: Jenkins, 1922).

Baden-Powell, Robert, *Scouting for Boys: A Handbook for Instruction in Good Citizenship* (London: Cox, 1908).

Bahnmaier, Jonathan Friedrich, 'Ein Wort für junge Töchter', *Cäcilia: Ein wöchentliches Familienblatt für Christensinn und Christenfreuden*, 1 (1817), 130–4.

Baker, Stephen, *How to Live with a Neurotic Dog* (Englewood Cliffs, N. J.: Prentice-Hall, 1960).

Ballantyne, R. M., *The Coral Island: A Tale of the Pacific Ocean* (1858; Edinburgh: Chambers, 1870).

Ballantyne, R. M., *Im Banne der Koralleninsel*, trans. Eugen von Beulwitz (Berlin: Deutsche Buch Gemeinschaft, n.d. [c.1965]) [Eng. orig., *The Coral Island: A Tale of the Pacific Ocean* (1858)].

Barrie, J. M., *The Little White Bird* (London: Hodder & Stoughton, 1902).

Barrie, J. M., *Peter and Wendy* (New York: Scribner, 1911).

Barrie, J. M., *Peter Pan*, trans. Ursula von Wiese (Düsseldorf: Hoch, 1964) [Eng. orig., *Peter and Wendy* (1911)].

Barrie, J. M., *Peter Pan in Kensington Gardens: From the Little White Bird* (London: Hodder & Stoughton, 1906).

Barrie, J. M., *Peter Pan oder Das Märchen vom Jungen der nicht gross werden wollte*, trans. Erich Kästner (Berlin: Bloch, n.d. [c.1950]) [Eng. orig., *Peter Pan, or, the Boy Who Wouldn't Grow Up* (1904)].

Barrie, J. M., *Peter Pan, or, the Boy Who Wouldn't Grow Up* (1904; London: Hodder & Stoughton, 1928).

Basu, Girindrasekhar (= Bose, Girindrasekhar), 'Śiśur man', *Prabasi*, 29 (1336 [1929]), 798–808.

Baum, L. Frank, *The Wonderful Wizard of Oz* (Chicago: Hill, 1900).

Becker, Liane, *Die Erziehungskunst der Mutter: Ein Leitfaden der Erziehungslehre* (München-Gladbach: Volksverein, 1908).

Beecher-Stowe, Harriet, *Uncle Tom's Cabin; or, Life Among the Lowly*, 2 vols (Boston: John P. Jewett, 1852).

Bell, Mary Hayley, *Whistle Down the Wind: A Modern Fable* (London: Boardman, 1958; London: Hodder Children's, 1997).

Blackwell, Elizabeth, *Counsel to Parents on the Moral Education of their Children, in Relation to Sex* (2nd rev. edn, London: Hatchards, 1879).

Blume, Judy, *Are You There, God? It's Me, Margaret* (New York: Dell, 1970; London: Macmillan, 2010).

Blume, Judy, *Blubber* (New York: Bradbury, 1974).

Blyton, Enid, *The Famous Five* series, 21 vols (London: Hodder & Stoughton, 1942–62).

Blyton, Enid, *First Term at Malory Towers* (London: Methuen, 1946).

Blyton, Enid, *Five on a Treasure Island* (1942; 6th edn, London: Hodder & Stoughton, 1949).

Blyton, Enid, *Hanni und Nanni gründen einen Klub* (Munich: Schneider, 1971).

Blyton, Enid, *Hanni und Nanni in tausend Nöten* (Munich: Schneider, 1974).

Blyton, Enid, *Malory Towers* series, 6 vols (London: Methuen, 1946–51).

Blyton, Enid, *The Six Bad Boys* (London: Lutterworth, 1951).

Blyton, Enid, *St. Clare's* series, 6 vols (London: Methuen, 1941–45).

Blyton, Enid, *The Twins at St. Clare's: A School Story For Girls* (1941; London: Methuen, 1953).

Boie, Kirsten, *Juli und das Monster* (Weinheim: Beltz & Gelberg, 1995).

Bonsels, Waldemar, *The Adventures of Maya the Bee*, trans. Adele Szold Seltzer and Arthur Guiterman (New York: Seltzer, 1922) [Ger. orig., *Die Biene Maja und ihre Abenteuer* (1912)].

Borchardt, Julian, *Wie sollen wir unsere Kinder ohne Prügel erziehen?* (Berlin: Buchhandlung Vorwärts, 1905).

Bose, Girindrasekhar (= Basu, Girindrasekhar), *Everyday Psychoanalysis* (Calcutta: Mis Susil Gupta, 1945).

Bovet, Theodor, *Von Mann zu Mann: Eine Einführung ins Reifealter für junge Männer* (Bern: Haupt, 1943; Tübingen: Katzmann, 1950).

Bowlby, John, 'The Influence of Early Environment in the Development of Neurosis and Neurotic Character', *International Journal of Psycho-Analysis*, 21 (1940), 154–78.

Bowlby, John, 'Maternal Care and Mental Health', in World Health Organization, ed., *Bulletin of the World Health Organization*, iii-3 (Geneva: WHO, 1951), 355–533.

Bowlby, John, *Child Care and the Growth of Love* (London: Penguin, 1953).

Bozhenko, Konstantin, *Prikliuchenie malen'kogo trubacha* (Moscow: Mirimanov, 1927).

Braun, Joachim, *Schwul und dann? Ein Coming-out-Ratgeber* (Berlin: Querverlag, 2006).

Brehm, Alfred Edmund, *The Animals of the World: Brehm's Life of Animals; A Complete Natural History for Popular Home Instruction and for the Use of Schools: Mammalia*, trans. from the 3rd German edition (Chicago: Marquis, 1895) [Ger. orig., *Brehms Tierleben: Allgemeine Kunde des Tierreichs*, 10 vols, Eduard Pechuel-Loesche, ed. (3rd rev. edn, 1890–3)].

Brehm, Alfred Edmund, *From North Pole to Equator: Studies of Wild Life and Scenes in Many Lands*, ed. J. Arthur Thomson, trans. Margaret R. Thomson (London: Blackie, 1896).

Brehm, Alfred Edmund, *Illustrirtes Thierleben: Eine allgemeine Kunde des Thierreichs*, 6 vols (Hildburghausen: Bibliographisches Institut, 1864–69).

Brink, Carol Ryrie, *Caddie Woodlawn* (New York: Macmillan, 1935).

Brock, Peter, *Bine und die Parkoma* (Berlin: Kinderbuchverlag, 1978).

Brock, Peter, *Ich bin die Nele* (Berlin: Kinderbuchverlag, 1975).

Brontë, Charlotte, *Jane Eyre: An Autobiography* (London: Smith, Elder, and Company, 1847).

Brown, Marc, *Arthur Goes To Camp* (Boston: Little, Brown, 1982).

Brückner, Heinrich, and Ingrid Blauschmidt, *Denkst Du schon an Liebe? Fragen des Reifealters—dargestellt für junge Leser* (Berlin: Kinderbuchverlag, 1976).

Bruckner, Karl, *The Day of the Bomb*, trans. Frances Lobb (London: Burke, 1962) [Ger. orig., *Sadako will leben* (1961)].

Bundesen, Hermann N., *Toward Manhood* (Philadelphia: Lippincott, 1951).

Burnett, Frances Hodgson, *Little Lord Fauntleroy* (New York: Scribner, 1886).

Burnett, Frances Hodgson, *The Secret Garden* (New York: Stokes, 1911).

Busch, Wilhelm, *Max and Maurice: A Juvenile History in Seven Tricks*, trans. Charles T. Brooks (New York: Roberts, 1871) [Ger. orig., *Max und Moritz: Eine Bubengeschichte in sieben Streichen* (1865)].

Campe, Joachim Heinrich, *Ueber Empfindsamkeit und Empfindelei in pädagogischer Hinsicht* (Hamburg: Herold, 1779).

Campe, Joachim Heinrich, *Robinson the Younger*, 2 vols (Hamburg: Bohn, 1781/2) [Ger. orig., *Robinson der Jüngere, zur angenehmen und nützlichen Unterhaltung für Kinder*, 2 vols (1779/80)].

Carroll, Lewis, *Alice's Adventures in Wonderland* (1865; London: Macmillan, 1866).

Caspari, Tina, *Bille und Zottel* series, 21 vols (Munich: Schneider, 1976–2003).

Chamberlain, V. C., *Adolescence to Maturity: A Practical Guide to Personal Development, Fulfilment, and Maturity* (London: Lane, 1952; Harmondsworth: Penguin, 1959).

Chapple, J. A. V., and Anita Wilson, eds., *Private Voices: The Diaries of Elizabeth Gaskell and Sophia Holland* (Keele: KUP, 1996).

Chaturbhuja Sahaya, *Maandan-e akhlaq*, 2 vols (Gujranwala: Matba-e Gyan, 1879).

Chomton, Werner, *Weltbrand von Morgen: Ein Zukunftsbild* (Stuttgart: Thienemann, 1934).

Clark, Ann Nolan, *Secret of the Andes* (New York: Viking, 1952).

Coerr, Eleanor, *Sadako and the Thousand Paper Cranes* (New York: Putnam, 1977).

Collodi, Carlo, *The Story of a Puppet, or, The Adventures of Pinocchio*, trans. M. A. Murray (London: Fisher Unwin, 1892) [Ita. orig., *Le avventure di Pinocchio* (1883)].

Combe, Andrew, *Principles of Physiology Applied to Health and Education: And the Improvement of Physical and Mental Education* (Edinburgh: Black, 1834).

Comfort, Alex, and Jane Comfort, *The Facts of Love: Living, Loving, and Growing Up* (New York: Ballantine, 1979).

Cooper, James Fenimore, *The Deerslayer, or, The First War-Path: A Tale* (Philadelphia: Lea and Blanchard, 1841).

Cooper, James Fenimore, *Leatherstocking Tales*, 5 vols (New York: Wiley/Philadelphia: Lea & Blanchard / Carey & Lea, 1823–41).

Darwin, Charles, 'A Biographical Sketch of an Infant', *Mind*, 2/7 (1877), 285–94.

Darwin, Charles, *The Voyage of the Beagle*, 3 vols, The Harvard Classics 29 (1838–9 as *Voyages of the Adventure and Beagle*; New York: Collier, 1937).

Datta, Arup Kumar, *The Kaziranga Trail* (New Delhi: Children's Book Trust, 1979).

Defoe, Daniel, *Robinson Crusoe* (London: Taylor, 1719 as *The Life and Strange Surprizing Adventures of Robinson Crusoe, of York, Mariner: Who Lived Eight and Twenty Years, All Alone in an Un-Inhabited Island on the Coast of America, Near the Mouth of the Great River Oroonoque; Having Been Cast on Shore by Shipwreck, Wherein All the Men Perished but Himself. With an Account How He Was at Last As Strangely Deliver'd by Pyrates*).

Derwent, Lavinia, *The Story of Peter Pan, retold by Lavinia Derwent, from the original story by J.M. Barrie* (Glasgow: Collins, 1957).

Dickens, Charles, *Bleak House*, 4 vols (Leipzig: Tauchnitz, 1852–3).

Dickens, Charles, *Oliver Twist, or, the Parish Boy's Progress* (London: Bentley, 1838).

Dielitz, Theodor, 'Alpen-Wanderung', in *Lebensbilder: Der Jugend vorgeführt* (Berlin: Winckelmann, n.d. [c.1840]), 64–86.

Diessel, Hildegard, *Resi hat Heimweh* (Göttingen: Fischer, 1971).

Dixon, Franklin W., *The Tower Treasure* (New York: Grosset & Dunlap, 1927).

Donnelly, Elfie, *So long, Grandpa*, trans. Anthea Bell (London: Anderson, 1980) [Ger. orig., *Servus Opa, sagte ich leise* (1977)].

Donovan, John, *I'll Get There: It Better Be Worth the Trip* (New York: Evanstone, 1969).

Dorokhov, P., *Syn bol'shevika* (Moscow: Gosudarstvennoe izdatel'stvo, 1928).

Druon, Maurice, *Tistou of the Green Fingers*, trans. Humphrey Hare (London: Hart-Davis, 1958) [Fre. orig., *Tistou les pouces verts* (1957)].

Dumont, Léon, *Théorie scientifique de la sensibilité: Le plaisir et la peine* (Paris: Baillière, 1875).

Durian, Wolf, *Kai aus der Kiste: Eine ganz unglaubliche Geschichte* (Leipzig: Schneider, 1926).

Dyer, E. P., 'Virtue', *Mother's Assistant and Young Lady's Friend*, 1 (1853), 191.

Edgeworth, Maria, 'Angelina, or, L'Amie Inconnue', in *Moral Tales for Young People*, ii (1801; 2nd edn, London: Johnson, 1806), 147–255.

Edgeworth, Maria, 'The Bracelets', in *The Parent's Assistant, or, Stories for Children*, iii (3rd edn, London: Johnson, 1800), 3–75.

Edgeworth, Maria, 'Frank', in *Early Lessons: In Four Volumes*, iii (4th edn, London: Hunter, 1821), 1–168.

Edgeworth, Maria, 'The Manufacturers', in *Popular Tales*, ii (London: Johnson, 1804), 283–367.

Edgeworth, Maria, 'Rosamond', in *Early Lessons: In Four Volumes*, ii (9th edn, London: Hunter, 1824), 1–167.

Edgeworth, Maria, 'Rosanna', in *Popular Tales*, ii (London: Johnson, 1804), 81–196.

Edgeworth, Maria, and Robert Lovell Edgeworth, *Practical Education* (London: Johnson, 1798).

Ende, Michael, *The Grey Gentlemen*, trans. Frances Lobb (London: Burke, 1974) [Ger. orig., *Momo: oder, Die seltsame Geschichte von den Zeit-Dieben und von dem Kind, das den Menschen die gestohlene Zeit zurückbrachte* (1973)].

Ende, Michael, *Jim Button and Luke the Engine Driver*, trans. Renata Symonds (London: Harrap, 1963) [Ger. orig., *Jim Knopf und Lukas der Lokomotivführer* (1960)].

Ende, Michael, *Jim Knopf und die Wilde 13* (Stuttgart: Thienemann, 1962).

Ende, Michael, *The Neverending Story*, trans. Ralph Manheim (London: Penguin, 1983) [Ger. orig., *Die unendliche Geschichte* (1979)].

Faber, Kurt, *Rund um die Erde: Irrfahrten und Abenteuer eines Greenhorns* (Ludwigshafen: Lhotzky, 1924).

Farley, Walter, *The Black Stallion* series, 31 vols (New York: Random House, 1941–).

Farman, John, *Keep Out of the Reach of Parents: A Teenager's Guide to Bringing Them Up* (London: Piccadilly, 1992).

Farningham, Marianne, *Girlhood* (London: Clarke, 1869).

Farrar, Frederic W., *Eric, or, Little by Little* (2nd edn, Edinburgh: Black, 1858).

Faßbinder, Nikolaus, *Am Wege des Kindes: Ein Buch für unsere Mütter* (Freiburg im Breisgau: Herdersche Verlagshandlung, 1916).

Fehrmann, Helma, and Peter Weismann, *Und plötzlich willste mehr: Die Geschichte von Paul und Paulas erster Liebe* (Munich: Weismann, 1979).

Fehrmann, Helma, Jürgen Flügge, and Holger Franke, *Was heisst hier Liebe? Ein Spiel um Liebe und Sexualität für Leute in und nach der Pubertät* (Munich: Weismann, 1977).

Finding Neverland, Marc Forster, dir. (Miramax, 2004) [film].

Fischer, Jochen, *Nicht Sex sondern Liebe: Eine Orientierungshilfe für junge Menschen* (Hamburg: Furche, 1966).

Flerov, A. E., *Ukazatel' knig dlia detskogo chteniia: V vozraste 7–14 let* (Moscow: Tikhomirov, 1905).

Foerster, Friedrich Wilhelm, *Jugendlehre: Ein Buch für Eltern, Lehrer und Geistliche* (51–55 Thousand edn, Berlin: Reimer, 1911).

Foerster, Friedrich Wilhelm, *Lebensführung* (Berlin: Reimer, 1909; 123–32 Thousand edn, Erlenbach-Zürich: Rotapfel, 1924).

Foerster, Friedrich Wilhelm, *Lebenskunde: Ein Buch für Knaben und Mädchen* (Berlin: Reimer, 1904).

Frenssen, Gustav, *Peter Moors Fahrt nach Südwest: Ein Feldzugsbericht* (New York: Holt, 1914).

Frenssen, Gustav, *Peter Moor's Journey to Southwest Africa: A Narrative of the German Campaign*, trans. Margaret May Ward (Boston: Houghton & Mifflin, 1908) [Ger. orig., *Peter Moors Fahrt nach Südwest: Ein Feldzugsbericht* (1906)].

Freud, Anna, *Introduction to the Technique of Child Analysis*, trans. L. Pierce Clark (New York: Nervous and Mental Disease Publishing, 1928) [Ger. orig., *Einführung in die Technik der Kinderanalyse: Vier Vorträge am Lehrinstitut der Wiener Psychoanalytischen Vereinigung* (1927)].

Freud, Sigmund, '"A Child is Being Beaten": A Contribution to the Study of the Origin of Sexual Perversions', in James Strachey, ed., *The Standard Edition of the Complete Psychological Works of Sigmund Freud, xvii, (1917–19): An Infantile Neurosis And Other Works*, trans. James Strachey (London: Hogarth, 1955), 179–204.

Freud, Sigmund, 'Analysis of a Phobia in a Five-Year-Old Boy', in James Strachey, ed., *The Standard Edition of the Complete Psychological Works of Sigmund Freud, x, (1909): Two Case Histories ('Little Hans' and the 'Rat Man')*, trans. James Strachey (London: Hogarth, 1975), 3–152.

Freud, Sigmund, *Three Essays on the Theory of Sexuality*, trans. James Strachey (London: Imago, 1949) [Ger. orig., *Drei Abhandlungen zur Sexualtheorie* (1905)].

Furman, Petr Romanovich, *Aleksandr Vasil'evich Suvorov* (Moscow: Stupin, 1914).

Gaidar, Arkady, *Chetvertyi blindazh* (Moscow: Izdatel'stvo detskoi literatury, 1936).

Gaidar, Arkady, *R. V.S.* (Moscow: n.p., 1926).

Gaidar, Arkady, *School*, trans. Bernard Isaacs (Moscow: Progress, 1967) [Rus. orig., *Shkola* (1930)].

Gaidar, Yegor, *Days of Defeat and Victory*, trans. Jane Ann Miller (Seattle: University of Washington Press, 1999) [Rus. orig., *Dni porazhenii i pobed* (1996)].

Garshin, Vsewolod, 'Four Days', in Stephen Graham, ed., *Great Russian Short Stories* (London: Benn, 1929; New York: Liveright, 1959), 476–89 [Rus. orig., *Chetyre dnia* (1877)].

Geifrig, Werner, *Bravo, Girl! Ein Stück für Lehrlinge, junge Arbeiter, Schulabgänger und ihre Eltern*, Reihe Materialien—Theater (Munich: Weismann, 1975).

Geißler, Maximilian, and Andrea Przyklenk, *Ich mach mir nichts aus Mädchen: Wenn Jungs schwul sind: Ein Ratgeber* (Munich: Kösel, 1998).

Gesell, Arnold, *Infancy and Human Growth* (New York: Macmillan, 1928).

Gesell, Arnold, *The Mental Growth of the Pre-School Child: A Psychological Outline of Normal Development from Birth to the Sixth Year, including a System of Developmental Diagnosis* (New York: Macmillan, 1925).

Gesell, Arnold, and Frances L. Ilg, *Infant and Child in the Culture of Today: The Guidance of Development in Home and Nursery School* (New York: Harper, 1943).

Gockel, Ottilie, 'Warum?', in Thekla von Gumpert, ed., *Herzblättchens Zeitvertreib: Unterhaltungen für kleine Knaben und Mädchen zur Herzensbildung und Entwickelung der Begriffe*, xxxvi (Glogau: Flemming, 1891), 34–8.

Godon, Ingrid, and André Sollie, *Hello, Sailor* (London: Macmillan, 2002) [Dut. orig., *Wachten op Matroos* (2000)].

Golding, William, *Lord of the Flies* (London: Faber & Faber, 1954).

Goscinny, René, *Young Nicolas*, trans. Stella Rodway (London: Hutchinson, 1961) [Fre. orig., *Le petit Nicolas* (1960)].

Grahame, Kenneth, *The Wind in the Willows* (New York: Scribner, 1908).

Gromov, A., *Za 'obchee delo' (Pet'ka Zhigan): Povest' dlia detei iz vremen bor'by sibirskikh partizans s Kolchakom* (Moscow: Mirimanov, 1926).

Grossmann, Thomas, *Schwul—na und?* (Reinbek bei Hamburg: Rowohlt, 1981).

Gumpert, Thekla von, *Die Herzblättchen: Erzählungen aus dem Familienleben und der Natur für kleine Kinder* (Glogau: Flemming, 1855–6×1857).

Haan, Linda de, *King & King* (Berkeley: Tricycle, 2002) [Dut. orig., *Koning en Koning* (2000)].

Haarer, Johanna, *Die deutsche Mutter und ihr erstes Kind* (1934; 500–32 Thousand edn, Munich: Lehmann, 1943).

Haarer, Johanna, *Unsere kleinen Kinder* (Munich: Lehmanns, 1936).

Hall, G. Stanley, *Adolescence: Its Psychology and Its Relations to Physiology, Anthropology, Sociology, Sex, Crime, Religion and Education*, 2 vols (New York: Appleton, 1904).

Hall, G. Stanley, *The Contents of Children's Minds on Entering School* (New York: Kellogg, 1893).

Hall, G. Stanley, 'A Study of Fears', *American Journal of Psychology*, 8/2 (1897), 147–249.

Hall, G. Stanley, *Youth: Its Education, Regimen and Hygiene* (New York: Appleton, 1906).

Hanswille, Reinert, *Liebe und Sexualität: Ein Buch für junge Menschen* (Munich: Kösel, 1986).

Härtling, Peter, *Ben Loves Anna*, trans. J. H. Auerbach (Woodstock, N.Y.: Overlook Press, 1990) [Ger. orig., *Ben liebt Anna* (1979)].

Härtling, Peter, *Crutches*, trans. Elizabeth D. Crawford (New York: Lothrop, Lee & Shepard, 1988) [Ger. orig., *Krücke* (1986)].

Härtling, Peter, *Theo Runs Away*, trans. Anthea Bell (London: Anderson, 1978) [Ger. orig., *Theo haut ab* (1977)].

Härtter, Richard, *Warum lieben sich Mann und Frau und woher kommen die Kinder? Eine Unterweisung für Jungen und Mädchen von 9 bis 11 Jahren* (Recklinghausen: Bitter, 1967).

Hassebrauk, Marianne, *Heimweh nach dem Rosenhof* (Munich: Schneider, 1962).

Hassencamp, Oliver, *Burg Schreckenstein* series, 27 vols (Munich: Schneider, 1959–88).

Haugen, Tormod, *The Night Birds*, trans. Sheila La Farge (London: Collins, 1985) [Nor. orig., *Nattfuglene* (1975)].

Heitefuß, Clara, *Mutter und Kind* (2nd edn, Barmen: Biermann, 1913).

Held, Kurt, *The Outsiders of Uskoken Castle*, trans. Lynn Aubrey (Garden City, N.Y.: Doubleday, 1967) [Ger. orig., *Die Rote Zora und ihre Bande* (1941)].

Hément, Félix, *Petit traité des punitions et des récompenses: À l'usage des maîtres et des parents* (Paris: Carré, 1890).

Hempe, Hans, *Pitzelchen hat kein Heimweh* (Göttingen: Fischer, 1969).

Henning, Frieda, *Fata Morganas alte und neue Heimat: Eine Kindergeschichte* (Bielefeld: Verlagshandlung der Anstalt Bethel, 1922).

Hesse, Hermann, *The Prodigy*, trans. W. J. Strachan (London: Owen & Vision, 1947) [Ger. orig., *Unterm Rad* (1906)].

Hetzer, Hildegard, *Seelische Hygiene! Lebenstüchtige Kinder! Richtlinien für die Erziehung im Kleinkindalter* (1930; 5th rev. edn, Lindau (Bodensee): Kleine Kinder, 1940).

Hilliard, Marion, *Problems of Adolescence: A Woman Doctor's Advice on Growing Up* (London: Macmillan, 1960).

Hitlerjunge Quex: Ein Film vom Opfergeist der deutschen Jugend, Hans Steinhoff, dir. (UFA, 1933, banned) [film].

Hoban, Russell, *Bedtime for Frances* (New York: Harper, 1960).

Hodann, Max, *Bub und Mädel: Gespräche unter Kameraden über die Geschlechterfrage* (1924; 5th edn, Rudolstadt: Greifenverlag, 1926).

Hodann, Max, *Woher die Kinder kommen: Ein Lehrbuch für Kinder lesbar* (Rudolstadt: Greifenverlag, 1926) repr. as *Bringt uns wirklich der Klapperstorch? Ein Lehrbüchlein für Kinder lesbar* (Berlin: Universitas, 1928).

Hofer, Johannes, *Dissertatio medica de nostalgia, oder Heimwehe* (Basel: Bertsche, 1688).

Hoffer, Eric, 'Long Live Shame!', *New York Times* (18 October 1974), 41.

Hoffmann, E. T. A., *The Life And Opinions of the Tomcat Murr Together with a Fragmentary Biography of Kappelmeister Johannes Kreisler on Random Sheets of Waste Paper*, trans. Anthea Bell (London: Penguin, 1999) [Ger. orig., *Lebens-Ansichten des Katers Murr nebst fragmentarischer Biographie des Kapellmeisters, Johannes Kreisler in zufälligen Makulaturblättern*, 2 vols (1819/21)].

Hoffmann, Heinrich, *Der Struwwelpeter oder lustige Geschichten und drollige Bilder* (Frankfurt am Main: Literarische Anstalt, [1858]).

Hoffmann, Heinrich, *Slovenly Peter (Struwwelpeter), or, Happy Tales and Funny Pictures Freely Translated by Mark Twain* (New York: Harper, 1935) [Ger. orig., *Struwwelpeter bzw. Lustige Geschichten und drollige Bilder mit 15 schön kolorierten Tafeln für Kinder von 3–6 Jahren* (1845)].

Holman, Felice, *Slake's Limbo* (New York: Scribner, 1974).

Hook, Steven Spielberg, dir. (Amblin Entertainment, 1991) [film].

Horney, Karen, 'On the Genesis of the Castration Complex in Women', *International Journal of Psycho-Analysis*, 5 (1924), 50–65.

Hornschuh, Heike, *Ich bin 13: Eine Schülerin erzählt: Aufgeschrieben von Simone Bergmann* (1974; 135–7 Thousand edn, Reinbek bei Hamburg: Rowohlt, 1993).

[Hughes, Thomas], *Notes for Boys (and Their Fathers) on Morals, Mind and Manners: By an Old Boy* (London: Stock, [1885]).

Hughes, Thomas, *Tom Brown's School Days: By an Old Boy* (Cambridge: Macmillan, 1857).

Hughes, Thomas, *True Manliness: From the Writings of Thomas Hughes* (Boston: Lothrop, 1880).

Huntingford, Edward, *Advice to School-Boys: Sermons on Their Duties, Trials, and Temptations* (London: Bickers, 1877).

Husain, Zakir, 'Abbu Khan ki bakri', in *Abbu Khan ki Bakri aur Chauda aur Kahaniyan* (1963; Delhi: Maktaba Jamia, 2009), 9–21.

Husain, Zakir, 'Akhri Qadam', in *Abbu Khan ki Bakri aur Chauda aur Kahaniyan* (Delhi: Maktaba Jamia, 2009), 64–70.

Husain, Zakir, *The Bravest Goat in the World*, trans. Samina Mishra, and Sanjay Muttoo (Delhi: Young Zubaan, Pratham, 2004) [Urd. orig., *Abbu Khan ki bakri* (2009)].

Husain, Zakir, 'The Final Step', in Saiyyida Hameed Saiyadain, ed., *Zakir Husain: Teacher Who Became President* (New Delhi: Indian Council for Cultural Relations, 2000), 136–8.

Isaacs, Susan, *The Nursery Years: The Mind of the Child from Birth to Six Years* (London: Routledge, 1929; repr. edn, London: Routledge & Paul, 1949).

Jahangir, Maqbul, *Amir Hamza ke karnameh*, 10 vols (Lahore: Ferozons, n.d. [c.1960s]).

Jahnke, Anneliese, *Neue Heimat: Ein Erstleseheft* (Berlin: Volk & Wissen, 1949).

Jalal ud Din, Muhammad, 'Tilismi dawa, Part 1', *Payam-e Ta'lim*, 22/9 (1939), 392–6.

Jalal ud Din, Muhammad, 'Tilismi dawa, Part 2', *Payam-e Ta'lim*, 22/10 (1939), 446–52.

James, Henry, *The Awkward Age* (London: Heinemann, 1899).

Janosch, *The Trip to Panama*, trans. Anthea Bell (London: Anderson, 1978) [Ger. orig., *Oh, wie schön ist Panama* (1978)].

Karim ud Din, *Pand-e sudmand* (Lahore: Matba-e Khurshid, 1866).

Kästner, Erich, *The 35th of May, or, Conrad's Ride to the South Seas*, trans. Cyrus Brooks (London: Cape, 1933) [Ger. orig., *Der 35. Mai oder Konrad reitet in die Südsee* (1933)].

Kästner, Erich, *The Animals' Conference*, trans. Zita de Schauensee (New York: McKay, 1949) [Ger. orig., *Die Konferenz der Tiere* (1949)].

Kästner, Erich, *Annaluise and Anton*, trans. Eric Sutton (London: Cape, 1932) [Ger. orig., *Pünktchen und Anton* (1930)].

Kästner, Erich, *Emil and the Detectives*, trans. May Massee (New York: Scholastic, 1930) [Ger. orig., *Emil und die Detektive* (1929)].

Kästner, Erich, *The Flying Classroom*, trans. Cyrus Brooks (London: Cape, 1934; Harmondsworth: Penguin, 1967) [Ger. orig., *Das fliegende Klassenzimmer* (1933)].

Kästner, Erich, *Lisa and Lottie*, trans. Cyrus Brooks (London: Cape, 1950 as *Lottie and Lisa*; New York: Knopf, 1969) [Ger. orig., *Das doppelte Lottchen: Ein Roman für Kinder* (1949)].

Kay, Carolin, 'How Should We Raise Our Son Benjamin? Advice Literature for Mothers in Early Twentieth-Century Germany', in Dirk Schumann, ed., *Raising Citizens in the 'Century of the Child': The United States and German Central Europe in Comparative Perspective* (New York: Berghahn Books, 2010), 105–21.

Kentler, Helmut, *Sexualerziehung* (Reinbek bei Hamburg: Rowohlt, 1970).

Kerr, Judith, *When Hitler Stole Pink Rabbit* (London: Collins, 1971).

Key, Ellen, *The Century of the Child*, trans. Marie Franzos (New York: Putnam, 1909) [Swe. orig., *Barnets århundrade* (1900)].

Kienast, Anton, *Gespräche über Thiere, oder Edmund und Emma, das mitleidige Geschwister-Paar* (Munich: Self-published, 1855).

Kinder und Jugendtheater Rote Grütze, *Darüber spricht man nicht!! Ein Spiel zur Sexualerziehung*, Reihe Materialien—Theater (1973; Munich: Weismann, 1976).

Kingsley, Charles, *Health and Education* (London: Isbister, 1874).

Kipling, Rudyard, *The Jungle Book* (London: Macmillan, 1894).

Kipling, Rudyard, *Kim* (New York: Doubleday, 1901).

Kipling, Rudyard, *Stalky & Co.* (London: Macmillan, 1899).

Klein, Carl, *Wie soll ich mich benehmen? Ein Buch über den guten Ton in der Familie, Gesellschaft und Öffentlichkeit* (Leipzig: Paul, n.d. [c.1899]).

Klein, Melanie, *The Psycho-Analysis of Children*, trans. Alix Strachey (London: Hogarth, 1932) [Ger. orig., *Die Psychoanalyse des Kindes* (1932)].

Klencke, H., *Die Mutter als Erzieherin ihrer Töchter und Söhne zur physischen und sittlichen Gesundheit vom ersten Kindesalter bis zur Reife: Ein praktisches Buch für deutsche Frauen* (Leipzig: Kummer, 1870).

Kloss, Erich, *In der wilden Klamm* (Leipzig: Schneider, 1934).

Knauth, P., *Lose Blätter und Blüten: Erzählungen, Gedichte, Fabeln, Schilderungen, Lehrbeschreibungen und dergleichen aus dem Leben der Tiere im Interesse des Tierschutz-Vereins* (Wiesbaden: Staudinger, 1883).

Knigge, Adolph, and P. Will, *Practical Philosophy of Life, or, The Art of Conversing With Men After the German Baron of Knigge*, 2 vols (1794; Lansingburgh: Penniman & Bliss, 1805) [Ger. orig., *Über den Umgang mit Menschen* (1788)].

Koch, Klaus, and Jörg Koch, *Bloss nicht wie 'die Alten'! Neue Wege zum Erwachsenweden* (Frankfurt am Main: Ullstein, 1991).

Kooistra, J., *Sittliche Erziehung*, trans. Eduard Müller (Leipzig: Wunderlich, 1899) [Dut. orig., *Zedelijke Opvoeding* (1894)].

Korschunow, Irina, *Adam Draws Himself a Dragon*, trans. James Skofield (New York: Harper & Row, 1986) [Ger. orig., *Hanno malt sich einen Drachen* (1978)].

Kozik, Christa, *Moritz in der Litfaßsäule* (Berlin: Kinderbuchverlag, 1980).

Kozyrev, N. G., *Soldatskie skazki* (Petrograd: n.p., 1915).

Kruse, Max, *Urmel aus dem Eis* (Reutlingen: Ensslin & Laiblin, 1969).

Kübler, M. S., *Das Buch der Mütter: Eine Anleitung zu naturgemäßer leiblicher und geistiger Erziehung der Kinder und zur allgemeinen Krankenpflege* (Zürich: Ernst, 1867).

Kunstmann, Antje, *Mädchen: Sexualaufklärung emanzipatorisch* (Starnberg: Raith, 1972).

Kurnin, S. V., *Chto chitat' detiam? Sbornik retsenzii iz zhurnalov, preimushchestvenno peda-gogicheskikh: Posobie pri izuchenii detskoi literatury* (Moscow: Solntsev, 1900).

Kutsche, Emil, Wilhelm König, and Robert Urbanek, *Frauen-Bildungsbuch: Ein Wegweiser, Ratgeber und Gesellschafter für die reifere weibliche Jugend* (1921; 5th rev. edn, Wittenberg: Herrose, 1926).

Ladiges, Ann, *Mann, du bist gemein!* (Reinbek bei Hamburg: Rowohlt, 1974).

Lagerlöf, Selma, *The Wonderful Adventures of Nils*, trans. Velma Swanston Howard (London: Penguin, 1907) [Swe. orig., *Nils Holgerssons underbara resa genom Sverige* (1906/1907)].

Lakhnavi, Ghalib, and Abdullah Bilgrami, *The Adventures of Amir Hamza: Lord of the Auspicious Planetary Conjunction*, trans. Musharraf Ali Farooqi (New York: Modern Library, 2008).

Lane, Homer Tyrrell, *Talks to Parents and Teachers* (London: Allen & Unwin, 1928).

L'Engle, Madeleine, *A Wrinkle in Time* (New York: Farrar, Straus & Giroux, 1962).

Lenski, Lois, *Strawberry Girl* (Philadelphia: Lippincott, 1945).

Lepper, Th., *Liebes und Leides für heranwachsende Mädchen* (Bochum: Verlag des Jungfrauenvereins, 1913; 23–7 Thousand edn, Bochum: Verbandsverlag weiblicher Vereine, n.d. [c.1914]).

Lewis, C. S., *The Chronicles of Narnia*, 7 vols (London: Bles / Bodley Head, 1950–6).

Lewis, C. S., *The Lion, the Witch and the Wardrobe* (London: Bles, 1950).

Lewis, C. S., *Prince Caspian: The Return to Narnia* (London: Bles, 1951).

Lhotzky, Heinrich, *The Soul of Your Child*, trans. Anna Barwell (London: Allen & Unwin, 1924) [Ger. orig., *Die Seele Deines Kindes: Ein Buch für Eltern* (1908)].

Lindenbaum, Pija, *Mini Mia and her Darling Uncle,* trans. Elisabeth Kallick Dyssegaard (Stockholm: R & S Books, 2007) [Swe. orig., *Lill-Zlatan och morbror raring* (2006)].

Lindgren, Astrid, *The Brothers Lionheart*, trans. Joan Tate (London: Hodder & Stoughton, 1975) [Swe. orig., *Bröderna Lejonhjärta* (1973)].

Lindgren, Astrid, *Confidences of Britt-Mari Hagström*, trans. Hanno Fischer (Cambridge: ExMundiLibris, 2005) [Swe. orig., *Britt-Mari lättar sitt hjärta* (1944)].

Lindgren, Astrid, *Emil in the Soup Tureen*, trans. Lilian Seaton (Chicago: Follett, 1970) [Swe. orig., *Emil i Lönneberga* (1963)].

Lindgren, Astrid, *Mio, My Son*, trans. Marianne Turner (New York: Viking, 1956) [Swe. orig., *Mio, min Mio* (1954)].

Lindgren, Astrid, *Pippi in the South Seas*, trans. Gerry Bothmer (London: Oxford UP, 1957; New York: Viking, 1981) [Swe. orig., *Pippi Långstrump i Söderhavet* (1948)].

Lindgren, Astrid, *Pippi Longstocking*, trans. Edna Hurup (London: OUP, 1945) [Swe. orig., *Pippi Långstrump* (1945)].

Lindgren, Astrid, *Ronia, the Robber's Daughter*, trans. Patricia Crompton (Harmondsworth: Puffin, 1983) [Swe. orig., *Ronja Rövardotter* (1981)].

Lindner, Gustav Ad., *Encyklopädisches Handbuch der Erziehungskunde mit besonderer Berücksichtigung des Volksschulwesens* (Vienna: Pichler, 1884).

Lindstroem, Kirstin, *Zauber der ersten Liebe: Ein Ratgeber für die heranwachsende Jugend* (Munich: Juncker, 1970).

Lofting, Hugh, *The Story of Doctor Dolittle: Being the History of His Peculiar Life at Home and Astonishing Adventures in Foreign Parts* (1920; 11th edn, New York: Stokes, 1923).

Loisel, Régis, *Peter Pan: Book Two Neverland*, trans. Mary Irwin (Northhampton, MA: Tundra, 1993) [Fre. orig., *Opikanoba* (1992)].

London, Jack, *The Call of the Wild* (New York: Macmillan, 1903).

London, Jack, *White Fang* (London: Macmillan, 1906).

The Lost Boys, Rodney Bennett, dir. (BBC, 1978) [docudrama mini-series].

Ludwig, Volker, and Uwe Friesel, *Die Geschichte von Trummi kaputt* (Reinbek bei Hamburg: Rowohlt, 1973).

Macaulay, Thomas, 'Indian Education: Minute of the 2nd of February, 1835', in G. M. Young, ed., *Macaulay: Prose and Poetry* (Cambridge: Harvard UP, 1967), 719–30.

Mai, Manfred, *Leonie ist verknallt* (Ravensburg: Ravensburger, 1997).

Mantegazza, Paolo, *L'Atlante delle espressioni del dolore: Fotografie prese dal vero e da molte altre opere d'arte* (Florence: Brogi, 1876).

Marcke, Leen van, *Nimm mich mit, Kapitän*, trans. Ilse van Heyst (Stuttgart: Boje, 1970) [Dut. orig., *O, die Pino* (1961)].

Marcus, Maria, *Das Himmelbett: Geschichten über Liebe, Lust und Sexualität*, trans. Lothar Schneider (Reinbek bei Hamburg: Rowohlt, 1982) [Dan. orig., *Himmelsengen: Noveller om sex for unge* (1979)].

Marcus, Maria, *Ein starkes Frühjahr*, trans. Jürgen Lassig (Reinbek bei Hamburg: Rowohlt, 1981) [Dan. orig., *Alle tiders forår* (1977)].

Marryat, Captain [Frederick], *Masterman Ready, or, the Wreck of the Pacific: Written for Young People*, 3 vols (London: Longman, Orme, Brown, Green & Longmans, 1841–2).

Matthias, Adolf, *Wie erziehen wir unsern Sohn Benjamin? Ein Buch für deutsche Väter und Mütter* (1897; 10th enl. edn, Munich: Beck, 1916).

May, Karl, *Winnetou I*, trans. Marlies Bugman (Copping, Tas.: Bugman, 2008) [Ger. orig., *Winnetou: Der Rote Gentleman I* (1893)].

May, Karl, *Winnetou III*, trans. Marlies Bugman (Copping, Tas.: Bugman, 2008) [Ger. orig., *Winnetou: Der Rote Gentleman III* (1893)].

McPhail, David, *Pig Goes To Camp* (New York: Dutton, 1983).

Meade, L. T., *A World of Girls: The Story of a School* (London: Cassell, 1886; Chicago: Donohue, n.d. [c.1900]).

Mebs, Gudrun, *Birgit: Eine Geschichte vom Sterben* (Berlin: Basis, 1982).

Melena, Elpis, *Gemma oder Tugend und Laster* (Munich: Franz, 1877).

Meyer, Emanuele, *Vom Mädchen zur Frau* (Stuttgart: Strecker & Schröder, 1912).

Michaelis, Karin, *Bibi: A Little Danish Girl*, trans. Lida Siboni Hanson (New York: Doubleday, 1927) [Dan. orig., *Bibi: En lille piges liv* (1929)].

Michaelis, Karin, *Bibi* series, 7 vols (Copenhagen: Jespersen, 1929–39).

Michaelis, Karin, *Bibi und die Verschworenen* (Berlin: Stuffer, 1932) [Dan. orig., *Bibi og de Sammensvorne* (1932)].

Miller, Albert G., *Fury: Stallion of Broken Wheel Ranch* (1959; New York: Grosset & Dunlap, 1971).

Miller, Albert G., *Fury* series, 5 vols (New York: Grosset & Dunlap, 1959–69).

Milne, Alan Alexander, *Winnie-the-Pooh* (London: Methuen, 1926).

Ministry of Education: Government of India, *Report of the Committee on Emotional Integration* (New Delhi: n.p., 1962).

Molter, Haja, and Thomas Billerbeck, *Verstehst du mich, versteh' ich dich: Von der richtigen Verständigung zum gegenseitigen Verstehen* (Würzburg: Arena, 1978).

Monroe, Paul, ed., *A Cyclopedia of Education*, v (New York: Macmillan, 1913).

Montgomery, L. M., *Anne of Green Gables* (Boston: Page, 1908).

Moulin Rouge, Baz Luhrmann, dir. (20th Century Fox, 2001) [film].

Mubarak Ullah, Muhammad, *Tanbih at talibin* (Agra: Educational Press, 1873).

Mühlen, Herminia zur, *Ali, der Teppichweber: Fünf Märchen* (Berlin: Malik, 1923).

Mühlen, Herminia zur, *Was Peterchens Freunde erzählen: Märchen* (Berlin: Malik, 1921).

Mukerji, Dhan Gopal, *Gay-Neck: The Story of a Pigeon* (New York: Dutton, 1927; 5th edn, New Delhi: National Book Trust, 2011).

Müller, Gerd-Gustl, *Der Job* (Munich: Weismann, 1977).

Müller, Gregor, 'Heimweh', in Heinrich Rombach, ed., *Lexikon der Pädagogik, ii: Fest Feier—Klug* (Freiburg im Breisgau: Herder, 1953), 657–8.

Munni Lal, *Shamin-e akhlaq* (Delhi: Matba-e Sayyid Mir Hasan Rizwi, 1877).

Munske, Hilde, ed., *Das bunte Jungmädelbuch* (1940; 11–39 Thousand edn, Berlin: Junge Generation, n.d. [c.1940]).

Murdoch, John, *The Indian Student's Manual: Hints on Studies, Moral Conduct, Religious Duties, and Success in Life* (Madras: Christian Vernacular Education Society, 1875).

Musil, Robert, *Young Törless*, trans. Eithne Wilkins and Ernst Kaiser (London: Secker & Warburg, 1955) [Ger. orig., *Die Verwirrungen des Zöglings Törleß* (1906)].

Necker de Saussure, Albertine-Adrienne, *L'Éducation progressive, ou Étude du cours de la vie*, i (Paris: Sautelet/Paulin, 1828).

Necker de Saussure, Albertine-Adrienne, *Progressive Education, Commencing with the Infant*, trans. Emma Willard and Lincoln Phelps (Boston: Ticknor, 1835) [Fre. orig., *L'Éducation progressive, ou Étude du cours de la vie*, i (1828)].

Nehru, Jawaharlal, 'Grow into the Heart of India' [2.10.1953], in S. Gopal, ed., *Selected Works of Jawaharlal Nehru: Second Series*, xxiv (Bombay: Oxford UP, 1999), 3–12.

Nehru, Jawaharlal, 'Making India Strong' [9.10.1952], in S. Gopal, ed., *Selected Works of Jawaharlal Nehru: Second Series*, xix (New Delhi: Jawaharlal Nehru Memorial Fund, 1996), 51–68.

Nehru, Jawaharlal, 'The Meaning of Culture' [3.9.1949], in S. Gopal, ed., *Selected Works of Jawaharlal Nehru: Second Series*, xiii (New Delhi: Jawaharlal Nehru Memorial Fund, 1992), 273–4.

Nehru, Jawaharlal, 'Unity and Harmony' [24.9.1949], in S. Gopal, ed., *Selected Works of Jawaharlal Nehru: Second Series*, xiii (New Delhi: Jawaharlal Nehru Memorial Fund, 1992), 276–80.

Neill, A. S., *The Last Man Alive: A Story for Children from the Age of Seven to Seventy* (London: Jenkins, 1938; repr. London: Gollancz, 1970).

Neill, A. S., *The Problem Child* (London: Jenkins, 1926).

Neill, A. S., *Summerhill: A Radical Approach to Child Rearing* (New York: Hart Publishing, 1960).

Nesbit, E., *The Railway Children* (London: Wells Gardner, Darton, 1906).

Nesbit, E., *The Story of the Treasure Seekers: Being the Adventures of the Bastable Children in Search of a Fortune* (London: Fisher Unwin, 1899).

Newcomb, Harvey, 'For Maternal Associations', *Mother's Assistant and Young Lady's Friend*, 2/3 (1842), 50–1.

Newcomb, Harvey, *How to be a Lady: A Book for Girls, Containing Useful Hints on the Formation of Character* (5th edn, Boston: Gould, Kendall, and Lincoln, 1848).

Newcomb, Harvey, *How to be a Man: A Book for Boys, Containing Useful Hints on the Formation of Character* (Boston: Gould, Kendall, and Lincoln, 1847).

Newcomb, Harvey, 'Rewards and Punishments', *Mother's Assistant and Young Lady's Friend*, 3/2 (1843), 29–32.

Newman, Lesléa, *Heather Has Two Mommies* (Boston: Alyson Wonderland, 1989).

Nordstrom, Ursula, *The Secret Language* (New York: Harper, 1960).

Nöstlinger, Christine, *Conrad*, trans. Anthea Bell (London: Andersen, 1976) [Ger. orig., *Konrad oder Das Kind aus der Konservenbüchse* (1975)].

Nöstlinger, Christine, *The Cucumber King: A Story with a Beginning, a Middle and an End, in which Wolfgang Hogelmann Tells the Whole Truth*, trans. Anthea Bell (London: Abelard-Schuman, 1975) [Ger. orig., *Wir pfeifen auf den Gurkenkönig* (1972)].

Nöstlinger, Christine, *Gretchen hat Hänschen-Kummer: Eine Familiengeschichte* (Hamburg: Oetinger, 1983).

Nöstlinger, Christine, *Gretchen, mein Mädchen* (Hamburg: Oetinger, 1988).

Nöstlinger, Christine, *Gretchen Sackmeier: Eine Familiengeschichte* (Hamburg: Oetinger, 1981).

Nur Ahmad Nur, *Anwar ul akhlaq* (Lahore: Matba Islamiya, 1893).

O'Connor, Daniel, *The Story of Peter Pan: Retold from the Fairy Play by Sir J. M. Barrie* (London: Bell, 1914).

Oppel, Karl, *Thiergeschichten: Erzählungen und Schilderungen aus dem Leben der Tiere* (Wiesbaden: Niedner, 1873).

Oppodeldok, Peter, 'Theater: Darüber spricht man nicht', *Das Blatt*, 67 (1976), 18.

Pausewang, Gudrun, *Auf einem langen Weg: Was die Adamek-Kinder erlebten, als der Krieg zu Ende ging* (Ravensburg: Maier, 1978).

Pausewang, Gudrun, *Etwas lässt sich doch bewirken: Ein Roman aus der Friedensbewegung* (Ravensburg: Maier, 1984).

Pausewang, Gudrun, *The Last Children*, trans. Norman M. Watt (London: McRae Books, 1989) [Ger. orig., *Die letzten Kinder von Schewenborn* (1983)].

Perez, Bernard, *The First Three Years of Childhood*, trans. Alice M. Christie (London: Swan Sonnenschein, 1885) [Fre. orig., *Les Trois premières années de l'enfant* (1878)].

Perez, Bernard, *L'Enfant de trois a sept ans* (Paris: Alcan, 1886).

Pergaud, Louis, *The War of the Buttons*, trans. Stanley Hochman and Eleanor Hochman (New York: Walker, 1968) [Fre. orig., *La guerre des boutons: Roman de ma douzième année* (1912)].

Perty, Maximilian, *Ueber das Seelenleben der Thiere: Thatsachen und Betrachtungen* (Leipzig: Winter, 1865).

Peter Pan, Herbert Brenon, dir. (Paramount, 1924) [silent film].

Peter Pan, P. J. Hogan, dir. (Universal Pictures, 2003) [film].

Petri, Horst, and Matthias Lauterbach, *Gewalt in der Erziehung: Plädoyer zur Abschaffung der Prügelstrafe: Analysen und Argumente* (Frankfurt am Main: Athenä um-Fischer-Taschenbuch-Verlag, 1975).

Petzel, Minna, 'Wie Hänschen das Lesen lernt', in Thekla von Gumpert, ed., *Herzblättchens Zeitvertreib: Unterhaltungen für kleine Knaben und Mädchen zur Herzensbildung und Entwickelung der Begriffe*, xxix (Glogau: Flemming, 1884), 91–5.

Pludra, Benno, *Insel der Schwäne* (Berlin: Kinderbuchverlag, 1980).

Pogoskii, A., *Aleksandr Vasil'evich Suvorov, Generalissimus russkikh voisk: Ego zhizn' i pobedy* (Saint Petersburg: n.p., 1875).

Post, Emily, *Children are People, and Ideal Parents are Comrades* (New York: Funk & Wagnalls, 1940).

Potter, Beatrix, *The Tale of Peter Rabbit* (London: Warne, 1902).

Powledge, Fred, *You'll Survive! Late Blooming, Early Blooming, Loneliness, Klutziness, and Other Problems of Adolescence, and How to Live Through Them* (New York: Scribner, 1986).

Preußler, Otfried, *The Little Witch*, trans. Anthea Bell (London: Abelard-Schuman, 1961) [Ger. orig., *Die kleine Hexe* (1957)].

Preußler, Otfried, *The Satanic Mill*, trans. Anthea Bell (London: Abelard-Schuman, 1972) [Ger. orig., *Krabat* (1971)].

Preyer, W., *The Mind of the Child: Observations Concerning the Mental Development of the Human Being in the First Years of Life*, 2 vols, trans. H. W. Brown (New York: Appleton, 1888–9) [Ger. orig., *Die Seele des Kindes: Beobachtungen über die geistige Entwicklung des Menschen in den ersten Lebensjahren* (1882)].

Ramakrishnan, Prema, *The Three Friends* (New Delhi: Children's Book Trust, 1969).

Ransome, Arthur, *Swallowdale* (Edinburgh: Gray, 1931).

Ravera, Lidia, and Marco Lombardo-Radice, *Pigs Have Wings*, trans. Jane Sebastian (New York: Pomerica, 1977) [Ita. orig., *Porci con le ali: Diario sussuo-politico di due adolescenti* (1976)].

Reed, Talbot Baines, *The Fifth Form at St. Dominic's* (1887; London: Religious Tract Society, 1890).

Reichsjugendführung, ed., *Pimpf im Dienst: Ein Handbuch für das Deutsche Jungvolk in der HJ* (1934; Potsdam: Voggenreiter, n.d. [c.1934]).

Return to Never Land, Robin Budd, and Donovan Cook, dirs. (Disney, 2002) [animation film].

Reuter, D., ed., *Pädagogisches Real-Lexicon oder Repertorium für Erziehungs- und Unterrichtskunde und ihre Literatur: Ein tägliches Hülfsbuch für Eltern und Erzieher* (Nuremberg: Campe, 1811).

Rhoden, Emmy von, *Der Trotzkopf: Eine Pensionsgeschichte für erwachsene Mädchen* (1885; 2nd edn, Stuttgart: Weise, 1886).

Rhoden, Emmy von, *Taming a Tomboy*, trans. Felix L. Oswald (1898; Chicago: Donohue, n.d. [c.1898]) [Ger. orig., *Der Trotzkopf: Eine Pensionsgeschichte für erwachsene Mädchen* (1885)].

Richardson, Justin, and Peter Parnell, *And Tango Makes Three* (New York: Simon & Schuster, 2005).

Robinson, Barbara, *The Best Christmas Pageant Ever* (New York: Harper & Row, 1972).

Rochefort, Christiane, *Encore heureux qu'on va vers l'été* (Paris: Galimard, 1975).

Rodrian, Irene, *Blöd, wenn der Typ draufgeht* (Reinbek bei Hamburg: Rowohlt, 1976).

Rodrian, Irene, *Viel Glück, mein Kind* (Munich: Weismann, 1975).

Rommel, Alberta, *Der goldene Schleier* (Stuttgart: Gundert, 1955).

Röttgen, Herbert, 'Kinderrevolution', *Das Blatt*, 92 (1977), 14–16.

Rousseau, Jean-Jacques, *Emile, or, On Education* (*Includes Emile and Sophie, or, The Solitaries*), ed. Christopher Kelly and Allan Bloom, trans. Allan Bloom (Hanover, N.H.: University Press of New England, 2010) [Fre. orig., *Émile, ou de l'éducation* (1762)].

Rousseau, Jean-Jacques, *Émile, ou de l'éducation* (Paris: Duchesne, 1762).

Rowling, J. K., *Harry Potter* series, 7 vols (London: Bloomsbury, 1997–2007).

Sachs, Marilyn, *Laura's Luck* (Garden City, N.Y.: Doubleday, 1965).

Saint-Exupéry, Antoine de, *The Little Prince*, trans. Katherine Woods (New York: Reynal & Hitchcock, 1943) [Fre. orig., *Le petite prince* (1943)].

Salten, Felix, *Bambi, a Life in the Woods*, trans. Whittaker Chambers (London: Cape, 1928) [Ger. orig., *Bambi: Eine Lebensgeschichte aus dem Walde* (1923)].

Sapper, Agnes, 'Bei der Patin', in *Das kleine Dummerle und andere Erzählungen: Zum Vorlesen im Familienkreise* (1904; Stuttgart: Gundert, 1915), 228–93.

Saunders, Marshall, *Beautiful Joe: An Autobiography* (Philadelphia: Banes, 1893).

Sautier, N., 'Ein Unglückstag', in Gumpert, Thekla von, ed., *Herzblättchens Zeitvertreib: Unterhaltungen für kleine Knaben und Mädchen zur Herzensbildung und Entwickelung der Begriffe*, xxix (Glogau: Flemming, 1884), 58–60.

Schenzinger, Karl Aloys, *Der Hitlerjunge Quex* (1932; 166–70 Thousand edn, Berlin: Zeitgeschichte, 1934).

Schick, Eleanor, *Katie Goes to Camp* (New York: Macmillan, 1968).

Schmid, Bastian, *Zur Psychologie unserer Haustiere* (Frankfurt am Main: Societäts-Verlag, 1939).

Schnell, Heinrich, *Ich und meine Jungens: Zufällige Gespräche über allerhand Erziehungsfragen von heute für die Eltern unserer Gymnasiasten* (Leipzig: Dieterich, 1914).

Schönstedt, Walter, *Kämpfende Jugend: Roman der arbeitenden Jugend*, Rote Eine-Mark-Roman 8 (Berlin: Internationaler Arbeiterverlag, 1932).

Schreiber, Adele, ed., *Das Buch vom Kinde: Ein Sammelwerk für die wichtigsten Fragen der Kindheit*, 2 vols (Leipzig: Teubner, 1907).

Schreiber, Adele, 'Kindesmißhandlung', in Adele Schreiber, ed., *Das Buch vom Kinde: ein Sammelwerk für die wichtigsten Fragen der Kindheit, ii: Öffentliches Erziehungs- und Fürsorgewesen, Das Kind in der Gesellschaft und Recht, Berufe und Berufswahl* (Leipzig: Teubner, 1907), 70–78.

Schreiber, Adele, 'Die soziale Erziehung des Kindes', in Adele Schreiber, ed., *Das Buch vom Kinde: ein Sammelwerk für die wichtigsten Fragen der Kindheit, i: Einleitung, Körper und Seele des Kindes, Häusliche und allgemeine Erziehung* (Leipzig: Teubner, 1907), 223–31.

Schwahn, Ottilie, 'Die kleinen Freundinnen', in Thekla von Gumpert, ed., *Herzblättchens Zeitvertreib: Unterhaltungen für kleine Knaben und Mädchen zur Herzensbildung und Entwickelung der Begriffe*, xxix (Glogau: Flemming, 1884), 73–7.

Scott, Gabriel, *Kari: A Story of Kari Supper from Lindeland*, Norway, trans. Anvor Barstad (Chicago: Hale, 1931) [Nor. orig., *Kari Kveldsmat* (1913)].

Seelmann, Kurt, *Wie soll ich mein Kind aufklären?* (Stuttgart: Klett, 1956).

Seelmann, Kurt, *Woher kommen die kleinen Buben und Mädchen? Ein Buch zum Vor- und Selberlesen für 8 bis 14jährige Mädchen und Buben* (Munich: Reinhardt, 1959).

Seelmann, Kurt, *Zwischen 15 und 19: Information über sexuelle und andere Fragen des Erwachsenwerdens* (Munich: Reinhardt, 1971).

Sewell, Anna, *Black Beauty: His Grooms and Companions: The Auobiography of a Horse* (London: Jarrold and Sons, 1877).

Shah Jahan, *Tahzib un Niswan wa Tarbiyat ul Insan* (Lahore: Numani Kutubkhana, 1881; repr. 1970).

Shankar Das, *Guldastah-e akhlaq* (Lahore: Islamiya, 1893).

Shcheglov, Ivan [Ivan L. Leont'ev], 'Pervoe srazhenie' (1881; Saint Petersburg: Tip. M. M. Stasiulevicha, 1887).

Sherwood, Mary Martha, *The Story of Little Henry and His Bearer Boosey. A Tale of Dinapore* (copyright edn, London: Houlston & Wright, 1866).

Shivkumar, K., *Krishna and Sudama* (1967; 20th edn, Delhi: Children's Book Trust, 2010).

Shkola muzhestva, Vladimir Basov and Mstislav Korchagin, dirs. (Mosfilm, 1954) [film].

Shmidt, O. I., *Galia* (Moscow: Sytina, 1886).

Siegert, Gustav, 'Heimweh', in W. Rein, *Encyklopädisches Handbuch der Pädagogik, iv: Handelsschulen—Klassenoberster* (2nd edn, Langensalza: Beyer & Mann, 1906), 185–6.

Siems, Martin, *Coming Out: Hilfen zur homosexuellen Emanzipation* (Reinbek bei Hamburg: Rowohlt, 1980).

Slaughter, John Willis, *The Adolescent* (London: Allen & Unwin, 1911).

Sorensen, Virginia, *Miracles on Maple Hill* (New York: Harcourt, Brace, 1956).

Spence, Robert, and Philip Spence, *Struwwelhitler: A Nazi Story Book By Doktor Schrecklichkeit* (London: Haycock Press, [c.1941]).

Sperry, Armstrong, *Call it Courage* (New York: Macmillan, 1940).

Spock, Benjamin, *The Common Sense Book of Baby and Child Care* (New York: Duell, Sloan and Pearce, 1946).

Spyri, Johanna, *Gritli's Children*, trans. Louise Brooks (New York: Grosset & Dunlap, n.d. [c.1920s]) [Ger. orig., *Wo Gritlis Kinder hingekommen sind & Gritlis Kinder kommen weiter* (1883/4)].

Spyri, Johanna, *Heidi*, trans. Elisabeth P. Stork (Philadelphia: Lippincott, 1915) [Ger. orig., *Heidi's Lehr- und Wanderjahre & Heidi kann brauchen, was es gelernt hat* (1880/1881)].

Spyri, Johanna, *Renz and Margritli, What happened in Waldhausen, Meieli*, trans. Helen B. Dole (New York: Grosset & Dunlap, 1931) [Ger. orig., *Daheim und wieder draußen* (1880)].

Stall, Sylvanus, *What a Young Boy Ought to Know* (Philadelphia: Vir, 1897).

Stall, Sylvanus, *What a Young Man Ought to Know* (Philadelphia: Vir, 1897).

Steinhöfel, Andreas, *The Center of the World*, trans. Alisa Jaffa (New York: Delacorte, 2005) [Ger. orig., *Die Mitte der Welt* (1998)].

Stengel, Hansgeorg, and Karl Scharder, *So ein Struwwelpeter: Lustige Geschichten und drollige Bilder für Kinder von 3 bis 6 Jahren* (Berlin: Kinderbuchverlag, 1970).

Steuben, Fritz, *Der Sohn des Manitu: Eine Erzählung vom Kampfe Tecumsehs: Alten Quellen nacherzählt* (1938; 7th edn, Stuttgart: Franckh, [1939]).

Steuben, Fritz, *Tecumseh* series, 7 vols (Stuttgart: Franckh, 1930–9).

Stevenson, Robert Louis, *Treasure Island* (London: Cassell, 1883).

Storr, Catherine, *Growing Up: A Practical Guide to Adolescence for Parents and Children* (London: Arrow, 1975).

Streatfeild, Noel, *Ballet Shoes* (New York: Random House, 1937).

Streatfeild, Noel, *The Circus Is Coming* (1938; rev. repr. edn, London: Dent, 1957).

Strittmatter, Erwin, *Tinko* (Berlin: Aufbau, 1954).

Subercaseaux, Benjamín, *Jemmy Button*, trans. Mary Del Villar, and Fred Del Villar (New York: Macmillan, 1954) [Spa. orig., *Jemmy Button* (1950)].

Sultan Jahan, *Tarbiyat ul atfal* (Bhopal: Matba Dar ul Iqbal, 1914).

Sultana, Khurshid, 'Nanha Tatu', *Payam-e Talim*, 22/7 (1939), 298–301.

Tesarek, Anton, and Wilhelm Börner, *Der Kinder-Knigge* (Wien: Saturn, 1938; 21–30 Thousand edn, Hamburg: Oetinger, n.d. [c.1948]).

Tetzner, Lisa, *Erlebnisse und Abenteuer der Kinder aus Nr. 67. Die Odyssee einer Jugend [Kinderodyssee]* series, 9 vols (1932–49) (Aarau: Sauerländer, 1944–9).

Tetzner, Lisa, *Die Kinder aus Nr. 67: Band 3 und 4* (Aarau: Sauerländer, 1944 as Erwin kommt nach Schweden; Munich: DTV, 1992).

Tiutchev, Fedor, 'Tovarishch', *Rodnik* (1888).

Tolkien, J. R. R., *The Hobbit, or, There and Back Again* (London: Allen & Unwin, 1937; Boston: Houghton & Mifflin, 1997).

Tolkien, J. R. R., *The Lord of the Rings: Part I: The Fellowship of the Ring* (London: Allen & Unwin, 1954).

Tolkien, J. R. R., *The Lord of the Rings* series, 3 vols (London: Allen & Unwin, 1954–5).

Trimmer, Sarah, *Fabulous Histories: Designed for the Instruction of Children Respecting their Treatment of Animals* (Dublin: Longman, 1791).

Trott, Magda, *Goldköpfchen: Erzählung für junge Mädchen* (Leipzig: Leipziger Graphische Werke, 1928).

Trott, Magda, *Pucki als junge Hausfrau* (Leipzig: Anton, 1937 as *Puckis junge Ehe*; Stuttgart: Titania, 1951).

Trott, Magda, *Pucki* series, 12 vols (Leipzig: Anton, 1935–41).

Trott, Magda, *Pucki und ihre Freunde* (Leipzig: Anton, 1936).

Twain, Mark, *The Adventures of Huckleberry Finn* (London: Chatto & Windus, 1884).

Twain, Mark, *The Adventures of Tom Sawyer* (Hartford: American, 1876).

Twain, Mark, *A Dog's Tale* (New York: Harper, 1904).

Ury, Else, *Nesthäkchen im Kinderheim: Eine Erzählung für Mädchen von 8–12 Jahren* (Berlin: Meidinger, 1915).

Ury, Else, *Nesthäkchen* series, 10 vols (Berlin: Meidinger, 1913–25).

Vallès, Jules, *The Child*, trans. Douglas Parmée (Newark: University of Delaware Press, 2003) [Fre. orig., *L'Enfant* (Paris: Charpentier, (1879)].

Varley, Susan, *Badger's Parting Gifts* (London: Anderson, 1984).

Verne, Jules, *Adrift in the Pacific* (London: Low, Marston, n.d.[c.1889]) [Fre. orig., *Deux ans de vacances* (1888)].

Verne, Jules, *Around the World in Eighty Days*, trans. George M. Towle (Boston: Osgood, 1873) [Fre. orig., *Le Tour du monde en quatre-vingts jours* (1873)].

Waechter, Friedrich Karl, *Der Anti-Struwwelpeter* (Frankfurt am Main: Melzer, 1970).

Watson, John B., *Behaviorism* (New York: Norton, 1924).

Watson, John B., 'Experimental Studies on the Growth of the Emotions', *Pedagogical Seminary and Journal of Genetic Psychology*, 32/2 (1925), 328–48.

Watson, John B., 'A Schematic Outline of the Emotions', *Psychological Review*, 26/3 (1919), 165–96.

Watson, John B., and Rosalie Rayner (= Rosalie Watson), 'Conditioned Emotional Reactions', *Journal of Experimental Psychology*, 3/1 (1920), 1–14.

Watson, John B., and Rosalie Watson (= Rosalie Rayner), *Psychological Care of the Infant and Child* (London: Allen & Unwin, 1928).

Weber, Clara, 'Marie und die beiden Sperlinge', in Thekla von Gumpert, ed., *Herzblättchens Zeitvertreib: Unterhaltungen für kleine Knaben und Mädchen zur Herzensbildung und Entwickelung der Begriffe*, xxix (Glogau: Flemming, 1884), 9–13.

Wedding, Alex, *Eddie and the Gypsy: A Story for Boys and Girls*, trans. Charles Ashleigh (New York: International Publishing, 1935) [Ger. orig., *Ede und Unku: Ein Roman für Jungen und Mädchen* (1931)].

Weidenmann, Alfred, *Jungzug 2: 50 Jungen im Dienst* (Stuttgart: Loewes, 1936).

Wellm, Alfred, *Kaule* (Berlin: Kinderbuchverlag, 1962).

Westecker, Grete, *Grita wächst heran* (Cologne: Schaffstein, 1939).

Wetherell, Elizabeth, *The Wide, Wide World* (1850; author's edn, Leipzig: Tauchnitz, 1854).

White, E. B., *Charlotte's Web* (New York: Harper, 1952).

Widmann, S. P., 'Heimweh', in Ernst M. Roloff, ed., *Lexikon der Pädagogik, ii: Fortbildung bis Kolping* (Freiburg im Breisgau: Herdersche Verlagshandlung, 1913), 704–5.

Wildermuth, Ottilie, *Aus Nord und Süd: Erzählungen der deutschen Jugend geboten* (Stuttgart: Kröner, n.d. [c.1874]).

Wildermuth, Ottilie, *Cordulas erste Reise* ([Hannover]: Neuer Jugendschriften-Verlag, n.d. [c.1954]).

Wildermuth, Ottilie, 'Kordulas erste Reise', in *Jugendgabe: Erzählungen für die Jugend* (Stuttgart: Union, [1867]), 67–84.

Wildhagen, Else, *Aus Trotzkopfs Ehe* (Stuttgart: Weise, 1895).

Wildhagen, Else, *Trotzkopfs Brautzeit* (Stuttgart: Weise, 1892).

Wildhagen, Else, *Trotzkopfs Nachkommen: Ein neues Geschlecht* (Stuttgart: Weise, 1930).

Willhoite, Michael, *Daddy's Roommate* (Boston: Alyson Wonderland, 1990).

Willhoite, Michael, *Daddy's Wedding* (Los Angeles: Alyson Wonderland, 1996).

Willis, Frederick, *A Book of London Yesterdays* (London: Phoenix House, 1960).

Wölfel, Ursula, *Tim Fireshoe*, trans. E. M. Prince (London: OUP, 1963) [Ger. orig., *Feuerschuh und Windsandale* (1961)].

Zagoskin, M. N., *Iurii Miroslavskii ili Russkie v 1612 godu: Istoricheskii roman s risunkami* (Moscow: Stepanova, 1829).

Zell, Th., *Seelenleben unserer Haustiere, das unsere Jugend kennen sollte* (Berlin: Bongs, 1922).

Zotov, N. A., ed., *Ukazatel' knig dlia vospitatel'skogo chteniia kadetam* (Saint Petersburg: Pedagogicheskii Sbornik, 1913).

SECONDARY LITERATURE

Ablow, Rachel, ed., *The Feeling of Reading: Affective Experience & Victorian Literature* (Ann Arbor: University of Michigan Press, 2010).

Abruzzo, Margaret, *Polemical Pain: Slavery, Cruelty, and the Rise of Humanitarism* (Baltimore: Johns Hopkins UP, 2011).

Abu-Lughod, Lila, *Veiled Sentiments: Honor and Poetry in a Bedouin Society* (rev. edn, Berkeley: University of California Press, 2007).

Adam, Christian, *Lesen unter Hitler: Autoren, Bestseller, Leser im Dritten Reich* (Cologne: Kiepenheuer, 2010).

Ahuja, Ravi, 'Mobility and Containment: The Voyages of South Asian Seamen, c.1900–1960', *International Review of Social History*, 51/S14 (2006), 111–41.

Altner, Manfred, ed., *Das proletarische Kinderbuch: Dokumente zur Geschichte der sozialistischen deutschen Kinder- und Jugendliteratur* (Dresden: Verlag der Kunst, 1988).

Anon., 'Adolescence, n.', in *OED Online* (Oxford University Press, 2013), <http://www.oed.com/view/Entry/2648?redirectedFrom=adolescence&> accessed 2 May 2013.

Anweiler, Oskar, and Klaus Meyer, eds., *Die sowjetische Bildungspolitik 1917–1960: Dokumente und Texte* (2nd rev. edn, Wiesbaden: Harrassowitz, 1979).

Appadurai, Arjun, *Modernity at Large: Cultural Dimensions of Globalization* (Minneapolis: University of Minnesota Press, 1996).

Appignanesi, Lisa, and John Forrester, *Freud's Women* (London: Weidenfeld and Nicolson, 1992).

Applegate, Celia, *A Nation of Provincials: The German Idea of Heimat* (Berkeley: University of California Press, 1990).

Apte, Mahadev L., *Humor and Laughter: An Anthropological Approach* (Ithaca, N.Y.: Cornell UP, 1985).

Archiv der Jugendkulturen e.V., ed., *50 Jahre BRAVO* (2nd rev. and enl. edn, Bad Tölz: Tilsner, 2006).

Arendt, Hannah, *The Human Condition* (Chicago: University of Chicago Press, 1958).

Ariès, Philippe, *Centuries of Childhood: A Social History of Family Life*, trans. Robert Baldick (New York: Knopf, 1962) [Fre. orig., *L'Enfant et la vie familiale sous l'ancien régime* (1960)].

Aspatore, Jilleen V., 'The Military-Patriotic Theme in Soviet Textbooks and Children's Literature', PhD thesis, Georgetown University, Ann Arbor, 1986.

Auerbach, Erich, *Mimesis: The Representation of Reality in Western Literature*, trans. Willard R. Trask (Princeton: PUP, 1953) [Ger. orig., *Mimesis: Dargestellte Wirklichkeit in der abendländischen Literatur* (1946)].

Baker, Steve, *Picturing the Beast: Animals Identity, and Representation* (Urbana: University of Illinois Press, 2001).

Bakhtin, Mikhail, *Rabelais and His World*, trans. Hélène Iswolsky (Bloomington: Indiana UP, 1984) [Rus. orig., *Tvorchestvo fransua rable* (1941, 1965)].

Bakker, Nellekke, 'The Meaning of Fear: Emotional Standards for Children in the Netherlands, 1850–1950: Was There a Western Transformation?', *Journal of Social History*, 34/2 (2000), 369–91.

Bänziger, Peter-Paul et al., eds., *Fragen Sie Dr. Sex! Ratgeberkommunikation und die mediale Konstruktion des Sexuellen* (Berlin: Suhrkamp, 2010).

Barnett, Douglas, and Hilary Horn Ratner, 'The Organization and Integration of Cognition and Emotion in Development', *Journal of Experimental Child Psychology*, 67/3 (1997), 303–16.

Barth, Susanne, *Mädchenlektüren: Lesediskurse im 18. und 19. Jahrhundert* (Frankfurt am Main: Campus, 2002).

Bayly, C. A., *Empire and Information: Intelligence Gathering and Social Communication in India, 1780–1870*, Cambridge Studies in Indian History and Society 1 (Cambridge: CUP, 1996).

Beck, Hall P., Sharman Levinson, and Gary Irons, 'Finding Little Albert: A Journey to John B. Watson's Infant Laboratory', *American Psychologist*, 64/7 (2009), 605–14.

Bénéï, Véronique, *Schooling Passions: Nation, History, and Language in Contemporary Western India* (Stanford: SUP, 2008).

Benjamin, Walter, 'The Task of the Translator: An Introduction to the Translation of Baudelaire's Tableaux Parisiens', in Lawrence Venuti, ed., *The Translation Studies Reader* (London: Routledge, 2000), 15–25.

Benz, Ute, 'Brutstätten der Nation: "Die deutsche Mutter und ihr erstes Kind" oder der anhaltende Erfolg eines Erziehungsbuches', *Dachauer Hefte*, 4 (1988), 144–63.

Berg, Christa, ' "Rat geben": Ein Dilemma pädagogischer Praxis und Wirkungsgeschichte', *Zeitschrift für Pädagogik*, 37/5 (1991), 709–34.

Berry, Nita, 'Value-Based Writing', in Navin Menon, and Bhavana Nair, eds., *Children's Literature in India* (Delhi: Children's Book Trust, 1999), 167–84.

Biess, Frank, 'Feelings in the Aftermath: Toward a History of Postwar Emotions', in Frank Biess, and Robert G. Moeller, eds., *Histories of the Aftermath: The Legacies of the Second World War in Europe* (New York: Berghahn Books, 2010), 30–48.

Biess, Frank, 'Die Sensibilisierung des Subjekts: Angst und "Neue Subjektivität" in den 1970er Jahren', *Werkstatt Geschichte*, 49 (2008), 51–71.

Biess, Frank et al., 'History of Emotions: Forum', *German History*, 28/1 (2010), 67–80.

Bilston, Sarah, *The Awkward Age in Women's Popular Fiction, 1850–1900: Girls and the Transition to Womanhood*, Oxford English Monographs (Oxford: OUP, 2004).

Bilston, Sarah, ' "It is Not What We Read, But How We Read": Maternal Counsel on Girl's Reading Practices in Mid-Victorian Literature', *Nineteenth-Century Contexts*, 30/1 (2008), 1–20.

Birkin, Andrew, *J. M. Barrie & The Lost Boys: The Real Story behind Peter Pan* (2nd edn, New Haven: Yale UP, 2005).

Biro, David, 'Is There Such a Thing as Psychological Pain? and Why It Matters', *Culture, Medicine and Psychiatry*, 34/4 (2010), 658–67.

Biro, David, *Listening to Pain: Finding Words, Compassion and Relief* (New York: Norton, 2011).

Biswas, A., and S. P. Agrawal, *Development of Education in India: A Historical Survey of Educacational Documents before and after Independence* (New Delhi: Concept, 1986).

Bixler, Phyllis, *The Secret Garden: Nature's Magic* (New York: Twayne, 1996).

Blickle, Peter, *Heimat: A Critical Theory of the German Idea of Homeland* (Rochester, N.Y.: Camden House, 2002).

Bloch, Ernst, *The Principle of Hope*, 3 vols, trans. Neville Plaice, Stephen Plaice, and Paul Knight (Oxford: Blackwell, 1985) [Ger. orig., *Das Prinzip Hoffnung*, 3 vols (1954–9)].

Blom, Amélie, 'The 2006 Anti-"Danish Cartoons" Riot in Lahore: Outrage and the Emotional Landscape of Pakistani Politics', *South Asia Multidisciplinary Academic Journal*, 2 (2008), <http://samaj.revues.org/1652> accessed 23 May 2013.

Blume, Svenja, *Pippi Långstrumps Verwandlung zur 'dame-bien-élevée': Die Anpassung eines Kinderbuchs an ein fremdes kulturelles System: Eine Analyse der französischen Übersetzung von Astrid Lindgrens Pippi Långstrump (1945–8)*, Schriftenreihe Poetica 58 (Hamburg: Kovac, 2001).

Boddice, Rob, *A History of Attitudes and Behaviours Towards Animals in Eighteenth- and Nineteenth-Century Britain: Anthropocentrism and the Emergence of Animals* (Lewiston, N.Y.: Mellen, 2009).

Boddice, Rob, 'In Loco Parentis? Public-school authority, cricket and manly character, 1855–62', *Gender and Education*, 21/2 (2009), 159–72.

Boehmer, Elleke, introduction in Robert Baden-Powell, *Scouting for Boys: A Handbook for Instruction in Good Citizenship: The Original 1908 Edition* (Oxford: OUP, 2004), xi–xxxix.

Bolius, Gisela, *Lisa Tetzner: Leben und Werk* (Frankfurt am Main: Dipa, 1997).

Bookhagen, Christl et al., *Kommune 2: Versuch der Revolutionierung des bürgerlichen Individuums: Kollektives Leben mit politischer Arbeit verbinden* (Berlin: Oberbaum, 1969).

Boone, Troy, *Youth of Darkest England: Working-Class Children at the Heart of Victorian Empire* (New York: Routledge, 2005).

Borgards, Roland, 'Tiere in der Literatur: Eine methodische Standortbestimmung', in Herwig Grimm and Carola Otterstedt, eds., *Das Tier an sich: Disziplinenübergreifende Perspektiven für neue Wege im wissenschaftsbasierten Tierschutz* (Göttingen: Vandenhoeck & Ruprecht, 2012), 87–118.

Borkfelt, Sune, 'Colonial Animals and Literary Analysis: The Example of Kipling's Animal Stories', *English Studies*, 90/5 (2009), 557–68.

Borutta, Manuel, and Nina Verheyen, ed., *Die Präsenz der Gefühle: Männlichkeit und Emotion in der Moderne* (Bielefeld: Transcript, 2010).

Bose, Pradip Kumar, 'Sons of the Nation: Child Rearing in the New Family', in Partha Chatterjee, ed., *Texts of Power: Emerging Disciplines in Colonial Bengal* (Minneapolis: University of Minneapolis Press, 1995), 118–44.

Bourdieu, Pierre, *The Logic of Practice*, trans. Richard Nice (Cambridge: Polity, 1990) [Fre. orig., *Le sens pratique* (1980)].

Bourke, Joanna, *Fear: A Cultural History* (London: Virago, 2005).

Bourke, Joanna, *An Intimate History of Killing: Face-to-Face Killing in Twentieth-Century Warfare* (London: Granta, 1999).

Bourke, Joanna, *What It Means to be Human: Reflections from 1791 to the Present* (London: Virago, 2011).

Boyd, Kelly, *Manliness and the Boys' Story Paper in Britain: A Cultural History, 1855–1940* (Basingstoke: Palgrave Macmillan, 2003).

Bradford, Clare, 'Children's Literature in a Global Age: Transnational and Local Identities', *Nordic Journal of ChildLit Aesthetics*, 2 (2011), 20–34 <http://www.childlitaesthetics.net/index.php/blft/article/view/5828> accessed 28 May 2013.

Braithwaite, John, *Crime, Shame and Reintegration* (Cambridge: CUP, 1989).

Breeuwsma, Gerrit, 'The Nephew of an Experimentalist: Ambivalences in Developmental Thinking', in Willem Koops and Michael Zuckerman, eds., *Beyond the Century of the Child: Cultural History and Developmental Psychology* (Philadelphia: University of Pennsylvania Press, 2003), 183–203.

Brehony, Kevin J., 'A New Education for a New Era: The Contribution of the Conferences of the New Education Fellowship to the Disciplinary Field of Education 1921–1938', *Paedagogica Historica*, 40/5–6 (2004), 733–55.

Breithaupt, Fritz, *Kulturen der Empathie* (Frankfurt am Main: Suhrkamp, 2009).

Briggs, John L., *Never in Anger: Portrait of an Eskimo Family* (Cambridge: Harvard UP, 1970).

Brock, Adrian C., ed., *Internationalizing the History of Psychology* (New York: NYUP, 2006).

Brockhaus, Gudrun, 'Lockung und Drohung: Die Mutterrolle in zwei Ratgebern der NS-Zeit', in Miriam Gebhardt and Clemens Wischermann, eds., *Familiensozialisation seit 1933: Verhandlungen über Kontinuität*, Studien zur Geschichte des Alltags 25 (Stuttgart: Franz Steiner, 2007), 49–69.

Bronfenbrenner, Urie, 'Ecological Systems Theory', in Ross Vasta, ed., *Six Theories of Child Development: Revised Formulations and Current Issues*, Annals of Child Development 6 (Greenwich: JAI, 1989), 187–251.

Brosius, Christiane, 'Love in the Age of Valentine and Pink Underwear: Media and Politics of Intimacy in South Asia', in Christiane Brosius and Roland Wenzlhuemer, eds., *Transcultural Turbulences: Towards a Multi-Sited Reading of Image Flows* (Heidelberg: Springer, 2011), 27–66.

Brown, Laura, *Homeless Dogs and Melancholy Apes: Humans and Other Animals in the Modern Literary Imagination* (Ithaca, N.Y.: Cornell UP, 2010).

Brückenhaus, Daniel, '"Every Stranger Must Be Suspected": Trust Relationships and the Surveillance of Anti-Colonialists in Early Twentieth-Century Western Europe', *Geschichte und Gesellschaft*, 36/4 (2010), 523–66.

Buchner, Jutta, *Kultur mit Tieren: Zur Formierung des bürgerlichen Tierverständnisses im 19. Jahrhundert* (Munster: Waxmann, 1996).

Budde, Gunilla-Friederike, *Auf dem Weg ins Bürgerleben: Kindheit und Erziehung in deutschen und englischen Bürgerfamilien 1840–1914* (Göttingen: Vandenhoeck & Ruprecht, 1994).

Bunke, Simon, *Heimweh: Studien zur Kultur- und Literaturgeschichte einer tödlichen Krankheit*, Rombach-Wissenschaften Reihe Litterae 156 (Freiburg im Breisgau: Rombach, 2009).

Burt, Jonathan, *Animals in Film* (London: Reaktion, 2002).

Butterworth, Charles E., 'Medieval Islamic Philosophy and the Virtue of Ethics', *Arabica*, 34/2 (1987), 221–50.

Butts, Dennis, 'The Birth of the Boys' Stories and the Transition from the Robinsonnades to the Adventure Story', *Revue de Littérature Comparée*, 304/4 (2002), 445–54.

Buzelin, Hélène, 'Translation Studies, Ethnography and the Production of Knowledge', in Paul St-Piere and Prafulla C. Kar, eds., *In Translation: Reflections, Refractions, Transformations*, Benjamins Translation Library 71 (Amsterdam: Benjamins, 2007), 39–56.

Carpenter, Humphrey, *Secret Gardens: A Study of the Golden Age of Children's Literature* (Boston: Houghton Mifflin, 1985).

Carpenter, Humphrey, and Mari Prichard, eds., *The Oxford Companion to Children's Literature* (Oxford: OUP, 1999).

Carroll, Noël, *Theorizing the Moving Image* (Cambridge: CUP, 1996).

Chatterjee, Partha, *The Nation and its Fragments: Colonial and Postcolonial Histories*, Princeton Studies in Culture/Power/History (Princeton: PUP, 1993).

Choudhury, Suparna, and Jan Slaby, eds., *Critical Neuroscience: A Handbook of the Social and Cultural Contexts of Neuroscience* (Chichester: Wiley-Blackwell, 2012).

Cipolla, Carlo M., *Literacy and Development in the West* (Harmondsworth: Penguin, 1969).

Clark, Beverly Lyon, *Regendering the School Story: Sassy Sissies and Tattling Tomboys* (New York: Garland, 1996).

Clifford, James, *Routes: Travel and Translation in the Late Twentieth Century* (Cambridge: Harvard UP, 1997).

Cohn, Bernard, 'Representing Authority in Victorian India', in Eric J. Hobsbawm and Terence Ranger, eds., *The Invention of Tradition* (Cambridge: CUP, 1983), 165–209.

Coplan, Amy, and Peter Goldie, eds., *Empathy: Philosophical and Psychological Perspectives* (Oxford: OUP, 2011).

Cosslett, Tess, *Talking Animals in British Children's Fiction, 1786–1914* (Aldershot: Ashgate, 2006).

Cunningham, Hugh, *Children and Childhood in Western Society since 1500*, Studies in Modern History (2nd edn, Harlow, England: Pearson Longman, 2005).

Cutt, M. Nancy, *Mrs. Sherwood and Her Books for Children: A Study* (London: OUP, 1974).

Dahrendorf, Malte, *Jugendliteratur und Politik: Gesellschaftliche Aspekte der Kinder- und Jugendliteratur*, Jugend und Medien 11 (Frankfurt am Main: Dipa, 1986).

Dally, Ann, *Inventing Motherhood: The Consequences of an Ideal* (London: Burnett, 1982).

Damousi, Joy, and Mariano Ben Plotkin, *The Transnational Unconscious: Essays in the History of Psychoanalysis and Transnationalism*, The Palgrave Macmillan transnational history series (Houndmills: Palgrave Macmillan, 2009).

Darnton, Robert, 'First Steps Toward a History of Reading', in *The Kiss of Lamourette: Reflections in Cultural History* (New York: Norton, 1990), 154–87.

Daston, Lorraine, and Gregg Mitman, eds., *Thinking With Animals: New Perspectives on Anthropomorphism* (New York: Columbia UP, 2005).

Davies, James, and Dimitrina Spencer, eds., *Emotions in the Field: The Psychology and Anthropology of Fieldwork Experience* (Stanford: SUP, 2010).

Davin, Anna, 'What Is a Child?', in Anthony Fletcher and Stephen Hussey, eds., *Childhood in Question: Children, Parents and the State* (Manchester: MUP, 1999), 15–36.

Davis, Belinda, 'What's Left? Popular Political Participation in Postwar Europe', *American Historical Review*, 113/2 (2008), 363–90.

Dekker, Rudolf M., and Hugo Rölling, 'Fear', in Paula S. Fass, ed., *Encyclopedia of Children and Childhood in History and Society*, ii (New York: Macmillan Reference, 2004), 353–6.

DeMello, Margo, ed., *Speaking for Animals: Animal Autobographical Writing*, Routledge Advances in Sociology 80 (New York: Routledge, 2013).

Demmerling, Christoph, and Hilge Landweer, *Philosophie der Gefühle: Von Achtung bis Zorn* (Stuttgart: Metzler, 2007).

Deonna, Julien A., Raffaele Rogno, and Fabrice Teroni, *In Defense of Shame: The Faces of an Emotion* (Oxford: OUP, 2012).

Dixon, Thomas, 'Educating the Emotions from Gradgrind to Goleman', *Research Papers in Education*, 27/4 (2012), 481–95.

Doderer, Klaus, *Erich Kästner: Lebensphasen—politsches Engagement—literarisches Wirken* (Weinheim: Juventa, 2002).

Duyvendak, Jan Willem, *The Politics of Home: Belonging and Nostalgia in Western Europe and the United States* (Basingstoke: Palgrave MacMillan, 2011).

Egoff, Sheila A., and Ronald Hagler, *Books That Shaped Our Minds* (Vancouver: University of British Columbia Library, 1998).

Eitler, Pascal, 'The "Origin" of Emotions: Sensitive Humans, Sensitive Animals', in Ute Frevert et al., *Emotional Lexicons* (Oxford: OUP, 2014) [Ger. orig., 'Der "Ursprung" der Gefühle: Reizbare Menschen und reizbare Tiere', in Ute Frevert et al., *Gefühlswissen: Eine lexikalische Spurensuche in der Moderne* (2011)].

Eitler, Pascal, ' "Weil sie fühlen, was wir fühlen": Menschen, Tiere und die Genealogie der Emotionen im 19. Jahrhundert', *Historische Anthropologie*, 19/2 (2011), 211–28.

Eitler, Pascal, and Monique Scheer, 'Emotionengeschichte als Körpergeschichte: Eine heuristische Perspektive auf religiöse Konversionen im 19. und 20. Jahrhundert', *Geschichte und Gesellschaft*, 35/2 (2009), 282–313.

Ekman, Paul, 'Basic Emotions', in Tim Dalgleish and Mick J. Power, eds., *Handbook of Cognition and Emotion* (Chichester: Wiley, 1999), 45–60.

Elberfeld, Jens, 'Subjekt/Beziehung: Patriarchat—Partnerschaft—Projekt: Psychowissen und Normalisierungspraktiken im Diskurs der Paartherapie (BRD 1960–90)', in Maik Tändler and Uffa Jensen, eds., *Das Selbst zwischen Anpassung und Befreiung: Psychowissen und Politik im 20. Jahrhundert* (Göttingen: Wallstein, 2012), 85–114.

Elias, Norbert, *The Civilizing Process: Sociogenetic and Psychogenetic Investigations*, ed. Eric Dunning, Johan Goudsblom, and Stephen Mennell, trans. Edward Jephcott (Oxford: Blackwell, 2010) [Ger. orig., *Über den Prozeß der Zivilisation*, 2 vols (1939)].

Engels, Friedrich, *The Origin of the Family, Private Property and the State: In the Light of the Researches of Lewis H. Morgan*, trans. Alick West and Dona Torr (London: Lawrence & Wishart, 1942) [Ger. orig., *Der Ursprung der Familie, des Privateigentums und des Staates: Im Anschluss an Lewis H. Morgan's Forschungen* (1884)].

Epstein, E. L., 'Afterword', in William Golding, *Lord of the Flies* (New York: Putnam, 1954), 203–8.

Ernst, Petra, ' "The World is my Country…": Heimat und Heimatlosigkeit in Lisa Tetzners Roman "Die Kinder aus Nr. 67" ', in Hans Joachim Nauschütz and Steffen Pelzsch, eds., *Heimat, Heimatverlust und Heimatgewinn als Thema und Motiv im europäischen Kinder- und Jugendbuch: Drittes internationales Symposium in Frankfurt (Oder) und Zbaszyn vom 24.–26. April 1995*, Internationales Symposium des Deutsch-Polnischen Literaturbüros in Frankfurt (Oder) 3 (Frankfurt (Oder): Dt.-Poln. Literaturbüro Oderregion, Haus der Künste, 1995), 7–15.

Ewing, Katherine Pratt, *Arguing Sainthood: Modernity, Psychoanalysis, and Islam* (Durham: Duke UP, 1997).

Eyer, Diane E., *Mother-Infant Bonding: A Scientific Fiction* (New Haven: Yale UP, 1992).

Eyre, Frank, *British Children's Books in the Twentieth Century* (rev. edn, London: Longman, 1971).

Faehndrich, Jutta, *Eine endliche Geschichte: Die Heimatbücher der deutschen Vertriebenen* (Cologne: Böhlau, 2011).

Faulstich, Werner, *Bestandsaufnahme Bestseller-Forschung: Ansätze—Methoden—Erträge* (Wiesbaden: Harrassowitz, 1983).

Feagin, Susan L., *Reading with Feeling: The Aesthetics of Appreciation* (Ithaca, N.Y.: Cornell UP, 1996).

Ferguson, Tamara J., Hedy Stegge, and Ilse Damhuis, 'Children's Understanding of Guilt and Shame', *Child Development*, 62/4 (1991), 827–39.

Ferrall, Charles, and Anna Jackson, *Juvenile Literature and British Society, 1850–1950: The Age of Adolescence*, Children's Literature and Culture 68 (New York: Routledge, 2010).

Fisman, Raymond, and Tarun Khanna, 'Is Trust a Historical Residue? Information Flows and Trust Levels', *Journal of Economic Behavior & Organization*, 38/1 (1999), 79–92.

Flanagan, Victoria, *Into the Closet: Cross-Dressing and the Gendered Body in Children's Literature and Film*, Children's Literature and Culture 47 (New York: Routledge, 2007).

Flegel, Monica, *Conceptualizing Cruelty to Children in Nineteenth-Century England: Literature, Representation, and the NSPCC*, Ashgate Studies in Childhood, 1700 to the Present (Farnham Surrey: Ashgate, 2009).

Freeman, Thomas, 'Heinrich Hoffmann's Struwwelpeter: An Inquiry into the Effects of Violence in Children's Literature', *Journal of Popular Culture*, 10/4 (1977), 808–20.

Frevert, Ute, *Does Trust Have a History?*, Max Weber Programme: Lecture Series 2009–1 (San Domenico di Fiesole: European University Institute, 2009).

Frevert, Ute, *Emotions in History: Lost and Found* (Budapest: Central European UP, 2011).

Frevert, Ute, ed., *Geschichte der Gefühle*, Geschichte und Gesellschaft 35/2 (Göttingen: Vandenhoeck & Ruprecht, 2009).

Frevert, Ute, 'Trust as Work', in Jürgen Kocka, ed., *Work in a Modern Society: The German Historical Experience in Comparative Perspective*, New German Historical Perspectives 3 (New York: Berghahn Books, 2010), 93–108.

Frevert, Ute et al., *Emotional Lexicons: Continuity and Change in the Vocabulary of Feeling 1700–2000* (Oxford: OUP, 2014) [Ger. orig., *Gefühlswissen: Eine lexikalische Spurensuche in der Moderne* (2011)].

Friedrichsmeyer, Sara, Sara Lennox, and Susanne Zantop, eds., *The Imperialist Imagination: German Colonialism and its Legacy* (Ann Arbor: University of Michigan Press, 1998).

Fuchs, Martin, 'Reaching Out, or, Nobody Exists in One Context Only: Society as Translation', *Translation Studies*, 2/1 (2009), 21–40.

Fuchs, Martin, 'Soziale Pragmatik des Übersetzens: Strategien der Interkulturalität in Indien', in Joachim Renn, Jürgen Straub, and Shingo Shimada, eds., *Übersetzung als Medium des Kulturverstehens und sozialer Integration* (Frankfurt am Main: Campus, 2002), 292–322.

Fuchs, Martin, 'Übersetzen und Übersetzt-Werden: Plädoyer für eine interaktionsana-lytische Reflexion', in Doris Bachmann-Medick, ed., *Übersetzung als Repräsentation fremder Kulturen*, Göttinger Beiträge zur internationalen Übersetzungsforschung 12 (Berlin: Schmidt, 1997), 308–28.

Fuchs, Michaela, *'Wie sollen wir unsere Kinder erziehen?': Bürgerliche Kindererziehung im Spiegel der populärpädagogischen Erziehungsratgeber des 19. Jahrhunderts* (Wien: Praesens, 1997).

Fukuyama, Francis, *Trust: The Social Virtues and the Creation of Prosperity* (New York: Free, 1995).

Gaddis, John L., *The Cold War: A New History* (London: Allen Lane, 2005).

Galbraith, Gretchen R., *Reading Lives: Reconstructing Childhood, Books, and Schools in Britain, 1870–1920* (New York: St. Martin's, 1997).

Gammerl, Benno, 'Emotional Styles: Concepts and Challenges', *Rethinking History*, 16/2 (2012), 161–75.

Garrels, Scott R., ed., *Mimesis and Science: Empirical Research on Imitation and the Mimetic Theory of Culture and Religion*, Studies in Violence, Mimesis, and Culture Series (East Lansing: Michigan State UP, 2011).

Gebauer, Gunter, and Christoph Wulf, *Mimesis: Culture, Art, Society*, trans. Don Reneau (Berkeley: University of California Press, 1995) [Ger. orig., *Mimesis: Kultur—Kunst—Gesellschaft* (1992)].

Gebhard, Gunther, Oliver Geisler, and Steffen Schröter, eds., *Heimat: Konturen und Konjunkturen eines umstrittenen Konzepts*, Kultur- und Medientheorie (Bielefeld: Transcript, 2007).

Gebhardt, Miriam, *Die Angst vor dem kindlichen Tyrannen: Eine Geschichte der Erziehung im 20. Jahrhundert* (Munich: Deutsche Verlagsanstalt, 2009).

Gebhardt, Miriam, 'Haarer Meets Spock: Frühkindliche Erziehung und gesellschaftlicher Wandel seit 1933', in Miriam Gebhardt and Clemens Wischermann, eds., *Familiensozialisation seit 1933: Verhandlungen über Kontinuität*, Studien zur Geschichte des Alltags 25 (Stuttgart: Franz Steiner, 2007), 87–104.

Geertz, Clifford, 'Thick Description: Toward an Interpretive Theory of Culture', in *The Interpretation of Cultures: Selected Essays* (New York: Basic, 1973), 3–30.

Geissmann, Claudine, and Pierre Geissmann, *A History of Child Psychoanalysis* (London: Routledge, 1998) [Fre. orig., *Histoire de la psychanalyse de l'enfant: Mouvements, idées, perspectives* (1992)].

Giloi, Eva, 'Socialization and the City: Parental Authority and Teenage Rebellion in Wilhelmine Germany', *Radical Historical Review*, 114 (2012), 91–112.

Girard, René, *Deceit, Desire, and the Novel: Self and Other in Literary Structure*, trans. Yvonne Freccero (Baltimore: Johns Hopkins UP, 1965) [Fre. orig., *Mensonge romantique et vérité romanesque* (1961)].

Girard, René, *Mimesis and Theory: Essays on Literature and Criticism, 1953–2005*, Cultural Memory in the Present (Stanford: SUP, 2008).

Goldsmith, Annette Y., 'Found in Translation: How US Publishers Select Children's Books in Foreign Languages', in Pat Pinsent, ed., *No Child is an Island: The Case of Children's Literature in Translation*, NCRCL Papers 12 (Lichfield: Pied Piper, 2006), 88–101.

Goodstein, Elizabeth S., *Experience without Qualities: Boredom and Modernity* (Stanford: SUP, 2005).

Gould, Stephen Jay, *Ontogeny and Phylogeny* (Cambridge: Belknap Press of Harvard UP, 1977).

Graebner, William, 'The Unstable World of Benjamin Spock: Social Engineering in a Democratic Culture', *Journal of American History*, 67/3 (1980), 612–29.

Grant, Julia, *Raising Baby by the Book: The Education of American Mothers* (New Haven: Yale UP, 1998).

Green, Roger Lancelyn, 'The Golden Age of Children's Books', *Essays and Studies*, 15 (1962), 59–73.

Grenby, M. O., and Andrea Immel, eds., *The Cambridge Companion to Children's Literature* (Cambridge: CUP, 2009).

Grenz, Dagmar, ' "Das eine sein und das andere auch sein…": Über die Widersprüchlichkeit des Frauenbildes am Beispiel der Mädchenliteratur', in Dagmar Grenz and Gisela Wilkending, eds., *Geschichte der Mädchenlektüre: Mädchenliteratur und die gesellschaftliche Situation der Frauen vom 18. Jahrhundert bis zur Gegenwart*, Lesesozialisation und Medien (Munich: Juventa, 1997), 197–216.

Grenz, Dagmar, ' "Der Trotzkopf": Ein Bestseller damals und heute', in Dagmar Grenz and Gisela Wilkending, eds., *Geschichte der Mädchenlektüre: Mädchenliteratur und die gesellschaftliche Situation der Frauen vom 18. Jahrhundert bis zur Gegenwart*, Lesesozialisation und Medien (Munich: Juventa, 1997), 115–22.

Grenz, Dagmar, 'Zeitgenössische Mädchenliteratur: Tradition oder Neubeginn?', in Dagmar Grenz and Gisela Wilkending, eds., *Geschichte der Mädchenlektüre: Mädchenliteratur und die gesellschaftliche Situation der Frauen vom 18. Jahrhundert bis zur Gegenwart*, Lesesozialisation und Medien (Munich: Juventa, 1997), 241–66.

Grier, Katherine C., 'Childhood Socialization and Companion Animals: United States, 1820–1870', *Society and Animals*, 7/2 (1999), 95–120.

Grieser, Dietmar, *Im Tiergarten der Weltliteratur: Auf den Spuren von Kater Murr, Biene Maja, Bambi, Möwe Jonathan und den anderen* (Munich: DTV, 1993).

Grima, Benedicte, *The Performance of Emotion among Paxtun Women: 'The Misfortunes Which Have Befallen Me'* (Austin: University of Texas Press, 1992).

Gross, James J., ed., *Handbook of Emotion Regulation* (New York: Guilford, 2007).

Große, Jürgen, *Philosophie der Langeweile* (Stuttgart: Metzler, 2008).

Gubar, Marah, '"Peter Pan" as Children's Theater: The Issue of Audience', in Julia L. Mickenberg and Lynne Valone, eds., *The Oxford Handbook of Children's Literature* (Oxford: OUP, 2011), 475–95.

Hale, Jr., Nathan G., *Rise and Crisis of Psychoanalysis in the United States: Freud and the Americans, 1917–1985* (New York: OUP, 1995).

Halfin, Igal, 'From Darkness to Light: Student Communist Autobiography During NEP', *Jahrbücher für Geschichte Osteuropas*, 45/2 (1997), 210–36.

Hall, Catherine, *Civilising Subjects: Metropole and Colony in the English Imagination, 1830–1867* (Chicago: University of Chicago Press, 2002).

Hall, Catherine, 'The Economy of Intellectual Prestige: Thomas Carlyle, John Stuart Mill, and the Case of Governor Eyre', *Cultural Critique*, 12/Spring (1989), 167–96.

Hanfi, Muzaffar, 'Urdu', in Kunniseri Akhileshwaram Jamuna, ed., *Children's Literature in Indian Languages* (New Delhi: Publications Division, Ministry of Information and Broadcasting, Government of India, 1982), 244–62.

Hannerz, Ulf, *Transnational Connections: Culture, People, Places* (London: Routledge, 1996).

Haraway, Donna J., *When Species Meet*, Posthumanities 3 (Minneapolis: University of Minnesota Press, 2008).

Hardyment, Christina, *Dream Babies: Child Care from Locke to Spock* (London: Cape, 1983).

Hasan, Mushir, and Rakshanda Jalil, *Partners in Freedom: Jamia Millia Islamia* (2nd edn, New Delhi: Niyogi, 2008).

Heidegger, Martin, *The Fundamental Concepts of Metaphysics: World, Finitude, Solitude*, trans. William McNeill and Nicholas Walker (Bloomington: Indiana UP, 1995) [Ger. orig., *Die Grundbegriffe der Metaphysik: Welt—Endlichkeit—Einsamkeit* (1929/30)].

Heinze, Martin, Dirk Quadflieg, and Martin Bühring, eds., *Utopie Heimat: Psychiatrische und Kulturphilosophische Zugänge*, Beiträge der Gesellschaft für Philosophie und Wissenschaften der Psyche 6 (Berlin: Parodos, 2006).

Herman, Ellen, 'Psychologism and the Child', in Theodore M. Porter and Dorothy Ross, eds., *The Cambridge History of Science, vii: The Modern Social Sciences* (Cambridge: CUP, 2003), 649–62.

Herman, Ellen, *The Romance of American Psychology: Political Culture in the Age of Experts* (Berkeley: University of California Press, 1995).

Herzog, Dagmar, 'Antifaschistische Körper: Studentenbewegung, sexuelle Revolution und anitautoritäre Kindererziehung', in Klaus Naumann, ed., *Nachkrieg in Deutschland* (Hamburg: Hamburger Edition, 2001), 521–51.

Heywood, Colin, 'Centuries of Childhood: An Anniversary—and an Epitaph?', *Journal of the History of Childhood and Youth*, 3/3 (2010), 343–65.

Heywood, Colin, *Growing Up in France: From the Ancien Régime to the Third Republic* (Cambridge: CUP, 2007).

Heywood, Colin, *A History of Childhood: Children and Childhood in the West from the Medieval to Modern Times* (Cambridge: Polity, 2001).

Höffer-Mehlmer, Markus, *Elternratgeber: Zur Geschichte eines Genres* (Baltmannsweiler: Schneider, 2003).

Höffer-Mehlmer, Markus, 'Erziehungsratgeber', in Jutta Ecarius, ed., *Handbuch Familie* (Wiesbaden: VS Verlag für Sozialwissenschaften, 2007), 669–87.

Höffer-Mehlmer, Markus, 'Sozialisation und Erziehungsratschlag: Elternratgeber nach 1945', in Miriam Gebhardt and Clemens Wischermann, eds., *Familiensozialisation seit 1933: Verhandlungen über Kontinuität*, Studien zur Geschichte des Alltags 25 (Stuttgart: Franz Steiner, 2007), 71–85.

Hollindale, Peter, 'A Hundred Years of Peter Pan', *Children's Literature in Education*, 36/3 (2005), 197–215.

Holmes, Martha Stoddard, 'Peter Pan and the Possibilities of Child Literature', in Allison B. Karvey and Lester D. Friedman, eds., *Second Star to the Right: Peter Pan in the Popular Imagination* (New Brunswick: Rutgers UP, 2009), 132–50.

Hosking, Geoffrey, 'Trust and Distrust: A Suitable Theme for Historians?', *Transactions of the Royal Historical Society (Sixth Series)*, 16/December (2006), 95–115.

Hourani, George F., *Reason and Tradition in Islamic Ethics* (Cambridge: CUP, 1985).

Hulbert, Ann, *Raising America: Experts, Parents, and a Century of Advice About Children* (New York: Knopf, 2003).

Humphrey, Judith, *The English Girls' School Story: Subversion and Challenge in a Traditional, Conservative Literary Genre* (Bethesda: Academica, 2009).

Hunt, Lynn, *Inventing Human Rights: A History* (New York: Norton, 2007).

Hunt, Peter, ed., *Understanding Children's Literature: Key Essays from the International Companion Encyclopedia of Children's Literature* (London: Routledge, 1999).

Illouz, Eva, *Consuming the Romantic Utopia: Love and the Cultural Contradictions of Capitalism* (Berkeley: University of California Press, 1997).

Ilsemann, Wilhelm von, ed., *Jugend zwischen Anpassung und Ausstieg: Ein Symposium mit Jugendlichen und Vertretern aus Wissenschaft, Wirtschaft, Politik und Verwaltung, vom 27. bis 30.5.1980 auf Schloß Gracht bei Köln* (Hamburg: Jugendwerk der Deutschen Shell, 1980).

Jaspers, Karl, *Heimweh und Verbrechen*, Archiv für Kriminalanthropologie und Kriminalistik 35 (Leipzig: Vogel, 1909).

Jensen, Uffa, 'Freuds unheimliche Gefühle: Zur Rolle von Emotionen in der Freudschen Psychoanalyse', in Uffa Jensen and Daniel Morat, eds., *Rationalisierungen des Gefühls: Zum Verhältnis von Wissenschaft und Emotionen 1880–1930* (Munich: Fink, 2008), 135–52.

Jones, Gregory, and Jane Brown, 'Wilhelm Busch's Merry Thoughts: His Early Books in Britain and America', *Papers of the Bibliographical Society of America*, 101/2 (2007), 167–204.

Justice, Keith L., *Bestseller Index: All Books, by Author, on the Lists of Publishers Weekly and the New York Times through 1990* (Jefferson, NC: McFarland, 1998).

Kaminski, Winfred, *Jugendliteratur und Revolte: Jugendprotest und seine Spiegelung in der Literatur für junge Leser* (Frankfurt am Main: Dipa, 1982).

Kamp, Johannes-Martin, *Kinderrepubliken: Geschichte, Praxis und Theorie radikaler Selbstregierung in Kinder- und Jugendheimen* (2nd edn, Wiesbaden: Self-published, 2006), <http://paed.com/kinder/kind/kinderrepubliken.pdf> accessed 4 Jan. 2013.

Kean, Hilda, *Animal Rights: Political and Social Change in Britain since 1800* (London: Reaktion, 1998).

Kelly, Catriona, *Children's World: Growing Up in Russia, 1890–1991* (New Haven: Yale UP, 2007).

Kessel, Martina, Langeweile*: Zum Umgang mit Zeit und Gefühlen in Deutschland vom späten 18. bis zum frühen 20. Jahrhundert* (Göttingen: Wallstein, 2001).

Kete, Kathleen, *The Beast in the Boudoir: Petkeeping in Nineteenth-Century Paris* (Berkeley: University of California Press, 1994).

Kete, Kathleen, 'Verniedlichte Natur: Kinder und Haustiere in historischen Quellen', in Dorothee Brantz and Christof Mauch, eds., *Tierische Geschichte: Die Beziehung von Mensch und Tier in der Kultur der Moderne* (Paderborn: Schöningh, 2010), 123–37.

Khan, Pasha Mohamad, 'A Handbook for Storytellers: The Tiraz al-akhbar and the Qissa Genre', in Satyanarayana Hegde, ed., *An Informal Festschrift in Honor of the Manifold Lifetime Achievements of Shamsur Rahman Faruqi* (2010), <http://www.columbia.edu/itc/mealac/pritchett/00urduhindilinks/srffest/> accessed 17 Apr. 2013.

Kiley, Dan, *The Peter Pan Syndrome: Men Who Have Never Grown Up* (New York: Dodd, Mead, 1983).

Kincaid, James R., *Child-Loving: The Erotic Child and Victorian Culture* (New York: Routledge, 1992).

Kirkpatrick, Robert J., *The Encyclopaedia of Boys' School Stories,* ed. Rosemary Auchmuty and Joy Wotton, The Encyclopaedia of School Stories 2 (Aldershot: Ashgate, 2000).

Kohli, Martin, 'Die Institutionalisierung des Lebenslaufs: Historische Befunde und theoretische Argumente', *Kölner Zeitschrift für Soziologie und Sozialpsychologie*, 37/1 (1985), 1–29.

Kokorski, Karin, 'The Invisible Threat: Symbolic Violence in Children's Literature and Young Adults' Fiction', in Thomas Kullmann, ed., *Violence in English Children's and Young Adult's Fiction* (Aachen: Shaker, 2010), 189–203.

Kössler, Till, 'Die Ordnung der Gefühle: Frühe Kinderpsychologie und das Problem kindlicher Emotionen (1880–1930)', in Uffa Jensen and Daniel Morat, eds., *Rationalisierungen des Gefühls: Zum Verhältnis von Wissenschaft und Emotionen 1880–1930* (Munich: Fink, 2008), 189–210.

Kucherenko, Olga, *Little Soldiers: How Soviet Children Went to War, 1941–1945* (New York: Oxford UP, 2011).

Kumar, Krishna, *Political Agenda of Education: A Study of Colonialist and Nationalist Ideas* (2nd edn, New Delhi: Sage, 2005).

Kumschick, Irina Rosa et al., 'Sheep with Boots': An Emotion-Centered Literary Intervention Designed to Increase Emotional Competence in Children* (under review).

Kupfer, Christine, 'Rabindranath Tagore's Bildung zum Weltmenschen: Ein Beispiel interkultureller Pädagogik', in Elisabeth Zwick, ed., *Pädagogik als Dialog der Kulturen: Grundlagen und Diskursfelder der interkulturellen Pädagogik*, Reform und Innovation 11 (Berlin: Lit, 2009), 227–59.

Kurme, Sebastian, *Halbstarke: Jugendprotest in den 1950er Jahren in Deutschland und den USA*, Campus Forschung 901 (Frankfurt am Main: Campus, 2006).

Kurzweil, Edith, *The Freudians: A Comparative Perspective* (New Haven: Yale UP, 1989).

Kutzer, M. Daphne, *Empire's Children: Empire and Imperialism in Classic British Children's Books* (New York: Garland, 2000).

Lal, Ruby, 'Recasting the Women's Question: The Girl-Child/Women in the Colonial Encounter', *Interventions: International Journal of Postcolonial Studies*, 10/3 (2008), 321–39.

Lal, Ruby, *Coming of Age in Nineteenth-Century India: The Girl-Child and the Art of Playfulness* (Cambridge: CUP, 2013).

Lambert-Hurley, Siobhan, *Muslim Women, Reform and Princely Patronage: Nawab Sultan Jahan Begam of Bhopal, Royal Asiatic Society Books* (London: Routledge, 2007).

Lathey, Gillian, *The Role of Translators in Children's Literature: Invisible Storytellers* (New York: Routledge, 2010).

Lawson, M. D., 'The New Education Fellowship: The Formative Years', *Journal of Educational Administration and History*, 13/2 (1981), 24–8.

Le Breton, David, *Anthropologie de la douleur*, Sciences humaines 12 (rev. and enl. edn, Paris: Métailié, 2006).

Lelyveld, David, *Aligarh's First Generation: Muslim Solidarity in British India* (Princeton: PUP, 1978; Delhi: Oxford UP, 1996).

Lethen, Helmuth, Cool Conduct: *The Culture of Distancein Weimar Germany*, trans. Don Reneau (Berkeley: University of California Press, 2002) [Ger. orig., *Verhaltenslehren der Kälte: Lebensversuche in der Weimarer Republik* (1993)].

Leutheuser, Karsten, *Freie, geführte und verführte Jugend: Politisch motivierte Jugendliteratur in Deutschland 1919–1989*, Literatur- und Medienwissenschaft 45 (Paderborn: Igel, 1945).

Levinson, Boris, *Pet-Oriented Child Psychotherapy* (Springfield: Thomas, 1969).

Levsen, Sonja, *Elite, Männlichkeit und Krieg: Tübinger und Cambridger Studenten 1900–1929*, Kritische Studien zur Geschichtswissenschaft 170 (Göttingen: Vandenhoeck & Ruprecht, 2006).

Lewis, Helen Block, 'Shame and the Narcissistic Personality', in Donald L. Nathanson, ed., *The Many Faces of Shame* (New York: Guilford, 1987), 93–132.

Lewis, Michael, Jeannette M. Haviland-Jones, and Lisa Feldman Barrett, eds., *Handbook of Emotions* (3rd edn, New York: Guilford, 2008).

Leys, Ruth, 'The Turn to Affect: A Critique', *Critical Inquiry*, 37/3 (2011), 434–72.

Lindenberger, Thomas, 'Einleitung: Physische Gewalt—Eine Kontinuität der Moderne', in Thomas Lindenberger and Alf Lüdtke, eds., *Physische Gewalt: Studien zur Geschichte der Neuzeit* (Frankfurt am Main: Suhrkamp, 1995), 7–38.

Lindholm, Charles, *Generosity and Jealousy: The Swat Pukhtun of Northern Pakistan* (New York: Columbia UP, 1982).

Lowenfeld, Henry, 'Notes on Shamelessness', *Psychoanalytic Quarterly*, 45 (1976), 62–72.

Luhmann, Niklas, 'Familiarity, Confidence, Trust: Problems and Alternatives', in Diego Gambetta, ed., *Trust: Making and Breaking Cooperative Relations* (Oxford: Blackwell, 1990), 94–107.

Lutz, Catherine A., *Unnatural Emotions: Everyday Sentiments on a Micronesian Atoll & Their Challenge to Western Theory* (Chicago: University of Chicago Press, 1998).

Lyons, Martyn, *A History of Reading and Writing in the Western World* (Basingstoke: Palgrave Macmillan, 2010).

Lyons, Martyn, *Readers and Society in Nineteenth-Century France: Workers, Women, Peasants* (Basingstoke: Palgrave, 2001).

Maasen, Sabine et al., eds., *Das beratene Selbst: Zur Genealogie der Therapeutisierung in den 'langen' Siebzigern* (Bielefeld: Transcript, 2011).

Maasen, Sabine, 'Das beratene Selbst: Zur Genealogie der Therapeutisierung in den "langen" Siebzigern: Eine Perspektivierung', in Sabine Maasen et al., eds., *Das beratene Selbst: Zur Genealogie der Therapeutisierung in den 'langen' Siebzigern* (Bielefeld: Transcript, 2011), 7–33.

McClintock, Anne, *Imperial Leather: Race, Gender and Sexuality in the Colonial Context* (New York: Routledge, 1995).

MacDonald, Geoff, and Lauri A. Jensen-Campbell, eds., *Social Pain: Neuropsychological and Health Implications of Loss and Exclusion* (Washington: American Psychological Association, 2011).

McHugh, Susan, *Animal Stories: Narrating Across Species Lines*, Posthumanities 15 (Minneapolis: University of Minnesota Press, 2011).

MacKenzie, John M., *Propaganda and Empire: The Manipulation of British Public Opinion, 1880–1960* (Manchester: MUP, 1984).

McLain, Karline, *India's Immortal Comic Books: Gods, Kings, and Other Heroes* (Bloomington: Indiana UP, 2009).

Maine, Henry Sumner, *Ancient Law: Its Connection with the Early History of Society, and its Relation to Modern Ideas* (London: Murray, 1861).

Malti, Tina, and Marlis Buchmann, 'Die Entwicklung moralischer Emotionen bei Kindergartenkindern', *Praxis der Kinderpsychologie und Kinderpsychiatrie*, 59/7 (2010), 545–60.

Mangum, Teresa, 'Dog Years, Human Fears', in Nigel Rothfels, ed., *Representing Animals* (Bloomington: Indiana UP, 2002), 35–47.

Mangum, Teresa, 'Narrative Dominion or The Animals Write Back? Animal Genres in Literature and the Arts', in Kathleen Kete, ed., *A Cultural History of Animals, v: A Cultural History of Animals in the Age of Empire* (Oxford: Berg, 2007), 153–73.

Markovits, Claude, Jacques Pouchepadass, and Sanjay Subrahmanyam, eds., *Society and Circulation: Mobile People and Itinerant Cultures in South Asia, 1750–1950* (Delhi: Permanent Black, 2003).

Marlow, Louise, 'Advice and Advice Literature', in Gudrun Krämer et al., eds., *Encyclopaedia of Islam* (3rd edn, Leiden: Brill Online, 2013), <http://referenceworks.brillonline.com/entries/encyclopaedia-of-islam-3/advice-and-advice-literature-COM_0026> accessed 17 Apr. 2013.

Marré, Beatrice, *Bücher für Mütter als pädagogische Literaturgattung und ihre Aussagen über Erziehung (1762–1851): Ein Beitrag zur Geschichte der Familienerziehung*, Beltz-Forschungsberichte (Weinheim: Beltz, 1986).

Marsden, Magnus, *Living Islam: Muslim Religious Experience in Pakistan's North-West Frontier* (Cambridge: CUP, 2005).

Martin, Luther H., Huck Gutman, and Patrick H. Hutton, eds., *Technologies of the Self: A Seminar with Michel Foucault* (Amherst: University of Massachusetts Press, 1988).

Martin, Maureen M., '"Boys Who Will Be Men": Desire in Tom Brown's Schooldays', *Victorian Literature and Culture*, 30/2 (2002), 483–502.

Martin, Michelle H., '"No One Will Ever Know your Secret!": Commercial Puberty Pamphlets for Girls from the 1940s to the 1990s', in Claudia Nelson and Michelle H. Martin, eds., *Sexual Pedagogies: Sex Education in Britain, Australia, and America, 1879–2000* (New York: Palgrave Macmillan, 2004), 135–54.

Matt, Susan J., *Homesickness: An American History* (Oxford: OUP, 2011).

Matt, Susan J., 'You Can't Go Home Again: Homesickness and Nostalgia in U.S. History', *Journal of American History*, 94/2 (2007), 469–97.

Messerli, Alfred, 'Zur Geschichte der Medien des Rates', in Peter-Paul Bänziger et al., eds., *Fragen Sie Dr. Sex! Ratgeberkommunikation und die mediale Konstruktion des Sexuellen* (Berlin: Suhrkamp, 2010), 30–57.

Metcalf, Thomas R., *Ideologies of the Raj* (Cambridge: CUP, 1994).

Metcalf, Thomas R., *An Imperial Vision: Indian Architecture and Britain's Raj* (Berkeley: University of California Press, 1989).

Michaels, Jennifer, 'Fantasies of Native Americans: Karl May's Continuing Impact on the German Imagination', *European Journal of American Culture*, 31/3 (2012), 205–18.

Midgley, David, '"Los von Berlin!": Anti-Urbanism as Counter-Culture in Early Twentieth-Century Germany', in Steve Giles and Maike Oergel, eds., *Counter-Cultures in Germany and Central Europe: From Sturm und Drang to Bader-Meinhof* (Oxford: Lang, 2003), 121–36.

Mieszkowski, Jan, 'Fear of a Safe Place', in Jan Plamper and Benjamin Lazier, eds., *Fear: Across the Disciplines* (Pittsburgh: University of Pittsburgh Press, 2012), 99–117.

Mignolo, Walter D., and Freya Schiwy, 'Double Translation: Transculturation and the Colonial Difference', in Tullio Maranhão and Bernhard Streck, eds., *Translation and Ethnography: The Anthropological Challenge of Intercultural Understanding* (Tucson: University of Arizona Press, 2003), 3–29.

Minault, Gail, *Secluded Scholars: Women's Education and Muslim Social Reform in Colonial India* (Delhi: Oxford UP, 1998).

Misztal, Barbara A., *Trust in Modern Societies: The Search for the Bases of Social Order* (Cambridge: Polity, 1996).

Mitchell, Sally, *The New Girl: Girls' Culture in England, 1880–1915* (New York: Columbia UP, 1995).

Mitchell, Stephen A., and Margaret J. Black, *Freud and Beyond: A History of Modern Psychoanalytic Thought* (New York: Basic, 1995).

Möllering, Guido, 'The Nature of Trust: From Georg Simmel to a Theory of Expectation, Interpretation and Suspension', *Sociology*, 35/2 (2001), 403–20.

Morris, David E., *The Cultures of Pain* (Berkeley: University of California Press, 1993).

Morse, M. Joy, 'The Kiss: Female Sexuality and Power in J. M. Barrie's Peter Pan', in Donna R. White and C. Anita Tarr, eds., J. M. Barrie's *Peter Pan: In and Out of Time: A Children's Classic at 100*, Children's Literature Association Centennial Studies 4 (Oxford: Scarecrow, 2006), 281–302.

Moscoso, Javier, *Pain: A Cultural History* (New York: Palgrave Macmillan, 2012).

Moskowitz, Eva S., *In Therapy We Trust: America's Obsession with Self-Fulfillment* (Baltimore: Johns Hopkins UP, 2001).

Mosse, George L., *Masses and Man: Nationalist and Fascist Perceptions of Reality* (New York: Fertig, 1980).

Müller, Helmut, 'Barrie, Sir James Matthew', in Klaus Doderer, ed., *Lexikon der Kinder- und Jugendliteratur, i: A-H* (special edn, Weinheim: Beltz, 1984), 108.

Munday, Jeremy, 'Issues in Translation Studies', in Jeremy Munday, ed., *The Routledge Companion to Translation Studies* (rev. edn, London: Routledge, 2009), 1–19.

Munns, David P. D., '"Gay, Innocent, and Heartless": Peter Pan and the Queering of Popular Culture', in Allison B. Karvey and Lester D. Friedman, eds., *Second Star to the Right: Peter Pan in the Popular Imagination* (New Brunswick: Rutgers UP, 2009), 219–42.

Nadel, Jacqueline, and George Butterworth, eds., *Imitation in Infancy*, Cambridge Studies in Cognitive and Perceptual Development (Cambridge: CUP, 2011).

Naim, C. M., 'Popular Jokes and Political History: The Case of Akhbar, Birbal and Mullah Do-Piyaza', *Economic and Political Weekly*, 30/24 (1995), 1456–64.

Naim, C. M., 'Prize-Winning Adab: A Study of Five Urdu Books Written in Response to the Allahabad Government Gazette Notification', in Barbara Daly Metcalf, ed., *Moral Conduct and Authority: The Place of Adab in South Asian Islam* (Berkeley: University of California Press, 1984), 290–314.

Nair, Janaki, *Women and Law in Colonial India: A Social History* (Delhi: Kali for Women, 1996).

Nash, David, and Anne-Marie Kilday, *Cultures of Shame: Exploring Crime and Morality in Britain 1600–1900* (Basingstoke: Palgrave MacMillan, 2010).

Nathanson, Donald L., 'A Timetable for Shame', in Donald L. Nathanson, ed., *The Many Faces of Shame* (New York: Guilford, 1987), 1–63.

Nehring, Holger, 'The British and West German Protests against Nuclear Weapons and the Cultures of the Cold War, 1957–64', *Contemporary British History*, 19/2 (2005), 223–41.

Nelke, Anne-Katrin, *Kind im Buch: Kindheitsdarstellungen in Kinderromanen der DDR* (Marburg: Tectum, 2010).

Nelson, Claudia, 'Jade and the Tomboy Tradition', in Julia L. Mickenberg and Lynne Valone, eds., *The Oxford Handbook of Children's Literature* (Oxford: OUP, 2011), 497–516.

Nelson, Claudia, 'Sex and the Single Boy: Ideals of Manliness and Sexuality in Victorian Literature for Boys', *Victorian Studies*, 32/4 (1989), 525–50.

Nelson, Claudia, and Michelle H. Martin, 'Introduction' in Claudia Nelson and Michelle H. Martin, eds., *Sexual Pedagogies: Sex Education in Britain, Australia, and America, 1879–2000* (New York: Palgrave Macmillan, 2004), 1–13.

Newsome, David, *Godliness and Good Learning: Four Studies on a Victorian Ideal* (London: Murray, 1961).

Noble, Marianne, *The Masochistic Pleasures of Sentimental Literature* (Princeton: PUP, 2000).

Noë, Alva, *Out of our Heads: Why you Are not your Brain, and Other Lessons from the Biology of Consciousness* (New York: Hill & Wang, 2009).

Notelle, Claudia, *Zwischen Pop und Politik: Zum Weltbild der Jugendzeitschriften 'Bravo', 'ran' und 'Junge Zeit'* (Munster: Lit, 1994).

Oelkers, Jürgen, 'Reformpädagogik vor der Reformpädagogik', *Paedagogica Historica*, 42/1–2 (2006), 15–48.

Oesterheld, Christina, 'Entertainment and Reform: Urdu Narrative Genres in the Nineteenth Century', in Stuart Blackburn and Vasudha Dalmia, eds., *India's Literacy History: Essays on the Nineteenth Century* (Delhi: Permanent Black, 2004), 167–212.

Oesterheld, Joachim, 'Zakir Husain: Begegnungen und Erfahrungen bei der Suche nach moderner Bildung für ein freies Indien', in Petra Heidrich and Heike Liebau, eds., *Akteure des Wandels: Lebensläufe und Gruppenbilder an Schnittstellen von Kulturen*, Zentrum Moderner Orient: Studien 14 (Berlin: Das Arabische Buch, 2001), 105–30.

Ohmer, Susan, 'Disney's Peter Pan: Gender, Fantasy, and Industrial Production', in Allison B. Karvey and Lester D. Friedman, eds., *Second Star to the Right: Peter Pan in the Popular Imagination* (New Brunswick: Rutgers UP, 2009), 151–87.

Olson, Richard G., *Science and Scientism in Nineteenth-Century Europe* (Urbana: University of Illinois Press, 2008).

Osella, Caroline, and Filippo Osella, *Men and Masculinities in South India*, Anthem South Asian Studies (London: Anthem, 2006).

Oswald, Lori Jo, 'Heroes and Victims: The Stereotyping of Animal Characters in Children's Realistic Animal Fiction', *Children's Literature in Education*, 26/2 (1995), 135–49.

Panandiker, Surekha, 'Soviet Literature for Children and Youth in Translation in the Language of Indian People', *Writer and Illustrator*, 4/2 (1985), 17–24.

Pearson, Susan J., *The Rights of the Defenseless: Protecting Animals and Children in Gilded Age America* (Chicago: University of Chicago Press, 2011).

Perkins, David, *Romanticism and Animal Rights*, Cambridge Studies in Romanticism 58 (digitally print edn, Cambridge: CUP, 2007).

Pernau, Margrit, 'Civility and Barbarism: Feelings as Criteria of Difference', in Ute Frevert et al., *Emotional Lexicons* (Oxford: OUP, 2014) [Ger. orig., 'Zivilität und Barbarei: Gefühle als Differenzkriterien', in Ute Frevert et al., *Gefühlswissen: Eine lexikalische Spurensuche in der Moderne* (2011)].

Pernau, Margrit, *Ashraf into Middle Classes: Muslims in Nineteenth Century Delhi* (Delhi: Oxford UP, 2013).

Pernau, Margrit et al., *Civilizing Emotions: Concepts in Asia and Europe 1870–1920* (forthcoming).

Peterson, Roger D., *Understanding Ethnic Violence: Fear, Hatred, and Resentment in Twentieth-Century Eastern Europe* (Cambridge: CUP, 2002).

Petzold, Dieter, 'Die Rezeption klassischer englischsprachiger Kinderbücher in Deutschland', in Hans-Heino Ewers, Gertrud Lehnert, and Emer O'Sullivan, eds., *Kinderliteratur im interkulturellen Prozess: Studien zur allgemeinen und vergleichenden Kinderliteraturwissenschaft* (Stuttgart: Metzler, 1994), 78–91.

Pfaff-Czarnecka, Joanna, *Multiple Belonging and the Challenges to Biographic Navigation*, Working papers / Max-Planck-Institute for the Study of Religious and Ethnic Diversity 13–05 (Göttingen: MPI zur Erforschung multireligiöser und multiethischer Gesellschaften, 2013), <http://www.mmg.mpg.de/fileadmin/user_upload/documents/wp/WP_13-05_Pfaff-Czarnecka_Multiple%20belonging.pdf> accessed 10 Apr. 2013.

Plamper, Jan, *Geschichte und Gefühl: Grundlagen der Emotionsgeschichte* (Munich: Siedler, 2012).

Plamper, Jan, 'The History of Emotions: An Interview with William Reddy, Barbara Rosenwein, and Peter Stearns', *History and Theory*, 49/2 (2010), 237–65.

Pleck, Elizabeth, *Domestic Tyranny: The Making of American Social Policy against Family Violence from Colonial Times to the Present* (New York: Oxford UP, 1987).

Pollock, Linda A., *Forgotten Children: Parent-Child Relations from 1500 to 1900* (Cambridge: CUP, 1983).

Preckel, Claudia, 'Islamische Bildungsnetzwerke und Gelehrtenkultur im Indien des 19. Jahrhunderts: Muhammad Siddiq Hasan Khan und die Entstehung der Ahl-e Hadith Bewegung in Bhopal', PhD thesis, Ruhr-Universität, Bochum, 2005, <http://www-brs.ub.ruhr-uni-bochum.de/netahtml/HSS/Diss/PreckelClaudia/diss.pdf> accessed 17 Apr. 2013.

Prieger, Almut, *Das Werk Enid Blytons: Eine Analyse ihrer Erfolgsserien in westdeutschen Verlagen*, Jugend und Medien 1 (Frankfurt am Main: Dipa, 1982).

Prinz, Jesse J., *The Emotional Construction of Morals* (Oxford: OUP, 2007).

Pritchett, Frances W., 'Afterword: The First Urdu Bestseller', in Maulvi Nazir Ahmad, *The Bride's Mirror: A Tale of Life in Delhi a Hundred Years Ago* (Delhi: Permanent Black, 2001), 204–21.

Pritchett, Frances W., *Marvelous Encounters: Folk Romance in Urdu and Hindi* (New Delhi: Manohar, 1985).

Prüfer, Fritz, and E. A. Schmid, 'Karl May in den Volksbüchereien', *Karl-May-Jahrbuch*, 13 (1930), 333–44.

Pugh, Tison, *Innocence, Heterosexuality, and the Queerness of Children's Literature* (New York: Routledge, 2011).

Putz, Christa, *Verordnete Lust: Sexualmedizin, Psychoanalyse und die 'Krise der Ehe', 1870–1930* (Bielefeld: Transcript, 2011).

Reckwitz, Andreas, *Das hybride Subjekt: Eine Theorie der Subjektkulturen von der bürgerlichen Moderne zur Postmoderne* (Weilerswist: Velbrück Wissenschaft, 2006).

Reddy, William M., 'Against Constructivism: The Historical Ethnography of Emotions', *Current Anthropology*, 38/3 (1997), 327–51.

Reddy, William M., *The Navigation of Feeling: A Framework for the History of Emotions* (Cambridge: CUP, 2001).

Redmann, Jennifer, 'Nostalgia and Optimism in Else Ury's Nesthäkchen Books for Young Girls in the Weimar Republic', *German Quarterly*, 79/4 (2006), 465–83.

Redmond, Gerald, 'The First Tom Brown's School Days: Origins and Evolution of "Muscular Christianity" in Children's Literature, 1762–1857', *Quest*, 30/Summer (1978), 4–18.

Reichardt, Sven, *Authentizität und Gemeinschaft: Linksalternatives Leben in den siebziger und frühen achtziger Jahren*, Suhrkamp Taschenbücher Wissenschaft 2075 (Berlin: Suhrkamp, 2013).

Reichardt, Sven, and Detlef Siegfried, eds., *Das Alternative Milieu: Antibürgerlicher Lebensstil und linke Politik in der Bundesrepublik Deutschland und Europa 1968–1983*, Hamburger Beiträge zur Sozial- und Zeitgeschichte 47 (Göttingen: Wallstein, 2010).

Reimer, Mavis, 'Introduction: Violence and Violent Children's Texts', *Children's Literature Association Quarterly*, 22/3 (1997), 102–4.

Richards, Jeffrey, *Happiest Days: The Public Schools in English Fiction* (Manchester: MUP, 1988).

Richman, Paula, ed., *Many Ramayanas: The Diversity of a Narrative Tradition in South Asia* (Berkeley: University of California Press, 1991).

Ricoeur, Paul, *A Ricoeur Reader: Reflection and Imagination*, ed. Mario J. Valdés, Theory/Culture series 2 (Toronto: University of Toronto Press, 1991).

Ricoeur, Paul, *Time and Narrative*, 3 vols, trans. Kathleen McLaughlin and David Pellauer (Chicago: University of Chicago Press, 1984–8) [Fre. orig., *Temps et récit*, 3 vols (1983–5)].

Ritvo, Harriet, *The Animal Estate: The English and Other Creatures in the Victorian Age* (Cambridge: Harvard UP, 1987).

Roberts, Robert, *The Classic Slum: Salford Life in the First Quarter of the Century* (Manchester: University of Manchester Press, 1971; repr. edn, London: Penguin, 1990)

Röhrs, Hermann, *Die Reformpädagogik: Ursprung und Verlauf unter internationalem Aspekt* (5th rev. and enl. edn, Weinheim: Deutscher Studien Verlag, 1998).

Röhrs, Hermann, and Volker Lenhart, eds., *Die Reformpädagogik auf den Kontinenten: Ein Handbuch*, Heidelberger Studien zur Erziehungswissenschaft 43 (Frankfurt am Main: Lang, 1994).

Romalov, Nancy Tillman, 'Unearthing the Historical Reader, or, Reading Girls' Reading', *Primary Sources & Original Works*, 4/1–2 (1997), 87–101.

Römhild, Dorothee, *Belly'chen ist Trumpf: Poetische und andere Hunde im 19. Jahrhundert* (Bielefeld: Aisthesis, 2005).

Roper, Michael, 'Between Manliness and Masculinity: The "War Generation" and the Psychology of Fear in Britain, 1914–1950', *Journal of British Studies*, 44/2 (2005), 343–62.

Roscher, Mieke, *Ein Königreich für Tiere* (Marburg: Tectum, 2009).

Rose, Jacqueline, *The Case of Peter Pan, or, The Impossibility of Children's Fiction*, New Cultural Studies (Philadelphia: University of Pennsylvania Press, 1993).

Rose, Jonathan, 'Arriving at a History of Reading', *Historically Speaking*, 5/36–9 (2004).

Rose, Jonathan, *The Intellectual Life of the British Working Classes* (2nd edn, New Haven: Yale UP, 2010).

Rose, Nikolas, *Governing the Soul: The Shaping of the Private Self* (London: Routledge, 1990).

Rose, Nikolas, *Inventing Our Selves: Psychology, Power, and Personhood* (Cambridge: CUP, 1998).

Ross, Dorothy, 'Hall, Granville Stanley', *American National Biography Online* [website], (2000), <http://www.anb.org/articles/14/14-00254.html;> accessed 7 May 2013.

Rothfels, Nigel, ed., *Representing Animals* (Bloomington: Indiana UP, 2002).

Rudd, David, 'Animal and Object Stories', in M. O. Grenby and Andrea Immel, eds., *The Cambridge Companion to Children's Literature* (Cambridge: CUP, 2009), 242–57.

Rudd, David, *Enid Blyton and The Mystery of Children's Literature* (Basingstoke: Palgrave, 2002).

Rutherford, Jonathan, 'The Third Space: Interview with Homi Bhabha', in Jonathan Rutherford, ed., *Identity: Community, Culture, Difference* (London: Lawrence & Wishart, 1990), 207–21.

Saarni, Carolyn, *Children's Understanding of Emotion* (Cambridge: CUP, 1989).

Sako, Mari, 'Does Trust Improve Business Performance?', in Roderick M. Kramer, ed., *Organizational Trust: A Reader*, Oxford Management Readers (Oxford: OUP, 2006), 267–92.

Salas, Angela M., 'Power and Repression/Repression and Power: Homosexuality in Subversive Picture Books and Conservative Youth Novels', in Claudia Nelson and Michelle H. Martin, eds., *Sexual Pedagogies: Sex Education in Britain, Australia, and America, 1879–2000* (New York: Palgrave Macmillan, 2004), 113–33.

Sammond, Nicholas, 'Dumbo, Disney, and Difference: Walt Disney Productions and Film as Children's Literature', in Julia L. Mickenberg and Lynne Valone, eds., *The Oxford Handbook of Children's Literature* (Oxford: OUP, 2011), 147–66.

Sarkar, Tanika, 'A Pre-History of Rights? The Age of Consent Debates in Colonial Bengal', in *Hindu Wife, Hindu Nation: Community, Religion, and Cultural Nationalism* (3rd edn, Delhi: Permanent Black, 2007), 226–49.

Sauerteig, Lutz, 'Die Herstellung des sexuellen und erotischen Körpers in der westdeutschen Jugendzeitschrift BRAVO in den 1960er und 1970er Jahren', *Medizinhistorisches Journal*, 42/2 (2007), 142–79.

Sauerteig, Lutz, ' "Wie soll ich es nur anstellen, ohne etwas falsch zu machen?" Der Rat der Bravo in Sachen Sex in den sechziger und siebziger Jahren', in Peter-Paul Bänziger et al., eds., *Fragen Sie Dr. Sex! Ratgeberkommunikation und die mediale Konstruktion des Sexuellen* (Berlin: Suhrkamp, 2010), 123–58.

Scarry, Elaine, *The Body in Pain: The Making and Unmaking of the World* (Oxford: OUP, 1985).

Scheer, Monique, 'Are Emotions a Kind of Practice (And is That What Makes Them Have a History)? A Bourdieuian Approach to Understanding Emotion', *History and Theory*, 51/2 (2012), 193–220.

Scheff, Thomas J., and Suzanne M. Retzinger, *Emotions and Violence: Shame and Rage in Destructive Conflicts*, Lexington Book Series on Social Theory (Lexington: Lexington, 1991).

Schenda, Rudolf, *Volk ohne Buch: Studien zur Sozialgeschichte der populären Lesestoffe 1770–1910*, Studien zur Philosophie und Literatur des 19. Jahrhunderts 5 (Frankfurt am Main: Klostermann, 1970).

Schilcher, Anita, *Geschlechterrollen, Familie, Freundschaft und Liebe in der Kinderliteratur der 90er Jahre: Studien zum Verhältnis von Normativität und Normalität im Kinderbuch und zur Methodik der Werteerziehung* (Frankfurt am Main: Lang, 2001).

Schneider, Wolfgang, ed., *Kindertheater nach 1968: Neorealistische Entwicklungen in der Bundesrepublik und West-Berlin* (Cologne: Prometh, 1984).

Schumann, Dirk, 'School Violence and its Control in Germany and the United States since the 1950s', in Wilhelm Heitmeyer et al., eds., *Control of Violence: Historical and International Perspectives on Violence in Modern Societies* (New York: Springer, 2011), 233–59.

Seligman, Adam B., *The Problem of Trust* (2nd edn, Princeton: PUP, 2000).

Shankar, Alaka, *Shankar* (New Delhi: Children's Book Trust, 1984).

Shapin, Steven, *A Social History of Truth: Civility and Science in Seventeenth-Century England* (Chicago: University of Chicago Press, 1994).

Shapiro, Kenneth J., 'Understanding Dogs Through Kinesthetic Empathy, Social Construction, and History', *Anthrozoos*, 3/3 (1990), 184–95.

Shimada, Shingo, 'Zur Asymmetrie in der Übersetzung von Kulturen: Das Beispiel des Minakata-Schlegel-Übersetzungsdisputs 1897', in Doris Bachmann-Medick, ed., *Übersetzung als Repräsentation fremder Kulturen*, Göttinger Beiträge zur internationalen Übersetzungsforschung 12 (Berlin: Schmidt, 1997), 260–74.

Shklovsky, Viktor, *Theory of Prose*, trans. Benjamin Sher (Elmwood Park, Ill.: Dalkey Archive, 1990) [Rus. orig., *O teorii prozy* (1925)].

Shuttleworth, Sally, *The Mind of the Child: Child Development in Literature, Science, and Medicine, 1840–1900* (Oxford: OUP, 2010).

Siegel, Lee, *Laughing Matters: Comic Tradition in India* (Chicago: University of Chicago Press, 1987).

Silver, Allan, 'Friendship and Trust as Moral Ideals: An Historical Approach', *European Journal of Sociology*, 30/2 (1989), 274–97.

Simmel, Georg, 'The Sociology of Secrecy and of Secret Societies', *American Journal of Sociology*, 11/4 (1906), 441–98.

Simpson, Elizabeth J., 'Advice in the Teen Magazines', *Illinois Teacher of Home Economics*, 7/6 (1964), 1–57.

Sims, Sue, and Hilary Clare, *The Encyclopaedia of Girls' School Stories*, ed. Rosemary Auchmuty and Joy Wotton, The Encyclopaedia of School Stories 1 (Aldershot: Ashgate, 2000).

Skiera, Ehrenhard, *Reformpädagogik in Geschichte und Gegenwart: Eine kritische Einführung* (2nd edn, Munich: Oldenbourg, 2010).

Smith, Michelle J., *Empire in British Girls' Literature and Culture: Imperial Girls, 1880–1915* (New York: Palgrave, 2011).

Spariosu, Mihai, ed., *Mimesis in Contemporary Theory: An Interdisciplinary Approach, i: The Literary and Philosophical Debate, Cultura Ludens: Imitation and Play in Western Culture* (Philadelphia: Benjamins, 1984).

Spector, Scott, Helmut Puff, and Dagmar Herzog, eds., *After the History of Sexuality: German Genealogies With and Beyond Foucault*, Spektrum (New York, N. Y.) 5 (New York: Berghahn Books, 2012).

Stallcup, Jackie E., 'Power, Fear, and Children's Picture Books', *Children's Literature*, 30/1 (2002), 125–58.

Stearns, Peter N., *American Cool: Constructing a Twentieth-Century Emotional Style* (New York: New York UP, 1994).

Stearns, Peter N., *American Fear: The Causes and Consequences of High Anciety* (New York: Routledge, 2006).

Stearns, Peter N., *Anxious Parents: A History of Modern Childrearing in America* (New York: NYUP, 2003).

Stearns, Peter N., 'Defining Happy Childhoods: Assessing a Recent Change', *Journal of Childhood and Youth*, 3/2 (2010), 165–86.

Stearns, Peter N., 'Girls, Boys, and Emotions: Redefinitions and Historical Change', *Journal of American History*, 80/1 (1993), 36–74.

Stearns, Peter N., and Timothy Haggerty, 'The Role of Fear: Transitions in American Emotional Standards for Children, 1850–1950', *American Historical Review*, 96/1 (1991), 63–94.

Steinlein, Rüdiger, 'Neubeginn, Restauration, antiautoritäre Wende', in Reiner Wild, ed., *Geschichte der deutschen Kinder- und Jugendliteratur* (3rd rev. and enl. edn, Stuttgart: Metzler, 2008), 312–42.

Stephens, John, and Robyn McCallum, *Retelling Stories, Framing Culture: Traditional Story and Metanarratives in Children's Literature* (New York: Garland, 1998).

Superle, Michelle, 'Animal Heroes and Transforming Substance: Canine Characters in Contemporary Children's Literature', in Aaron Gross and Anne Vallely, eds., *Animals and the Human Imagination: A Companion to Animal Stories* (New York: Columbia UP, 2012), 174–202.

Suzuki, Shoko, and Christoph Wulf, eds., *Mimesis, Poiesis, and Performativity in Education* (Munster: Waxmann, 2007).

Tangney, June Price, 'The Self-Conscious Emotions: Shame, Guilt, Embarassment and Pride', in Tim Dalgleish and Mick J. Power, eds., *Handbook of Cognition and Emotion* (Chichester: Wiley, 1999), 541–68.

Tanner, Jakob, 'Körpererfahrung, Schmerz und die Konstruktion des Kulturellen', *Historische Anthropologie*, 2 (1994), 489–502.

Tarde, Gabriel, *The Laws of Imitation*, trans. Elsie Clews Parsons (New York: Holt, 1903) [Fre. orig., *Les lois de l'imitation: Étude sociologique* (2nd rev. edn, 1895)].

Tebbutt, Melanie, *Being Boys: Youth, Leisure and Identity in the Inter-War Years* (Manchester: MUP, 2012).

Thomson-Wohlgemuth, Gaby, 'Flying High: Translation of Children's Literature in East Germany', in Jan van Collie and Walter P. Verschueren, eds., *Children's Literature in Translation: Challenges and Strategies* (Manchester: St. Jerome, 2006), 47–59.

Tomkins, Silvan S., *Affect, Imagery, Consciousness, ii: The Negative Affects* (New York: Springer, 1963).

Tosh, John, *Manliness and Masculinities in Nineteenth-Century Britain,* Women and Men in History (Harlow: Pearson, 2005).

Trepanier, Mary L., and Jane A. Romatowski, 'Classroom Use of Selected Children's Books: Prosocial Development in Young Children', *Journal of Humanistic Education and Development*, 21/1 (1982), 36–42.

Trotha, Trutz von, 'Violence', in George Ritzer, ed., *The Blackwell Encyclopedia of Sociology* (Malden, Mass.: Wiley-Blackwell, 2007), 5193–9.

Urwin, Cathy, and Elaine Sharland, 'From Bodies to Minds in Childcare Literature: Advice to Parents in Inter-War Britain', in Roger Cooter, ed., *In the Name of the Child: Health and Welfare 1880–1940, Studies in the Social History of Medicine* (London: Routledge, 1992), 174–99.

Vallone, Lynne, *Becoming Victoria* (New Haven: Yale UP, 2001).

Vallone, Lynne, *Disciplines of Virtue: Girls' Culture in the Eighteenth and Nineteenth Centuries* (New Haven: Yale UP, 1995).

Vallone, Lynne, 'Grrrls and Dolls: Feminism and Female Youth Culture', in Beverly Lyon Clark and Margaret R. Higonnet, eds., *Girls, Boys, Books, Toys: Gender in Children's Literature and Culture* (Baltimore: Johns Hopkins UP, 1999), 196–209.

Vallone, Lynne, '"The True Meaning of Dirt": Putting Good and Bad Girls in Their Place(s)', in Claudia Nelson and Lynne Vallone, eds., *The Girl's Own: Cultural History of the Anglo-American Girl, 1830–1915* (Athens, GA: University of Georgia Press, 2010), 259–83.

Vanden Bossche, Chris R., 'Moving Out: Adolescence', in Herbert F. Tucker, ed., *A Companion to Victorian Literature & Culture*, Blackwell Companions to Literature and Culture 2 (Malden, Mass.: Blackwell, 1990), 82–96.

Venuti, Lawrence, *The Scandals of Translation: Towards an Ethics of Difference* (London: Routledge, 1998).

Venuti, Lawrence, *The Translator's Invisibility: A History of Translation* (2nd edn, London: Routledge, 2008).

Verheyen, Nina, *Diskussionslust: Eine Kulturgeschichte des 'besseren Arguments' in Westdeutschland*, Kritische Studien zur Geschichtswissenschaft 193 (Göttingen: Vandenhoeck & Ruprecht, 2010).

Vicedo, Marga, 'The Social Nature of the Mother's Tie to her Child: John Bowlby's Theory of Attachment in Postwar America', *British Journal for the History of Science*, 44/3 (2011), 401–26.

Virilio, Paul, *Open Sky*, trans. Julie Rose (London: Verso, 1997) [Fre. orig., *La vitesse de libération: Essai* (1995)].

Vogt-Praclik, Kornelia, *Bestseller in der Weimarer Republik 1925–1930: Eine Untersuchung* (Herzberg: Bautz, 1987).

Volck, Adolf, 'Begleiterscheinungen zur Absatzstatistik', *Karl-May-Jahrbuch*, 11 (1928), 149–52.

Voss, Julia, *Darwins Jim Knopf*, S. Fischer Wissenschaft (Frankfurt am Main: Fischer, 2009).

Waal, Frans de, *The Age of Empathy: Nature's Lesson for a Kinder Society* (New York: Harmony, 2009).

Wallace, Doris B., Margery B. Franklin, and Robert T. Keegan, 'The Observing Eye: A Century of Baby Diaries', *Human Development*, 37/1 (1994), 1–29.

Wallace, Jo-Ann, 'Describing "The Water-Babies": "The Child" in Postcolonial Theory', in Chris Tiffin and Alan Lawson, eds., *De-Scribing Empire: Post-Colonialism and Textuality* (London: Routledge, 1994), 171–84.

Watanabe-O'Kelly, Helen, ' "Angstapparat aus Kalkül": Wie, wozu und zu welchem Ende erregt die Literatur Angst?', *Zeitschrift für Erziehungswissenschaft*, 15/1 Supplement (2012), 115–24.

Whitley, David, *The Idea of Nature in the Disney Animation*, Ashgate Studies in Childhood, 1700 to the Present (Aldershot: Ashgate, 2008).

Wikan, Unni, 'Managing the Heart to Brighten Face and Soul: Emotions in Balinese Morality and Health Care', *American Ethnologist*, 16/2 (1989), 294–312.

Wild, Markus, *Tierphilosophie zur Einführung* (Hamburg: Junius, 2008).

Williams, Bernard, *Shame and Necessity* (1993; Berkeley: University of California Press, 2008).

Wilson, Anita, 'Critical Introduction', in J. A. V. Chapple and Anita Wilson, eds., *Private Voices: The Diaries of Elizabeth Gaskell and Sophia Holland* (Keele: KUP, 1996), 11–47.

Wolman, Benjamin B., ed., *Handbook of Child Psychoanalysis: Research, Theory, and Practice* (New York: Van Nostrand Reinhold, 1972).

Wulf, Christoph, 'Mimetic Learning', *Designs for Learning*, 1/1 (2008), 56–67.

Wurmser, Léon, *The Mask of Shame* (Baltimore: Johns Hopkins UP, 1981).

Zaidi, Khushhal, *Urdu men bachon ka adab* (New Delhi: n.p., 1989).

Zantop, Susanne M., *Colonial Fantasies: Conquest, Family, and Nation in Precolonial Germany, 1770–1870* (Durham: Duke UP, 1997).

Zembylas, Michalinos, 'Emotional Capital and Education: Theoretical Insights from Bourdieu', *British Journal of Educational Studies*, 55/4 (2007), 443–63.

Zerbel, Miriam, *Tierschutz im Kaiserreich: Ein Beitrag zur Geschichte des Vereinswesens* (Frankfurt am Main: Lang, 1993).

Index of Names

Index of Subjects

Index of Work Titles

For non-English books we have used the title of the English translation, or of the original if there is no English translation.